Child Pornography

Child Pornography: Law and Policy draws together literature from law, criminology, sociology and psychology to examine this controversial subject. The book begins by examining what child pornography is and how it is currently defined. By drawing upon the laws in four different countries, the book identifies the different methods of classification and the scope of legal intervention. The second part of the book critically examines each offence and assesses whether it is effective at countering child pornography. The text contains an essential chapter on young people who are complicit in the production and distribution of child pornography, raising interesting questions about the interface between law and child sexual experimentation. Finally, the book considers international responses to child pornography and the actions of the police in investigating and prosecuting such crimes. *Child Pornography: Law and Policy* provides a detailed analysis of the legal and policy framework and examines whether the current system is at all effective at tackling the production and dissemination of abusive material.

Alisdair A. Gillespie is Professor of Criminal Law and Justice at De Montfort University, Leicester. He has published widely in the field of the sexual exploitation of children and has advised national and international bodies, including criminal justice agencies and child protection charities, on this area.

Child Pornography

Law and Policy

Alisdair A. Gillespie

Routledge
Taylor & Francis Group
a GlassHouse book

First published 2011
by Routledge
2 Park Square, Milton Park, Abingdon, Oxon OX14 4RN

Simultaneously published in the USA and Canada by
Routledge
711 Third Avenue, New York, NY 10017

A GlassHouse book

Routledge is an imprint of the Taylor & Francis Group, an informa business

British Library Cataloguing in Publication Data
A catalogue record for this book is available from the British Library

Library of Congress Cataloging in Publication Data
Gillespie, Alisdair
    Child pornography: law and policy / Alisdair A. Gillespie.
        p. cm.
    "A GlassHouse book."
    1. Child pornography—Law and legislation—England.   I. Title.
    KD8075.G55 2011
    345.41'0274083—dc22

                                                        2010044332

ISBN: 978-0-415-49987-3 (hbk)
ISBN: 978-0-415-66741-8 (pbk)
ISBN: 978-0-203-81810-7 (ebk)

Typeset in Times
by RefineCatch Limited, Bungay, Suffolk

Contents

13 Conclusion

List of figures and tables

Figure

Tables

Acknowledgements

I wish to thank a number of people who have assisted me, not only in the production of this book, but also over the years I have worked in this area. It is almost impossible to divide the help between those who have assisted me whilst writing the book and those who have helped me in wider research in this area.

I particularly wish to thank Dr Angela Carr, Terry Jones, Lars Lööf, Professor David Ormerod, Tink Palmer and especially Dr Ethel Quayle for all the help they have given me. I would also like to thank colleagues at my university, notably Professor Michael Hirst and Gavin Dingwall, and also to thank the Department of Law for providing me with a sabbatical that allowed me to write the bulk of this book. I would also like to thank Esther George and Harry Hadfield of the Crown Prosecution Service and to acknowledge the assistance of the numerous police officers I have talked to and worked with in this area over the years. I have tremendous respect for the work of those officers who dedicate themselves to combating child pornography. It is not an easy task and pressures on police budgets and misunderstanding of their work means that regrettably it is rarely resourced appropriately, yet most officers work against these constraints and develop new techniques to detect offenders and identify and assist victims.

I should also like to acknowledge the Internet Watch Foundation. In January 2010 I was privileged to be appointed to the board of the IWF. The Foundation acts as the industry self-regulator, and its activities have made a significant impact on the proliferation of child pornography, not only in the United Kingdom but in other parts of the world.

I also acknowledge the assistance of Routledge, who have stayed with me during the project. It was subject to delays and changes of substance but the editorial staff stayed with me, for which I am very grateful.

It goes without saying that all errors, confusions and misunderstandings are, of course, my own.

A.A.G.

Chapter 1

Introduction

This is a book about child pornography, which is an issue that still provokes considerable debate, as will be noted throughout this book, and which defies a definition. The purpose of this book is to examine the existing literature on child pornography and consider what implications this has on the law. Whilst the book will be based on the law in England and Wales, as this is the jurisdiction the author is most familiar with, a number of other jurisdictions (Australia, Canada and the United States) will be examined along with international policy and legal instruments.

Throughout the book a number of focuses are used to scrutinise the legal position in respect of child pornography. The first focus is its definition and Chapters 2–5 present a variety of definitions, including considering the controversial subject of virtual child pornography. The next focus is the criminalisation of child pornography and Chapters 6–8 consider what offences are created in the various jurisdictions. Chapter 9 considers the specific issue of children becoming involved in the creation of child pornography and Chapter 10 examines how offenders are sentenced. The third focus considers how child pornography is policed and thus an examination is made of how international law and policy affects the legal position of child pornography and Chapter 12 considers how law enforcement bodies tackle child pornography.

Terminology

It was said that child pornography is something that continues to provoke debate and this is true even of the terminology. Whilst this book is called *Child Pornography: Law and Policy* the term 'child pornography' is extremely contentious and many believe that it should no longer be used.

Edwards argues that the term is an oxymoron arguing that it is not pornography but rather it is the representation of the rape, abuse and torture of children (Edwards, 2000: 1). Taylor and Quayle expand on this by noting that the term 'child pornography' is offensive because of the juxtaposition of 'child' with 'pornography' with the latter term being aligned to erotica, something that is clearly inappropriate when considering the depiction of the sexual abuse of children (Taylor and Quayle,

2003: 4). It is the fact that modern pornography presumes consensual activity that is what makes many argue that the term child pornography is wrong. An example of this is presented by Ost who notes that the Metropolitan Police, when giving evidence to a parliamentary select committee, stated that the term 'child pornography' presents the child as a consensual and willing partner in sexual relations (Ost, 2009: 31). However Ost continues by questioning whether prefixing the word 'pornography' with 'child' would bring a different reaction from the public than if it was prefixed by the word 'adult' (Ost, 2009: 32). It is submitted that a different reaction is more likely. Whilst in the 1970s – when child pornography legislation was first developed – few outside of child protection and law enforcement would have understood what this meant, the same is not true today.

Newspapers frequently report child pornography convictions and well known operations such as Operation Ore (discussed in Chapter 12) mean that public understanding of child pornography is becoming more developed. The reality of child pornography is reported freely by the press. In 2006 Alan Webster and Tanya French were jailed for the rape, and photographing, of a 12 week-old baby girl. In 2009 Vanessa George was jailed for photographing children, including babies, which she looked after at a nursery in Plymouth. These cases, together with others, present the reality of child pornography. They were widely reported in the media and so it could be argued that the public are able to differentiate between adult and child pornography. That said, perhaps it is irrelevant whether people can differentiate between adult and child pornography if the term itself is suggestive of consensual sexual activity.

If the term child pornography is considered inappropriate then what should be used instead? Common alternatives are 'images of sexual abuse' or 'child abuse images' (Taylor and Quayle, 2003: 7) and certainly the latter has found favour with law enforcement agencies with both the Child Exploitation and Online Protection Centre (CEOP) and the Internet Watch Foundation (IWF) using this term (CEOP, website; IWF, website). However there are undoubted difficulties with this term. The first is that it limits the material. It will be seen from the later chapters of this book that whilst the law tends to focus on photographic representations of child abuse this is only one form of material. Other forms of material exist, including sound, text and pictorial representations. If the label 'child abuse images' is used, therefore, this is overly limiting. Of course this can be solved by referring to material rather than images, thus one possible label could be 'child abuse material'.

Whilst it may seem that 'abuse' is the least controversial part of this alternative definition it does, in fact, raise questions. It has been noted that academic definitions of child pornography emphasise the impact it has on a child and the fact that a child must be abused in its production (Beech et al., 2008: 218) but it will be noted later in this book that this is not true of all material. Even if we focus on photographic material it does not follow that a child must be abused to produce the material. It will be noted in Chapter 2 that a wide range of material is used as child pornography. Taylor and Quayle note that the common thread in all material is that they provide sexual gratification for the producer and viewer (Taylor and Quayle, 2003: 5). Tate, in one of the earliest studies on child pornography, noted that offenders use a broad range of material (Tate, 1990) and this was further developed by the COPINE unit at University College Cork who produced a typology of child pornography (Taylor *et al.*, 2001 discussed in Chapter 2). Research notes that offenders will use indicative material including, for example, pictures of children in underwear (Taylor *et al.*, 2001) which could come from clothing catalogues. It is difficult to say that such children have been abused in the production of such images.

The view that child pornography intrinsically involves the abuse of children also raises difficult issues in terms of children who voluntarily participate in the production of material. This is a sensitive topic and one that is discussed more extensively in Chapter 9 but it must be recognised that some adolescents are producing their own material. An example would be two 16 year-olds who film themselves having consensual sexual intercourse. In many countries, including England and Wales, two 16 year olds can legally have sexual intercourse but it is prohibited to take an indecent photograph of a child under 18. Thus the 16 year-olds could be guilty of infringing child pornography laws. Can we really say that these adolescents have abused each other? By calling it child abuse images this is exactly what we would be stating: those adolescents would be guilty of child abuse. Of course a solution would be to decriminalise the example discussed above (something developed further in Chapter 9) but even if this were done it does not answer the point about the broad range of material noted above.

Taylor and Quayle argue that an essential feature of child pornography is that there is a power imbalance between adult and child (Taylor and Quayle, 2003: 2) and this is developed by Ost who notes that the inherent power imbalance means that a child is, at the very least, exploited by either the production or use of the material (Ost, 2009). Exploitation arguably bears a wider definition than abuse (see the discussion in Buck, 2010: 262–263) and certainly in the context of sexual exploitation it is considered to include situations where a child is unaware that they are being used for a person's own deviant purposes. In the context of child pornography it is submitted that this could include situations where a person takes an innocent picture of a child and places it within a sexualised context. For example, the actions of the offender in *R v H* [2005] EWCA Crim 3037 involved a teacher, who was also the school photographer, who took pictures of school children and then, using a graphic manipulation program, added images of semen on to their faces, the resultant image making it appear that they had been engaging in sexual activity (this case is discussed in more depth during Chapter 5). It would be difficult to say that the children featured in those images have been abused but it may be more realistic to say that they have been exploited. If we return to the issue of adolescents filming themselves having sexual intercourse, it would be difficult to say that they have either abused or exploited each other. However if the image was then disseminated or shown to another without both parties' consent then whilst it is unlikely to transform this into abuse it may be appropriate to think of this as exploitation. The footage was recorded for private purposes and the breach of trust involved in disseminating the photograph could be considered exploitative.

Accordingly it could be argued that a better term for child pornography is 'child exploitative material'. However a difficulty with avoiding the term 'child pornography' in a book like this is that, as will be seen, many legal instruments specifically refer to child pornography and this does not appear to be changing. The latest international instrument is the proposal by the EU for a new Directive on combating the sexual abuse, sexual exploitation of children and child pornography (COM (2010) 94; 2010/0064 (COD) discussed more extensively in Chapter 11) and this expressly uses the term 'child pornography' as do many other international and national laws. Some authors, to acknowledge the difficulty of the term, use 'child pornography' only when the instruments themselves use the term (e.g. Middleton *et al.*, 2009: 6) but in a book such as this it is likely that it would become confusing. Therefore this book will continue to use the term 'child pornography' although it will also use the other terms that exist within legal instruments. By using the term it is not intended to downplay the behaviour of those who engage with this material or minimise the impact on victims. It will be clear throughout this book that the author believes that child pornography does amount to the sexual abuse or exploitation of a child and that children are harmed by its production, dissemination and viewing. However as the term bears currency in legal instruments it must be used.

Child pornography in modern society

As Ost notes, the sexual abuse of children, including through their prostitution, has occurred throughout history (Ost, 2009: 25). There is a long and inglorious history relating to the sexual subjugation of children and this includes the portrayal of child pornography that can be found in ancient works of art (Ost, 2009: 25). However notwithstanding this, the issue of child pornography had probably not reached the attention of the general populace until the latter part of the twentieth century and, in particular, the first part of the twenty-first century. Why is this? During that period there was certainly an increase in media attention on the subject (Sheldon and Howitt, 2007: 26–27) but why? During the latter half of the twentieth century the issue of censorship began to be reconsidered and increased liberalisation allowed for restricted and censored works to appear. Whilst censorship receded there was, at the same time, recognition that certain forms of material could be exploitative and in the 1970s countries, most notably England and Wales and the United States, developed specific laws to tackle child pornography.

It has been noted that once law highlights an issue its incidence increases, probably not because its commission is necessarily more frequent but rather because law enforcement agencies now have an incentive to act on that material, meaning more offences are detected and prosecuted (Adler, 2001: 231). However, communication technologies have certainly revolutionised the manner in which child pornography operates and the growth of the internet and digital technologies has meant the amount of child pornography material has grown exponentially (Taylor and Quayle, 2003). The growth in material led to it featuring more prominently on the public policy agenda. It is notable, for example, that England and Wales introduced a law, *inter alia*, tackling the production and dissemination of child pornography in 1978 (Protection of Children Act 1978) and possession in 1988 (s. 160, Criminal Justice Act 1988). Yet its increasing prominence on the public policy agenda is perhaps demonstrated by the fact that these laws have been amended by no less than six statutes since 1988, with five of these amendments taking place since 2000.

The increased prominence of child pornography and an increased prosecution rate for the offences (see Akdeniz, 2008: 25) meant that media interest was sparked and thus the reporting of the matters increased, also raising public consciousness of the issue. It can be concluded therefore that although, as will be seen later in this book, child pornography is certainly not necessarily a 'hi-tech' crime, the use of technology has radically transformed its incidence and, to an extent, also its very nature.

Prosecutions

The transformation in child pornography can, to an extent, become evident by the growth in prosecutions. Reference in this section will be made to the position in England and Wales but it is illustrative of the general position. Identifying the precise numbers of people who have been convicted is somewhat difficult. Whilst Parliament has occasionally published detailed figures, obtaining annual figures is almost impossible. The most comprehensive crime data presentation is made in the *Criminal Statistics* publication each year. The latest, at the time of writing, is 2008 (published in 2010). However despite the fact that individual offences relating to, for example, the adulteration of food (category 89) or allowing a chimney to be on fire (category 161) are included there is no single category for child pornography. Instead offences relating to indecent photographs of children are included within category 86 ('obscene publications, etc., and protected sexualised material'). This includes not only offences relating to indecent photographs but also, *inter alia*, displaying an indecent matter, supplying video recordings of an unclassified work, having protected material in possession and been given or shown protected material.

In Chapter 12 it will be noted that there is no single approach taken to policing child pornography and the absence of statistics makes it difficult to assess trends in the effectiveness of policing. It is submitted that it would be helpful if statistics relating to indecent photographs of children (the relevant offences for child pornography in England and Wales: see Chapters 3 and 6) were kept separately. There is sufficient difference between protected material and indecent photographs of children to justify a separate analysis.

In this section, therefore, reference will be made to two sources. The first is a House of Commons written answer from 2009 (Hansard, HC Written Answers,

13 October 2009, col. 846W). This dealt with statistics relating to the years 2003–2007 inclusive. The second source is Akdeniz, 2008, who has analysed earlier data, and the figures for the years 1994 to 2003 were taken from this source. In Table 1.1 the data relate to convictions (including those who plead guilty) for offences under either s. 1, Protection of Children Act 1978 or s. 160, Criminal Justice Act 1988. The detail of these offences is set out in Chapter 6 but broadly speaking s. 160 relates to the possession of child pornography whereas s. 1 relates to its taking, making and distribution (but see the ruling in *R v Bowden* [2000] QB 88 discussed in Chapter 6 which blurs the distinction between the two offences in relation to material downloaded from the internet). The trend can perhaps be better seen in graph form (Figure 1.1).

It can be seen that there has been a general upward trajectory, with the trajectory starting to climb steeply at around the time of the millennium. This corresponds with the take-up of technology and, especially, the growth of broadband technology that allowed quick access to the internet and the ability to speedily download large image files. There is a definite spike between 2003 and 2006 which is probably explainable by Operation Ore. This was the UK version of the operation that arose after the US Postal Inspection Service arrested the operators of Landslide Productions. Ore is the largest police operation in this area to have ever been undertaken and it will be discussed in Chapter 12. Over 7,000 names were contained on the Landslide lists and the police began to work through this list at around the time of the millennium. It took some time for the matter to come before the courts and this will explain the delay. The conduct of Ore will be

Table 1.1 Convictions, 1994–2007

	Section		
Year	1	160	Total
1994	27	36	63
1995	44	37	81
1996	69	79	148
1997	103	81	184
1998	82	105	187
1999	139	99	238
2000	217	77	294
2001	289	75	364
2002	434	97	531
2003	1048	239	1287
2004	978	184	1162
2005	958	196	1154
2006	768	166	934
2007	782	185	967

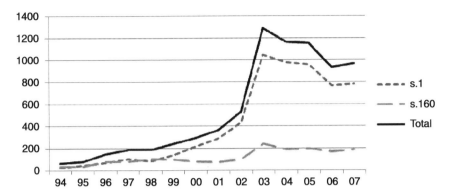

Figure 1.1 Convictions, 1994–2007.

discussed in Chapter 12 but by 2006 the operation was winding down and this would seem to be represented in the graph.

There has not been another large-scale operation like Ore since, in part because there was some doubt as to whether people would ever access sites in the same way again (Bains, 2008 reports that most distribution of child pornography exists through peer-to-peer technology although the IWF report that commercial websites are beginning to increase once again: IWF, 2010). This means that the police are unlikely to identify a large number of persons from a single source again. However reference to the graph and table shows that the reduction in prosecutions has not been dramatic and prosecutions remain relatively high, especially when compared to the early 1990s when home internet was in its infancy.

Whilst the latest prosecution statistics are not available, it would appear the position is remaining true to this trend. *Criminal Statistics 2008*, discussed above, states that the total number of convictions for 'possession of obscene material, etc.' is 1,285. Whilst some of these crimes will relate to the offences relating to restricted material it is more likely that the vast majority of them will refer to offences relating to child pornography. It would seem therefore that the number of crimes is beginning to rise once again. This will be in part because of the resources that were put into this area by the police (discussed in Chapter 12) and the increase in knowledge in this area. A completely unscientific manner of gauging law enforcement action is to consult newspapers. A simple search of newspaper indices (which will, of course, show duplicated cases although this particular search index did have a duplication filter) reports 1,700 stories for a search entitled ' "child pornography" and guilty'. As noted above it is not suggested that this result has any empirical validity but it does suggest that the reporting of convictions relating to child pornography is an almost weekly occurrence. The realisation that people access child pornography has entered the public consciousness and attracts significant media attention.

Moral panic

The increased media attention has led to questions being raised as to whether a moral panic exists in respect of child pornography. The classic formulation of a moral panic remains that put forward by Stanley Cohen who studied the response to the Mods and Rockers in the 1960s, especially the reaction to relatively limited outbreaks of violence that occurred between them at Brighton. His work set the foundation for what has become a separate area of study (Garland, 2008) the sub-discipline of moral panic studies. Cohen summarised a moral panic as:

> A condition, episode, person or group of persons emerges to become defined as a threat to societal values and interests; its nature is presented in a stylized and stereotypical fashion by the mass media; the moral barricades are manned by editors, bishops, politicians and other right-thinking people; socially accredited experts pronounce their diagnoses and solutions; ways of coping are evolved or (more often) resorted to; the condition then disappears, submerges or deteriorates and becomes more visible.
>
> (Cohen, 2002: 1)

The term quickly entered the lexicon and somewhat ironically even the media use the term (Altheide, 2009: 80) often inappropriately. This is something that Cohen himself has identified: in the introduction to the third edition he notes that after thirty years of study the concept has become more refined and has entered media discourse (Cohen, 2002: vii).

Garland cites Hall *et al.*, who note that the essence of the moral panic is that those in authority and influence (e.g. police, politicians and the press) begin to talk 'with one voice' about a particular phenomenon, its damage and required solutions (Garland, 2008: 10). After Cohen the most widely accepted definition is that by Goode and Ben Yehuda (Garland, 2008: 10) who state that there are five elements to a moral panic:

- Concern.
- Hostility.
- Consensus.
- Disproportionality.
- Volatility.

Garland is concerned that this definition neglects the moral core at the heart of a moral panic and also the fact that the concern is symptomatic, i.e. that those in authority will claim it is part of a wider problem (Garland, 2008: 11).

Does child pornography amount to a moral panic? Certainly some accept that it does (Cavanagh, 2007 although she cites no evidence as to why this amounts to a moral panic, merely claiming that it does, see p. 5). There would appear to be a broad consensus that the paedophile (used in its societal rather than clinical sense, something discussed later in the book) can amount to a folk devil (Critcher, 2002; Ost, 2009 although cf Collier, 2001 who disagrees) and certainly Cohen, in his third edition of his book, refers specifically to the issue of the paedophile (Cohen, 2002: xiv f.) although in a careful way and not suggesting that all matters relating to paedophiles amount to a panic. Some argue that the moral panic on child pornography is when it is seen in the context of a wider panic about the internet and the safety of children (Cavanagh, 2007). However others argue that whilst there are aspects of the discourse that could amount to a moral panic the issue has not truly become one (see, most notably in this regard, Jenkins, 2009).

Ost, in a careful analysis, suggests that there is a moral panic surrounding child pornography but that it is part of a wider moral panic surrounding sex offenders (Ost, 2009: 177). This suggestion receives support from other commentators who have suggested that recent law and policy regarding sex offences, particularly against children, has been shaped by a moral panic (Critcher, 2002). Certainly, in respect of child pornography, the basis for a moral panic would seem to be present. In England and Wales, for example, it is clear that there was a strong moral rationale behind the passing of legislation relating to child pornography (McCarthy and Moodie, 1981; Ost, 2009) and it has been noted already that the spectre of the 'paedophile' does, in many people's eyes, meet the criteria for a folk devil.

However others are less sure and suggest that the essence of a moral panic is missing. Jenkins notes that many of the constituent elements are present but that the issue has simply failed to detonate as one would expect of a moral panic (Jenkins, 2001: 38). It is the absence of panic that is perhaps missing. Garland notes that Cohen never explained what he meant by panic (Garland, 2008: 10) but it must mean a sense of disproportionality, alarm and exaggeration ('disproportionality' as Goode and Ben Yehuda summarise it). Garland does not believe that there has been the disproportionate hysterical reaction typically found in a moral panic:

> Unlike the fantasy of 'satanic ritual abuse' ... more mundane practices involving the 'abuse' of children . . . are all too real, and, having been rendered visible, would undoubtedly prompt condemnation and efforts at control with or without the hysterical outcries and exaggerated reporting.
>
> (Garland, 2008: 16)

This probably also applies to child pornography. It is certainly possible to find moralistic comments and exaggerated and inflamed comments (Ost, 2009) but arguably these are isolated examples and reinforce Jenkins' arguments about the moral panic failing to detonate. A moral panic leads to right-thinking people manning the barricades, fuelling an ever-more hysterical debate and leading to grossly disproportionate action. It will be seen in later chapters of this book that there have undoubtedly been some overreactions but in many instances this has not been an institutional way. Perhaps the classic examples of overreactions that have led to charges of a moral panic have been the police seizure of apparently innocuous photographs. Chapter 3 will discuss occasions where the work of

Tierney Gearon and Nan Goldin have been the subject of police action. This has, in some instances, led to accusations that child pornography amounts to a moral panic (Kleinhans, 2004). However it will be submitted in Chapter 3 that the action of the police, whilst regrettable, had more to do with the way in which the law in England and Wales is framed than any manning of the barricades. In any event these are more likely to be considered isolated incidents and whilst the images have been the subject of police action in some instances, on other occasions no action has been taken. It is submitted that a moral panic requires widespread disproportionality. This has not happened here. Most police action in respect of child pornography is, it will be submitted, legitimate and there are only occasional lapses. This does not suggest a moral panic.

In terms of systematic disproportionality it will be seen that in the arguments surrounding so-called virtual child pornography there has been a number of exaggerations and hyperbole but the majority of action at the legislative and policy level have been appropriate or designed to anticipate loopholes before they can be exploited.

Perhaps a good example of anticipatory action is the legislative action within the Police and Justice Act 2009 which amended Part III of the Regulation of Investigatory Powers Act 2000. Part III of RIPA allows the police to demand, in certain circumstances, that encrypted data is either presented in an unencrypted way or that the 'key' is handed over. There was concern that the sentence for non-compliance under RIPA (originally two years imprisonment) was so low compared to the sentence an offender would receive for child pornography offences that no offender would hand over their key. Ost notes that the police pushed hard for this amendment and that such claims were readily accepted by the media and those in government (Ost, 2009: 167). Whilst there has been scepticism as to the extent at which encryption is used it has been suggested by some that this is because it is easier for law enforcement agencies to concentrate on the 'easy' targets (Jenkins, 2009: 38) and that a core of offenders do now use security and encryption to hide their behaviour (Jenkins, 2009; Eneman, 2009). The Police and Justice Act 2009 amendments could have been considered a disproportionate reaction to the reality that few offenders who are caught use encryption (in part because it is time-consuming and burdensome to properly encrypt a whole computer) or it could be said to be an appropriate response to evidence that offenders were beginning to use such technology, and it was an attempt by the legislature to ensure that the law was 'fit for purpose' before encryption becomes standard practice. The fact that such actions can be construed in these two ways perhaps suggests that there is not a moral panic: it does not meet the hysterical overreaction common within moral panics.

Other aspects of a moral panic are also missing. An essential aspect of a moral panic is its transient nature – it flares up and then disappears from sight. It is difficult to suggest that the issue of child pornography is transient; it has remained on the policy agenda since the 1990s. Ost does not deny this but suggests that child pornography is a recurring moral panic. That rather than its longevity militating the belief that it amounts to a moral panic, it is a moral panic that continues to exist as new threats are identified (Ost, 2009: 177). Of course the counter-argument is that, as suggested at the beginning of this paragraph, the absence of a transient nature means that it is less likely that a moral panic exists in respect of child pornography.

Perhaps a difficulty with this is that the concept of moral panic has changed. In particular the term 'moral panic' has taken on a meaning that does not necessarily reflect what was originally intended. Ost, when concluding that a moral panic does exist in respect of child pornography, states 'my argument that evidence exists which is indicative of a moral panic about child pornography . . . does not lead to the conclusion that they are not real phenomenon' (Ost, 2009: 177). This is an important statement and perfectly correct. Ost cites Cohen, arguably the 'father' of moral panic, who confirms that the fact that a moral panic exists should not mean that there is no harm at the centre of the panic. However has the concept itself changed beyond what Cohen envisaged it to be? It would now seem more common to suggest that a moral panic means something more than a concern being exaggerated; it is one that has been blown out of all proportion and leads to inappropriate reactions (see the discussion in Jenkins, 2009: 36). This is perhaps reinforced by the fact that reactions are now not uncommonly being dismissed as 'merely a moral panic' (Garland, 2008: 9) which implies that it is not a 'real' problem. Perhaps this is now a problem with affixing the label 'moral panic' to any phenomenon; it carries with it a stigma that it is a trivial issue that is the subject of disproportionate overreactions.

As noted already, it will be argued in this book that whilst there have been some overreactions and exaggerated claims in respect of child pornography, it cannot be said that the law and policy initiatives that have been taken, when looked at as a whole, amount to a disproportionate reaction. In general the legislative and policy actions have been appropriate to reacting to the real harm that is caused to children in the production and dissemination of child pornography, and to developing new strategies to counter the new techniques used by offenders exploiting technological advances. Accordingly it is submitted that there is not a moral panic surrounding child pornography, although it is conceded that there are some, particularly in the press, who make exaggerated claims about the prevalence of the phenomenon.

Chapter 2

What is child pornography?

Any examination of the law of a subject must first consider the focus of the legal instrument, in the context of this book that being child pornography. This chapter considers two distinct yet interconnected issues. The first is the definition of child pornography. This may seem superfluous since many would argue they know what child pornography is but, as will be seen, this is not necessarily correct. 'Child pornography' is a difficult term to define with the precision required by the law and, in essence, this means that the laws which will be examined in the coming chapters do not necessarily tackle all child pornography.

The second issue is to examine who is involved with child pornography and, therefore, what types of conduct should be criminalised. Whilst Chapters 6 and 7 will examine what is currently criminalised, the point of this second part of the chapter is to consider the issue from a policy stance.

Defining child pornography

It has been noted that 'the terms "child" and "pornography" on their own are themselves contentious, with complex and sometimes contradictory meanings' (Taylor and Quayle, 2003: 2). It was noted in Chapter 1 that the term 'child pornography' is shunned by many in the law enforcement and child protection arenas. However the term and its two constituent elements do act as the starting point to any definition. In reality there are three elements to any definition. Those are:

- *Child.* What do we mean by 'child'?
- *Type of material.* What types of material should be considered to be child pornography?
- *Nature of material.* What is it about the material that makes it deviant and subject to regulation?

Obviously there is a link between the three parts to the definition but each will be examined separately initially.

Child

There is no agreed definition of a 'child' perhaps because the concept of child-hood is itself vague: 'childhood . . . is a social construction, subject to continuous process of (re)invention and (re)definition' (Jewkes, 2010: 8). Certainly society has a significant say in what a child is and it has been suggested that the concept of childhood will continually change according to our perceptions and under-standing (King, 2007: 402) and this must, of course, include cultural and ethical ideas. A difficulty in constructing childhood in the Western World for the purposes of sexuality is that much of our understanding is tempered by nineteenth century notions of childhood innocence (Egan and Hawkes, 2008: 317) yet the sexually active minor has been illustrated throughout history (Evans, 1993: 210) and certainly in recent years it would appear that adolescents have become more aware of their sexuality and are increasingly sexually active (discussed by Waites, 2005).

There are, in essence, three ways of deciding who should be a child for the purposes of child pornography. The first two methods examine the individual and decide whether their characteristics are such that they should be classified as a child. The first method is to use biological characteristics and the second is to consider the maturity of the individual. The third approach rejects this subjective approach and operates on the basis of prescribing an age under which an individual is classed as 'a child'.

Biological

The first method of construing a child is to use biology in its definition. Society has adopted stages of development (e.g. baby, infant, child and adolescent) but perhaps biology can be used to distinguish between the different phases of an individual's life. Within the field of child sexual abuse the most relevant biological factor to consider is puberty, something that leads us to the concept of the paedophile.

The term 'paedophile' is now used almost interchangeably with 'child sex offender' in some writings and yet it is also a recognised clinical disorder and it is in this context that it may be relevant here. A paedophile is someone who suffers from paedophilia, which is considered to be a clinical paraphilia (DSM IV 302.2). Whilst there has been some controversy over the precise characteristics of paedophilia (Seto, 2008: 176) it is commonly accepted to mean the sexual preference for pre-pubescent children (Seto, 2004: 322). Puberty marks the point at which a body is capable of sexual reproduction and the sexual preference for sexual activity with someone below that age is considered to be deviant (Seto, 2004: 323). It would follow there-fore that linking child pornography to the concept of puberty would, at least, provide some link to psychological understanding of paedophilia. Another advantage is that, as will be seen, aging a child can be somewhat difficult but puberty is something that can be objectively identified (Seto, 2008: 165). Accordingly basing the concept of childhood on puberty would allow material to be judged effectively.

There are drawbacks in the use of puberty in child pornography however. There is evidence that the age of puberty is decreasing in the developed world (see, for example, Herman-Giddens and Slora, 1997) and that factors such as race and body mass index may even influence the onset of puberty (Kaplowitz *et al.*, 2001). If this is true, then it would mean that basing child pornography on puberty could mean that it would protect a reducing number of children.

A stronger argument however is that although puberty marks the point at which a person is biologically ready for sexual reproduction it does not follow that the person is. A person needs to be emotionally and psychologically ready for sexual contact and as puberty could occur in young children, it is not clear that a pubertal child is ready for sexual contact. Some psychologists believe that restricting the DSM criteria to those with a sexual interest in pre-pubescent children is overly limiting (see, for example, Marshall, 1997) and others have argued that alongside paedophilia is another deviant sexual interest known as hebephilia.

Hebephilia was first coined in the 1950s and was used to describe those who have a sexual interest in pubescent children (Blanchard *et al.*, 2009: 336) but its use is not widespread. It can be immediately contrasted with paedophilia in that it is designed to apply to those who have begun puberty. As noted above, paedophilia is clinically the sexual attraction to pre-pubescent children and thus where they have begun puberty the clinical definition no longer applies. A criticism of using puberty as the basis of 'childhood' is that it means that a significant proportion of individuals that we would perhaps think of as children would be outside of this definition. Hebephilia recognises this and suggests that a sexual attraction to those who are pubescent may be problematic.

However not everyone necessarily believes that hebephilia amounts to a mental disorder or, indeed, that it is a problematic sexual interest. Whilst some argue that paedophilia is not a mental disorder (Tromovitch, 2009) most would disagree and its place within DSM IV as a paraphilia has not been seriously questioned. However the status of hebephilia is certainly more controversial. Whilst some suggest that DSM IV should be widened to include hebephilia (Blanchard *et al.*, 2009) this suggestion provoked considerable backlash with many noting that the mere fact that a person has a sexual interest in pubescent children does not mean that he is necessarily suffering from a mental disorder (Moser, 2009; DeClue, 2009; Zander, 2009). Moser notes that having sexual intercourse with a child is wrong but this by itself does not suggest that a person is suffering from a recognised mental disorder (Moser, 2009: 323). Of course it could be argued that its status as a mental disorder is irrelevant to whether it should be criminalised and indeed some have noted that the law appears to draw improper conclusions from clinical diagnoses (Moser, 2009: 323). However its status may be relevant if we are considering biological classifications. If it were recognised as a deviant mental disorder then it could perhaps extend our understanding of what a 'child' is, in that what makes it deviant could be relevant to childhood. However without a consensus on whether it is a mental disorder there are questions as to how useful hebephilia would be towards our understanding of a 'child'.

A further difficulty with hebephilia is that it arguably does not stand by itself. If the term is recognised then it would appear other categories of sexual interest would seem to exist too. The term epheophilia is used to denote those who have a sexual interest in adolescents although there is confusion as to what this means. Some argue that it applies to those who have a sexual interest in those aged between 15 and 19 (Blanchard *et al.*, 2009: 336) whereas others argue that it is more limited and it applies to those typically aged 15 to 16, with telophilia meaning those with a sexual interest in those over 17 (DeClue, 2009: 317). Where would this fit into our understanding of what a 'child' is?

The different classifications demonstrate the most problematic issue for recognising hebephilia and the other sexual interests in the context of child pornography. It is that in terms of developing a definition of a 'child' it creates a circular argument. It has been noted that the onset of puberty is a distinctive physiological factor and this is a point recognised even by those who advocate the inclusion of hebephilia (Blanchard *et al.*, 2009: 336). There is no distinctiveness with hebephilia or epheophilia. It was noted above that people cannot even agree the age bands of these terms but it is notable that age becomes a key factor, unlike biology which is the issue in terms of paedophilia. The fact that children will progress through puberty at different speeds has led some to suggest that hebephilia should be identified by a sexual preference for children of a certain age (Blanchard *et al.*, 2009: 348). That being the case, for our context this would mean that in order to decide when a person is a 'child' we would consider whether they were below a certain age. This approach ceases to be based on biological/physiological characteristics and instead becomes an issue of prescribing the age of a child; something discussed below as the third method of definition.

It would appear therefore if biology is to be used as the definition of a child then the differentiation is that of puberty (the distinction being between paedophilic and non-paedophilic material). This does not however move us away from the crucial problem with using puberty as the criterion for 'child' which is that it leads to the situation where child pornography would become separated from the other sexual offences against children where the age of consent is commonly used. If it is illegal to have sexual contact with a pubescent child below the age of consent, should it not also be illegal to take a sexualised picture of a child of the same age?

Maturity

It would seem that biology by itself cannot act as an appropriate way of construing childhood, in part because our moral and cultural tradition is such that we cannot accept that puberty (which would appear to be occurring earlier) marks the point at which it is acceptable to have sexual intercourse. Perhaps what is necessary is to take an additional element – the maturity of a child – into consideration. We can accept that sexual intercourse with a child before (s)he has reached puberty is wrong in terms of nature, but if we are concerned for the vulnerability of a child then it is perhaps their competence that we doubt.

It is known that individuals mature at different rates and that therefore some individuals will be more capable of making decisions and understanding the consequences of their decisions. Should this be taken into account when construing a 'child'? Should a child be someone who does not have the maturity and capacity to understand the consequences of the decision they reach, e.g. to have sexual intercourse? In many countries, including England and Wales, it has been increasingly common in recent years to recognise that adulthood is not something that descends upon an individual at the age of majority. Many legal systems recognise that children are able to take responsibility for some of their actions and in England and Wales the House of Lords judgment in *Gillick v West Norfolk and Wisbech AHA* [1986] AC 112 was a landmark in children's rights.

The case of *Gillick* gave rise to what is known as the Gillick-competent child, i.e. a person of sufficient age and understanding as to be responsible for the consequences of their actions. Of course it is not a simple concept and it has been remarked that it is often misunderstood (Fortin, 2009) and the House of Lords was never suggesting that the individual was not a child, only that they could begin to take responsibility for some aspects of their life. The courts have not extended this to all aspects of the child's welfare and the so-called retreat from Gillick led to situations where the courts would not allow a Gillick-competent child to make decisions that it (the court) considered were detrimental to the child's welfare (Fortin, 2009).

Gillick itself creates an interesting paradox. As is well known it was the issue of contraception that was at the heart of this decision. The decision in *Gillick* has meant that some children are considered to be sufficiently mature to make decisions as to whether they should be entitled to take medical contraception. So the law is, on the one hand, deciding that a child is capable of understanding the consequences of sexual intercourse and yet on the other hand stating that a person under the age of consent may not have sexual intercourse (discussed more fully in Waites, 2005). Of course this is for pragmatic reasons; it is easier for the law to set an arbitrary rule than for the law to investigate the competence of a child each time there is sexual activity. It is for this same reason that maturity and competence cannot be used for the purposes of child pornography. It must be accepted that at least some adolescents will be aware of the consequences of being photographed in a sexual way. Chapter 9 will detail situations where adolescents have done this. It would be incredible if each and every child mentioned was naïve and suddenly accrued the maturity to make their decisions on their eighteenth birthday. It is more likely that at least some individuals will fully understand what it is they are doing.

However maturity could not be used for the purposes of child pornography. Whilst, as conceded above, certain adolescents may have the maturity and capability to make this decision, how would the viewer of an image know whether that child was sufficiently mature? Basing child pornography laws on maturity would mean that the law sought to protect those that did not have the maturity or capacity to make those decisions. Accordingly a photograph of, for example, a 16 year-old girl posed sexually on a bed would be lawful where it depicted X, who was sufficiently mature to understand what she is involved in, but unlawful where it depicted Y, who was not. However how could anyone other than the photographer know what the maturity of the child is? It is not possible to know the circumstances under which a photograph was taken merely by examining the resultant image (King, 2008: 332). Certainly basing any analysis on the apparent enjoyment or compliance by the child would be flawed since we know that compliance can be brought about by drugs, coercion, grooming or long-term abuse (King, 2008: 333; Lanning, 2005). Accordingly maturity must be rejected as a method of construing childhood.

Prescribing an age

It has been seen that the two subjective approaches of considering the characteristics of a specific child will not lead to a suitable definition of a 'child'. Accordingly the law takes the approach of prescribing an age. Realistically this is a pragmatic decision and at least ensures that there is certainty as to who is a child, at least when their age is known.

If an age is to be prescribed then the first issue to be discussed is what age to prescribe. The age at which a person is considered to be a 'child' differs between jurisdictions and indeed between contexts. So, for example, the age of majority may well be different to the age of consent and both may differ from, for example, the age of criminal responsibility (in England and Wales for example, these ages would be 18, 16 and 10 respectively). Even when one examines a single context – e.g. the age of consent – there is no agreement as to what this is and it may differ depending on the activity (some countries continue to differentiate between homosexual and heterosexual acts), whom the sexual activity is with (e.g. in England and Wales there are certain individuals who are deemed to be in a position of trust where the age of consent is raised from 16 to 18) and indeed it may differ between countries (for example, in both the United States and Australia there is no single age of consent, with each state or territory having the right to set their own).

The Convention on the Rights of the Child defines a 'child' as anyone under the age of 18 unless domestic legislation says to the contrary (Article 1). The Optional Protocol to the CRC on the sale of children, child prostitution and child pornography (A/RES/54/263) echoes this position by, in essence, linking the definition of child pornography to that of a child within the CRC itself. Other international instruments adopt similar reasoning, with both the ILO Convention on the Worst Forms of Child Labour (C 182) and the [EU] Council Framework Decision 2004/68/JHA on combating the Sexual Exploitation of Children and Child Pornography (OJ: 13/44) setting the definition of a 'child' for the purposes of child pornography at 18. However other instruments adopt a slightly different approach. The Convention on Cybercrime (CETS No. 185) provides that the definition of a 'child' should ordinarily be 18 but can be reduced to 16 by signatory states (Article 3) and the Convention on the Protection of Children against Sexual Exploitation and Sexual Abuse (CETS No. 201) sets the age ordinarily at 18 but allows this to be reduced for some activities where the person portrayed has reached the age of consent (Article 3(a)).

International law therefore uses the age of majority for the purposes of defining a 'child' although this may, in part, be as a result of the fact that there has been no serious attempt at arriving at a uniform age of consent. The age of majority (18) is a controversial choice to many. Perhaps the most notable critic is Jenkins:

> Seventeen-year-olds are not children, and it is ludicrous to try to impose upon them the same limitations that apply to seven-year-olds . . . we cannot carry on pretending that sexuality is a mysterious force that descends on a person suddenly on his or her eighteenth birthday, prior to which the individual remains in pristine innocence.
>
> (Jenkins, 2001: 220)

There is some force to this argument. Choosing 18 does, at least ostensibly, treat 17 year-olds and young children in the same way. In reality the law will often differentiate through sentencing and prosecutorial discretion, but as a matter of definition this is correct. However the difficulty with Jenkins' argument is that it could be used against almost any age beyond puberty. It was noted in the previous section that children mature at different rates and this will mean that some adolescents at a particular age may be mature enough to understand what sexual activity involves and others will not. Therefore picking any age could lead to the same criticism being levelled.

Perhaps a better way to construe Jenkins' argument is to view it as an argument against differentiating between the age of consent (which in most countries would seem to be below 18) and the age of majority. Certainly a difficulty with using the age of majority over the age of consent is that it creates a paradox whereby a 19 year-old man can lawfully have sexual intercourse with his 17 year-old girlfriend but if she were to give him a topless photograph of herself, both would be committing serious criminal offences in many jurisdictions. However supporters of using the age of majority point to the fact that children 'still lack the mature judgement to decide whether or not to allow themselves to be photographed or filmed in such situations' (Carr, 2001: 12). It is known that once a sexualised photograph is placed on the internet it is highly unlikely that it will ever be recovered since it will be mirrored, downloaded and distributed (Taylor and Quayle, 2003: 24). Certainly therefore the argument of Carr is strengthened by the fact that the decision is permanent and there is some clear evidence emerging that adolescents do not necessarily understand the risks they are taking (see the discussion in Chapter 9). However the same is true of many situations, including other sexual contact. There is clear evidence that adolescents do not fully understand the dangers of pregnancy or sexually transmitted diseases, both of which could have permanent consequences, but few have suggested raising the age of consent.

It is not necessary in this chapter to consider what an appropriate age should be but it is submitted that differentiating between the age of consent and age of majority is not ideal. It sends out the wrong message and potentially criminalises adolescents who have a lawful active sexual life. That is not to minimise the harm that can be caused by the dissemination of the recording of private sexual activity but there is perhaps a question as to whether the criminal law is the appropriate tool to address this if it is at the expense of criminalising adolescents.

Type of material

Most of the literature that exists on child pornography is focused on photographs and movies. To an extent this is somewhat understandable as it would appear that this is the most prolific form of child pornography and is arguably the form that is most damaging to a child, in that it is a permanent record of the exploitation or abuse of a child. However child pornography is not restricted to photographs or indeed images at all. This is recognised in at least some instruments. The definition of child pornography contained in the Optional Protocol to the UNCRC is:

> ... any representation, by whatever means, of a child engaged in real or simulated explicit sexual activities or any representation of the sexual parts of a child for primarily sexual purposes.
>
> (Article 2(c))

The reference to 'whatever means' clearly covers more than just photographs as does the expansion to include simulated activities. Interpol has interpreted this in a wider way:

> ... any means of depicting or promoting the sexual exploitation of a child, including written or audio material, which focuses on the child's sexual behaviour or genitals.
>
> (cited in Carr, 2001)

Whilst this continues to make reference to 'any means of depicting the sexual exploitation of a child' the definition expressly considers non-image based forms of material. According to this definition it can be said that there are three forms of material:

- Visual representations.
- Written representations.
- Audio representations.

Visual representations

The first form to discuss is visual representation and this is undoubtedly the most prolific form of material. It must also be accepted that it is a very broad category and can be subdivided to include:

- Photographs.
- Manipulated photographs.
- Drawings (including computer-generated images).
- Cartoons.

Photographs are arguably the least problematic to criminalise (subject to the discussion on 'nature' below). Where a photograph shows the sexual exploitation or abuse of a child then the person who takes the photograph is complicit in their abuse or exploitation and many would argue that the person accessing or distributing the photograph is also complicit (discussed more extensively in the second half of this chapter below). Included within photographs would be negatives and moving films. The latter can arguably raise issues for the law. Should an entire film be classed as child pornography if a single scene depicts the sexual abuse of a child? How should the law treat a film for sentencing purposes? For example, should it be considered differently to 'still' photographs? This issue will be discussed more fully in Chapter 10 but if a distinction is made then this raises further questions since it is known that many static photographs will actually be images taken from a movie (Taylor and Quayle, 2003: 39). Indeed, it has been suggested that this fact is used by some offenders to compile a 'theme' of images focusing on, for example, oral sex, masturbation or other categories (Taylor and Quayle, 2003: 38).

Whilst digital technology has revolutionised the creation and dissemination of child pornography, advances in computing have created the situation whereby images can be easily altered or a realistic image of a child be created. The consequences of these manipulations is that it is possible to create an image that appears to be a child engaged in sexual activity without a child ever being involved or allow an image to suggest that a real child is engaging in sexual activity when, in fact, they are not. This issue will be explored in more depth in Chapters 3 and 5 but it is notable that they pose a distinct challenge to the law in terms of justifying their criminalisation.

Alongside manipulated and computer-generated images of children, the issue of cartoons and drawings has also been raised in recent years. Whilst the portrayal of child pornography dates back to ancient times (Ost, 2009: 25) the new millennia has seen the discussion on its regulation reappear on the public agenda. One of the most prominent forms of drawings to be discussed in recent times is the issue of Manga cartoons. Manga is a popular and ancient form of art in Japan (Ito, 2005) but its popularity has increased in recent years beyond Asian countries. A species of Manga cartoons is Hentai, which are sexually explicit forms of Manga. It is not uncommon for Hentai to focus on aggressive sex, portraying rape and also involve the use of young-looking characters, including those portrayed as girls or schoolchildren (Jones, 2003). Some countries are concerned about this form of expression but there is some evidence to suggest that its status is accepted in Japan (Jones, 2003) even though it would appear that Hentai is a relatively modern phenomenon dating from the 1970s or 1980s

(Ito, 2005). What should the status of Hentai be? If one recalls the UN definition then it undoubtedly conforms with that in that it is a representation, but
it is also undoubtedly a product of a person's imagination, a fantasy. The consequences of considering Hentai to be a form of child abuse will be discussed in
Chapter 5.

Written representations

It has been noted that although the term 'pornography' originally meant writing,
the issue of text has tended to be overlooked in understandings of child pornography (NGO, 2005: 27). It is known that a considerable body of written material
exists, with Jenkins noting that a significant proportion of this amount is written
by sex offenders themselves, who then place it on the internet where it is copied
and downloaded by others (Jenkins, 2001: 57). Jenkins notes that much of the
material presented could be classified as extreme and involve fantasies about
rape (Jenkins, 2001: 134) although other material may be non-violent. Along with
ad hoc production there is also a body of text-based work that is created and hosted
by more formal organisations, such as NAMBLA (the North American Man/Boy
Lovers Association, an organisation that campaigns to permit sexual relationships
to exist between adults and children). Such organisations try to justify themselves
as putting forward 'cross-generational' or 'love' stories but their content remains
the description of sexual acts between adults and minors, therefore amounting
to a 'representation' within the meaning of, for example, the definition of child
pornography put forward in the Optional Protocol.

As will be seen from Chapter 7 the law struggles with text-based forms of
pornography and few countries specifically address this issue (a notable exception
being Ireland: see s. 2(1), Child Trafficking and Pornography Act 1998). The
reason for this is that it is the form of material that raises most prominently
the issue of freedom of speech/expression. Most countries still bear the scars of
the debate over the legitimateness of publishing books that challenge society's
views of morality. Whilst, in practical terms, we can draw a distinction between
stories created by those with a sexual interest in children and literary works such
as Nabokov's *Lolita* or the Marquis de Sade's *Juliette*, it is less easy for the law to
draw this distinction. How does one frame a law that criminalises the former but
not the latter? It is this balance that will be discussed in more depth in Chapter 7.

Audio representations

Perhaps one of the forms of material that is least discussed is that of audio
representations although there is some evidence to suggest that they exist with,
for example, Interpol expressly noting their existence in their definition of
child pornography (Interpol website). There would also appear to be psychological evidence to show that offenders can find sound files sexually arousing
(Quayle *et al.*, 2006: 60). However it is an issue that is rarely discussed and, as

will be seen from the later chapters of this book, it is uncommon for legal instruments to tackle this material.

Of course a difficulty with sound is deciding what it is that should be classed as child pornography. For example, should it only be the audio representation of a child engaging in sexual activity? Where, for example, a person receives sexual gratification from a child being spanked or beaten then should an audio-representation of this be classed as child pornography? What of the recording of a sexually explicit conversation with a child? Is that child pornography? Another difficulty is ascertaining whether it is a child. Visual representations allow a person to assess the age of a child but it is perhaps more difficult to do this with sound. Does this mean that any definition should be based on the presentation of the matter – i.e. if the subject is being portrayed as a child then it is a child – irrespective of the reality? If the object of the law is to protect actual children how would such an approach fit in? What would the position be of extracts from films? Some released films do broach the subject of sexual contact with a child (for example, the film version of *Lolita*) so would a sound-only recording of the film amount to child pornography?

As noted few jurisdictions expressly tackle sound and the author is aware of no case within those jurisdictions where audio-only material has been prosecuted, perhaps because of the difficulties suggested above.

Nature or purpose of the material

The final aspect of the definition is to consider what it is about the material that justifies its criminalisation. This section will simply highlight this issue as it is something that will be discussed in more depth in later chapters, particularly Chapters 3 and 4 where the legal tests for the nature of material will be discussed in more depth.

It has been noted already that the term 'child pornography' is very controversial and, realistically, it is the term 'pornography' that is objectionable. To many pornography is considered to be the visual depiction of sexualised behaviour between consenting adults. Whilst, of course, not everybody agrees with this and many feminists argue that it is about the subjugation of women (Easton, 1994, and see, in particular, the work of Catherine MacKinnon) it has to be accepted that this is true for at least some forms of behaviour. However this is not true of child pornography as in many instances the material depicts non-consensual behaviour and many would argue that a child lacks the capacity to consent to their depiction (Carr, 2001, discussed above). More than this, it has been noted that most definitions of child pornography are premised on the basis of the harm that is caused to the child in the production of child pornography (Beech *et al.*, 2008: 218). The same is undoubtedly true of laws. The international instruments that seek to regulate child pornography all provide some reference to this notion and the law in England and Wales adopts the same approach: indeed it will be seen in Chapter 3 that the name of the legislation – Protection of Children Act 1978 – was not accidental.

Whilst a significant amount of the material that constitutes child pornography will depict clear harm being caused to a child it must be noted that not all material does this. Tate, in one of the earlier studies on child pornography, noted that offenders use a broad range of material (Tate, 1990: 15) and not all of it necessarily shows a child being sexually assaulted. The UN Special Rapporteur on the sale of children, child prostitution and child pornography classified material into 'hardcore' and 'child erotica' (Petit, 2004: 7–8). He defined hardcore material as that which 'depicts a child engaged in real or simulated explicit sexual activities or lewdly depict parts of a child's body' (Petit, 2004: 7). He defined 'child erotica' as 'images of children posing half dressed or naked with an emphasis on sexualizing the child' (Petit, 2004: 8) and he noted that much of the material was not illegal under many countries' laws.

Some academics have suggested that definitions of child pornography should be focused not on the material itself but on its effect on its consumers. Perhaps the most notable of these was the work of Svedin and Back, 1996 who suggest that child pornography could be defined as material that is intended to invoke a sexual reaction from the viewer. An advantage of this approach is that it allows for a wider base of material to be included but a significant disadvantage is that of certainty. Offenders are not an ubiquitous group and offenders will react differently and in respect of different material (Taylor and Quayle, 2003: 30) and this would raise questions as to how to classify material.

Perhaps the most notable analysis of material was undertaken by the COPINE unit, then based on Cork, Ireland. Their research entailed building up a database of child pornography photographs that was freely available from the internet (the majority of the images were taken from newsgroups). By analysing the images they were able to identify the characteristics of images and they produced a ten-point taxonomy (Taylor et al., 2001). The ten-point scale is shown in Table 2.1.

Chapter 10 will note that this scale has been misrepresented by, amongst others, the Sentencing Advisory Panel/Sentencing Guidelines Council in that the scale was never intended to suggest an indication of either the dangerousness of a person or the seriousness of an offence committed. The taxonomy was based on the victimisation suffered in the production of the image (Taylor et al., 2001: 100) and it is for this reason that sexual activity between minors (level 7) is lower than non-penetrative activity involving an adult (level 8) since the latter involves the breach of a position of power. A simple reading of the taxonomy demonstrates the broad range of material and it is notable that it contains images that could be classed as innocent. Indeed, the full explanation of level 1 notes that the photographs may come from legitimate sources.

Can level 1 and 2 images be considered child pornography? Certainly it is unlikely that it would be considered to be within any legal definition but Taylor and Quayle note:

The reasons for inclusion of these kinds of photograph … is that the extent to which a photograph may be sexualised and fantasised over lies not so much in its objective content, but in the use to which the picture might be put.

(Taylor and Quayle, 2003: 33)

Table 2.1 Scale of images

Level	Name	Description
1	Indicative	Non-erotic and non-sexualised pictures showing children in their underwear, swimming costumes, etc.
2	Nudist	Pictures of naked or semi-naked children in appropriate nudist settings
3	Erotica	Surreptitiously taken photographs of children in appropriate nudist settings
4	Posing	Deliberately posed pictures of children fully clothed, partially clothed or naked
5	Erotic posing	Deliberately posed pictures of children fully clothed, partially clothed or naked in sexualised or provocative poses
6	Explicit erotic posing	Emphasising genital areas where the child is either naked, partially clothed or fully clothed
7	Explicit sexual activity	Involves touching, mutual and self-masturbation, oral sex and intercourse by child, not involving an adult
8	Assault	Pictures of children being subject to a sexual assault, involving digital touching, involving an adult
9	Gross assault	Grossly obscene pictures of sexual assault, involving penetrative sex, masturbation or oral sex involving an adult
10	Sadistic/ Bestiality	(a) Pictures showing a child being tied, bound, beaten, whipped or otherwise subject to something that implies pain (b) Pictures where an animal is involved in some form of sexual behaviour with a child

In other words, psychologically it is relevant that offenders may misuse these types of images even if the law may not currently recognise this fact. The same can be said of the other lower level images and Taylor and Quayle note, for example, that level 2 is perhaps problematic in that a number of sexualised photographs have been used in the context of advertisements (Taylor and Quayle, 2003: 34). Certainly a number of advertisers have pushed the boundaries in the past and played on adolescent sexuality to promote their products (see Adler, 2001: 252 f.). However the 'legitimateness' of the material may be irrelevant to an offender since it is clear that offenders will use perfectly legitimate material for masturbation to fulfil sexual fantasy (Howitt, 1995, cited in Sheldon and Howitt, 2007: 113).

Given the broad range of material that will encompass even legitimate images, how should the law approach the nature of child pornography? It has been suggested that legal systems tend to divide material into three categories:

- *Indicative.* Material depicting clothed children which suggests a sexual interest in children.
- *Indecent.* Material depicting naked children which suggests a sexual interest in children.
- *Obscene.* Material which depicts children in sexual acts (Taylor and Quayle, 2003: 27).

The same authors suggest that the former category – indicative – is unlikely to be illegal. Whilst this may well be true, a difficulty with this approach is that the categories are broad. For example, the range of material within the 'indecent' category will encompass both innocent and problematic pictures, not all of which will be illegal. It is also doubtful that such broad categories tell us anything about the use of material by offenders (Taylor and Quayle, 2003: 27).

Child pornography laws in most jurisdictions appear to be derivatives of obscenity legislation (Gillespie, 2010a). This approach is also reflected in international instruments where, for example, the EU Framework Decision makes reference to images of a child 'involved or engaged in sexually explicit conduct, including lascivious exhibition of the genitals or the pubic area of a child' (Article 1(a)). 'Lasciviousness' is directly related to obscenity although in the United States, where the term is also used, the courts have suggested that it need not bear the same gravity as obscenity and covers a broader range of material (see, for example, *US v Rayl* 270 F3.d. 709 (2001), *US v Dost* 636 F. Supp. 727 (1986) and Gillespie, 2010b). The Australian state of Victoria, and England and Wales adopt a similar approach but choose the term 'indecent' instead of lascivious (see s. 67A, Crimes Act 1958 (Victoria) and s. 1, Protection of Children Act 1978 (England and Wales)). These concepts will be explored in later chapters but it is worth noting that it would seem that indecency is a derivative of obscenity.

Whilst the detail of the tests relating to lasciviousness and indecency will be explored elsewhere it is worth noting here that the law does appear to limit the categories of material that are considered to constitute child pornography. Not all material that offenders use for sexual gratification will be illegal. It will be seen from the following chapters that a degree of objectivity is required in deciding whether the test is satisfied and this may introduce uncertainty as to what constitutes child pornography.

Involvement in child pornography

It is not enough that child pornography is defined, it is also necessary to understand how child pornography is used by offenders. By understanding this use it will be possible to assess how, and to what extent, the law should intervene.

Sheldon and Howitt suggest that there are four uses of child pornography:

- Pornography as a means of sexual arousal and aid to fantasy.
- Pornography as a way of avoiding real life.

- Pornography as a collecting behaviour.
- Pornography as a way of facilitating social relationships. (Sheldon and Howitt, 2007: 109.)

Taylor and Quayle argue that some claim there is an additional use: accessing child pornography as therapy (Taylor and Quayle, 2003: 80). This use is the suggestion by some offenders that they use child pornography as a form of therapeutic treatment to prevent them from committing contact offences. The existence of such use is controversial and it will be explored briefly below.

Taylor and Quayle noted that of these different types, the use of child pornography for sexual arousal was the most dominant (Taylor and Quayle, 2003: 80), something also found by Sheldon and Howitt who noted that 75 per cent of internet offenders they questioned admitted to using it for this purpose (Sheldon and Howitt, 2007: 109). It is notable that many offenders would download large quantities of material for their sexual arousal, allowing them to choose the images which they wished to use for sexual gratification (Sheldon and Howitt, 2007: 109; Taylor and Quayle, 2003: 182). Those that accessed child pornography as an aid to sexual gratification would, perhaps not unsurprisingly, be quite specific in terms of what they looked for and noted that some images they found distasteful and indeed morally wrong (Sheldon and Howitt, 2007: 110; Taylor and Quayle, 2003: 83). A common selecting factor was the issue of enjoyment (Taylor and Quayle, 2003: 82) and it has been noted that many offenders will rely on the child smiling or perhaps enjoying themselves as a justification for the images, implying that it is not rape because the child is clearly enjoying it (Sheldon and Howitt, 2007: 111; Winder and Gough, 2010: 130).

Believing the child is consenting is not the only cognitive distortion suffered by offenders. It is notable that offenders will often choose to justify their use of child pornography as harmless (Winder and Gough, 2010: 130). Howitt and Sheldon note that comments such as 'having sexual thoughts and fantasies about a child isn't that bad because at least it is not really hurting the child' and 'just looking at a child is not as bad as touching and will not affect the child as much' are commonly made by offenders (Sheldon and Howitt, 2007: 191) and they criticise them as 'self-serving excuses by internet-only offenders to justify their offences'.

The second use of the material identified is that of avoiding life. It has been noted that the internet provides 'a world which is very unproblematic compared with the real word with all of its difficulties' (Sheldon and Howitt, 2007: 113). This is perhaps best reflected by the popularity of 'alternative worlds' such as 'Second Life' which allows users to interact with persons in alternative worlds by creating representations of themselves ('avatars') which will frequently bear no resemblance to themselves (for an interesting discussion on child pornography within Second Life see Coleman, 2008).

A common feature of emotional avoidance is that offenders report that they were able to go to the room where they accessed the internet and shut themselves away from the world (Taylor and Quayle, 2003: 89; Sheldon and Howitt, 2007:

114). Offenders found themselves in control of an aspect of their life in a way that they did not necessarily have in real life (Sheldon and Howitt, 2007: 115). Often the control would be sexual control and the offenders would believe they could obtain sexual gratification in a way that they could not in real life (Taylor and Quayle, 2003: 90). Such belief could combine with the cognitive distortions identified above, leading people to decide that they were acting in a harmless way. A difficulty with using pornography as a means of emotional avoidance is that, as with some forms of addiction, it appears that the 'fix' required to obtain the avoidance becomes bigger and there is some evidence to suggest that offenders begin to look for more depraved, more sexual and younger children in order to produce the release (Sheldon and Howitt, 2007: 115).

The third identified behaviour is collecting. Some offenders would attempt to suggest that collecting child pornography was no different to other forms:

> we were trading pictures . . . it's as much as it pains me to say . . . kinda like trading baseball cards.

> and there was also the thrill in collecting them. You wanted to get complete sets so it . . . was a bit like stamp collecting as well.
>
> (Taylor and Quayle, 2003: 83)

Of course such comments belie the reality of the position and the fact that it can serve as a powerful cognitive distortion in attempting to normalise the behaviour. It is telling that 'when talking about the pictures [collected], invariably no reference was made to the content as being child pornography' (Taylor and Quayle, 2003: 83). It appears that to some offenders the process of collecting is an important feature of their behaviour and this will involve the quest to complete a collection. The process of collecting would sometimes be part of the pleasure an offender received but there is also evidence to suggest that it was often used for other reasons. It was noted that collecting and organising the collection would allow for an offender to identify new material and also would facilitate the trading and dissemination of material (Taylor and Quayle, 2003: 84).

The fourth behavioural type identified is the use of pornography as a way of facilitating societal relationships. This will not apply to every offender but it identifies the position whereby many offenders will form collectives or join groups that will allow them to communicate with each other and trade images. To an extent this behaviour can be a development of emotional avoidance as some offenders would join these collectives because it allowed them to believe they were not alone and others shared their sexual interest (Taylor and Quayle, 2003: 88; Sheldon and Howitt, 2007: 119). Many would find the group as exciting as the material and desire being accepted within the group (Sheldon and Howitt, 2007: 119; Sheehan and Sullivan, 2010: 163).

Some collectives are relatively informal with low levels of security but it is also clear that others are quite sophisticated with a series of 'rules' being developed by which the collective functions (Taylor and Quayle, 2003: 94). Some of these rules would relate to the type of material that would be accepted, or rules governing how the images are traded. It may also involve how new members can join the collective, in part to ensure the security of the group.

Whilst these four behaviours focus on the reasoning of the offender, others believe that an analysis of what the offender does could be useful. Taylor and Quayle identify two broad categories which they characterise as 'producer' and the 'viewer' (Taylor and Quayle, 2003). The distinction between the two categories is based on the premise of creation with the latter, viewing, including possession, collection and distribution (Taylor and Quayle, 2003: 23). Some would no doubt question whether distribution can realistically be separated from production as there would appear to be an inextricable link between them. Others believe that the use is more complicated and Krone has produced a typology of behaviour (Table 2.2).

Krone suggests there is progression in severity between the levels (Krone, 2004: 4) but it is not immediately clear what the basis of the severity is. Krone argues there is a progression from offences that do not involve direct contact with children to those which do involve direct contact but if victimisation is the key it

Table 2.2 Krone's typology of behaviour

Type of involvement	Features
Browser	Response to spam, accidental hit on suspect site – material knowingly saved
Private fantasy	Conscious creation of online text or digital images for private use
Trawler	Actively seeking child pornography using openly available browsers
Non-secure collector	Actively seeking material often through peer-to-peer networks
Secure collector	Actively seeking material but only through secure networks. Collector syndrome and exchange as an entry barrier
Groomer	Cultivating an online relationship with one or more children. The offender may or may not seek material in any of the above ways. Pornography may be used to facilitate abuse
Physical abuser	Abusing a child who may have been introduced to the offender online. The offender may or may not seek material in any of the above ways. Pornography may be used to facilitate abuse
Producer	Records own abuse or that of others (or induces children to submit images of themselves)
Distributor	May distribute at any one of the levels above

Source: Krone (2004: 4).

is difficult to understand why it is that the distributor is listed as the most serious offender when many would argue the producer is. Questions are perhaps also asked about the lower levels, as some argue that the creation of fantasy material is a concern although this is a matter that is discussed more fully in Chapter 5.

The typology is useful in identifying the different types of conduct that offenders undertake. It is notable that the first level – browsing – is premised on the basis that the material is encountered innocently but that the offender consciously decides to save the material. Many offenders argue that they started off their viewing of child pornography through initially accessing adult pornography (Sheldon and Howitt, 2007: 100) and coming across child pornography through pop-ups or posted material on those sites (see also Seto *et al.*, 2010: 175). Many jurisdictions will probably criminalise trawling as possession (discussed in Chapters 6 and 8) but probably only where it can be proven that the images were deliberately saved or kept for an inappropriate amount of time.

It is interesting that Krone distinguishes between a trawler and a collector. In later writings he notes that a trawler may include the 'libertarian' who is someone who is not necessarily sexually interested in child pornography but someone who 'asserts a claim to be free to access whatever material they wish' (Krone, 2005: 25). A trawler is somebody who is seeking out child pornography but only in publicly available manners. Whilst Krone refers to the use of web browsers it is also likely that it would include the use of Usenet (see Sheldon and Howitt, 2007: 94). Being a trawler does not necessarily mean that the offender is not technologically aware since some will be sufficiently aware to evade age verification or payment systems (Sheldon and Howitt, 2007: 101). A collector differs from a trawler in that he will access peer-to-peer networks and actively trade with other offenders. It is quite possible that a collector is more likely to be using child pornography as a way of facilitating a social relationship and is talking with other offenders. The secure collector is careful as to who he trades material with. He is conscious of the illegality of his behaviour and will use encryption or collectives with high degrees of security to minimise his chances of being detected by law enforcement (something discussed in Chapter 12).

The online groomer and physical abuser uses child pornography in one of two ways. The first is that there is some suggestion that they may use child pornography as a way of justifying their contact offending. This is something that will be addressed below where the discussion of contact offending is expanded upon. The second way of using child pornography is to facilitate their contact offending. There is some evidence to suggest that offenders use child pornography to de-sensitise children, making them believe that sexual relationships below the age of consent (or indeed before puberty) is neither wrong nor unusual (Taylor and Quayle, 2003: 23). Alternatively where a child has sent an image of itself to an offender, this could be used as blackmail by the offender to coerce the child into acquiescing into sexual contact (Ost, 2009: 47).

Closely related to the groomer and the physical abuser is the producer of child pornography. Krone is careful to state that a producer is 'involved in the physical abuse of children' (Krone, 2004: 5) because it does not necessarily follow that the producer will be the person who is actually undertaking the abusive acts. It is quite possible that the production of child pornography is a commercial enterprise and thus the person who is ultimately producing the material is not sexually interested in the child and views it simply as a commercial enterprise (Beech *et al.*, 2008). That said, there appears to be some evidence that a considerable amount of child pornography is not commercial (Wolak *et al.*, 2005: 43 but see IWF, 2010 which suggests that the amount of commercially traded and produced material is increasing). Whilst it may seem that a producer will necessarily wish to distribute the material he has produced there is no clear evidence base to show this (Wolak *et al.*, 2005: 41). This may in part be explained by the fact that offenders may be unlikely to admit distribution in that it could lead to an increased sentence (discussed more extensively in Chapter 10). Of those who do disseminate their production, some will release the material to a limited number of people (Wolak *et al.*, 2005: 43) although, of course, there is no guarantee that the recipients will not themselves then distribute the images.

Krone's typology is useful in identifying the key uses of child pornography by offenders. How should the law react to these? The specifics will be dealt with in the subsequent chapters but the public policy justification for criminalisation should be addressed, albeit briefly, here. When one looks at the behaviour and use of the material it can be said that there are, in reality, four actions:

- Production.
- Dissemination.
- Possession.
- Viewing.

The justification for criminalising each may differ and so each will be examined in turn. Separate to this is the use of child pornography to groom children. However this will not be explored in this book as it is arguably a different behaviour – it is the solicitation of a child for sexual gratification – and the child pornography is simply a tool that an offender uses as part of this solicitation. This is not to minimise the behaviour, far from it, but this chapter is examining offender behaviour in respect of child pornography in its own right rather than as a means of facilitating other crimes.

Production

The first of the four behaviours to examine is that of the production of child pornography. In this context production means the creation of child pornography that does not previously exist. Production covers a broad range of behaviour, from commercial production to the individual offender recording his own material. The latter is particularly interesting since whereas commercial producers may not find the material sexually interesting, smaller producers are more likely to be users of child pornography themselves (Wolak *et al.*, 2005: 34 noted that 73 per cent of producers in their study also possessed material produced by others). The majority of small-scale producers sexually assaulted the victim that was portrayed within it (Wolak *et al.*, 2005: 39) although approximately one-third did not. Those that did not were more likely to use 'covert' methods of producing child pornography through, for example, hidden cameras (Wolak *et al.*, 2005: 40). Voyeurism is considered to be a paraphilia in its own right (DSM IV §302.82) and questions may be raised as to when it amounts to child pornography and when it is the desire to meet voyeuristic demands (see Gillespie, 2008). The answer probably depends on the purpose of the recording and perhaps whether the material was distributed. If it was distributed then its classification could perhaps be gleaned from that (i.e. is it distributed as part of a wider voyeuristic collection (including adults) or is it distributed to those with a sexual interest in children).

Why should production be criminalised? The justification will differ depending on the type of material but in this section the justification for criminalising photograph-based child pornography (which is almost certainly the most prolific type) will be discussed, with the criminalisation of non-photograph-based forms being discussed elsewhere in the book.

To an extent the justification for criminalising the production of photograph-based forms of child pornography is the easiest of the four types of behaviour. As has been noted already in this chapter, its production involves a real child. Subject to the discussion on the nature of the material which was presented earlier in this chapter, the production of child pornography requires a real child to be abused or exploited. The latter part is important in that even where the subject is not engaging in sexual activity, the picture is exploitative in that viewers will be able to access images of the subject that should be inherently private. It is submitted that such images undermine the sexual autonomy and identity of the child.

Where the child has been sexually assaulted, the production of child pornography aggravates this harm. Whilst there have been few studies that have examined the victimisation of the subject of internet child pornography (Palmer, 2005: 63) studies that pre-date the internet show that children suffer psychological harm from the process of the abuse being filmed (Quayle *et al.*, 2006: 48). Indeed, the studies noted that the production of child pornography meant that it was less likely that a child would disclose the abuse (Quayle *et al.*, 2006: 48) in part because they were afraid that they would be viewed as complicit in their abuse or acquiesced to it (Palmer, 2005: 63). The internet ensures that these images can now circulate perpetually (Taylor and Quayle, 2003: 24) and thus the long-term consequences for the victim can be profound (Taylor and Quayle, 2003: 211). A victim will never know when someone known to them will see the photograph and possibly recognise them (Palmer, 2005) causing additional psychological distress and harm (von Weiler *et al.*, 2010: 216). Accordingly an additional reason for criminalising the production of child pornography is this additional psychological harm that is caused separate to the harms caused by the initial abuse.

A third justification for the criminalisation of the production of child pornography is that it objectifies children as sexual objects. Arguably the justification could apply to all the actions relating to child pornography but it is perhaps most relevant to the production of child pornography.

Dissemination

The second of the four identified actions is that of dissemination, i.e. the proliferation of child pornography. There are two aspects of distribution that need to be considered: the proliferation of original material (i.e. by a producer) and the proliferation of existing material (i.e. by someone other than a producer).

Whilst we may think of a producer of child pornography necessarily distributing the material they create, one major study showed that only a minority actually do so (Wolak *et al.*, 2005: 41). However this conclusion is premised by the qualification that in approximately one-half of the cases law enforcement agencies could not identify whether there had been distribution. Whilst as a matter of law this would mean that a person could not be charged with distribution it does not mean that there has been no distribution, merely it may not have been detected. A number of producers state that they undertook a restricted form of distribution where they passed the material on to a small number of people, although this shows a degree of naivety as it is impossible to be assured that those recipients would not themselves then distribute the material (although it would appear such naivety does exist: Sheehan and Sullivan, 2010: 163).

The second, and perhaps more common, form of distribution is when someone other than the producer distributes the material. It has been noted that the dissemination of child pornography can be lucrative (Taylor and Quayle, 2003: 6) although there is doubt as to how extensive commercial child pornography is. Whilst some believe that it accounts for only a minor part (O'Donnell and Milner, 2007: 20; Wolak *et al.*, 2005: 43) others believe that it is starting to become more extensive, with the UN Special Rapporteur on the sale of children, child pornography and child prostitution stating there is evidence that organised crime is becoming increasingly involved (Petit, 2004: 8). This change appears to be borne out by the latest Internet Watch Foundation report where it is stated that 'over half of the material we deal with is related to commercial payment mechanisms' (IWF, 2010: 6). This being the case then the potential for human misery increases. Commercial child sexual exploitation has been likened to the slave trade and there is no reason to consider that child pornography is any different: it involves a child being treated as a commodity.

When one thinks of distribution it is relatively easy to think of it as a simple process: person X sends child pornography to person Y. However it may be more sophisticated than this. It was noted earlier in this chapter that one recognised use of child pornography was to facilitate social relationships. Distribution is central to this behaviour and it is notable that often the purpose of the distribution was as much about the normalisation of their behaviour as it was the trading of images (Taylor and Quayle, 2003: 184). For some offenders who were part of a collective, the trading of images (particularly new images) gave them a status within the collective (Taylor and Quayle, 2003: 185). It should not be thought that all offenders seek to become involved in trading as many do not (the research of Sheldon and Howitt showed few people who were actively 'trading' images although they concede this was because their subjects were not part of a collective: see Sheldon and Howitt, 2007: 108) but it can be questioned whether the law necessarily understands the different behavioural aspects of distribution, including those within an organised ring.

What is the justification for criminalising distribution? Where it is the producer who is distributing child pornography then it acts as a direct additional harm to the abuse suffered. It was noted above that the impact a child suffers with the knowledge that their abuse was recorded is considerable. What of those situations where it is not the producer who is distributing the image but a third party? It can be said that they are complicit in the continuing harm that a child suffers. The distribution of images means that the secondary harm caused by the production of child pornography continues to exist many years after the victim's assault, and there continues to be a risk that the child will be identified. A third party who distributes this material is contributing to this secondary harm and is thus also culpable.

What of the more indirect harms? The most relevant is that distribution encourages offenders to believe that the use of child pornography for sexual gratification is normal or acceptable. This is perhaps difficult to justify criminalisation. It has been noted already that some offenders use the trading of child pornography as part of a social interaction whereby they encourage each other in their behaviour and consolidate the belief that it is correct. However can this really be said to be a justification for the criminalisation of all distribution? Arguably not because it must be remembered that even where offenders are paedophiles (in its clinical sense), paedophilia itself is not illegal nor is being a paedophile. Unless the social interaction amounts to the encouragement to commit a crime then this element cannot realistically be considered criminal.

An issue that will be picked up in Chapter 10, when discussing the issue of sentencing, is whether the distribution of particular types of images necessarily demonstrates the risk of harm they pose. There is some evidence to suggest that offenders were prepared to trade images that they themselves found uninteresting or objectionable in order to obtain images that they were interested in (Taylor and Quayle, 2003: 185).

Possession

The third form of behaviour identified is that of possession and, as will be seen, the criminalisation of possession has proved somewhat controversial. In the context of the internet it is most likely that this will be downloading material (although as will be seen in Chapter 6 the law in England and Wales will not necessarily consider this to be possession) but in offline offending this could be through retaining material in magazines, photographs, drawings or videos.

The criminalisation of possession remains somewhat controversial. Not every country criminalises the possession of child pornography and international law is somewhat opaque as to its status. The Optional Protocol to the CRC requires States to criminalise 'producing, distributing, disseminating, importing, exporting, offering, selling or possessing for the above purposes child pornography . . .' (Article 3.1). This would seem to mean that simple possession is not included within the Optional Protocol. The Convention on Cybercrime does prohibit simple possession (Article 9.1(e)) although the Convention allows Member States to choose not to do so (Article 9.4). The Convention on the sexual exploitation of children adopts a slightly more restricted approach in that although simple possession is criminalised (Article 20.1(e)) Member States can choose not to criminalise simple possession where the offender has reached the age of consent and the child consents to the possession (Article 20.3).

Should possession be criminalised? Notwithstanding the wording of the Optional Protocol the Special Rapporteur on the sale of children, child prostitution and child pornography has stated:

> The possession of child pornography creates demand for such material. An effective way to curtail the production of child pornography is to attach criminal consequences to the conduct of each participant in the chain from production to possession.
>
> (Petit, 2004: 10)

It has to be acknowledged that not everybody necessarily agrees that the possession of child pornography can be necessarily justified. Separate arguments exist in respect of virtual child pornography and this will be explored in Chapter 5. What of the possession of material that does depict the abuse of (real) children? There are four possible justifications that are ordinarily put forward:

- The suggestion that there is a link between the possession of child pornography and contact offending.
- The argument that the possession of child pornography fuels demand for new images.
- That secondary harm is caused to victims by the possession of child pornography.
- That the material is justified on the basis of morality.

Contact offending

It is not uncommon to hear articulated the belief that there is a link between the possession of child pornography and contact sexual offences being committed against children. Certainly the link exists in at least one direction in that it has been noted already that photograph-based child pornography involves a real child being abused or exploited to produce child pornography (subject to the discussion on virtual child pornography in Chapter 5). What is contested however is whether there is a link in the other direction: i.e. whether it can be shown that a person who possesses child pornography is more likely to offend against a child.

The research on the existence of such a link is equivocal at best. What does appear clear is that possession of child pornography can be an effective indication of whether someone is a paedophile (Seto *et al.*, 2006). This research does not however show the existence of a link between possession and offending. The research was focused not on contact offending but on paedophilia itself. As noted earlier in this chapter, paedophilia is a paraphilia and not necessarily an indication of offending behaviour. The authors note that their research has a practical implication in that it can be of use where an offender denies that he has a sexual interest in children (Seto *et al.*, 2006: 614); something that will be discussed in the context of sentencing in Chapter 10. However the authors expressly noted that their research did not demonstrate anything about sexual recidivism or the risk of sexual contact (Seto *et al.*, 2006: 614).

What of studies that have sought to specifically explore the link? There are different approaches to considering any link. One is to look at re-offending rates. A notable study in this regard is Seto and Eke, 2005 which concluded that the recidivism rate was low and they specifically concluded that their findings 'contradict the assumption that all child pornography offenders are at [a] very high risk to commit sexual offences involving children' (Seto and Eke, 2005: 208). Other studies have reached similar conclusions. Endrass *et al.* examined the files relating to 231 Swiss men who were convicted of child pornography offences after accessing the American website Landslide Productions. The study revisited the offenders some six years after they were convicted and they found that none of the offenders had subsequently committed a contact sex offence (Endrass *et al.*, 2009: 4). It is perhaps surprising that there were no offenders convicted of a contact offence since Seto and Eke, in a smaller sample, noted at least some re-offending (Seto and Eke, 2005: 206).

A difficulty with using recidivism as evidence of a link is that it is believed that there is a disproportionately low reporting rate for sexual crimes, including offences against children. Also the standard of proof required to convict an offender is, in most countries, normally high and thus the mere fact that an offender has not been convicted of a sex offence does not mean that one has not been committed. Endreass *et al.* noted this and when the data was re-examined and investigations and charging decisions were taken into account then some offenders were found to have potentially progressed to contact offending (Endrass *et al.*, 2009: 4) although not in a statistically relevant number. The difficulty with recidivism rates as a methodology is that some studies look at alternative methods of categorising future offending. An interesting study in this regard is Bourke and Hernandez, 2009. This study examined, *inter alia*, the offending history of a group of offenders who had been convicted of child pornography offences. The study consisted of 155 offenders who were the subject of a residential sex offender treatment programme (SOTP). The results were quite startling. Prior to entering the SOTP some 74 per cent of offenders had no documented history of contact offending and yet by the end of the programme 85 per cent of the offenders admitted a contact offence, an increase of 59 per cent (Bourke and Hernandez, 2009: 187). Where this research differs from other studies is that the offenders had not been convicted of the offences – they were making admissions. Whilst it is, of course, possible that some people made a statement because they wanted to show co-operation with the SOTP it seems unlikely that this will account for the entirety of this sudden transformation. Indeed, the authors of the study expressly state that their findings challenge the suggestion that some people are 'only' involved with child pornography (Bourke and Hernandez, 2009: 188).

It is clear that the evidence is somewhat disparate. Hanson attempted to recon-cile many of the conflicting studies but noted that the results were equivocal:

> These findings suggest that a significant proportion, but not all, online sex offenders commit hands-on sexual offences in addition to internet sex offences. Even under conditions that would be expected to produce high disclosure rates ... approximately half of the online offenders reported no contact with live victims. Consequentially, it is possible that there is a rela-tively distant group of offenders whose only crimes involve internet or pornographic materials.
>
> (Hanson, 2009: 6)

These findings are supported by others. Sheldon and Howitt argue that their research showed 'most of the internet offenders either had no interest in, or avoided for some other reason, sexual contacts with children' (Sheldon and Howitt, 2007: 234). That said, they noted that where an offender was convicted of both an internet and contact offence, there was some evidence to believe that the pornography had played a role in the cycle of abuse leading to offending (Sheldon and Howitt, 2007: 235). They note that this is because of the role sexual fantasy can play in some sex offending. The difficulty is in identifying who those offenders are and what the link between fantasy and offending is (Quayle et al., 2006: 61). The position is perhaps further complicated by the fact that it would appear to depend on whether a person had a sexual interest in a child before engaging with child pornography (Quayle et al., 2006: 63; Bourke and Hernandez, 2009: 188).

Where does this leave us? It can be said that the evidence is equivocal at best. Whilst there would seem to be some evidence of a risk it is difficult to quantify this risk and it would seem that a significant number – and possibly the majority of offenders – do not seem to progress from child pornography to contact offences. It has been stated that '[g]iven the importance of this issue and the absence of definite knowledge, for practical purposes prudence suggests that we must err on the side of caution' (Taylor and Quayle, 2003: 195) and this must be correct. The law however requires proof of harm in order to justify criminalisation. That is not to say that the proof must be to the criminal standard or possibly even to the civil standard: given the nature of this behaviour it is quite likely that a significant risk could justify criminalisation. It is not however clear that we are at this stage now as the research is so inconclusive. That said, it is clear that the research should not be ignored and whilst it is so disparate as to preclude criminalisation solely on this basis it may be unwise to suggest that it can have no impact, and it is perhaps a more general factor that should be taken into account when deciding whether to criminalise possession.

Fuel argument

It was noted above that the UN Special Rapporteur on the sale of children, child prostitution and child pornography clearly believes that the possession of child pornography creates a demand for new material (Petit, 2004: 10) and he puts forward this argument as a justification for criminalising possession. Ost notes that this 'demand' argument is readily accepted by the courts who will frequently refer to this concept when sentencing those who are in possession of child pornography (Ost, 2009: 114).

There would seem to be some evidence to support the contention that possession can lead to a demand for new material. Quayle *et al.* state:

> What is apparent is that downloading behaviour, and the fantasies that it fuels, rarely remains a static response. If nothing else, offenders may get bored by the images they have downloaded and find that they lose the capacity to sexual arousal . . . Given the endless availability of pornographies on the internet, one natural consequence of this may be to seek more arousing images . . .
>
> (Quayle *et al.*, 2006: 61)

Since, with the exception of child pornography, the creation of child pornography requires a child to be abused or exploited it could follow that this demonstrates that possession does fuel the demand for new images and that this could justify the criminalisation of possession.

Ost approaches the same issue from a slightly different angle, which she describes as the 'market reduction' argument (Ost, 2009: 113). In this way she queries whether a justification for criminalising possession is that doing so will reduce the demand for new images which would, in turn, mean that less people would produce child pornography. Ost notes that the argument is best applied to commercial child pornography and that the research was unclear as to what extent a commercial market exists (Ost, 2009: 116) although, as noted earlier, there now seems evidence that commercial child pornography is on the increase (see, for example, IWF, 2010: 6).

Ost notes that some question whether the influence of the market is a justification for criminalising the possession of material (Ost, 2009: 117) although she concludes that it is possible to justify on the basis that possessors 'benefit from and take advantage of the actions of the producers of such material who cause the major, direct harm to the children involved' (Ost, 2009: 117–118). However this conclusion is premised on the existence of a link that the possessor is influencing the actions of the producer. Certainly such a link is likely to be present in commercial transactions – the possessor buys the new material – but it may also be present in other contexts, where for example a producer can see that people are 'consuming' his material and thus he feels more inclined to produce more material (on this see Sheehan and Sullivan, 2010: 163–164). It will be remembered from earlier in this chapter that a use of pornography can be to facilitate social relationships (Sheldon and Howitt, 2007: 109) and this may assist in demonstrating this link.

Secondary victimisation

The third justification that is put forward for the criminalisation of possession relates to secondary victimisation. The concept of secondary victimisation has been discussed already but it also could apply to the possessor. It will be remembered that it has been shown that child pornography is the re-victimisation of the child by serving as a permanent record of abuse (Taylor and Quayle, 2003: 24). The courts have adopted this logic and have, for example, noted that a child can be caused serious psychological harm by the knowledge that 'people out there [were] getting a perverted thrill from watching them forced to pose and behave in this way' (*R v Beaney* [2004] EWCA Crim 449 at [8]).

Ost agrees and notes that 'the possessor of child pornography directly harms the child in the image by exacerbating the primary harm . . . if the child is aware that the image is possessed by others' (Ost, 2009: 123). Of course this raises the issue about what happens where the child is not aware of the image. Certainly there can be no secondary harm where a child has no knowledge that the abuse was recorded or distributed. However as child pornography is a permanent record it is likely that the potential for secondary harm will continue to exist. If a person is not told that an image exists until 20 years later it is unlikely that this will affect their response, and the trauma that could be caused by that revelation. The same is likely to be true where the child is not aware of the initial abuse or exploitation (either because it was taken in a voyeuristic manner (e.g. a hidden camera in a bedroom or bathroom) or because the child was so young as not to recall the abuse (e.g. because it was a baby or toddler)). That said, the harm could arise where the child discovers, at a later date, the fact that the abuse or exploitation was recorded and this could include situations where the police or other law enforcement agency contacts the victim (something that will be discussed in Chapter 12). In any event in terms of the general offence of possession the fact that secondary harm is caused to those who appear in the photographs is, it is submitted, sufficient justification for criminalisation.

Morals

The final, and perhaps most controversial, reason advanced for justifying the criminalisation of possession is based on the concepts of morality. Williams, in particular, believes that it is inappropriate to justify criminalisation merely on what society finds inappropriate (Williams, 2004). As Ost notes, however, Devlin, amongst others, has argued that even private acts of immoral behaviour can amount to a threat to society justifying criminalisation (Ost, 2009: 120 f.). Whilst criminalising possession purely on the basis of morality may be problematic, Ost notes that it is more usually cited as an *additional* basis (Ost, 2009: 122). This perhaps illustrates the point about criminalisation. Whilst it may be difficult to identify a single justification for the criminalisation of possession, each of the factors identified contributes something to the argument and the combination suggests that there is a real risk of harm to children. As Ost notes, it should not be necessary to find direct proof of harm, it should suffice that there is a real risk of harm (Ost, 2009: 122) and this must be correct.

Viewing

The final behaviour to consider is that of viewing child pornography. It will be remembered from earlier in this chapter that Taylor and Quayle used the term 'viewing' as a broad category to encompass all forms of behaviour other than the production of material. However in this section the literal meaning will be adopted: i.e. an offender who is simply browsing the internet for child pornography material without intentionally downloading them ('intentional' is deliberately used since it is likely that the internet browser will save images automatically in the cache).

Should viewing child pornography be criminalised? As an initial step it should be noted that an element of *mens rea* would be required in that it should apply only to those who deliberately browse the internet with the intention of seeking child pornography. It was noted above that Krone and others believe that some offenders will initially obtain child pornography by chance and it is important that those who innocently come across child pornography (through pop-ups or illegal content being posted on legal sites) are not criminalised (but see *R v Harrison* [2008] 1 Cr App R 29 discussed in Chapter 6, one reading of which would appear to suggest that those who are merely reckless as to whether child pornography will be obtained may be culpable in England and Wales).

Should, or indeed could, deliberately accessing child pornography on the internet be criminalised? It will be seen in Chapter 6 that the courts in England and Wales have, somewhat controversially, decided that deliberately opening an indecent image of a child on a computer screen does amount to a criminal offence (*R v Jayson* [2002] EWCA Crim 683). It is also reported that legislation in Denmark covers those who 'deliberately access' child pornography and this must include viewing (Petit, 2004: 13). The Convention on the Protection of Children against Sexual Exploitation and Sexual Abuse calls on Member States to restrict, 'knowingly obtaining access, through information and communication technologies, to child pornography' (Article 20.1(f)) although the Convention allows Member States to choose not to apply this provision in whole or in part (Article 20.4). Knowingly accessing child pornography through ICT must mean viewing and it is notable that the Council of Europe has chosen to criminalise this. The EU has followed their lead. The Commission is currently consulting on replacing Council Framework Decision 2004/68/JHA (COM (2010) 94; 2010/0064(COD)) and Article 5.3 of the proposed text uses almost identical wording to the Convention on sexual exploitation but without offering Member States the right to opt out of such criminalisation.

Can this step be justified? Realistically the justification for criminalising viewing will be analogous to that of possession because they are, to an extent, similar. Arguably viewing is more transient since a person is not keeping or storing images, they are simply viewing them. This could be important because research appears to suggest that an offender who organises his collection in a systematic way is of greater concern (Wolak *et al.*, 2005: 10; Taylor and Quayle, 2003: 210) not least because it may be easier to disseminate the work. That said, however, this difference should not be overstated since a lot of offenders do not organise their collections and there is, for example, no evidence that an offender who systematically organises their collection is of greater risk of sexually assaulting a child (Wolak *et al.*, 2005: 11).

Our understanding of who is a 'possessor' and who is a 'viewer' will also adapt with technological change. In recent years there has been a growth in so-called 'cloud storage'. This is a term that is used to denote where files, etc., are stored—not on a local computer but on the internet itself. The data is stored on multiple servers and accessible through an FTP program. Where a user keeps his child pornography in cloud-based storage is he in possession of the material or is he merely viewing it? Also, if the former, then is the material possessed in this country or another? What is the position where it is hosted in a country where child pornography is lawful? These are issues that will be picked up elsewhere in the book.

Child pornography as therapy

Although the previous sections have discussed how child pornography is used and the behaviour of offenders, one final issue should be discussed, that of whether child pornography can be used in a therapeutic way.

Williams puts forward the argument that possession of child pornography could act as a therapeutic resource (Williams, 2004: 253) although she appears to concentrate on virtual child pornography in this regard. That said, some have put forward the belief that even child pornography involving actual children can act as a therapeutic means of preventing sexual-contact offending. Offenders will sometimes put this justification forward:

> Our main aim in collecting the child pornography is that we weren't involved with kids . . . it was helping . . . I didn't feel the urge as strongly as I do now to try and start something with a child
>
> ('EI' presented by Taylor and Quayle, 2003: 81)

Taylor and Quayle note that this is an offender seeking to minimise the inherent harm that is involved in the production of child pornography. They also note that such discourse allows offenders to present themselves as 'ill' and not deviant (Taylor and Quayle, 2003: 91). This 'pseudo-medicine' merely demonstrates that some offenders will evade the reality of what they are doing.

There is no substantive research that validates the idea that child pornography, in whatever form, can act as a therapeutic medium. Whilst studies such as Kutchinksy, 1985 are sometimes cited the results of such work have never been confirmed and they do not always differentiate between adult and child pornography or indeed between deviant fantasy and deviant behaviour (Sheldon and Howitt, 2007: 189). Seto, one of the most authoritative experts on paedophilia, concludes:

> A cathartic effect of child pornography would not be consistent with evidence regarding the impact of sexually explicit media.
>
> (Seto, 2008: 68)

Even without this conclusion it must be seriously questioned whether the inherent harm involved in child pornography could be offset by any possible therapeutic benefit. The issue of secondary victimisation has been rehearsed several times in this chapter and it has been noted that the victim portrayed in this image could suffer serious consequences from the knowledge that some are using their abuse and exploitation as a masturbatory aid. Is it likely that this trauma would be less if an offender states, 'Ah, but it stops me abusing another child'? It is submitted that it is unlikely to do so and that an unproven hypothesis that child pornography may have cathartic benefits will not depose the proven harms caused by the creation, dissemination and possession of child pornography.

Chapter 3

Defining indecent photographs of children

Chapter 2 considered the definition of child pornography and why it should be the subject of criminal sanctions. The chapter noted that whilst there are a variety of different types of material that could be criminalised, photograph-based forms of child pornography are arguably the most prominent form. In this chapter a discussion will be had of how the law in England and Wales defines photograph-based forms of child pornography.

In England and Wales photograph-based forms of child pornography are classed as 'indecent photographs of children' (s. 1, Protection of Children Act 1978) (PoCA 1978). PoCA 1978 is the primary piece of legislation in this area although it will be seen in the later chapters that other legislation (most notably the Criminal Justice Act 1988 and Sexual Offences Act 2003) also have an impact. PoCA 1978 provides the key definitions which are shared by other pieces of legislation.

The genesis and detail of PoCA 1978 will be expanded upon in other chapters of this book but in terms of defining child pornography there are three issues that need to be considered; that is, the meaning of 'child', 'photograph' and 'indecent'.

Child

As was the case in Chapter 2, the first issue to consider is what a 'child' is. It will be remembered that in Chapter 2 there was discussion about whether a child should be defined through biological characteristics or through the prescription of age. The Protection of Children Act 1978 always adopted the approach of specifying the age of a child. When originally drafted, a child was considered to be a person under the age of 16. There was little discussion in Parliament about why this age was taken although this was, in part, because the legislation itself was the subject of little scrutiny, with it being suggested 'the Bill passed through the House of Commons without any detailed discussion of its content or any possibility of improving it by amendment' (McCarthy and Moodie, 1981: 59). Certainly the second reading of the Bill passed without a vote and the third reading without debate. Certain members of the House of Lords itself deprecated the state the Bill arrived in when it was discussed in the House (see, for example, Hansard, HL Deb, vol. 391, col. 535 f., 5 May 1978) although, at least, the House of Lords was instrumental in undertaking any necessary revisions.

In the absence of any clues from Hansard, it is likely that the age of 16 was chosen during the drafting of PoCA 1978 because that was (and largely remains) the age of consent in England and Wales. However this changed in 2003 with the passing of the Sexual Offences Act 2003. One of the effects of the SOA 2003 was to raise the definition of a 'child' to 18 (s. 45, SOA 2003). The government premised the argument of raising the age on the need to act compatibly with the international instruments discussed in Chapter 2.

Little objection was made to the raising of the age with almost universal consensus that 18 was the more appropriate level. Dominic Grieve MP, the then shadow Home Secretary, stated:

> I do not find anything philosophically wrong in providing restrictions on what is permissible with a child under eighteen, even though I may be perfectly content and comfortable with the idea that sixteen is the age of consent. [These] two things are very different.
>
> (Hansard, Standing Cttee B Debates, 18 September 2003, col. 248)

Sandra Gidley MP, a Liberal Democrat Member of Parliament, had earlier made similar comments and noted that she would not necessarily wish 'some of the decisions that I made at that age to be with me for the rest of my life' (ibid., col. 247). Where any concern was shown by Parliament as to the consequences of raising the age to 18 it was in respect of adolescents taking photographs of each other. This is a point that will be discussed in Chapter 9.

Accordingly the age of a 'child' for the purposes of indecent photographs of a child is now 18 notwithstanding the fact that this means it is inconsistent with the age of consent. The difficulty that this brings was discussed in Chapter 2 and the argument will not be rehearsed here. That said, it is worth echoing the comments of academics in other jurisdictions who have said, 'there's something deeply anomalous about a law that criminalises the representation of a non-criminal act. Since two 16 year-olds are legally free to engage in sexual acts, why should it be a crime to represent those acts?' (Persky and Dixon, 2001: 210). The government and supporters of the change will, of course, point to cases where the sexual activities being depicted were coerced. Certainly it will be difficult to tell from a photograph whether the 16 year-olds were exercising free control to engage in sexual activities, but there is something contrary about criminalising all representations of what could be lawful behaviour.

Ascertaining age

Whilst it is clear that the law prescribes an age – eighteen – how does the court decide whether a child is under that age? Section 2(3), PoCA 1978 provides:

In proceedings under this Act . . . a person is to be taken as having been a child at any material time if it appears from the evidence as a whole that he was under the age of [eighteen].

It should be noted at the outset that s. 2(3) is *not* criminalising all images that *appear* to be a child. Jenkins, amongst others, has criticised laws that seek to criminalise the appearance of childhood:

> . . . appears to whom? Some years ago, millions of people worldwide saw the film Titanic, in which Kate Winslet plays a seventeen-year-old girl who has sex during the course of the story. Nobody was troubled by this incident, as the actress herself is well over the age of consent, but the film probably violated [US law] by simulating a sex act by someone presented . . . as a minor. Other recent films, such as Lolita and American Beauty, have faced similar dangers.
>
> (Jenkins, 2001: 220)

This is not the position with s. 2(3) however. The reference in that section to 'taken as a whole' must mean that where it is known that a person is *not* a child – so, to take the example used by Jenkins, it was known that Kate Winslet was not under 18 when *Titanic* was filmed – then s. 2(3) does not apply. Of course the converse is not true. As noted above, where the age of the child is known then the wording of s. 2(3) – 'evidence taken as a whole' – will mean that even where a person looks over 18 the fact that they are a child will not mean they are treated as though they are an adult (see also *R v Owen* [1988] 1 WLR 134 discussed further below). Not every jurisdiction operates this rule and Eneman notes, for example, that in Sweden there has been at least one case where a conviction was quashed because a child appeared to be over the age of 18 notwithstanding the fact that the person taking the photograph knew the subjects were aged only 16 (Eneman, 2005: 35). If the object of child pornography laws (in whole or in part) are to protect children from exploitation then such an approach fails children and the approach of s. 2(3) is more preferable.

It is a sad reality that most children in photographs are not identified (Holland, 2005; Elliot and Beech, 2009: 181) and so the age of the child will ordinarily not be known. Section 2(3) caters for this by allowing the tribunal of fact to look at the evidence as a whole – which in many cases is likely to simply be the photo-graph itself – to decide the age of the child. How does the tribunal of fact make this finding?

In some jurisdictions a jury is entitled to receive expert evidence on the issue of age. Usually this is a medically qualified person who is able to comment on the physiological characteristics of children and who can provide evidence to suggest the age of the child. In England and Wales this does not happen. In *R v Land* [1999] QB 65 the Court of Appeal rejected two principal submissions of rele-vance here. The first is that they rejected the contention that a person found in possession of child pornography should be convicted only where it was proven that he *knew* the photographs were of children. Judge LJ (as he then was) stated, 'a glance will quickly show whether the material is or may be depicting someone who is under sixteen' (p. 70) although it is less than clear that this is the case. In fairness, Judge LJ was arguing that where a person is unsure as to the age of a child (rather than knowing it) then it would be prudent to be safe and destroy material that could be considered to be of children. The consequences of this will be explored more fully in respect of possession but it is submitted that it is some-what naive to suggest that a quick glance will allow someone to decide whether photographs are of persons aged above or below the age of 18.

The second submission rejected by the Court of Appeal, and the one most relevant here, is whether expert evidence is admissible. The court held that '[t]he purpose of expert evidence is to assist the court with information which is outside the normal experience and knowledge of the judge or jury . . . the jury is as well placed as an expert to assess any argument addressed to the question whether the prosecution has established . . . that the person depicted in the photograph is under sixteen years of age' (p. 71). The court is stating that each juror is capable of deciding whether the person depicted in the photograph appears to be under the age of 18. Was the court correct to reach this decision? It may seem somewhat optimistic to suggest that the average person should have 'experience and knowl-edge' of aging people and such experience that receiving expert evidence would not assist them.

One of the difficulties in providing expert testimony is in respect of agreeing what the basis for the expertise is. Many experts use Tanner staging to identify the age of a child (Cattaneo *et al.*, 2009: e22). The Tanner staging method describes the different stages of sexual maturation and can be used to map pubertal develop-ment but it has been stated that Tanner himself suggests that using the Tanner stages to identify the chronological age of a child is illegitimate (Cattaneo *et al.*, 2009: e22). This is because pubertal development is different for each individual and depends on a number of factors. Accordingly ascertaining age through pubertal development would be problematic although there is some evidence to suggest that in jurisdictions that do allow expert evidence, this is one of the methods used (Lueher, 2005: 15).

Few studies have been conducted on the reliability of ascertaining age but an interesting study was conducted by Cattaneo *et al.* (2009). This study specifically addresses the issue about whether lay persons are any better than experts at ascertaining age. The experts used were forensic pathologists, paediatricians and gynaecologists, all people that would be expected to be familiar with methods of aging children. The assessment was relatively crude in that the participants were shown eleven photographs of nude women (all of which were aged over 18). The participants were asked to simply decide whether a person was aged above or below 18. The stark conclusion of the study is that no category did particularly well at identifying age. Forensic psychologists performed best but they correctly identified age in only 55 per cent of cases (Cattaneo *et al.*, 2009: e22–e23). In other words they got almost as many wrong as they did right. Lay persons correctly identified age in 37 per cent of cases and in Italy they correctly identified them in 50 per cent of cases. Paediatricians were worst at identifying age, with the study showing that they were wrong up to 95 per cent of the time.

Of course a weakness with the Cattaneo study is that it focused simply on the age of 18 and so it does not suggest that, for example, a person would not recognise a pre-pubescent individual as a child. However in such cases the age of a child would never be in doubt (save for issues of sentencing). The cases where age is relevant are where there is doubt as to whether a child (who may be well developed in terms of post-puberty sexual physiology) is above the age of 18. The Cattaneo study suggests that neither lay persons nor experts were particularly good at identifying whether a person was aged above or below 18. To an extent it can be argued therefore that the Court of Appeal was right in *Land* to suggest that expert evidence would not be of assistance since the experts could be equally wrong.

The findings of the study do raise significant questions in respect of the prosecution of child pornography. The difficulty in ascertaining age has led some to note that law enforcement agencies will be slow to tackle 'borderline' images (Wells *et al.*, 2007: 276). This is something that will be considered in Chapter 12 but the position in England and Wales is complicated slightly by the fact that age is relevant to the sentencing of offenders. This is something that will be discussed in Chapter 10 but it does mean identifying the broad age of a child can be necessary.

Photograph

The second issue to discuss is that of what constitutes a photograph. It will be remembered that notwithstanding the points made in Chapter 2 about the breadth of material available, the law in England and Wales focuses specifically on the issue of photographs. This was a deliberate choice by those that framed the legislation and it was considered at the time to be a reflection of the problem at the time.

The meaning of a photograph will be considered below but it certainly applies to a photograph in the ordinary sense of the word. It was always intended, however, to be not restricted to still photographs, with the legislation stating:

> Reference to an indecent photograph include a film, a copy of an indecent photograph or film, and an indecent photograph comprised in a film.
>
> (s. 7(2), PoCA 1978)

Accordingly a moving film is also considered to be a photograph as is a photograph produced by creating a 'still' of a film. This is of particular importance as research suggests that a considerable proportion of 'still' photographs are, in fact, images taken from a film (Taylor and Quayle, 2003: 39).

Technological advancements have been breathtaking since the 1970s and the technology that we use now was not even considered feasible only a couple of decades previously. The advance in technology brought about challenges to law enforcement, not least the question of whether digital representations amounted to a photograph. The original wording of the Protection of Children Act 1978 stated that a photograph included, *inter alia*, a 'copy of a photograph' and Manchester had suggested that digital scans of photographs, including reproductions thereof, could amount to a copy (Manchester, 1995: 124).

The issue of computer-based child pornography first came to the attention of the courts in the case of *R v Fellows and Arnold* [1997] 1 Cr App R 244. The principal offender – Fellows – was a computer expert at the University of Birmingham. He stored computer pornography on the computer server and provided access to others, including the second appellant. The first appellant was charged with offences under the Protection of Children Act 1978 and he attempted to argue, *inter alia*, that the image stored on a computer disc and sent to others who called it up on to a computer screen did not amount to a 'photograph' for the purposes of PoCA 1978. Part of his argument was based on the fact that Parliament had inserted the concept of 'pseudo-photograph' into PoCA 1978 by the Criminal Justice and Public Order Act 1994 (see below). Fellows argued that this insertion meant that the digital storage of images could not therefore amount to a photograph but only a pseudo-photograph (*R v Fellows and Arnold* at p. 249).

The Court of Appeal emphatically rejected the argument of the appellant. They noted that similar issues had arisen under the Obscene Publications Act 1959 when video-recorders first appeared. The original wording of that legislation suggested that a film was something that was projected. A video cassette, on the other hand, did not project but translated magnetic signals into pictures and sounds. In Attorney General's Reference (No. 5 of 1980) (1981) 72 Cr App R 71 the Court of Appeal held that this was irrelevant and that Parliament had intended that the showing of all films be covered and that the wording used was simply a result of the understanding of technology at that time. In *Fellows* the Court of Appeal held that the same logic could be applied to PoCA 1978. In 1978 Parliament could not conceive that a photograph could be digitally scanned and then sent around the world via the internet. The court rejected the suggestion that the insertion of pseudo-photographs by the 1994 legislation was an admission by Parliament that such matters were not included ([1997] 1 Cr App R 244 at p. 253) and noted it is for the courts, not Parliament, to decide what the interpretation of a statute is.

Counsel for Fellows attempted to argue that a photograph was, in fact, the negative on which the picture was stored, and that the physical photographs produced from that negative were in fact copies of photographs (at p. 253). The court rejected this and noted that in ordinary parlance a photograph was considered to be the actual physical photograph: i.e. the paper with the image displayed (at p. 254). This must be correct, not least because the original wording of s. 7(4) expressly stated, 'references to a photograph include the negative as well as the positive version' meaning Parliament itself considered the positive (the photograph) to be a photograph and not just a mere copy of a photograph.

The court ruled that the hard disc, on which the images were stored, was either a photograph (in a different form) or, more likely, a copy of a photograph and they held that nothing within the Act required a copy of a photograph to be a photograph itself (at p. 254). It has been suggested that the Court of Appeal was wrong when it suggested that the disc was either a photograph or a copy of a photograph and that it is the file – the actual data – that is relevant not the technology it is stored on (Manchester, 1996: 6). This must be correct but it is submitted that nothing turns on this point and it was simply a misunderstanding by the judges who, at that time, may not have known enough about how the technology operates.

It may be thought that *Fellows* is now an irrelevant case, not least because the CJPOA 1994 ended any uncertainty by amending s. 7(4) to say references to a photograph include, 'data stored on a computer disc or by other electronic means which is capable of conversion into a photograph' (s. 7(4)(b)). This belief may be reinforced by the fact that old-fashioned film cameras have largely died away and we now have digital cameras that store images on solid-state media. It would be difficult in this day and age to suggest that when one takes a picture with a digital camera one is not taking a photograph. The importance of *Fellows* however is that PoCA 1978 can respond to technological advancements. The essence of the *Fellows* case is that Parliament, in PoCA 1978, sought to tackle the production and dissemination of indecent photographs of children and that if technology changes the manner in which this occurs, the courts can interpret the legislation to take account of the advances of technology. Given technological advancement shows no signs of slowing – with 3D/hologram photography looking increasingly possible – the statutory interpretation point of *Fellows* may remain of consequence.

Pseudo-photograph

If, as was held in *Fellows*, a digital storage of a photograph is not a pseudo-photograph, what is a pseudo-photograph? In *Fellows* the court stated, albeit *in dicta*, that 'it seems to us to be concerned with images created by computer processes rather than the storage and transmission by computers of images created originally by photography' ([1997] 1 Cr App R 244 at p. 255). Surprisingly there have been few reported decisions on what a pseudo-photograph is. The *dicta* of the Court of Appeal in *Fellows* would seem to be supported by a reading of Hansard. The Home Secretary at the time, Michael Howard MP, stated, '[the CJPOA 1994] will ensure that there is no legal loophole for paedophiles who create indecent images of children though the use of computers' (Hansard, HC Deb, 11 January 1994, vol. 235, col. 31). Ann Winterton MP welcomed the legislation, noting that she had organised a presentation by the Metropolitan Police which had shown that they were concerned it was difficult for them to differentiate between a photograph and an image produced by computers (ibid., col. 81).

Section 7(7) of the Act, which was inserted by the CJPOA 1994, states:

> 'Pseudo-photograph' means an image, whether made by computer graphics or otherwise howsoever, which appears to be a photograph.

Whilst s. 7(7) refers to the creation of an image by, *inter alia*, a computer-graphics program it is commonly thought that a pseudo-image is where an original photograph has been manipulated or a collage of photographs have been used to create a photograph (Akdeniz, 2001: 253). Pseudo-photographs generally fall into two principal forms. The first is where a picture of a nude adult is loaded into a graphic manipulation package and, through manipulation, altered so that the image now appears to be of a child through, for example, thinning the hips, reducing the breast size and airbrushing out pubic hair. The second principal form is where a child's head is superimposed on to the body of an adult picture so that, in a crude manner, it will look as though the child is posing nude. A variation of the second form would be to superimpose an 'innocent' picture of a child on to a sex scene. For example, a picture of a child licking an ice cream is cut and imposed on to a pornographic picture so it appears as though the child is performing fellatio on an adult. A derivative of this can be seen from the case of *R v H* [2005] EWCA Crim 3037 where the offender took (legitimate) photographs of school children and later electronically added the image of semen on to the photographs so it would appear that the child had been involved in sexual activity. The resultant images must be classed as pseudo-photographs.

A key phrase within s. 7(7) is 'appears to be a photograph' and it is contended that this means that drawings, cartoons and some computer-generated images of abuse will not be pseudo-photographs as they do not appear to be a photograph (in its normal sense of the word). Support for this contention can be found from the case of *Goodland v DPP* [2000] 1 WLR 1427. This is one of the few cases to have specifically considered the issue of a pseudo-photograph. It concerned what the court described as a 'pitiful' image comprised of two separate photographs 'hinged' together. One photograph was of a naked adult woman and the other was the head of a young child. If the 'hinge' was closed then it would appear (very crudely) that the child's head was on the adult's body. The Divisional Court quashed Goodland's conviction for possession of a pseudo-photograph stating that the article obviously did not look like *a* photograph: it was quite clearly two. *In dicta* they suggested that if the image was photocopied whilst hinged then this may amount to a pseudo-photograph (p. 1442) because it could then perhaps appear to be a photograph. Drawings and most computer-generated images are not sophisticated enough to be mistaken for a photograph and so they would not, it is submitted, come within s. 7(7).

That said, there are some very sophisticated computer-generated images which do appear to be of photographic quality and it is only with a forensic examination that it can be seen it is not a photograph. It is submitted that these would come within s. 7(7) even where it can be proven that a real child is not involved. Section 7(7) clearly applies to images created solely by a computer-graphics program and s. 7(8) states that the resultant image should be considered a child where the 'impression conveyed . . . is that the person showed is a child'. The fact that it is not a real child will not negate the fact that the impression is that it is of a child and thus it would be classed as a pseudo-photograph, indeed it will be remembered that this was (apparently) the very reason why the CJPOA 1994 amendments were made in the first place. The consequences and justification of criminalising such images is discussed in Chapter 5 but it should be noted here that the obvious solution is to ensure that the quality of the computer-generated image is slightly poorer than that which could be considered to be a photograph.

An important issue arises in respect of pseudo-photographs and that is the concept of age. Section 7(8) states:

> If the impression conveyed by a pseudo-photograph is that the person shown is a child, the pseudo-photograph shall be treated for all purposes of this Act as showing a child and so shall a pseudo-photograph where the predominant impression conveyed is that the person shown is a child notwithstanding that some of the physical characteristics shown are those of an adult.

Section 7(8) is required because of the fact that some pseudo-photographs will, as noted above, be a composite picture of an adult and a child where, crudely, it would appear that the child is more sexually mature than she is. In those situations s. 7(8) allows a prosecution where the 'predominant' impression is of a child. A more profound implication of s. 7(8) is where a photograph has been manipulated so as to make an adult look like a child. It was noted above that this is technically feasible and constitutes one form of pseudo-photograph. The person charged might be able to say, 'Yes, but this is person X and she is aged twenty-one.' It will be remembered from the discussion in the preceding section that ordinarily this would be a defence to a photograph (see the discussion surrounding Kate Winslet on p. 44) but where the image is a pseudo-photograph, i.e. it is no longer a photograph but has been manipulated, then this defence is unlikely to succeed since s. 7(8) clearly applies where the image *appears* to be of a child.

Tracings

The most recent amendment of the meaning of 'photograph' was brought about by the Criminal Justice and Immigration Act 2008. That legislation inserted a new subsection within s. 7 of PoCA 1978, subsection 4A which states:

References to a photograph also include –

(a) a tracing or other image, whether made by electronic or other means (of whatever nature) –

    (i) which is not itself a photograph or pseudo-photograph, but

    (ii) which is derived from the whole or part of a photograph or pseudo-photograph (or a combination of either or both); and

(b) data stored on a computer disc by other electronic means which is capable of conversion into an image within paragraph (a) . . .

This amendment was not debated in Parliament, it was merely accepted, but its genesis is put forward in the explanatory notes. In essence there was some concern that traced images were not illegal. Tracings could occur in a number of different ways but two were of concern. The first is the 'traditional' method of tracing an image – i.e. using tracing paper. If an offender were to trace around a photograph and then colour in this photograph it would appear that they would have created a lawful image. The resultant image is patently not a photograph and neither is it a pseudo-photograph since it does not appear to be a photograph. The same result can also be achieved by computers: some scanners allow a person to 'trace' the outlines of an image and, if this was then sent on to someone else, it would probably not be considered either a photograph or pseudo-photograph for the same reasons. There was some doubt as to whether it would amount to a 'copy' of a photograph and interestingly at the time of the CJPOA 1994 it was questioned whether a drawing of a photograph would itself be a 'copy of a photograph' (Manchester, 1995: 124). It was suggested that if copy was given its literal meaning – 'thing made to . . . be identical to another' (*Concise Oxford English Dictionary*) – then drawings and pictures of a photograph would not be included. Certainly there is no record of any prosecution arising out of a tracing and the doubt as to whether it amounts to a 'copy' was a principal reason why s. 7(4A) was inserted. It is questionable whether any prosecution will take place in respect of a tracing but its inclusion does mean that where they are discovered within a collection they can now be lawfully seized and destroyed whereas prior to this amendment they probably could not.

Indecent

Of the three definitional aspects perhaps 'indecent' is the most problematic. The Protection of Children Act 1978 did not provide a definition of 'indecent', something that was considered controversial at the time (see, in particular, the proceedings of the House of Lords in committee at Hansard, HL Deb, vol. 392, cols 558 f. 18 May 1978). The term 'indecent' was chosen because it had already been used in other statutes concerning pornography, most notably s. 11, Post Office Act 1953 which criminalised the sending of an indecent article through the postal system. However that legislation did not define the term either but in *R v Stamford* [1972] 2 QB 391 the Court of Appeal held that indecency and obscenity are at either end of the same scale with obscenity being the graver of the two (at p. 398). Obscenity, and therefore indecency, is considered against recognised standards of propriety and is a matter purely for the jury.

The objective approach derived from the laws of obscenity has been challenged on three separate occasions. The first, and perhaps most important, was in *R v Graham-Kerr* [1988] 1 WLR 1098. The appellant had been convicted of taking indecent pictures of a boy. The facts were that the boy belonged to a naturist club. On the night in question a public swimming pool had been closed to the public to allow naturists to meet and swim. There was an official photographer who took photographs of the victim (a 7 year-old boy) but the appellant, without the permission of the victim's parents, took pictures of the boy in the changing room area. He had met the boy earlier that evening when, with the parent's permission, he had taught the boy to swim. In interview, the appellant admitted that he found the boy sexually attractive and that he received sexual gratification by the taking and viewing of pictures of naked boys (at p. 1100).

At his trial, the judge argued that a recent ruling of the House of Lords (*R v Court* [1989] AC 28 discussed below at p. 59) permitted the jury to consider the context in which the photographs were taken. The appellant was convicted and appealed to the Court of Appeal who quashed his conviction. The court disagreed that *Court* applied (for reasons explored below) and instead suggested that it was a purely objective approach to deciding indecency. The court noted that a difficulty with adopting a different approach is that the indecency of a photograph would differ depending on the motivation (p. 1104) and that this could cause difficulties for the application of the other offences under the Act (p. 1106). The court therefore upheld the application of the *Stamford* test and stated that the jury must consider recognised standards of propriety when deciding the indecency or otherwise of the test (p. 1105).

The second challenge came over a decade later. In *R v Smethurst* [2002] 1 Cr App R 6 the appellant did not seek to challenge that the objective approach was not intended when the legislation proceeded through Parliament but rather was based on the premise that the Human Rights Act 1998 required a different approach to be taken. The appellant in this case had downloaded a series of naked photographs of young girls from the internet. He stated that he had downloaded them from a site which indicated the girls were all aged at least 16 and he believed them to be 16. He denied he found them sexually stimulating and stated he was a photographer and was interested in the female form.

The appellant contended the images were not indecent but the jury obviously found otherwise. He appealed his conviction alleging that the objective approach to the meaning of indecency was contrary to Article 10 of the ECHR. In particular, the appellant noted that the phrase 'in accordance with the law' within Article 10(2) requires, *inter alia*, that it is sufficiently precise that a citizen can foresee which of his actions infringe the law (at p. 55). The importance of this argument is that if Article 10(1) is engaged – that downloading child pornography can be considered a part of the freedom of expression – the State can only interfere with this right if, *inter alia*, it is done in accordance with the law. Reliance was placed on a number of decisions of the European Court of Human Rights but, in particular, the decision in *Steel v United Kingdom* (1998) 5 BHRC 339 which challenged the ability to be bound over 'to be of good behaviour'. The ECtHR in that case found that this did not meet the test of certainty and forseeability.

The Court of Appeal, however, disagreed that such analysis was applicable in this case stating that 'the fact that what is or what is not indecent very much depends on the judgment of the individual' (p. 57 per Lord Woolf CJ). This can be contrasted with, for example, expectations of what is good behaviour. As with

Graham-Kerr, the Court of Appeal was concerned that allowing a subjective approach may mean that the same photograph may, or may not, be indecent depending on the circumstances (p. 58) and suggested that this could cause problems where the creator of the photograph had legitimate reason to do so but later users did not. This is something that will be discussed below as it is, with respect, only one possible interpretation. The court conceded that a difficulty with the objective approach is that there must be some legitimate actions which a jury may find indecent. It pointed out, however, that proceedings under PoCA 1978 can only be instigated with the permission of the DPP (s. 1(3), PoCA 1978) and the court believed this provided appropriate protection where a prosecution would not be appropriate (p. 58).

The third, and most recent challenge, was again brought under the auspices of the Human Rights Act 1998. In *R v O'Carroll* [2003] EWCA Crim 2338 the appellant was convicted of three counts contrary to s. 170(2)(b), Customs and Excise Management Act 1979. Section 170(2)(b) concerns the importation of prohibited goods: in this context an indecent or obscene article (s. 42, Customs Consolidation Act 1876). In this case the articles were a number of photographs of 'a young naked child engaging in normal outdoor activity such as playing on a beach' (at [2]). The application of the term 'indecency' to nudity is considered below (p. 55) but what is relevant in this case was that the appellant sought, *inter alia*, to argue that the objective approach was a breach of Article 7 of the ECHR in that it did not allow the context of the actor to be taken into account. The Court of Appeal gave short shrift to the argument referring to the ECtHR judgment in *Müller v Switzerland* (1991) 13 EHRR 212, which concerned an obscenity case. Swiss law, like English law, did not have a fixed definition of 'obscenity' but the ECtHR held that the requirement of foreseeability is not a fixed concept (p. 226) and noted this is particularly true 'in fields in which the situation changes according to the prevailing views of society' (at [29]).

The courts have thus been quite clear that the objective approach should be adopted but they are less clear as to why that is the case. The *Stamford* decision is perhaps the most telling in that it decided that indecency and obscenity were on the same scale. Whilst this is undoubtedly true it set the train by which indecency would be treated the same as obscenity: a purely objective approach would be adopted with the quest of ensuring that an article would be judged decent or indecent irrespective of the circumstances surrounding it. Whilst this decision is understandable, it does have consequences which will be examined below.

Whilst it is clear that an objective test is being used, the case of *R v Murray* [2004] EWCA Crim 2211 clarified that it is the article itself that must be considered indecent rather than, for example, any original material. In this case the appellant had recorded a documentary film broadcast on terrestrial television that showed a gynaecological examination of a young child. The appellant had then, using motion software, cut the soundtrack (in which a gynaecologist was commentating on the examination), slowed down the footage and cut it so that it only showed the genitalia of the child. He was charged with making an indecent photograph of a child (it will be remembered that 'photograph' includes a film (s. 7(3), PoCA 1978)) and attempted to argue that he could not be guilty of the offence as the original footage was taken from a legitimate film. The Court of Appeal rejected that argument and stated that the appellant had, quite clearly, made a new photograph (the film) through his modifications and that the jury simply had to examine whether that film was indecent, ignoring whether the original film was decent or indecent. This is obviously a sensible decision and is logical given the ordinary meaning of the word 'made'. It cannot be argued that the modifications did anything other than produce new footage and quite clearly the jury should be able to decide whether that new footage is indecent.

One issue that does arise from a purely objective stance is whether the age of the victim should be relevant. In *R v Owen* [1988] 1 WLR 134 the Court of Appeal was called upon to rule as to whether knowledge of age was relevant. The appellant was a professional photographer who was engaged to produce a portfolio of photographs for a 14 year-old girl who wished to be a model. Most of the photographs were innocuous but some showed her breasts exposed. The appellant sought to argue that the jury should be told not to take account of the age of the child but rather consider whether the photograph was indecent *per se*. If it was indecent and was of a child then he was culpable. If, however, it was not indecent then the mere fact that it was of a child could not make it indecent. In support of this argument, the appellant sought to rely on s. 7(3), PoCA 1978 which states, 'Photographs . . . shall, if they show children and are indecent, be treated for all purposes of this Act as indecent photographs of children' which appears to suggest that the question of age is separate from indecency. The Court of Appeal disagreed and stated that the term 'indecent' qualified the words 'photograph of a child' meaning that the jury could take account of the age when deciding whether something was indecent.

The decision of the Court of Appeal was questioned by Sir John Smith who noted that this meant that, if there were two photographs similar in all respects except one was of an 18 year-old and one was of a 14 year-old, the latter would be illegal whereas the former would not. He suggested that this was inappropriate as there was no difference between the two photographs and that any indecency would relate only to the conduct of the photographer (Smith, 1998: 120, 482). The counter-argument, of course, is that if the mischief of PoCA 1978 was to protect children from, *inter alia*, exploitation then the issue of age must be relevant since the 14 year-old is being presented in a sexualised way, something the law is seeking to prevent.

Indecency and the breadth of material

In most cases of child pornography the meaning of indecency will not be problematic. It will be remembered from Chapter 2 that there is a wide range of material used by offenders and that a taxonomy (the 'COPINE scale') was created to present this (p. 24 above). Realistically level 5 images (erotic posing) and above will be considered indecent and without a jury having to wonder too much about the standards of propriety. At the other end of the scale are pictures that could simply never be considered indecent. Level 1 images (those that depict children in their underwear or swimwear) could realistically never be considered indecent. More problematic, however, are those images between these two points on the scale. The most troublesome (for the law) are images that depict nudism (without any sexualised posing) or those where there has been the sexualised posing of non-naked children.

Addressing the second of these categories first, it should be noted that there is nothing within the legislation that requires a child to be naked. It would follow therefore that where a clothed (or partially clothed) child is depicted in a sexualised way it is quite possible that this would amount to an indecent photograph of a child. Given that the current definition of indecency relies on the concept of infringing recognised standards of propriety it would be easy to see how, for example, a picture of young children posed to indicate sexual acts could be indecent notwithstanding their genitalia may be covered.

What of more generic pictures depicting children in underwear? In *R v Henderson* [2006] EWCA Crim 3264 the appellant was charged with filming up the skirts of women using a covert camera. One of the photographs was described as showing the 'upper thighs [of a fourteen-year-old] from below' (at [7]) and it was charged as taking an indecent photograph of a child. *R v Hamilton* [2007] EWCA Crim 2062 involved similar behaviour and when one of his victims was identified and found to be aged 14, a charge of outraging public decency was altered almost automatically to one of taking an indecent photograph of a child (at [11]). Can it really be said that these pictures amount to child pornography? It will still be for the jury to decide whether they infringe contemporary standards of decency, but in both cases this appeared to be almost taken for granted. Whilst there is no doubt that the behaviour is problematic (indeed would seem to fall within the diagnosis of voyeurism (DSM-IV §302.82) and see Gillespie, 2008, for discussion on the application of the law to such behaviour) and it could even be argued that the *behaviour* is indecent, does it necessarily follow that the *photograph* itself is? If the objective approach is ignoring context and focusing only on the resultant image then it may seem somewhat difficult to suggest that the upper thighs of a teenager or a picture of her underwear are truly indecent.

Adler has noted a difficulty of ignoring context and widening the definition of child pornography to include the clothed or coy child which is that everything becomes pornographic (Adler, 2001: 264) and we start to consider children themselves as sexual objects. This would be ironic since the sexualisation of children has been deprecated by those in authority (see, for example, Adler, 2001: 252 and the decision of the Advertising Standards Authority to ban an advert for American Apparel in September 2009).

The most problematic issue is where a child is nude. This has proven controversial from the very inception of the legislation and continues to be so today.

Some members of the legislature were concerned that by passing the Protection of Children Act 1978 they were criminalising simple nudist pictures, including those that could be considered innocent. Lord Houghton criticised the concept of indecency and noted that 'I have in my hands, as I had before, photographs which probably some noble Lords would think are indecent and which others would think are beautiful' (Hansard, HL Deb, 28 June 1978, vol. 394, col. 347). Pictures depicting the nudity of children have existed for many thousands of years and sometimes depict the most profound of situations. Perhaps one of the most famous is that of 'a naked young Vietnamese girl running toward the camera after a napalm bomb attack' (Kleinhans, 2004: 21). This image can be found everywhere and few would consider it a sexualised picture, more a depiction of the horror of war and how it can hound the vulnerable and innocent.

Of course it could be argued that the nakedness of the Vietnamese child was incidental to the shot but art regularly focuses on the nudity of children. Some contemporary examples have highlighted the tension that exists between art and the law. Perhaps the classic example is the 'I am Camera' exhibition by Tierney Gearon which depicted her own children naked (Smith, 2004: 5). Whilst some argued her children were too young to be able to take the conscious decision of whether they wanted their naked bodies to be displayed forever (Smith, 2004: 6) few would suggest that they were harmful photographs or amounted to child pornography. Yet the exhibition was the subject of a police investigation, including having the images (temporarily) seized (Smith, 2004: 5). In 2007 Northumbria police entered the Baltic Art gallery in Gateshead and seized a photograph by the controversial artist Nan Goldin arguing that it was indecent. The work of Sally Mann is also controversial with commentators noting that they can be construed as either pornography or art (Edge and Baylis, 2004: 87), in part because they are terms that bear no fixed meaning and shift with society's acceptance.

In none of the situations above were the images the subject of a criminal prosecution but the controversy sparked a debate about the limits of child pornography. Some used these incidents as evidence that there was a moral panic (a point discussed in Chapter 1) and certainly there are some who argue quite cogently that extending child pornography laws too far can actually be counterproductive (Adler, 2001), ultimately causing children harm (Ost, 2009: 133 and 177 f.). Is mere nudity sufficient for the purposes of an indecent photograph? Whilst the Protection of Children Act 1978 was ultimately a private member's Bill, in the House of Lords the government, through Lord Harris of Greenwich (Minister of State at the Home Office), led most of the process. Lord Harris said, 'I have already made clear, as I did in a fair degree of detail in Committee, that photographs of naked children are by themselves unlikely to be indecent' (Hansard, HL Deb, 28 June 1978, vol. 394, col. 335). Support for this was found, in part, from the first-instance decision in *Commissioners of Customs and Excise v Sun and Health Ltd* (1973) (see the comments of Lord Harris of Greenwich at Hansard, HL Deb, vol. 392, col. 563, 18 May 1978) where the High Court had held that mere nudity was not indecent. However others disagreed and Lord Beaumont of

Whitley had suggested that Lord Parker, the then Lord Chief Justice, had stated, 'if you are on the beach with your children and a woman takes off her clothes, that is indecent' (ibid., col. 560).

In *R v Oliver et al.* [2003] 1 Cr App R 28 the Court of Appeal issued sentencing guidelines for offences relating to child pornography. This followed advice received from the Sentencing Advisory Panel (something discussed in Chapter 10). The SAP had suggested using a modified version of the COPINE scale, something the Court of Appeal agreed with. However the court stated that levels 1–4 should not form part of the scale because it doubted that they would amount to indecency. However in *R v O'Carroll* [2003] EWCA Crim 2338 the Court of Appeal stated that those comments were said *in obiter* (at [17]) and upheld a conviction that related specifically to the importation of naturist photographs of children playing on a beach. The Court of Appeal did not hold expressly that naturist photographs were indecent but rather held that a jury were entitled to find them indecent.

The fact that nude images can be considered indecent is problematic when the purely objective approach is adopted. It will be remembered from the above that *Graham-Kerr* held that the motivation of the offender was irrelevant (something confirmed in *Smethurst*). The implication of this when it is decided that mere nudity suffices can be extremely problematic. It has already been noted that art exhibitions were the subject of police investigation but what of parents who take pictures of their own children? The possibility that they could be the subject of criminal investigation was the subject of some disquiet when the Protection of Children Act 1978 was progressing through Parliament (see Hansard, HL Deb, vol. 392, col. 561, 18 May 1978) but it is certainly not a theoretical possibility. In 1995 the television newsreader Julia Sommerville and her partner were arrested by the police, who wished to question them about a picture of their naked daughter in the bath (Fowler, 1995). Neither Sommerville nor her partner was prosecuted for the photographs but Alan Levy QC, a prominent authority on child protection, stated:

> Clearly there is a risk innocent parents may be drawn in, and there is a grey area here on what indecency means ... What it must rely on is common sense. If you are taking naked pictures of a seven-year-old, which seems older than usual, you are playing with fire – not because you are necessarily doing anything indecent, but because it might be construed that way.
>
> (Fowler, 1995)

Many would perhaps find these comments surprising – especially the comment that taking pictures of one's own 7 year-old child amounts to playing with fire – but it is undoubtedly an accurate statement of the law as it currently is. If, as is currently the case, the objective approach is adopted then the fact that a parent has decided to take a family photograph is irrelevant: the jury are called upon simply to consider whether the photograph is indecent. If it is capable of being indecent, then, according to the then Lord Chief Justice, they must rely on the sensibility of the Director of Public Prosecutions. Lord Woolf stated that a family photograph is an example of a situation when it would be clearly inappropriate to prosecute (*R v Smethurst* [2002] 1 Cr App R 6 at p. 58 per Lord Woolf CJ). That may be the case but it does not stop the family being arrested and interviewed, with the inevitable consequence that the civil child protection system may well begin a parallel investigation.

Relying on the sensibilities of the DPP was questioned even in 1978 when the legislation was progressing through Parliament:

> ... I do not think, as a matter of public policy, that it is right that people should be put in the position of finding that they have quite inadvertently and innocently committed criminal offence and should have to rely on the goodwill of the Director of Public Prosecutions in order to avoid prosecution.
>
> (Hansard, HL Deb, 18 May 1978, vol. 392, col. 543,
> per Lord Wigoder)

The position is particularly onerous in respect of the making or taking of an indecent photograph (s. 1(1)(a), PoCA 1978) since, as will be seen, few defences exist to this offence. The amendments put forward by the Sexual Offences Act 2003 arguably make the position more troublesome. It will be seen below that one defence created by the SOA 2003 exempts, *inter alia*, law enforcement officers from PoCA 1978 when the creation or distribution of material is necessary for the investigation or prosecution of crime. This is, to an extent, a perfectly sensible defence and its inclusion was relatively uncontroversial (Gillespie, 2004). However is a legitimate law enforcement operation not a prima facie case of when it would never be in the public interest to prosecute? That being the case, then why is it that relying on the goodwill of the DPP was considered insufficient? Why is it that law enforcement personnel should be protected from the subjective action of prosecutorial discretion whereas a parent taking a legitimate picture of their child in a bath is not?

It is submitted that a person taking a photograph of a child should be aware whether they are breaking the law, something that is not currently possible as the law is currently interpreted. During the original drafting there had been an attempt to include a defence by criminalising only those images that were taken 'without lawful authority or reasonable excuse' but Lord Scarman, one of the leading Lords of Appeal in Ordinary of the time, noted that this would be problematic in the extreme. His Lordship noted that the term 'reasonable excuse' would be likely to be interpreted more widely than would be appropriate in the context of child pornography. His most powerful argument however was:

> The parent [possessing a photograph of his child] may say, 'I have a legitimate reason for having that photograph of my child in my hands.' Why should a parent be forced on to the defensive, talking about excuse, reasonable or otherwise?
>
> (Hansard, HL Deb, 18 May 1978, vol. 392, col. 546)

This is a very salient point. The law, as it is currently interpreted, starts with the presumption that a parent has committed an offence and needs to rely on prosecutorial discretion or, had the original amendments been passed, rely on a defence. Surely this is inappropriate? The images should not be the subject of a criminal inquiry in the first place.

A different approach

If, and it is submitted that it is appropriate to do so, legitimate family photographs are to be removed from the gaze of the criminal justice system, how can this be achieved? It would seem from the preceding analysis that the difficulty is the objective approach to determining what is indecent. However adopting a purely subjective approach would be problematic too. It would require, in essence, the police to conduct an interview with each offender to identify the purpose for which the image was taken or held. The prosecution could be put to the test on the issue of purpose which, in circumstances where the image is obscene, would be pointless and a waste of resources and time. The law of sexual offences has, for some time, allowed for a hybrid approach. The classic formulation was set forward by the House of Lords in *R v Court* [1989] AC 28 in respect of the offence of indecent assault. It is notable that the central term in both offences was indecency but the use of *Court* was specifically rejected by the Court of Appeal in *Graham-Kerr*. The *Court* test was, of course, then encapsulated in statute in s. 78, Sexual Offences Act 2003 when it defines 'sexual' as:

(a) whatever its circumstances or any person's purpose in relation to it, it is because of its nature sexual, or
(b) because of its nature it may be sexual and because of its circumstances or the purpose of any person in relation to it (or both) it is sexual.

If 'sexual' were replaced with 'indecent' once more, could this test provide a more satisfactory approach to the definition of indecency for the purposes of child pornography?

In *Graham-Kerr* the Court of Appeal doubted its use primarily on the basis that they believed that there was a fundamental difference between an indecent assault and an indecent photograph. The court stated that the decision in *Court* was, in essence, a matter of *mens rea*. Ormerod succinctly summarises the difficulty as:

... with indecent assault the activity of assault is the matter criminalised; with the present offence it is not the taking but the image that is indecent.
(Ormerod, 2001: 658)

This is of course correct and it explained why, for example, the Court of Appeal in *Graham-Kerr* held that they were not bound by the House of Lords decision in that case. However by itself it does not automatically require an objective approach to be taken. Ormerod continues:

In practical terms it would be difficult to prove the motivations and circumstances of the images being created. It would be impossible to prove such
matters where the prosecution was for possession/distribution by someone
other than the creator.

(Ormerod, 2001: 658)

The simple fact that something is difficult to prove is, of course, not necessarily an
obstacle to it being used and, as noted above, in the vast majority of child pornography cases the motivation of the offender is unlikely to be in doubt (where the
material can only be considered indecent or obscene). However it would certainly
require the police to look for supporting evidence and Ormerod notes that the facts
of *Smethurst* demonstrate an additional difficulty where, because of technological
advancements, any making is more likely to be as a result of downloading an image
from the internet than the taking of a photograph. In *Smethurst* the defendant
advanced an argument that he downloaded the images for legitimate, rather than
sexual, purposes.

If the focus is on the image then the latter point also becomes relevant. It is the
possession or distribution of an indecent photograph that is illegal. If the photograph
was taken in a legitimate setting then it would not be an indecent photograph (under
the subjective test) and so the possession or distribution of the image would
not therefore be illegal irrespective of the motivation of the possessor or distributor.
This would clearly be a significant flaw in any law and it is thus understandable
that the Court of Appeal did not choose to accept the invitation to depart from the
objective test on any of the three times they were asked.

Where does this leave those such as parents who are, theoretically at least, liable
for what could be innocent activities? Ormerod suggests that the better approach
would be to extend the defences contained in s. 1(4), PoCA 1978 (discussed in
Chapter 6) to the taking of photographs for legitimate reasons (Ormerod, 2001: 658)
but it has already been noted that this was rejected at the time of the legislation, in
part on the advice of one of the leading jurists of the time, Lord Scarman.

Ost suggests that the objection of the courts and Ormerod would fall away if
only the creation of an image were criminlised (Ost, 2009: 135). This argument is
premised on the basis that only the creator causes direct harm (Ost, 2009: 144)
although as was noted in Chapter 2, Ost later finds a justification for criminalising
the other forms of behaviour. Whilst it would be difficult to accept only the creation of images as being criminalised (for the reasons discussed in Chapter 2) Ost's
point demonstrates a flaw in the existing legislation.

It has been noted, both in this chapter and Chapter 2, that laws of child
pornography – and most certainly the law relating to indecent photographs of children in England and Wales – are derived from obscenity legislation. The emphasis
of the legislation is therefore very much on the image itself and this justifies the use
of the objective test to decide whether something is indecent. However has this reliance on obscenity meant that the law has become displaced from our knowledge
of offender behaviour and, indeed, the purpose of the legislation?

At the heart of this is the question as to what we are concerned with: is it the photograph or is it what happens with that photograph? This may seem an obtuse point but it is submitted that it is in fact fundamental. Whilst obviously the photograph is important it is submitted that it is less clear that it is the photograph itself that we are concerned with. It has been noted that (at least some) photographs depict a crime taking place against a child. The child in the photograph is unquestionably a victim, either of abuse or exploitation but this does not necessarily mean that it should be the focus of our attention. Is it not more likely that we are concerned with those actions of the offender discussed in Chapter 2? If, as appears likely, the ultimate aim of child pornography legislation is to protect children, is this necessarily achieved by focusing criminal attention on the photograph rather than on the conduct of the offender?

Let us take an example. A picture depicts a 13 year-old girl being penetrated by an adult. This is undoubtedly a distressing image and depicts an illegal act. Reference to the COPINE scale would suggest that it amounts to a level 9 image. It is unquestionably indecent and would be, regardless of which test is used. What is it about the picture that makes us consider it worthy of criminalisation? It must be the fact that it shows a child being sexually assaulted. The photographer who has taken this image has contributed to the abuse or exploitation of that child by taking the photograph. The child suffers harm from this action. No one would question that the photographer should be criminalised but it is submitted that the justification for the criminalisation is as much about the fact that he has caused harm to the victim as it is to the production of an image that is objectively considered indecent or obscene.

The focus on the activities of the offender could be taken further with this photograph. The person who took the photograph sends it to a third party who he knows has a sexual interest in children and that person sends it to three other people. Again it can be argued that this causes harm through secondary victimisation. The people who distribute this image have done so in a way that revictimises the child and which allows for her original victimisation to become permanent. They did so deliberately and either knowing, or not caring, that such harm would be caused. It does not follow however that every distribution is wrong. Let us assume that this image comes to the attention of a police officer. He forwards it to the Child Exploitation and Online Protection Centre (CEOP: discussed in Chapter 12) who attempt to trace the victim. The original police officer has distributed an indecent image of a child. We would not be concerned about this distribution however. That distribution has not caused harm to the child; in fact it has occurred in order to identify the child so that appropriate help can be given to that individual. Using the objective test the officer has distributed an indecent image of a child although he would not be guilty of an offence because s. 1(4)(a), PoCA 1978 provides him a defence: he had a legitimate reason for distributing the image.

However is this not an example of the problem presented by Lord Scarman? Why is it that the police officer needs a defence? A defence operates only where the prosecution have proven the *actus reus* and *mens rea* of an offence. The *mens rea* of the offence of distribution would appear to be intentionally distributing an indecent article (discussed in Chapter 6) which would appear to be satisfied subject to any discussion about the issue of the doctrine of double effect (Ormerod, 2009: 194 f.). Why should this be a position of a defence however? Whilst in practice it may make little difference, the law is stating that the action is wrong but subject to a justification or excuse. It was not wrong however, it was the correct action to take. Instead of acting to harm a child, it was an action that was taken to benefit a child.

What of more legitimate photographs? The subjective approach would, of course, ensure that photographs taken by parents, for example, would not be considered indecent. It will be remembered that an objection to the use of the subjective test is that it would mean that those who later possess or distribute the image may not be culpable. If the emphasis is taken away from the photograph and placed on to the activities of the person the result may be different. If possession is to be illegal – and the justification for this was discussed in Chapter 2 – then should it not be the possession for an improper purpose that should be criminalised? Arguably this must be what Parliament intended when it provided for the defence of, for example, legitimate reason (s. 160(2)(a), Criminal Justice Act 1988).

The disadvantage of altering the current approach is that it could lead to the position where the same photograph could be either decent or indecent depending on the context. It would also be necessary to prove, in some circumstances, the purpose of the person who takes, possesses or distributes the image. However it should be remembered that the *Court*/s.78 test is not purely subjective, it has both an objective and subjective limb. Where, regardless of the motivation of the actor, the picture is obviously sexual/indecent then the purpose is irrelevant. In reality this is likely to cover all those images that relate to COPINE level 6 or above. Similarly where a photograph is never capable of being indecent (COPINE level 1 images and possibly some level 2 images) then again the motivation of the offender will not matter. It could be considered that this is a weakness of the argument but realistically there has to be a minimum threshold. The remaining photographs are where the motivation has to be shown. Whilst some have questioned whether this will be easily provable in the modern internet era (Ormerod, 2001: 658) it is submitted that it should be possible to do so. The investigative interview can put matters to the suspect and an analysis of the computer may show other evidence. It was noted in Chapter 2 that behaviours such as cataloguing, etc., are relevant and this can be put in evidence.

Moving away from the subjective test which is required by the focus on the image rather than the behaviour of the defendant would, it is submitted, be a useful step forward. Whilst it is true to say that there has been no recorded prosecution of a parent being charged with the offence of taking an indecent photograph of a child in legitimate circumstances, a prosecution is not the only criminal justice response. It was noted above that Julia Sommerville was arrested and two separate art exhibitions were the subject of a police investigation, all three cases attracting significant media commentary. It is submitted that in none of the three cases was it ever likely that there would be a prosecution, nor do they amount to behaviour that was ever contemplated by Parliament. A family who is investigated by the police will suffer, at the very least, inconvenience and possible distress, not least because it is likely that the criminal investigation will be accompanied by a parallel civil child protection investigation. More than this, however, is that each of the cases noted above (and any subsequent cases) leads to considerable debate about the effectiveness and appropriateness of the law in the media. In Chapter 1 it was argued that child pornography does not amount to a moral panic *per se* but that does not mean that some aspects do not have some of its characteristics. An overreaction could lead to apathy about the issues and the aim of the legislation which can only be deeply unhelpful to the protection of children. Focusing on the behaviour and actions of the offender and using a (partially) subjective test (as in *Court*/s. 78) would, it is submitted, have meant that neither Julia Sommerville nor the two art exhibitions would have faced police action. It would also bring the law and our understanding of deviant offending behaviour closer together. The move would also be compatible with the Optional Protocol to the UNCRC which refers to a representation 'for primarily sexual purposes' (Article 2(c)) which suggests that purpose could, and arguably should, be considered in some contexts.

Other legal definitions of child pornography

Chapter 3 considered how the law in England and Wales defined photograph-based forms of child pornography. The purpose of this chapter is to consider how other countries define child pornography. As with Chapters 2 and 3, the issue of virtual child pornography will not be examined because this will be dealt with more fully in Chapter 5 which examines this specific issue.

Selecting the countries to examine is to an extent somewhat arbitrary and is dictated, in part, by access to material, the size of the book and an understanding of the legal systems for each country. The United States has been chosen since this has some of the older child pornography laws and because, in part, a lot of academic material is focused on that jurisdiction. Canada has been chosen since, as will be seen, it adopts an approach different to others and Australia has also been chosen because it adopts a varied approach across its jurisdictions.

In a single chapter it is not possible to examine the legal approaches in great depth but it is to be hoped that an overview can be presented of how the legal systems tackle the phenomenon, which allows comparisons to be drawn to the law in England and Wales. For each of the countries selected the same process will be adopted as with Chapter 2, i.e. three aspects will be examined; who is a child, what type of material is covered and what it is about the nature of the material that makes it constitute child pornography.

United States

The first jurisdiction to examine is that of the United States. As is well known, the United States adopts a duality system of laws in that the law exists at both federal and state level. In a book of this size it is not possible to consider the law in each of the 50 states and the federal law. I decided, with some reluctance, to concentrate purely on the federal law. This is, in part, because it will be seen that the federal law applies wherever the internet or US Mail exists and so it is the provision that is perhaps most commonly violated. However the decision was also taken because choosing which of the 50 states to examine would have been extremely arbitrary and it would not necessarily have added anything to the discussion. It is apparent that many state laws do differ in their subtleties and so a discussion of a significant number of these laws would be necessary. Sadly this book does not have the space to devote to such an extensive examination. The pragmatic decision was therefore to examine the federal law and the remainder of this section will do this.

Federal law applies only in defined circumstances. The Constitution of the United States ensures that state law applies as the 'default' position and only where the matter can be said to affect federal interests will that law apply. The trigger for this will be discussed in Chapter 8 but in the context of child pornography this will ordinarily be where there is an interstate issue, something that has been given a wide definition when making reference to information and communication technologies.

America was one of the first countries to adopt specific legislation in respect of child pornography. As with other countries it is clear that the legislation is a derivative of obscenity legislation, in part because the Supreme Court had held that obscenity could be restricted in a way compatible with free speech (*Miller v California* 93 S.Ct. 2607 (1973)). The Supreme Court, in the landmark decision of *New York v Ferber* 102 S.Ct. 3348 (1982), held that child pornography was not protected by the First Amendment to the US Constitution (which provides for the freedom of speech). The Supreme Court noted that whilst in *Miller* they had decided the obscene material was not protected by the first amendment, the harm caused to children by the production of child pornography meant that a lesser standard could be used without it being rendered unconstitutional (see especially p. 3358). This position continued until the second landmark decision of the Supreme Court in this area, *Ashcroft v Free Speech Coalition* 122 S.Ct. 1389 (2002). This case will be discussed both in this chapter and, in more detail, during Chapter 8, but in essence it was a case where the Supreme Court struck down as unconstitutional provisions of federal law that sought to criminalise the possession of virtual child pornography, i.e. material that did not involve real children.

The first issue is to decide which provisions of the US federal law are to be examined. In common with some jurisdictions, there are a number of offences that could be considered to criminalise sexualised representations of children. All offences are within Title 18 of the United States Code and are within Chapter 110 of that Title. The most relevant are 18 USC §2252 which is entitled 'certain activities relating to material involving the sexual exploitation of minors' although the main provision is 18 USC §2252A which is entitled 'certain activities relating to material constituting or containing child pornography'. It is this latter provision that will be examined in most detail as it is the one that is primarily intended to cover the material that was identified in Chapter 2. In addition to this, there are provisions relating to obscenity (contained within Chapter 71 of the Title 18) and it is quite possible that these provisions could also cover some aspects of child pornography. For example 18 USC §1466A relates to 'obscene visual representations of the sexual abuse of children' which is intended primarily to deal with non-photographic visual depictions. In common with other aspects of this chapter and the approach adopted in Chapters 2 and 3, this provision will not be examined in detail during this chapter as this deals with matters relating to so-called 'virtual child pornography'.

Accordingly the emphasis in this section is on 18 USC §2252A. It is notable that the Code refers to 'child pornography'. It was noted in Chapter 1 that the term is disliked by many professionals but this is an example of a legislature (in this case the US Congress) using the term in its legal sense. Unlike with some other jurisdictions it is not intended to exhibit all of the statutory material verbatim in this section because it takes up two sides of A4 paper and is extremely complicated. Instead relevant extracts are included where appropriate in this chapter.

Age

The first issue to discuss is that of the age of a child. 18 USC §2256(1) defines a minor as someone under the age of 18 years of age. Unlike in many other legislative instruments there appears to be no express statement that a person is a child if they appear to be a child or are represented as a child, it simply states that a minor is someone under the age of 18. The sole exception to this is 18 USC §2256(8)(B) which states that child pornography includes where, *inter alia*, 'such visual depiction is a digital image, computer image, or computer-generated image that is, or is indistinguishable from, that of a minor engaging in sexually explicit conduct'. The meaning of this term will be explored below but the syntax suggests that it could include material that is not only of a minor, but of that which is not a minor but which is indistinguishable from a minor. This applies to digital or computer images and is, in effect, covering material that relates to computer-generated images of abuse. Accordingly it is more relevant to the discussion of virtual child pornography, not least because it does not seem to cover photographs.

The requirement that a photograph covers a child is, in part, a result of the decision of the Supreme Court in *Ashcroft v Free Speech Coalition* 122 S.Ct. 1389 (2002) which held that child pornography laws are only constitutional where they depict actual minors. Whilst this decision primarily related to so-called virtual child pornography it also affects those cases where an adult poses as a child: post-Ashcroft the prosecution need to prove to the required standard that the person depicted is an actual child and not an adult.

Ascertaining age

It will be remembered from Chapter 3 that the position in England and Wales is that expert evidence is not admissible as to the age of the child. The same is not true in America. Whilst it has been held that it is not always necessary to adduce expert evidence (*US v Rearden* 349 F.3d 608 (2003) where the Ninth Circuit held that expert evidence is not needed where it is obvious from the photographs that those portrayed are children (p. 614)) the law provides discretion to prosecutors to adduce expert evidence as to the age of a child where they believe it necessary (see *US v Rayl* 270 F.3d 709 (2001) where the Eighth Circuit held that the prosecution were justified in adducing medical testimony).

Expert evidence is, of course, merely opinion evidence and therefore the tribunal of fact can choose to ignore this evidence (see, for example, *US v Shipe* (2001) unreported where the US Air Force Court of Criminal Appeals quashed a conviction for child pornography holding that, contrary to what an expert had testified, the prosecution had not proven that the images contained in a photograph were actually of females under 18). There has been no clear direction as to how expert evidence should be given. Whilst it will ordinarily be a medically qualified person giving evidence the use of lay experts has also been upheld (*US v Davis* 41 Fed. Appx. 566 (2002)) and this could mean that, for example, a specialist police officer who has experience of aging children could testify.

There are no clear rules on how the expert should gauge the age of a child. In many reported cases the prosecution call a medically qualified practitioner who uses the 'Tanner scale' to identify children (a useful summary of the practice of the Sixth Circuit is presented in *US v Noda* 137 Fed Appx 856 (2005) at 864). The 'tanner scale' evaluates the progression of a person through the stages of puberty. It is possible to compare this to the 'typical' pubertal development of a child to estimate the age although Cattaneo *et al.* have suggested this use is controversial and note that the developer of the Tanner Scale has argued that using the scale to provide expert evidence as to age is 'wholly illegitimate' (Cattaneo *et al.*, 2009: e22). That said, the mere fact that the person who develops a system disagrees with its use cannot be conclusive as it is possible that other, equally qualified persons, can show that it can be used in this modified way.

Since an expert is simply putting forward his or her expert opinion, the reliability of the methodology they used to arrive at this opinion is something that can be put to the expert in cross-examination. Accordingly, for example, where they use the Tanner Scale and the defendant believes that this use is inappropriate or has led to a false result then those questions can be put to the witness during the trial (see the discussion in *US v Hamilton* 413 F.3d 1138 (2005) at pp. 1143–1144). The tribunal of fact can decide what weight (if any) to place on this expert evidence and can, in any event, make their own opinion on the matter from seeing the material (*US v Rayl* 270 F.3d 709 at 714) and decide whether the prosecution have proven, beyond all reasonable doubt, that the person depicted is under the age of 18.

Type of material

Federal law defines child pornography as:

> …any visual depiction, including any photograph, film, video, picture, or computer or computer-generated image or picture, whether made or produced by electronic, mechanical, or other means…
>
> (18 USC §2256(8))

This provides for a wide range of material to be covered by federal law although it should be noted that the emphasis is on visual depictions and thus, as with the position in England and Wales, sound and text representations are excluded from the definition.

Computer-generated images

The inclusion of photographs and films, etc., are uncontroversial but what of the inclusion of computer-generated images? In *Ashcroft v Free Speech Coalition* 122 S.Ct.1389 (2002) the US Supreme Court held that child pornography laws could not apply to fictitious child pornography. However it should be noted that the ruling did not restrict material to photograph-based forms, it merely stated that the law may only apply to depictions of real children or material indistinguishable from real children. In terms of the former, it is certainly possible to create a computer-generated image of a real child and this would continue to be prohibited even after the ruling in *Ashcroft*, something seen from the face of the legislation:

> ... such visual depiction has been created, adapted or modified to appear that an identifiable minor is engaging in sexually explicit conduct.
>
> (18 USC §2256(8)(C))

The term 'identifiable minor' is then defined as:

(A) a person –
   (i) (I) who was a minor at the time the visual depiction was created, adapted, or modified; or (II) whose image as a minor was used in creating, adapting, or modifying the visual depiction; and
   (ii) who is recognisable as an actual person by the person's face, likeness, or other distinguishing characteristic, such as a unique birthmark or other recognisable feature; and

(B) shall not be construed to require proof of the actual identity of the identifiable minor.

This would cover, for example, situations where a person uses a computer-graphics program to produce a representation of a real child or where they use graphic conversion programs to convert a photograph into, for example, a cartoon (cf the position in England and Wales where it was seen in Chapter 3 that the Protection of Children Act 1978 does not include a comparable provision). The inclusion of paragraph (B) is important as it shows that proof of identity is not necessary. Whilst in some instances identity will be possible it allows for situations where a person has produced the computer-generated image from a photograph of an unknown child.

The legislation would also encompass so-called morphed images. It will be remembered in Chapter 2 that the example was given of an image of a child purportedly performing a sex act but which is, in fact, a composite involving the picture of a child eating an ice cream and a (lawful) adult pornographic image. By using a computer manipulation program it would be possible to 'cut' the image of the child and superimpose it on to the adult photograph so that it now looks as though the child is performing a sex act. In *Ashcroft* the US Supreme Court expressly distanced their conclusion from morphed images:

> Rather than creating original images, pornographers can alter innocent pictures of real children so that the children appear to be engaged in sexual activity. Although morphed images may fall within the definition of virtual child pornography, they implicate the interests of real children and are in that sense closer to the images in Ferber.
>
> (122 S.Ct. 1389 (2002) at p. 1397)

However this is premised on the basis that a real child was involved. Accordingly pseudo-photographs that show, for example, a child's head on an adult's body will be culpable as will those where the child is superimposed on to a porno-graphic image to make it appear that a child is engaged in sexual activity. What will not be covered, however, are those situations where an image of an adult is taken and graphically altered to represent a child (cf the position in England and Wales discussed in Chapter 3).

Identifying the child

It was noted above that there is a requirement that either a child is involved or the material is indistinguishable from a child. The question arises whether, following the decision in *Ashcroft*, it is necessary for the prosecution to always prove that the material is real rather than a fictitious person or an adult. It would seem that the prosecution do not have an obligation to raise positive evidence of this in every case (see Buckman, 2009: I §3 and see *US v Farrelly* 389 F.3d 649 (2004) where the Sixth Circuit held that it was not necessary where the jury had access to the photographs themselves and where the defendant did not challenge the reality of the children (p. 653)). Where there is any doubt it is often safer to present an expert who can testify that the images are not virtual as to do otherwise may mean that the prosecution has not discharged its evidential burden. As with expert evidence of age (discussed above) there is no prescription as to who the expert should be and in *US v Rearden* 349 F.3d 608 (2003) the prosecution called an employee of a visual effects studio who testified that the material was consistent with a photo-graph and not a graphic or manipulated image (p. 613). As with all expert evidence, it is for the tribunal of fact to decide whether to accept this evidence and they could instead form their own opinion having seen the material.

Hyperlinks

18 USC §2256 is clear that the material must be a visual representation and in *US v Navrestad* 66 MJ 262 (2008) the US Court of Appeals for the Armed Forces

quashed a conviction for distributing child pornography where the appellant transmitted a hyperlink to child abuse to another person. No actual image was transmitted but it was accepted that if the hyperlink was clicked whilst a user was connected to the computer then child pornography would be displayed. The prosecution sought to argue that as child pornography included data capable of conversion into a photograph, the hyperlink should be so construed since once clicked an image would be displayed.

Interestingly the Court of Appeals in *Navrestad* noted an unpublished decision of the Eleventh Circuit (*US v Hair* 178 Fed Appx 879 (2006)) where an appellant's conviction for attempted transportation of material was upheld even though it was simply a hyperlink. The court in *Navrestad* suggested that the key issue was that the appellant was charged with distribution and not attempted distribution (66 MJ 262 at 266) which suggests the prosecution made an error. That said, it is still difficult to see how this could amount to an attempt since a person is not attempting to transport a visual representation since it continues to be simply a link to photographs: a visual representation will never be sent. If this is to be criminalised then surely it should be on an alternative basis.

Nature of the material

The final issue to examine is what it is about the nature of the material that makes it constitute child pornography. 'Child pornography' is defined as a visual representation where:

> (A) the production of such visual depiction involves the use of a minor engaging in sexually explicit conduct;
> (B) such visual depiction is a digital image, computer image, or computer-generated image that is, or is indistinguishable from, that of a minor engaging in sexually explicit conduct; or
> (C) such visual depiction has been created, adapted or modified to appear that an identifiable minor is engaging in sexually explicit conduct.
>
> (18 USC §2256(8))

'Sexually explicit conduct' is defined separately for paragraphs (A) and (C) on the one hand and paragraph (B) on the other (see 18 USC §2256(2)). This is because paragraph (B) deals with computer-generated imagery.

For paragraphs (A) and (C) the following definition is used:

> 'sexually explicit material' means actual or simulated –
>
> (i) sexual intercourse, including genital–genital, oral–genital, anal–genital, or oral–anal, whether between persons of the same or opposite sex;
> (ii) bestiality;
> (iii) masturbation;

(iv) sadistic or masochistic abuse; or

(v) lascivious exhibition of the genitals or pubic area of any person.

(18 USC §2256(2)(A))

The definition for paragraph (B) is almost identical:

'sexual explicit conduct' means –

(i) graphic sexual intercourse, including genital–genital, oral–genital, anal–genital, or oral–anal, whether between persons of the same or opposite sex, or lascivious simulated sexual intercourse where the genitals, breast, or pubic area of any person is exhibited;

(ii) graphic and lascivious simulated;

(I) bestiality;

(II) masturbation;

(III) sadistic or masochistic abuse; or

(iii) graphic or simulated lascivious exhibition of the genitals or pubic area of any person.

(18 USC §2256(2)(B))

In essence the principal difference between the two is the requirement that computer-generated imagery must be 'graphic' which is itself defined as:

'graphic' ... means that a viewer can observe any part of the genitals or pubic area of any depicted person or animal during any part of the time that the sexually explicit conduct is being depicted.

(18 USC §2256(10))

At first sight it may not seem to add much to the definition since the depiction of the genitals or pubic area of a child would seem to be a fundamental part of the definition of sexually explicit conduct but the addition is that the genitals must be shown whereas without this requirement the definition would be satisfied where the depiction showed an adult and a child obviously having sexual intercourse but without showing their genitals.

In the vast majority of situations the definition of sexually explicit conduct will not pose any difficulties: certainly the inclusion of masturbation and sexual intercourse (broadly defined) will mean that most explicit behaviour is caught.

Lascivious exhibition of the genitals or pubic area

Whilst there is no difficulty in identifying what amounts to sexually explicit conduct where it involves some sort of sexual act, the law is perhaps less certain when it comes to the lascivious exhibition of the genitals or pubic area. The first issue is to identify what is meant by this term. The term 'genitals' is not defined although the dictionary defines it as 'relating to the human or animal reproductive organs' (*Concise Oxford English Dictionary*) which would suggest that the exhibition of the female breast is not within the definition (save where it is expressly mentioned in 18 USC §2256(B)(i)). This would appear to be in direct contrast to the position in England and Wales where no reference is made to the genitalia of a child, with the question simply being whether the photograph is indecent and with case law holding that this can include the exhibition of a female minor's breasts (see, perhaps most notably, *R v Owen* [1988] 1 WLR 134).

What does the term 'lascivious' mean? As with 'indecent' in the Protection of Children Act 1978 the term is not defined in statute and it has been for the courts to decide what is, or is not, lascivious. The starting point is that, as with indecency, it is not restricted to obscene material (*US v Arvin* 900 F.2d 1385 (1990)) and child pornography will include material that is of a lesser standard. It will be remembered from earlier in the chapter that obscenity is a much higher standard and the purpose of the federal legislation was to allow for the criminalisation of material of a lesser standard where it related to children (something that the US Supreme Court upheld in *Ashcroft*).

The courts have held that 'lascivious' is not easily defined (see *US v Villard* 885 F.2d 117 (1989)) and although Congress replaced the term 'lewd' with 'lascivious' (suggesting that 'lewd' was too connected with obscenity) the dictionary suggests that a definition of lascivious is 'lewd'. In *US v Horn* 187 F.3d 781 (1999) the Eighth Circuit held that lascivious meant it is when:

> ...the child is nude or partially clothed, when the focus of the depiction is the child's genitals or pubic area, and when the image is intended to elicit a sexual response in the viewer.

(p. 789)

and in *US v Nemuras* 740 F.2d 286 (1984) the Second Circuit held that naked or semi-naked pictures of a 4 year-old in poses that suggested sexual availability were lascivious. Perhaps the most notable attempt to define the term lasciviousness was performed by Thompson CJ of the S.D. California District Court in *US v Dost* 636 F. Supp. 828 (1986) where the judge suggested that six factors could be used by the tribunal of fact to decide lasciviousness. The six factors are whether:

1   The focal point of the visual depiction is on the child's genitalia or pubic area.
2   The setting of the visual depiction is sexually suggestive, i.e. in a place or pose generally associated with sexual activity.
3   The child is depicted in an unnatural pose, or in inappropriate attire, considering the age of the child.
4   The child is fully or partially clothed or nude.
5   The visual depiction suggests sexual coyness or a willingness to engage in sexual activity.

6   The visual depiction is intended or designed to elicit a sexual response in
     the viewer.

(p. 832)

The judge expressly stated that 'a visual depiction need not involve all of these
factors' but they are a series of factors that could assist in making a judgment. The
factors have been broadly adopted by the judiciary with them being specifically
approved by the Ninth Circuit in *US v Wiegand* 812 F.2d 1239 (1987) although some
other courts have shown a degree of scepticism (for a summary see *US v Rivera* 546
F.3d 245 at p. 250). That said, the scepticism is more that the *Dost* factors will be
considered a limiting factor in that juries may believe that all six factors need to be
present when that was never the intention. The fifth and sixth factors have been
particularly criticised. In terms of the fifth factor the Ninth Circuit have rejected the
suggestion that a child must appear to be a sexual temptress and instead focus on how
the photographer presents the image and whether sexuality is demonstrated from that
(*Rivera* p. 251). The sixth factor has been criticised as making it unclear whether it
was an objective or subjective approach (*Rivera* pp. 251–2) but the Second Circuit
noted that much of the criticism of the sixth factor relates to its application to possession whereas Dost himself was convicted of producing child pornography. This is
not to say that a different standard of lasciviousness is established between possession and production but perhaps allows a jury to consider the context in assisting
them in deciding whether the presentation of the material is lascivious.

Other decisions have concentrated on the idea of lasciviousness being the
presentation of a child as a sexual object (*US v Wiegand* 812 F.2d 1239 (1987) at
p. 1244). Where the photograph is based on nudity then certainly a sexualised
context must be identified (*US v Rayl* 270 F.3d 709 (2001) at p. 714) and this will
include an examination of the pose of the child (*US v Boudreau* 250 F.3d 279
(2001)) and whether the image concentrated on the genitalia of the child (*US v
Kemmerling* 285 F.3d 644 (2002)).

The requirement to concentrate on the genitalia of the child and the sexual nature
of the photograph (including, for example, the way that a child has been posed, etc.,)
will mean that some photographs depicting nudity will not be considered lascivious.
(See, in particular, *US v Vilard* 885 F.2d 117 at p. 124 when discussing a picture of
a naked boy. The court held that the mere fact that the boy was nude with a (partial)
erection did not mean that the focal point of the photograph was his genitals. They
noted *in obiter* that the naked picture of a girl may not be lascivious without some
element of sexual suggestiveness.) In *US v Grimes* 24 F.3d 375 (2001), which will
be discussed further below, it was suggested that this means that innocent photographs, for example photographs taken by a parent of their child in the bath, will not
be considered lascivious (p. 382). It will be remembered from Chapter 3 that
the same cannot be said in England and Wales, where, at least theoretically, such
photographs may be the subject of criminal intervention.

Given that it would appear that mere nudity will not necessarily constitute
child pornography, a surprising decision is *US v Knox* 32 F.3d 733. Here the Third

Circuit Court of Appeals was asked to consider whether the lascivious exhibition of genitals or the pubic area required that they were visible. *Knox* was an unusual situation in that it was the government rather than the defendant who were seeking to limit the extent of the statute. The offender had been convicted, *inter alia*, of child pornography offences relating to a video described thus:

> The tapes contained numerous vignettes of teenage and preteen females, between the ages of ten and seventeen, striking provocative poses for the camera. The children were obviously being directed by someone off-camera. All of the children wore bikini bathing suits, leotards, underwear or other abbreviated attire while they were being filmed.
>
> (p. 737)

There was no doubt therefore that the images were in a sexualised context but their genital and pubic areas where covered, albeit sometimes with opaque matrial. The government sought to argue that the wording of §2256 requires the genital or pubic area to be visible or discernible through the clothing but the Court of Appeals rejected this argument. The court specifically rejected the argument that there was a nudity requirement noting the plain wording of the statute did not require this (p. 744). They premised their argument on the basis of exploitation:

> Although the genitals are covered, the display and focus on the young girls' genitals or pubic area apparently still provides considerable interest and excitement for the pedophile observer, or else there would not be a market for the tapes in question in this case. Thus the scantily clad genitals or pubic area of young girls can be 'exhibited' in the ordinary sense of that word, and in fact were exhibited in the tapes which are the subject of Knox's conviction.
>
> (p. 745)

Whilst this is an interesting argument – and it will be remembered from Chapter 2 that the COPINE scale expressly covers such indicative content – the same argument can be used as regards virtually all forms of material. Those with a sexual interest in children may find gratification in all forms of material: should shops be prevented from displaying advertisements showing children in underwear (e.g. catalogues) and these be banned because offenders may find such imagery sexually gratifying?

The court notes that the dictionary definition of lascivious merely means tending to excite, lust, lewd or indecent and concludes that the term means depicting the genitals or pubic area of a child 'in order to excite lustfulness or sexual stimulation in the viewer' (p. 745). Combining this definition with the harm argument discussed above, the court concludes that there is no necessity for nudity or the direct exposure of genitals to amount to lascivious exhibition so long as the film concentrates on the regions. In respect of the tape in *Knox* the court notes:

The genitals and pubic area of the young girls in the ... tapes were certainly 'on display' as the camera focused for prolonged time intervals on close-up views of these body parts through their thin but opaque clothing.

(p. 746)

They conclude:

... a 'lascivious exhibition of the genitals or pubic area' of a minor necessarily requires only that the material depict some 'sexually explicit conduct' by the minor subject which appears to the lascivious interest of the intended audience.

To define lascivious to include material that concentrates on the genital or pubic area of a clothed (or partially clothed) child (other than when depicted in real or simulated activity) is extremely controversial and it has been suggested by one eminent writer that the consequences of the decision are that the law itself is sexualising children (Adler, 2001: 261) and Adler suggests that this could ultimately harm children as the law begins to see children as sexualised objects rather than focusing on offenders who exhibit sexual behaviour towards children. Others disagree and argue that the material in *Knox* did show problematic behaviour. The children were posing in a sexualised way and the material did show that the person who took the filming was concentrating on the genitalia of the children, albeit this was obscured. The question that *Knox* poses is to what extent lasciviousness is based on express or implied sexuality.

Pixillation

An interesting decision was made by the Fifth Circuit in *US v Grimes* 244 F.3d 375 (2001). The appellant had been convicted of the possession of child pornography, the specifics being that there were 17 images of naked girls but with pixillated boxes over the genital area. A pixillated box is a box produced by a graphics program that increases the pixillisation of a given area leading to it being blurred (as is common on television programmes to obscure a person's face). The appellant sought to argue that the pixillisation meant that the genitals were not being exhibited and/or it prevented them from being lasciviously exhibited. The Court of Appeals rejected this argument saying:

It is plain to any viewer that the producing of these visual depictions involved the use of minors engaging in sexually explicit conduct and that the visual depictions captured that activity.

(p. 380)

The court made reference to the decision in *Knox* and noted that it stated that the actual exhibition of the genitals or pubic area was not necessary, Applying this, they noted that the pixillisation may have prevented the genitals from being clearly seen but it remained obvious what was happening to the child and where the genitals and pubic region was (p. 382).

Grimes is interesting because whilst the genitalia is not visible the court is correct to state that it was obvious what the images presented. The children depicted had obviously been photographed naked and somebody pixillated the genitalia for reasons unknown. If at least one purpose of criminalising child pornography is the direct harm that it causes to a child (in both its primary and secondary sense) then the decision in *Grimes* must be correct. It will be remembered from Chapter 2 that one reason for criminalising the possession of child pornography is due to secondary victimisation. Does the fact that the genitalia is pixillated detract from this secondary victimisation? The exploitation (it is not clear whether there was any abuse inflicted in terms of contact abuse to the child) the child suffered is being enticed or coerced into being photographed nude. The pixillation does not alter the fact that this is what happened and that people are gaining sexual gratification from viewing these images even with the pixillisation. If lasciviousness is to be broadly construed as the sexual posing of a child then the images in *Grimes* would, it is submitted, meet this criterion.

Does the rationale of *Grimes* mean that there should be a reconsideration of the criticisms of *Knox*? It could be argued that in both sets of images the child is being portrayed as a sexual object and that in each the child's body is being used for sexual gratification. Does the fact that in one the child is nude (albeit with the genitalia obscured) and in the other the child is clothed make a difference? It is submitted that it does. For the reasons set out above there must be a minimum threshold for what constitutes child pornography. It was noted in Chapter 2 that an offender can gain sexual gratification from a wide range of images, including innocuous material but criminalising all material on the basis that it could be misused would be highly problematic. If the law is to retain integrity it is submitted that there must be a minimum threshold for it to amount to child pornography. In England and Wales this is the concept of indecency and in the United States it is lasciviousness: both indicate a recognition that material is beyond recognised standards of propriety. Whilst it is possible that clothed depictions can meet this criteria (where, for example, it depicts a child engaged in sexual activity) it is submitted that it is more difficult to do so where there is no overtly sexualised act taking place. Nudity, on the other hand, may transform the image. For reasons already discussed enticing or coercing a child into posing nude may be exploitative and pixillating the images does not alter the inherent nature of the image which is that it is an image of a naked child who has been enticed or coerced into displaying their genitalia, presumably for the purposes of sexual gratification.

Canada

The second jurisdiction to examine in this chapter is that of Canada. As compared to the United States and the United Kingdom, Canada adopted child pornography laws comparatively late. Despite two reports in the 1980s and one in 1990 calling for specific child pornography laws to be adopted (Curry, 2005: 143) it was not until a new minister was appointed in 1993 that dedicated legislation was introduced (Curry, 2005; Persky and Dixon, 2001).

Whilst Canada is a federation of ten provinces and three territories its criminal law is, unlike the United States, federal-based. The criminal law is codified and the legislation of 1993 inserted a new section into the Criminal Code, that being section 163.1. This defines child pornography and establishes the offences and defences relating to it.

Section 163.1(1) defines child pornography as:

  (a) a photographic film, video or other visual representation, whether or not it was made by electronic or mechanical means,

      (i) that shows a person who is or is depicted as being under the age of eighteen years and is engaged in or is depicted as engaged in explicit sexual activity, or

     (ii) the dominant characteristic of which is the depiction, for a sexual purpose, of a sexual organ or the anal region of a person under the age of eighteen years;

  (b) any written, visual representation or audio recording that advocates or counsels sexual activity with a person under the age of eighteen years;

  (c) any written material whose dominant characteristic is the description, for a sexual purpose, of sexual activity with a person under the age of eighteen years that would be an offence under this Act; or

  (d) any audio recording that has as its dominant characteristic the description, presentation or representation, for a sexual purpose, of sexual activity with a person under the age of eighteen years that would be an offence under this Act.

As with the federal law in America the legislation expressly uses the term 'child pornography'. It has been noted by some commentators that this is perhaps unsurprising, given that even the distasteful term 'kiddie porn' was used comparatively widely in Canada, including in official policy documents (Persky and Dixon, 2001: 4, 41 where they adduce a quote including the terms 'kiddie porn'). However as was discussed in Chapter 1 the term 'child pornography' is not infrequently used in legal instruments and Canada is a good example of this.

Age

Section 163.1(1) makes clear that the age of a child is under 18 although the decision of the Canadian Supreme Court in *R v Sharpe* 2001 SCC 2 does alter this in respect of possession. The choice of the age of 18 is perhaps surprising since until 2008 the age of consent in Canada was 14. The Tackling Violent Crime Act 2008 raised the ordinary age of consent to 16 although subject to an exemption for near-age participants.

The choice of 18 continues to mean that the age of a child for the purposes of child pornography is above the age of consent. The consequences for this where adolescents are filming themselves as part of consensual sexual contact will be discussed more extensively in Chapter 9 but in *R v Sharpe* 2001 SCC 2 the Canadian Supreme Court held that exceptions to s. 163.1 would be needed so as to make it compatible with constitutional protections. One exception was described by McLachlin CJC as:

> ...privately created visual recordings of lawful sexual activity made by or depicting the person in possession and intended only for private use. Sexually explicit photographs taken by a teenager of him or herself, and kept entirely in private, would fall within this class of materials. Another example would be teenaged couple's private photographs of themselves engaged in sexual activity.
>
> (at [76])

The Supreme Court so ruled because it was thought that including such material within the definition of child pornography would be an unjustified interference with the right to freedom of expression (contained within s. 2(b) of the Canadian Charter of Rights and Freedoms). The expression of lawful sexual activity must mean that those who are aged 16 to 18 are allowed to be depicted in material that would otherwise be considered child pornography so long as it is for their own private use and kept privately. The limits and implications of this will be discussed further in Chapter 9.

Ascertaining age

Section 163 of the Code does not expressly state how the age of the child should be ascertained. Section 163.1 adopts two positions in terms of age. Where the depiction is of explicit sexual activity (which is discussed below) then the person must be either under 18 or depicted as being under 18. Where, however, the material is the depiction of the sexual organs or anal region, then it is only where the person is under 18 that the material is illegal and not, therefore, where the person is depicted as being under 18. However it was noted in Chapter 2 – during the discussion of ascertaining age – that some (most prominently Jenkins, 2001) argue that criminalising the depiction of a child is problematic. Certainly if depiction is to be given its literal interpretation then the argument by Jenkins that films such as *Titanic* could infringe child pornography laws would prove true.

In *Sharpe* McLachlin CJC held that the issue of age is one of fact and that it is an objective test: 'would a reasonable observer perceive the person in the representation as being under eighteen and engaged in explicit sexual activity?' (at [43]). However this does not answer the challenge posed by Jenkins. To take the example of the 1997 film adaptation of *Lolita* it is clear that this is the depiction of an under-18 engaged in sexual activity. Whilst it is true to say that there would be a defence of artistic merit – discussed in Chapter 8 – this starts with the presumption that the material is illegal and only becomes lawful where evidence can be adduced as to its artistic merit. Where it can be proven that a person is aged at least 18 when filmed why should it be illegal if the movie depicts the person as being under the age of 18? McLachlin CJC suggested that it can be justified because representation could be used for deviant purposes such as solicitation (*Sharpe* 2001 SCC 2 at [43]) but is this not an argument for criminalising the *use* of material rather than its possession or distribution?

Representation is wider than mere appearance (the test used in some other jurisdictions) and potentially it could be wider than is necessarily desirable. In *R v Garbett* 2008 ONCJ 97 MacDonnell J raised the issue of whether s. 163.1 meant that so-called 'dress down' pornography (i.e. pornography where adults are depicted as being minors) is caught within the provisions. Counsel for both the appellant and Crown suggested that a 'photograph of explicit sexual activity involving a person who is clearly an adult but is dressed in a childlike fashion – perhaps wearing a primary school uniform ... would constitute child pornography because the person is depicted as being under that age' (at [71]). MacDonnell J argued that counsel were wrong because the test enunciated by McLachlin CJC in *Sharpe* was whether a reasonable person would consider the person depicted to be under 18 (*Garbett* at [74]). It is less clear that this is what McLachlin CJC meant but it is submitted that the conclusion of MacDonnell J is appropriate as to do otherwise could lead to the position whereby material that depicts persons who are obviously adult in childlike clothing would be criminalised. Save where such material is being used to solicit sexual activity from minors – which is the subject of separate offences – it would be difficult to justify such an approach.

There is a statutory defence for someone who makes a mistake as to age. This will be discussed in Chapter 8 as it relates not to the definition of the offence but rather whether an offender is guilty of an offence relating to child pornography.

Type of material

Section 163.1(1) makes clear that the Canadian definition includes material much wider than mere visual depictions. Sections 163.1(1)(b) and (c) expressly refer to written material meaning that text-based child pornography is also included within the provisions. Sections 163.1(1)(b) and (d) expressly refer to audio recordings meaning that sound-based child pornography is included within the definition. This is clearly a much broader definition than that adopted in either England and Wales or America. Chapter 2 discussed the difficulty of criminalising text-based child pornography and issues such as conflicts with the freedom of expression are certainly raised. It will be seen from Chapter 8 that some of the difficulties highlighted in Chapter 2 concerning text and sound recordings are dealt with by defences and these will be explored there.

In terms of visual representations, s. 163.1(1)(a) states that 'a photographic film, video or other visual representation, whether or not it was made by electronic or mechanical means' is included. This clearly covers not only photographs and morphed images but also computer-generated images and even drawings. The reference to 'mechanical' means would also include paintings, drawings or cartoons. Thus the type of material covered in Canada is extremely wide. Its wide definition means that there has not, so far as the author has been aware, been any difficulty in identifying whether a particular type of material (rather than its nature) is within the definition of child pornography, in part because of the clarity and comprehensiveness of s. 163.1(1).

Nature of the material

The final aspect therefore is the nature of the material. Section 163.1(1) is interesting in that it classifies a wide range of material as child pornography, including material that would not necessarily be considered child pornography in other jurisdictions.

Counselling or advocating sexual activity.

Section 163.1(1)(b) states child pornography includes (b) 'any written, visual representation or audio recording that advocates or counsels sexual activity with a person under the age of eighteen years'. It is not uncommon for countries to criminalise actions that advocate or counsels illicit sexual activity but it is not ordinarily classed as child pornography. Realistically this type of material is beyond that which is contemplated in this book which is material that, broadly speaking, equates to the definitions contained within Chapter 2. It is nonetheless very interesting that Canada classifies this as child pornography. Given the age of consent is currently 16 (as identified above) it is also interesting that they chose the age of 18 for the purposes of paragraph 18. Given that it is perfectly lawful to have sexual intercourse with a person aged 17 why should it be illegal to advocate or counsel sexual activity with a 17 year-old? As stated above this is outside the scope of this book but paragraph (b) does raise some interesting questions.

Sexual activity

There are two principal types of representation contained within s. 163.1(1), those that relate to the depiction of sexual activity (contained within paragraphs (a), (c) and (d)) and the depiction of the sexual organs. The depiction of sexual activity will be examined first.

In *Sharpe* 2001 SCC 2 McLachlin CJC considered the meaning of these words. She referred to the dictionary and noted that, in the context of sexual, it meant, 'describing or representing nudity or intimate sexual activity' (at [45]). If this is correct then it could be questioned what the point of paragraph (ii) is since nudity is apparently within the definition in paragraph (i). However McLachlin CJC then noted Parliament must have intended there to be a difference and she suggested that paragraph (ii) referred to the 'static depiction' of the sexual organs or anal regions of the child (at [47]), implying that the emphasis in paragraph (i) is, in part, on the term *activity*. She continued by noting:

> I conclude that 'explicit sexual activity' refers to acts which viewed objectively fall at the extreme end of the spectrum of sexual activity – acts involving nudity or intimate sexual activity, represented in a graphic and unambiguous fashion, with persons under or depicted as under eighteen years of age.
>
> (at [49])

In many instances this will be unproblematic but McLachlin CJC appeared concerned to ensure to establish a *de minimis* and noted that activities such as kissing or holding cannot amount to sexual activity.

Representation of sexual organs

The second type of representation is restricted to visual representations and it is where 'the dominant characteristic of which is the depiction, for a sexual purpose, of a sexual organ or the anal region of a person under the age of eighteen years' (s. 163.1(1)(a)(ii)). What does 'dominant characteristic' mean? In *Sharpe* McLachlin CJC stated that an objective approach should be taken to this:

> The question is whether a reasonable viewer, looking at the depiction objectively and in context, would see its 'dominant characteristic' as the depiction of the child's sexual organ or anal region. The same applies to the phrase 'for a sexual purpose' which I would interpret in the sense of reasonably perceived as intended to cause sexual stimulation to some viewers.
>
> (at [50])

The term 'dominant characteristic' means taking the image in its context rather than, for example, deciding whether the majority of an image is the depiction of the child's sexual organs or anal region. The requirement that its dominant characteristic must be for a sexual purpose must, as McLachlin CJC later states, mean that innocent pictures will not be included within the provisions. In Chapters 2 and 3 considerable attention was, for example, placed on the possibility of parents taking photographs of their children in, for example, the bath being prosecuted for the production of child pornography. McLachlin CJC makes clear that she believes that this could not happen under Canadian law as it would not be for a sexual purpose (at [51]). Interestingly McLachlin CJC noted that the context is important and thus placing a photograph in an album of sexual photographs or adding a sexual caption to a photograph could transform an image into one whose dominant characteristic are for a sexual purpose.

The wording of paragraph (ii) was explored further in *R v I(JE)* 2005 BCCA 584 where the appellant was convicted of child pornography offences relating to secret camera footage taken of four teenage girls and an adult woman. The footage was recorded surreptitiously in the bathroom and show the women nude. It was accepted the footage did not show anything overtly sexual but the trial judge held that the dominant characteristic of the footage was images of the young women for a sexual purpose. The British Columbia Court of Appeal stated that mere nudity may not necessarily infringe child pornography but noted that context is important and they held it was of importance here that the images 'were not taken innocently. They constitute a serious violation of the privacy and dignity of these four young women' (at [17]). Whilst this may be true, it must be questioned whether this *by itself* is for a sexual purpose. That said, it must be evidence for the tribunal of fact to consider but the essential test must, as McLachlin CJC stated, be whether the image, viewed objectively, would seem to be for a sexual purpose.

Australia

The third country to examine is Australia, which is a federal country consisting of six states and two self-governing territories (the Australian Capital Territory and the Northern Territory). As with the United States, and unlike Canada, the criminal law operates on two planes; the federal law (known as Commonwealth law) and state law. Given that there are a relatively small number of states and territories in Australia it will be possible to discuss the law in each and provide a more detailed understanding than was possible in respect of the United States.

As with the United States it is not possible to provide the full text of each jurisdiction's laws verbatim and instead extracts will be reproduced. The position in Western Australia should also be noted. The current law of child pornography in this state is contained within s. 60, Classification (Publications, Films and Computer Games) Enforcement Act 1996 but in 2009 a Bill, known as the Child Exploitation Material and Classification Legislation Amendment Bill was introduced into the Western Australia Parliament. At the time of writing it has not been passed and accordingly the law in this chapter will make reference to the 1996 Act. However where it is possible to do so, a commentary on the effect that the current Bill will have on the legal position if it were passed in its current form will be made.

Terminology

Not only do the different jurisdictions have different definitions, there are different terms used to describe material. Table 4.1 shows the different terms used. It is interesting that whilst a majority of jurisdictions continue to use the term 'child pornography', three have decided not to use this title and to refer to it as either 'child abuse' or 'child exploitation' material. It will be remembered from Chapter 1 that these are the alternative names preferred by many in the law enforcement and

Table 4.1 Terminology used to describe 'child pornography'

Jurisdiction	Terminology
Australian Capital Territory	Child pornography
Commonwealth	Child pornography
New South Wales	Child pornography
Northern Territory	Child abuse material
Queensland	Child exploitation material
South Australia	Child pornography
Tasmania	Child exploitation material
Victoria	Child pornography
Western Australia	Child pornography[a]

Note
a If the *Child Exploitation Material and Classification Legislation Amendment Bill* is passed into
  law then the term will change to 'child exploitation material'.

child protection fields. It is perhaps notable that the Child Exploitation Material and
Classification Legislation Amendment Bill intends to change the terminology used
in the legislation of Western Australia and this perhaps demonstrates a trend in
Australia to move away from the label 'child pornography'.

Age

There is no single definition of a 'child' for the purposes of child pornography in
Australia, with each jurisdiction setting its own age. The age of majority in Australia
is 18 and to allow a comparison to be drawn with the age of a child for the purposes
of sexual intercourse (as discussed in Chapters 2 and 3) Table 4.2 presents the
various ages. It can be seen from Table 4.2 that five of the jurisdictions use the
age 18, in common with England and Wales, Canada and America. The other four
jurisdictions define a child as being someone under the age of 16. In all but three
jurisdictions there is a difference in the age. The disparity between the age of consent
and the age of child pornography raises issues that were rehearsed in Chapter 2 and
which will be explored in more detail in Chapter 9.

The position of South Australia is perhaps the most interesting in that it defines
a child for the purposes of child pornography as someone under the age of 16 but
the age of ordinary consent in the State is 17. This is the only jurisdiction within
Australia, and indeed the other countries that are examined in this book, where the
ordinary age of consent is higher than the age at which a person is 'a child' for the
purposes of child pornography. It is not clear why this position arose.

It is perhaps worth noting that the Child Exploitation Material and Classification
Legislation Amendment Bill will not, if passed in its current form, raise the age of
'a child' for these purposes in Western Australia. The Bill continues to state that
a child will be under 16. This is perhaps surprising since Australia is a signatory

Table 4.2 Age of a 'child'

Jurisdiction	Age	
	CP	Consent
Australian Capital Territory	18	16
Commonwealth	18	16
New South Wales	16	16
Northern Territory	18	16
Queensland	16	16
South Australia	16	17
Tasmania	18	17
Victoria	18	16
Western Australia	16	16

to various international conventions that stipulate a child should be aged 18 for these purposes (most notably the Optional Protocol to the Convention on the Rights of the Child on the sale of children, child prostitution and child pornography). International arrangements are a federal matter and this is perhaps why the Commonwealth law uses the age of 18 but it does demonstrate that the individual states are willing to legislate on their own terms and, in the case of Western Australia, ensure that there is no disparity between the age of a child for the purposes of child pornography and the ordinary age of consent.

Appearance

All but the Australian Capital Territories define a child in an equivocal way. Section 64(5) of the Crimes Act 1900 of the Australian Capital Territories defines child pornography as certain types of material that relate to a 'child'. The dictionary contained at the end of the Act (and which under s. 4 of the Act is considered to be part of the Act) simply defines a child as a 'person who has not attained the age of eighteen'. It would appear therefore that the prosecution must prove that the person depicted in the photograph *is* a child rather than, for example, appears to be a child or is depicted as a child. This could conceivably cause difficulty in terms of proving the offences relating to child pornography since it was noted in Chapter 2 that proving age in a post-pubescent child may not be easy.

The remaining jurisdictions in Australia expressly tackle the issue of age. The States of South Australia and Queensland state that a child is someone who is 'under, or apparently under,' the age of 16. Commonwealth law, the States of Tasmania, Victoria and the Northern Territory all define a child as someone under the designated age or 'who appears to be' under the designated age. 'Appears to be' is clearly equivocal language and is designed to tackle situations where the prosecution cannot prove the exact age of the child but who wishes to lead the prosecution on the basis that the person appears to be a child. Whether, as with Canada, this could potentially include so-called 'dress-down pornography' has not been resolved by the courts but certainly the language would appear to suggest that it could include adults who appear to be younger. The alternative construction would be to follow the logic of the United Kingdom and state that proof that the subject is over the designated age means the material is not criminal. The use of the term 'apparently' is slightly less equivocal but it is submitted that it too is designed to tackle situations whereby the prosecution cannot prove the age of the child but wishes to lead on the basis that the person is likely to be a child.

The law in Western Australia is that a child is someone 'who is, or who looks like, a child under sixteen years of age' (s. 3, Classification (Publications, Films and Computer Games) Enforcement Act 1996). The term 'who looks like' is, it is submitted, analogous to 'appears to be' and thus the comment that applies to the legislation of the Northern Territory will also apply to Western Australia. If the Child Exploitation Material and Classification Legislation Amendment Bill is passed in its current form then the wording will change to 'appears to be', a term discussed above.

Ascertaining age

The legislation in no territory explains how the age of a child should be ascertained. In *Police v Kennedy* (1998) 71 SASR 175 Bleby J, sitting in the Supreme Court of South Australia, held that the question of age is for the tribunal of fact to decide without recourse to expert evidence (at p. 191). This position was supported by a later decision of that court in *R v Clarke* (2008) 100 SASR 363 (at 371). The author was not able to find a case that suggested that an alternative approach is taken to the other jurisdictions in Australia and therefore it would seem that the question of age is a matter of fact and one that should ordinarily be undertaken without recourse to expert evidence. It will be remembered from Chapter 3 that this is the position in England and Wales too.

Type of material

The jurisdictions differ between what type of material is covered by the definitions of child pornography contained within the legislation. There are a number of different approaches. The Australian Capital Territory and the States of New South Wales, Victoria and Western Australia have their own unique definition. The remaining jurisdictions use an approach based on 'depicts or describes' and those jurisdictions will be examined as a whole. It will be seen that in general the Australian jurisdictions adopt a wide meaning of the type of material included.

Australian Capital Territory

The Australian Capital Territory uses a definition that is not shared by any other jurisdiction. Section 67A, Crimes Act 1900 states that it includes 'anything that represents', *inter alia*, the sexual parts of, or sexual activity with, a child. The reference to 'anything' would seem to be very wide-ranging and could cover all material. However what does the term 'represent' mean? Will this include all forms of material? Whilst it will clearly apply to visual depictions it is perhaps more questionable whether it applies to text or sound-based child pornography. Can they be said to be representations? The dictionary definition of 'represent' is 'a representation, an image, an impression' (*Oxford English Dictionary*) which would appear to suggest the answer is 'no'. This would seem to be confirmed by 'representation' which means 'something which stands for or denotes another symbolically' which again suggests image-based forms only.

There is, to the author's knowledge, no case law that states whether the term includes non-visual representations but it would seem from a literal stance at least that it may not.

New South Wales

New South Wales adopts its own unique definition but it is much wider than that adopted by the Australian Capital Territory. Section 91FA, Crimes Act 1900 states that material includes 'any film, printed matter, electronic data or any other thing of any kind (including any computer image or other depiction'. This is obviously an extremely wide definition. The reference to 'printed matter' will, it is submitted, be sufficient to include text-based material. However the inclusion of the words 'any other thing of any kind' would in any event mean it is clear that all forms of material including sound and internet-based material will be covered.

Victoria

The State of Victoria defines child pornography as 'a film, photograph, publication or computer game that describes or depicts a person' (s. 67A, Crimes Act 1958). The term 'publication' is defined as that which is contained within the Commonwealth Classification (Publications, Films and Computer Games) Act 1995. That Act defines a publication as 'any written or pictorial matter' but not a film or computer game (s. 5). As the legislation of Victoria includes films, photographs and computer games the consequence of this is that all written and pictorial matters are within the meaning of the legislation. This does, however, mean that sound-based depictions do not appear to be included within the definition of child pornography in the State of Victoria.

Western Australia

The position adopted in Western Australia is perhaps one of the most comprehensive definitions. Section 3, Classification (Publications, Films and Computer Games) Enforcement Act 1996 defines child pornography as 'an article that describes or depicts' offensive material. The term 'article' is then defined so as to include a publication, film, computer programme and associated data, photograph, object, sound recording and an advertisement for any article. Accordingly it can be seen that 'article' encompasses virtually all types of material and that it specifically covers photographs, computer data and sound recordings. The type of material is widened when one notes that 'publication' is defined under s. 3 as having the same meaning as in the Commonwealth Classification (Publications, Films and Computer Games) Act 1995, i.e. that described above for Victoria except, of course, sound-based recordings are included within the definition included in the Western Australia legislation. The effect of the Commonwealth legislation is, in essence, to bring text-based and all other visual depictions within the definition.

If the Child Exploitation Material and Classification Legislation Amendment Bill currently before the Western Australia Parliament is passed as currently drafted then the definition will change. The new definition will be much clearer:

> material includes –
>
> a   any object, picture, film, written or printed matter, data or other thing; and
> b   any thing from which text, pictures, sound or data can be produced or reproduced, with or without the aid of anything else.

All forms of material will thus come within the definition of child pornography, including all visual representations, text and audio-based child pornography.

Depicts or describes

The most popular method of describing the type of material is to use the form 'depicts or describes' which is used in the following jurisdictions:

- Commonwealth law (s. 473.1, Criminal Code Act 1995).
- Northern Territory (s. 125A, Criminal Code Act).
- Queensland (s. 20A, Criminal Code Act 1899).
- South Australia (s. 62, Criminal Law Consolidation Act 1935).
- Tasmania (s. 1A, Criminal Code Act 1924).

Some of the jurisdictions go further by expressly covering certain types of material. For example, South Australia expressly covers an 'image' (s. 62, Criminal Law Consolidation Act 1935). The terms 'describe' and 'depict' are rarely defined but it is submitted that they are terms of ordinary usage and it is quite clear that they are wider than the term 'representation' used in the Australian Capital Territory. The term 'describes' can quite clearly refer to text-based material and the term 'depicts' is wide enough to cover both visual and, it is submitted, sound-based depictions. Thus it would seem that those jurisdictions that use this term will potentially cover all forms of material.

Nature of the material

Whilst there are similarities between the different approaches adopted as to the nature of the material, there would appear to be five broad approaches. Four are based on:

- Offensive sexual activity or its context (used by New South Wales, the Northern Territory, Queensland and Tasmania).
- Offensive sexual activity or the depiction of the genitalia (used by the Commonwealth).
- Sexual activity or the depiction of a child for sexual gratification (used by South Australia).
- Depiction of the sexual parts of a child or activity of a sexual nature (used by the Australian Capital Territory).

The fifth is the law of Western Australia. This currently has a unique definition although, as will be seen, it is planned to bring the definition in line with the first form of definition noted above.

Each of the approaches will be examined in turn although it should be noted that there is a degree of similarity and overlap between the various methods.

Offensive sexual activity and context

The first approach is based on the premise of offensiveness and sexual context. The language used in each of the jurisdictions adopting this approach are broadly similar and for simplicity the legislation of New South Wales will be exhibited:

> Child pornography means material that depicts or describes ... in a manner that would in all the circumstances cause offence to reasonable persons, a person who is (or appears to be) a child:
>
> (a) engaged in sexual activity, or
> (b) in a sexual context, or
> (c) as the victim of torture, cruelty or physical abuse (whether or not in a sexual context)
>
> (s. 91H(1), Crimes Act 1900)

It can be immediately seen from this definition that the focus on the legislation is not the sexualised representation of a child in that s. 91H(1)(c) includes the depiction of a child 'as the victim of torture, cruelty or physical abuse (whether or not in a sexual context)'. This is an interesting approach and is one that is not adopted by many other jurisdictions. Whilst such material may well contravene legislation relating to obscenity in many jurisdictions, this is rarely as extensive as child pornography legislation. The inclusion of what can be broadly referred to as sadism is interesting since it will be remembered from Chapter 2 that the COPINE scale includes sadism in its topography of child pornography. Its inclusion within this legislation is perhaps non-controversial given the harm that must be caused in its production but it is worth noting that it applies whether or not there is a sexual context. This perhaps raises questions over what the purpose of this legislation is and whether it is a sex offence or a different type of offence.

If, for these purposes, we focus on the sexual element then there are three elements to this definition:

- The material is such that it would cause offence to reasonable persons.
- The child is engaged in sexual activity.
- The child is shown in a sexual context.

The term 'sexual activity' is not defined in that section although it is defined in an earlier section relating to the grooming of children (see s. 66EB(1)) although it is, in essence, simply defined as a criminal offence under the Act. 'Sexual context' is, however, not defined although it would seem a term of ordinary usage.

The requirement that the material must be offensive to reasonable persons would seem to cater for those situations where an image may be classed as pornographic but it was taken for legitimate purposes. The classic example of this, as noted in Chapters 2 and 3, was the issue of a parent taking a picture of a child in the bath. Depending on whether the child is moving at the time it is quite possible that the child's genitals, etc., may be seen in the photograph but it would seem unlikely that reasonable persons would be offended by it. That said, it is not clear whether the context of the photograph changes matters. So, for example, reasonable persons may not be offended if the parent takes or has possession of such photographs but would they be offended if someone unknown to the child had this photograph and used it for the purposes of sexual gratification? The legislation refers to 'in all the circumstances', and so could the identity of the offender and the circumstances in which it is made or possessed be taken into account in deciding its offensiveness?

The issues of offensiveness and context were addressed, in part, by the New South Wales Court of Criminal Appeal in *DPP v Annetts* [2009] NSWCCA 86. The respondent (the appellant in this matter was the DPP) had been found to be in possession of video images that he was alleged to have taken, using a concealed camera, of boys under the age of 16 dressing and undressing in the local swimming pool, including showing some of the boys in a state of nudity and with some focusing on the genitalia of some of the boys (at [4]). The Court of Appeal stated that the questions as to offensiveness and context were objective and considered by reference to their content. McClellan CJ at CL said:

> The fact that the images were secretly recorded is not relevant to whether or not the material is child pornography. Furthermore, the reasons which motivated the photographer are not relevant. These matters may inform an understanding of the context in which the film was made but are not relevant to an understanding of whether the video depicts boys in a 'sexual context'.
>
> (at [10])

She continued, however, by saying:

> The fact that all the images were of young boys and the camera has concentrated on their genitalia are both relevant to the question of whether or not the images depicted are of a person or persons in a 'sexual context' ... a conclusion that the images depict persons under sixteen in 'sexual context' may be informed by the number of images, the gestures of those photographed and the portion or portions of the body, including the genitalia, depicted.
>
> (at [11])

The essence of this judgment is that it would seem that the law in New South Wales (and presumably those other jurisdictions that adopt similar wording) is that the decision as to sexual context is purely objective and a direct analogy can be drawn to the definition of indecency contained within England and Wales (see *R v Graham-Kerr* [1988] 1 WLR 1098). The same logic appears to hold and, in particular, the Chief Justice at Common Law is stating that the motivations of an offender are irrelevant in this context. Whether the motivations are relevant to offensiveness is perhaps less clear although the tone of the judgment implies not.

Offensive sexual activity or the depiction of the genitalia

The second approach is related to the first approach and is used by the Commonwealth, i.e. federal law. Section 473.1 of the Criminal Code defines child pornography as:

(a) material that depicts a person ... under eighteen years of age and who:

    (i) is engaged in, or appears to be engaged in, a sexual pose or sexual activity (whether or not in the presence of other persons); or

    (ii) is in the presence of a person who is engaged in, or appears to be engaged in, a sexual pose of sexual activity;

and does this in a way that reasonable persons would regard as being, in all the circumstances, offensive; or

(b) material the dominant characteristic of which is the depiction, for a sexual purpose, of:

    (i) a sexual organ or the anal region of a person who is, or appears to be, under eighteen years of age; or

    (ii) a representation of such a sexual organ or anal region, or

    (iii) the breasts, or a representation of the breasts, of a female person who is, or appears to be, under eighteen years of age;

in a way that reasonable persons would regard as being, in all the circumstances, offensive...

There also exists paragraphs (c) and (d) which have not been reproduced because they refer to the description of behaviour contained in paragraphs (a) and (b). For the reasons given earlier, text-based forms of child pornography are not being discussed in this chapter.

The Commonwealth definition is, broadly speaking, similar to that undertaken by the states discussed above in that it is based on the concept of sexual representations and offensiveness. It does not, unlike the jurisdictions of South Australia or the Australian Capital Territory (discussed below), draw upon the intentions or purpose of the material. Paragraph (a) focuses on the activity of a person whereas paragraph (b) focuses on the representation of the sexual parts of a child. That said, it should be noted that paragraph (a)(i) expressly includes the sexual posing of a child and this implies that the child need not be involved in a sexual activity: a sexual pose for a still photograph would suffice. An interesting question that arises in this context is whether this would apply to clothed children. Nothing within paragraph (a) requires the child to be nude or semi-nude (unlike the language expressed in paragraph (b)) and so it is possible that a pose involving a clothed (or semi-clothed) child may suffice. Such an interpretation would be controversial although it would, presumably, depend on what the sexual posing amounts to. For example:

V, a 15 year-old child, is pictured kneeling on the floor with her head near a man who is shown unzipping his trousers.

An image such as this is unlikely to amount to child pornography in many jurisdictions but an argument can be made out that it is exploitative: especially if it is a 'still' from a film and the child is later abused. Is this sexual posing? Almost certainly and under the Commonwealth law it may well amount to child pornography.

Paragraph (a)(ii) includes material where the child is represented as watching others engaged in sexual activity. A similar definition is adopted in England and Wales (discussed in Chapter 3) and it is undoubtedly because this can amount to the sexual exploitation of a child itself. It is perhaps reinforced by the fact that some countries criminalise the intentional causing of a child to watch sexual activity, as it could be used to help normalise a child to sexual activities, potentially as part of a grooming process.

Paragraph (b) operates on a slightly different basis. The emphasis of this paragraph is on the depiction of the sexual parts of the child. The wording states that the 'dominant' characteristic must be for 'a sexual purpose'. This is very similar to the test used in Canada (discussed above). Presumably, as with Canada, this phrasing is intended to mean that it need not be the sole purpose of the depiction. The requirement for it to be for a sexual purpose will mean, for example, that legitimate representations of the sexual parts of a child (for example, in a medical lecture or text) will not be caught by these provisions nor would legitimate photographs taken by, for example, parents. Given the phrasing of the legislation it would seem that, as is the position in England and

Wales, a decision is taken as to whether the material is for a sexual purpose not its use (cf the position in South Australia following the decision in *R v Murdock* [2009] SADC 109 discussed below). Accordingly if a person misuses a legitimate photograph it would seem that this will not amount to child pornography.

The list of circumstances under sub-paragraphs (i)–(iii) are uncontroversial and mirror the position in other jurisdictions. The distinction between sub-paragraphs (i) and (ii) would seem to be that paragraph (i) would seem to require an actual depiction of the sexual parts of a child (i.e. a photograph) whereas sub-paragraph (ii) is concerned with a depiction (for example, a CGI image). Given that sub-paragraph (iii) deals with actual depictions and representations in the same text it may be questioned why it was necessary to differentiate between them but it may simply have been for clarity.

The second part of the test in both paragraph (a) and (b) is the requirement that reasonable persons would find the depictions offensive. The nature of this has been discussed already.

Sexual activity or the depiction of a child for sexual gratification

The third approach does not emphasise the sexual activity of a child, it concentrates more on the intended gratification of the material. This approach can be found in South Australia where child pornography is defined as material:

(a) that –

   (i) describes or depicts a child engaging in sexual activity; or
   (ii) consists of, or contains, the image of a child or bodily parts of a child ... or in the production of which a child has been or appears to have been involved; and

(b) that is intended or apparently intended –

   (i) to excite or gratify sexual interest; or
   (ii) to excite or gratify a sadistic or other perverted interest in violence or cruelty.

This is quite a complicated provision, especially in respect of paragraph (b). This paragraph places paragraph (a) into context and so it is not enough that the material meets the criteria in paragraph (a); it must also, in effect, be for sexual gratification or sadism. Paragraph (b)(ii) is slightly wider than the provision contained in Commonwealth law but its purpose is undoubtedly the same.

If, as with previous decisions, we concentrate on the sexual context it would appear that a two-part test is created. The first is that the child should be depicted engaged in sexual activity or that it contains the image of a child or parts of the body of a child. The second part of the test (irrespective of which of the first part is satisfied) is that it must be intended (or apparently intended) to 'excite or gratify sexual interest'. As with other jurisdictions the term 'sexual activity' is not defined but it is unlikely that this would cause any difficulty in interpretation. The requirement that there be an intention for sexual gratification is also unlikely to cause much difficulty where the footage portrays explicit sexual activity. Of more interest is the second alternative. The phrasing of paragraph (a)(ii) is extremely wide. It talks about the image of a child or the body parts of a child or an image where the child has been involved in its production. At no point does it require, for example, that the image should be of the sexual parts of a child or that the picture itself needs to be sexual. The only reference to sexual is in respect of paragraph (b) where the intention of the maker is relevant. Potentially this makes the definition extremely wide and could include pictures of a fully clothed child (as that is an image of a child) so long as the intention to gratify sexually is satisfied.

The potential breadth of the material was highlighted in *R v Murdock* [2009] SADC 109. The defendant in this matter was convicted of the production and possession of child pornography. The material related to a 9 year-old child who resided with the defendant at the time it was produced. The material included video footage of the victim in various states of undress, including those that showed her vagina, breasts and buttocks. Other footage showed the victim topless and pulling her underwear down and, at the same time, pulling her bottom cheeks apart so as to expose her anal and vaginal regions. In other words the footage was reasonably explicit but His Honour Judge Muecke, giving judgment, considered the basic definition contained in the legislation. The judge noted that the definition was potentially extremely wide but noted (citing comments of the Attorney General from when the legislation was passed by the State Parliament) that it was intended to be broad and that the requirement for sexual intent was designed to ensure that innocent material, including brochures advertising children's clothing or underwear, was not captured by the provisions (at [54]).

Accordingly it would seem that it is the mental element (that contained within paragraph (b)) that is the key part of this definition. Judge Muecke noted that there did not appear to be much difference between an intention to excite or gratify sexual interest and *apparently* intending to do the same (at [71]) but, again after referring to comments from the Attorney General, he decided that it was intended to encompass situations where the tribunal of fact decided it was the actor's purpose and situations where the sexual interest is apparent on the face of the material itself (at [72]). The judge decided the test was as follows:

> I may, as a finder of fact, find that the material the subject of this case is child pornography if (a) the accused intended it to excite or gratify sexual interest when he produced it or possessed it (taking into account the circumstances of its production or possession); or (b) it is either inherently pornographic, in the sense that it excites or gratifies sexual interest, or that an intention to excite or

gratify sexual interest is apparent on the face of the material (taking into account the circumstances of its production or possession).

(at [79])

This test is thus partly objective and partly subjective. Where it is apparent from the face of the material that the sexual interest is present then the intention of the offender does not appear strictly relevant (save where it was produced or possessed for a legitimate purpose) but where it is not obviously sexual it is necessary to look at the intentions of the producer *or possessor*. The latter is interesting as it suggests that the intentions of the producer and possessor could be different. For example:

X, a parent, takes a picture on her mobile phone of her 2 year-old daughter in the bath. Y steals X's phone. He finds the photograph and transfers it to his machine so that he can masturbate to the image.

In the circumstances above it would seem that X has not produced child pornography in that it is not obviously sexual and it was not her intent to produce it for the purposes of sexual gratification. Y, on the other hand, has the same photograph but he does possess it for the purposes of sexual gratification and accordingly the image does, in respect of him, amount to child pornography.

An interesting aside in *Murdock* is that the judge questions whether he can hear expert evidence about the prurient nature of the material (at [99]). The judge says 'there seems to me to be no reason in principle why I could not take these opinions into account'. This is perhaps surprising since it must be expert opinion as to whether the material is obviously sexual. Given that this is an objective stance it would perhaps be expected that the matter would be heard by the tribunal of fact without recourse to expert evidence (as is the case in England and Wales: see *R v Land* [1999] QB 65). Given it would seem that expert evidence is inadmissible in respect of ascertaining age it would perhaps be surprising if expert evidence as to the prurient nature of the material was admissible.

Depiction of the sexual parts of a child or activity of a sexual nature

The final approach adopted is that used in the Australian Capital Territory. This provision is perhaps closer to the definitions used in Canada and the United States in that it refers expressly to sexual activity and the sexual parts of a child. Section 64(5), Crimes Act 1900 states:

Child pornography means anything that represents –

(a) the sexual parts of a child; or
(b) a child engaged in an activity of a sexual nature; or

(c)   someone else engaged in an activity of a sexual nature in the presence of
the child

substantially for the sexual arousal or sexual gratification of someone other
than the child.

Section 64(5) creates a two-part test. The first part relates to the depiction and is
that which is contained within paragraphs (a)–(c). The term 'sexual parts' is not
defined by the legislation. It may be thought that the term is readily understandable and, to an extent, it is. However the legislation does not, for example, say the
naked sexual parts of a child so would an image of the covered sexual parts of a
child be included? It was noted earlier in this chapter that this is currently under
debate in, for example, the United States. In *R v Thompson* [2009] ACTSC 23
Higgins CJ acquitted an offender of child pornography offences in circumstances
where the sexual parts were not clearly visible. The learned judge said, 'there is
filming of where the sexual parts of a child might be, but, it is no more or less so
than if the child was fully clothed' (at [4]). Accordingly it would seem that the
material has to either represent or display the sexual parts of the child and not
merely the area of the child where the sexual parts are to be found.

The requirement in paragraph (b) that the child be performing an activity of a
sexual nature is unlikely to cause any problems of construction. As with the
Commonwealth legislation (discussed above), it is notable that paragraph (c) covers
material that shows people engaging in sexual activity in the presence of a child.

The second part of the definition is that the material is represented 'substantially
for the sexual arousal or sexual gratification of someone other than the child'. The
exemption for the child is, presumably, seeking to exempt self-produced imagery
that could amount to child pornography (an issue which is discussed more extensively in Chapter 9). The use of the term 'substantially' presumably means that it
need not be the sole reason for its production or possession. Whilst the legislation
does not use the term 'intent' (unlike the position in South Australia) it would seem
implicit that where that is a person's intention that it would satisfy the test. In *R v
Thompson* [2009] ACTSC 23 Higgins CJ noted that this mental element cannot
transform innocuous material into child pornography. He also noted that it is the
intention that is relevant not the circumstances:

> ...if you take a film of a child with a view to later viewing it for sexual
> arousal then the mere fact that that does not happen or that it is ineffectual for
> that purpose for whatever reason is not a course to take anybody out of the
> section.
>
> (at [3])

Clearly this has to be correct. The decision in *Thompson* does not answer how the
purpose is to be identified but the absence of the word intention could be taken
to mean that the approach adopted by the South Australia Supreme Court in

R v Murdock [2009] SADC 109 (discussed above) could apply: i.e. that some material will be obviously for the purposes of sexual gratification but other types may require an understanding of the offender's intention.

Western Australia

The final approach is that adopted in Western Australia. The current definition is contained within s. 3, Classification (Publications, Films and Computer Games) Enforcement Act 1996 as:

> ...an article that describes or depicts, in a manner that is likely to cause offence to a reasonable adult, a person who is, or who looks like, a child under sixteen years of age (whether the person is engaged in sexual activity or not).

Accordingly the definition is not based on any sexual representation, indeed the concluding words of the definition make that clear, although obviously a child engaging in sexual activity is likely to cause offence to a reasonable adult. This is the broadest definition used in any of the legislation and could conceivably cover depictions of, for example, a child being involved in drugs, etc. It could certainly cover acts of sadism and violence, something noted in relation to other Australian jurisdictions. The breadth however does perhaps call into question whether all the material can truly be said to be 'child pornography' as the term is generally understood.

As has been mentioned several times in this chapter, the Western Australia Parliament is currently considering the Child Exploitation Material and Classification Legislation Amendment Bill which, if passed in its current form, will alter the definition (inserting s. 216 into the Criminal Code). The proposed definition will be:

> Child exploitation material means material that, in a way likely to offend a reasonable person, describes, depicts or represents a person, or part of a person, who is, or appears to be, a child –
>
> (a) engaging in sexual activity; or
> (b) in a sexual, offensive or demeaning context; or
> (c) being subjected to abuse, cruelty or torture (whether or not in a sexual context).

It can be seen that the proposed definition is perhaps closer to the first approach to the nature of the material discussed above. That said, paragraph (b) remains wider than, for example, the legislation in New South Wales as it continues to refer to 'offensive or demeaning' contexts rather than just sexual contexts. Accordingly even with the new definition it is quite possible that it will include material that is non-sexual but neither is it cruel or sadistic (e.g. the depiction of children taking drugs). It is not the place of this book to consider the justification for such a move (as this book is, realistically, concentrating on child pornography as understood in Chapter 2) but it does raise questions about what the purpose of the legislation is. There may be a number of offensive depictions that do not directly harm a child, so is the purpose of the legislation to protect children or is it, for example, based on morality or some other approach?

Chapter 5

Virtual child pornography

The preceding chapters have discussed the definition of child pornography but in each chapter the issue of so-called virtual child pornography was not included. Discussing virtual child pornography in a chapter by itself is warranted because it is the source of perhaps the biggest contemporary argument in the law relating to child pornography. Whilst in the 1980s the argument was whether the simple possession of child pornography should be criminalised it is now largely accepted that it is appropriate to do so because of the harm that can be caused by this (discussed in Chapter 2). However since the turn of the new millennia techno-logical advancements have been significant and the production of virtual child pornography began to feature on the political agenda. The landmark decision of the US Supreme Court in *Ashcroft v Free Speech Coalition* 122 S.Ct. 1389 (2002) heightened this debate. The merits of the arguments in favour and against criminalising virtual child pornography will be discussed in this chapter.

Defining virtual child pornography

Before turning to the merits of the arguments it is first necessary to define what is meant by virtual child pornography. It may seem that this will be easy to do but much of the literature, especially that which compares US and UK laws, confuses the issue (see, for example, Peysakhovich, 2004 who does not distinguish between virtual and pseudo images). This is in part because there is no single definition of virtual child pornography.

Computer graphics programs can operate in a number of ways. However it is submitted that the methods can be divided into two broad categories: computer-*manipulated* images and computer-*generated* images. Each are distinct but there is a considerable overlap between them.

Computer-manipulated images

The first category that can be identified is computer-manipulated images. It is submitted that in the vast majority of cases images that are classed as pseudo-images (the definition of which was discussed in Chapter 3) will be computer-manipulated images although it should be noted that the legislation in England and Wales states that computer-generated images can amount to a pseudo-photograph so long as it appears to be a photograph (the meaning of this is discussed below). A computer-manipulated image, as its name suggests, has as its base a real image. There are two broad types of manipulation that are relevant here; splicing and morphing.

Splicing is where two (or more) photographs are taken and are spliced together to create a new image. A crude method of splicing would be where a child's face is 'cut' from one image and 'pasted' on to the body of an adult who is posed in a sexual way (e.g. a pornographic picture). The crude appearance will therefore show the features of a child on the body of an adult. Splicing need not actually involve any form of computer manipulation. One of the earliest cases under English law to consider splicing was *DPP v Goodland* [2000] 1 WLR 1427 where the Divisional Court was called upon to rule upon a 'pitiful' image that the appellant had created. The image consisted of the head of a child being 'hinged' by sticky tape on to a picture of a naked adult woman (p. 1442). When the hinge was 'closed' it would thus appear that the head of the child was on the naked body of the adult. The Divisional Court in this case quashed the conviction deciding that it was patently not 'an image' (as it was two) but did note, albeit *in dicta*, that had he photocopied the image a different result may have been achieved. In the modern communication age it is more likely that splicing will take place using a computer-graphics program where the results can be more realistic depending on the age of the person.

The second form of splicing does not involve two images of different people but rather splices an innocent photograph on to a sexualised situation. Perhaps the classic example of this is someone who, through graphic manipulations software, takes a picture of a child eating an ice cream and 'cuts' the image before 'pasting' it on to a pornographic scene. The resultant image makes it appear that the child is performing a sex act on the adult. There are obviously a variety of different types of situations where this second form of splicing can take place.

The second form of manipulation is morphing. In this context this means taking a pornographic picture of an adult and manipulating its context to create an image of a child. This could typically be done through, for example, airbrushing the pubic hair of the adult, reducing the breast and hip sizes of the female and thinning the body. The resultant image will have the impression of a pubescent child rather than the appearance of an adult.

Computer-generated images

The second category of images is computer-generated images. Again there are two types of computer-generated images. The first can be considered to be computer-created images and the second can be classed as rendered images.

In this context the first category are those images that are created exclusively by computer-graphics programs. By this it is meant that there was never an original photograph in the first place and the resultant image is, in essence, one that has been 'drawn' by the computer. Some of these images can be extremely realistic. (For an early production of these images see 'Kaya' by the artist Alceu Baptistã, produced in 2001, and for more recent work see the artist Max Edwin Wahyudi.)

The second category, rendered images, is probably a derivative of manipulated images but is considered here as it can arguably be said to be a creation rather than a manipulation. Computer software exists that can turn a photograph or other image into something that has the appearance of a computer-generated image. Instead of a photograph a person is rendered into a 3-D computer-generated image. The resultant rendered image may look like a cartoon or a realistic computer-generated image. The rendered image can then be manipulated by, for example, changing the physical attributes of the person (including skin colour and sizes).

Virtual child pornography

Of the four categories of images identified above only one will be classed purely as virtual child pornography and feature within the discussion in this chapter. That category is computer-created images: i.e. those where there was never an original image in the first place. These images are, in essence, fictitious child pornography in that a child was never involved. Arguably a second class can also be placed within this category, that of morphed images. Where a pornographic image of an adult is altered so as to take on the appearance of a child then it can similarly be argued that this is fictitious child pornography (in that no child was actually involved) but, for reasons explained momentarily, there may be a reason to classify this separately.

Depiction of a real child

Of the remaining two classes, splicing and rendered images, it is submitted that these are not truly virtual child pornography. In each case a real child is involved. Whilst it is true to say that a child has not been physically harmed in the production of the image and therefore it could be argued that no abuse occurs (although that is subject to the discussion of emotional harm below) it is submitted that the child has been exploited. Defining 'exploitation' is never easy and its precise relationship with abuse is the subject of some debate (see Ost, 2009: 240 f. for a definition of exploitation in the context of child pornography) but the splicing and rendering of images can impact on the individual presented.

A person has their own sexual identity and autonomy. Could it be argued that the creation of an image that sexualises the child in this way is an infringement of the autonomy and identity of that individual, leading to the exploitation of a child? Of course it is true to say that even innocent pictures can be used for sexual gratification but the manipulation that is occurring here is at a different level. The image is seeking to present the child being complicit in sexual activity that did not happen. Would a person who sees the image understand that it did not happen or would they believe it did? It is known that considerable psychological distress can be caused to victims of child pornography (Palmer, 2005) not just because it aggravates the distress caused by the original harm caused to the child but also because of the realisation that their image and degradation is being used for the purposes of sexual gratification (Taylor and Quayle, 2003: 211).

Whilst the primary harm caused by the sexual abuse would not take place in splicing or rendered images, it is submitted that this secondary harm can still exist (for judicial recognition of this see *R v H* [2005] EWCA Crim 3037. This case concerned a school teacher who spliced pictures of the children in his class on to pornographic images. Victim impact statements are referred to in the judgment of the Court of Appeal (see [7])). Of course Ost notes that a difficulty with this premise is that the harm will only be caused where the person identified is made aware of the image (Ost, 2009: 128). In *H* had the police not told the parents or children about these images (which they were bound to do as they will no doubt have been trying to assess whether the teacher had committed any contact sex offences in respect of the children) then the children would not have suffered any psychological harm as a result of these images being created (although one image was disseminated (at [6]) and so it is possible that this individual could have been harmed if the image was circulated freely). Does this mean that images not seen by the victim do not cause harm?

Ost puts forward an alternative basis of distinction. She notes it may be possible to construe an argument that a child should not be defamed through their image (Ost, 2009: 128 citing *Tolley v J.S. Fry & Sons Ltd* [1931] AC 333). The argument of Ost is that if the image purports to show a person's image in a way that would cause her to be represented negatively then this would amount to defamation regardless of whether the child is aware of the image. However a difficulty with using defamation is that it is commonly accepted that defamation exists when someone is made aware of the negative image, i.e. it requires someone to be aware of it. Whilst there is no requirement for the child to be aware of the image, it does mean that at least one other has to be aware of it. Where the image has been placed on the internet then this is considered to be publishing it (*R v Waddon* [2000] All ER (D) 502) irrespective of whether it is proved that anyone has, in fact, seen it, but what of the situation where the image is not published? Ost notes that if virtual child pornography was considered lawful then it is perhaps more likely that the images would be published (Ost, 2009: 129) and this must be correct. Whilst pseudo-photographs are illegal then persons will be more cautious about publishing or disseminating them whilst the same is unlikely to be true if they are lawful and all they have to fear is a civil defamation action (the funding of which can be expensive).

It is submitted that the potential psychological harm that can be caused to a child by the production of these images means that they do not constitute virtual child pornography *per se* and that they should be treated in the same way as photographic-based child pornography. It is notable that in *Ashcroft v Free Speech Coalition* 122 S.Ct. 1389 (2002) neither the Free Speech Coalition nor the Supreme Court questioned the propriety of criminalising these types of images (p. 1397) with the court noting that they do implicate the interests of real children.

Interestingly it will be remembered from Chapter 3 that the current law of England and Wales may not necessarily cover the situations identified above. Whilst it is clear from cases such as *Goodland* and *H* that splicing will be covered under the provisions of pseudo-photographs it is quite likely that rendering will not be covered. An image that is clearly a drawing or computer-generated image would, it is submitted, not come within the definition of a pseudo-photograph because it does not 'appear to be a photograph'. Where the quality is extremely high (e.g. the image of 'Kaya') and it is not easy to differentiate between the image and a photograph then it may be a pseudo-photograph but the implication of *Goodland* is that something that obviously does not appear to be a photograph cannot be a pseudo-photograph.

Non-existent children

For the purposes of this chapter, therefore, virtual child pornography is defined as an image that does not involve the image of an identifiable child. However this in itself can be problematic. In terms of morphed images it will be remembered that a picture of an adult could be morphed through airbrushing to depict a child. If the face is not altered and remains identifiable then does this also cause questions to be raised about exploitation? Whilst X may be perfectly comfortable to be photographed nude as an adult would she be equally happy if a representation purported to show her nude or engaged in sexual activity at the age of 13 or 14? Could we apply Ost's theory of defamation here? (Ost, 2009: 128) Certainly if the image is published (rather than held privately) then it could be argued that in this context the individual's character has suffered interference. Perhaps therefore virtual child pornography should be restricted to situations where it does not include an identifiable person.

Of course the difficulty with defining an image in the absence of identification is that, as will be seen in Chapter 12, few children are ever identified (see also Maalla, 2009: 15–16). If the prosecution had to prove the identity of the subject then this would cause real practical difficulties to law enforcement. Some have suggested that a solution to this difficulty would be to place a reverse burden on the defence: that the defendant must prove that it did not involve a real child (Ost, 2009) and this could be extended to include a real person if morphed images of an identifiable person are also to be included. The US Supreme Court in *Ashcroft v Free Speech Coalition* rejected this approach (122 S.Ct. 1389 (2002) pp. 1404–1405) in part because they believed that if proving the existence of a real child would be difficult for the prosecution then disproving it is likely to be (at least) as difficult for the defendant. Whilst this is likely to be less problematic for those who create the images it would certainly be problematic for those who downloaded the images. How would a person who downloads an image know whether it depicts a real child or not?

However Ost believes that a reverse burden of proof can be justified. She does not minimise the difficulty that could be caused to someone who possesses an image that they did not create, but argues that it can be justified on the basis that the possessor is taking a risk that their behaviour underwrites primary harm and accordingly they should be prepared to take the risk of being punished if it transpires that it involves a real child (Ost, 2009: 131). This is certainly an interesting argument and it places the onus of responsibility on to the offender. If a person is engaging in material that is, at the very least morally suspect, is it objectionable for the law to require that the offender satisfies himself that the images does not involve a real child? In *Ashcroft* the Supreme Court argued that it would be extremely difficult for any offender to discharge such an obligation but could there be a requirement that an offender takes reasonable steps to ascertain the legality of images that he downloads? There is an attraction to such arguments because of our understanding of the harm that can be caused by the sexualised representations of an individual.

Of course many would argue that this turns around the free speech argument. Freedom of speech is ordinarily guaranteed by requiring the State to prove that the speech is harmful, not requiring the individual to prove, even to a civil standard, that it is not. However it has been noted already that photographs are ordinarily outside the protection of freedom of speech/expression and it could be questioned whether this should be any different for other representation of a real child? It is submitted that Ost is correct to state that the harm that can be caused by, for example, a computer-generated image of a real child engaging in sexual activity, is as grave as a photograph. Earlier chapters of this book have noted the primary and secondary harm that can be caused by visual depictions and it is submitted that computer-generated images can cause harm and accordingly can be the subject of limitations. Of course the harm justification is premised solely on the basis that it is a representation of a real child. Where it does not involve a real child then no harm is caused and therefore the argument could not be used.

It has been seen therefore that defining what constitutes virtual child pornography is not easy. At a simple level it can be said to include any computer-generated image, which would exclude computer-manipulated images (especially those currently known, in England and Wales, as pseudo-photographs). However the rationale for excluding pseudo-photographs of children from the definition of virtual child pornography may also apply to other forms of visual representations of a real child. Indeed, it is suggested that it would be appropriate to cease focusing on the type of material and instead on the subject. Where it involves a real child then there is a risk of harm that can arise and thus a justification for regulating such imagery exists. However it must also be accepted that there are visual images that do not involve real individuals, i.e. images that are purely fictitious. The remainder of this chapter will consider the arguments surrounding the regulation of this type of material.

Competing arguments

Now that virtual child pornography has been defined it is necessary to consider what action, if any, the law should take in respect of it. This section will examine how legislatures have sought to criminalise child pornography and the arguments for and against its criminalisation. As will be seen, the principal battleground in this area relates to whether the criminalisation of child pornography infringes the rights and freedoms of an individual.

Legislative responses

Increasing attention is being paid to virtual child pornography with significant legislative action. In international law there has been a desire to criminalise virtual child pornography for some time. The Optional Protocol to the CRC would appear to cover virtual child pornography as it refers to a representation by 'whatever means' but it will be remembered from Chapter 2 that it requires that it relates to a 'child' which may (indeed arguably does) relate to a real child. Accordingly it may mean that computer-generated images of a fictitious child are not covered but those that relate to an identifiable child (e.g. a rendered image) will be within the provisions (something supported by the NGO Subgroup on sexual exploitation who imply, in a report on definitions, that the Optional Protocol does not include all forms of virtual child pornography whereas other instruments do (NGO, 2005: 27)).

Other international instruments are clearer as to their desire to include virtual child pornography. The Council of Europe Convention on Cybercrime (CETS No. 185) expressly refers to virtual child pornography (Article 9(2)(c)) although it does allow signatory states to 'opt out' of this provision should they so wish (Article 9(4)). In the Explanatory Report that accompanied the Convention it was stated that the prohibition of virtual child pornography could be justified because it 'might be used to encourage or seduce children into participating in [sexual] acts' (para.. 102). The scheme of prohibiting virtual images but allowing a reservation to be made is carried forward into the new Council of Europe Convention on the Protection of Children against Sexual Exploitation and Sexual Abuse (CETS No. 201). Article 20 clearly covers virtual child pornography although Article 20(3) provides signatory states with the opportunity to opt out of criminalising the possession or production of material that consists 'exclusively of simulated representations or realistic images of a non-existent child'. Again there is no detailed explanation as to why these images should be criminalised and indeed the explanatory report cautions states against making a reservation under Article 20(3):

> States Parties should be aware of the rapid developments in technology, which allow producing of extremely lifelike images of child pornography where in reality no child was involved and should avoid covering such productions by their reservation.
>
> (para. 144)

Domestic legislation has also turned its attention to the issue of child pornography. In England and Wales the Coroners and Justice Act 2009 has criminalised, for the first time, the possession of some forms of virtual child pornography (ss. 62–68, CJA 2009). The detail of these provisions will be discussed in Chapter 7 but for the purposes of this chapter it should be noted that little reasoning was put forward for criminalising the images. In the original consultation for the documents the government expressly noted that there was no evidence to suggest that the images caused harm (Home Office, 2007: 6) and so the decision to criminalise them seems to be one of moral taste. The responses to the consultation paper showed support from law enforcement and child protection bodies (MoJ, 2008). The primary justification put forward by many respondents were:

- It reinforces negative views and feelings towards children.
- It could be used by offenders to groom children.
- It was frequently found alongside 'real' child pornography. (MoJ, 2008: 6.)

The government signalled that it accepted that certain forms of virtual child pornography – those for which the publishing, or dissemination of, would be caught by obscenity legislation – should be criminalised. It did not however state whether it believed the justifications put forward by the respondents noted above were correct or not, or indeed signal on what basis it was seeking to justify the material.

That said, it is clear from Parliamentary proceedings that little scrutiny of the justification was given. For example, in the House of Lords the opposition stated, 'we entirely accept the necessity for these [provisions]' (Hansard, HL Deb, vol. 710, col. 1212, 18 May 2009, Lord Kingsland). Similarly in the House of Commons, Sir Paul Beresford MP, a Conservative politician who is well known for his interest in tackling child pornography, noted that the proposals were welcome because of the quality of images produced by technology (Hansard, HC Deb, vol. 487, col. 75, 26 January 2009). The cross-party consensus on the legislation would seem to indicate that the legislative justification is the same as that contained within the government proposals.

Perhaps the most cogent set of reasons were those put forward by the United States Congress. Congress, when passing the Child Pornography Prevention Act 1996, issued a series of congressional findings (s. 1, CPPA 1996). Most of the findings relate to child pornography in its general sense rather than specifically to virtual child pornography. So, for example, the first to fourth refer to how child pornography harms children, creates a permanent record, can whet an offender's appetite or be used to assist in the solicitation of a child. The seventh notes that child pornography involving an identifiable child infringes the child's privacy whilst the tenth and eleventh findings note that the possession of images creates a market and sexualises children. The twelfth finds that criminalising possession will encourage possessors to destroy material and the thirteenth finds that the elimination of the child pornography provides a justification for criminalising all forms of child pornography.

The remaining findings relate the general findings specifically to the issue of virtual child pornography. The fifth finding notes that new technologies can produce child pornography that is indistinguishable from real child pornography.

This is expanded upon by the sixth finding which explains how technology can be used to create or modify child pornography. The eighth and ninth findings are perhaps the most notable in that they find that the stimulation of an offender through whetting their appetite with virtual child pornography is just as potent as with real child pornography, and the ninth states that the use of virtual child pornography poses the same risk for the seduction or solicitation of children.

These findings were used by Congress to justify enacting the 1996 legislation and, as will be seen below, some were used before the US Supreme Court when attempting to defend the constitutionality of the legislation.

Human rights and freedoms

Those that challenge the criminalisation of virtual child pornography base their arguments on the fundamental freedoms acknowledged by law. The relevant freedoms are ordinarily based on the premise of the right to free speech/freedom of expression or the right to privacy, the latter being (in essence) the notion that the State should only interfere with the autonomy of an individual where it can prove a pressing need to do so.

The exact nature of these freedoms will differ between the jurisdictions but for the purposes of this book two will be examined. The first is the right to free speech contained within the First Amendment of the US Constitution. The second issue is the right to Freedom of Expression under Article 10 of the European Convention on Human Rights (ECHR).

The First Amendment is considered to be one of the most important freedoms enshrined in the American Constitution. Its origins lay in the tensions over whether the States would ratify the US Constitution. The First Amendment, protecting freedom of religion and speech, marked a deliberate break from the colonial past where English laws suppressing speech were commonplace. The freedom is jealously guarded and in *Roth v United States* 77 S.Ct. 1304 (1957) the US Supreme Court noted that it applied to 'unorthodox ideas, controversial ideas, even ideas hateful to the prevailing climate of opinion' (p. 1309). Similarly the right to freedom of expression contained within Article 10 of the European Convention on Human Rights is considered to be one of the most important principles and essential to the workings of a democracy (*Handyside v UK* (1976) 1 EHRR 737). The Court has been clear as to its scope:

> Article 10 is applicable not only to information or ideas that are favourably received or regarded as inoffensive or as a matter of indifference, but also to those that offend, shock or disturb the State or any sector of the population.
>
> (Handsyide at [49])

However neither the US nor ECHR model of freedom of speech/expression claim their respective freedoms to be an absolute right. Article 10 is expressly qualified by Article 10(2) which explains the circumstances under which a state can interfere with the right encapsulated in Article 10(1). Whilst the First Amendment is not qualified in the same way, the US Supreme Court has held that the freedom of speech is not absolute and they recognise categories of material that are not protected by the First Amendment, including obscenity (*Roth v United States* 77 S.Ct. 1304 (1957) and, most notably, *Miller v California* 93 S.Ct. 2607 (1973)). The consensus that the freedoms are not absolute however masks an inherent difference in approach between the US and European models. The position in America is that the Supreme Court will recognise that certain forms of speech are outside of the protection of the First Amendment: i.e. the freedom is simply not engaged. By necessity these exceptions will be tightly constrained as it leaves such expression without protection. The ECHR approach however operates on the basis of qualifying the right. That is to say the right will still ordinarily be engaged (although some forms of expression will fall outside its scope: Harris *et al.*, 2009: 445) but that freedom can be interfered with by the State so long as it is justified on the basis of a pressing social need and subject to its necessity and proportionality.

Any justification under Article 8(2) requires the measure to be for a legitimate aim, necessary in a democratic society and to be proportionate. Article 8(2) lists the legitimate aims and those relevant here would include ' . . . the protection of health or morals, for the protection of the reputation or rights of others . . .' The precise meaning of these terms will be discussed later but certainly where it could be shown that there was a link to harm then a justification under Article 8(2) is likely to succeed.

The justifiable interference is perhaps more profound a difference than would ordinarily be thought because of the doctrine of the margin of appreciation that applies to such matters (for a discussion see Harris *et al.*, 2009: 349–351). Put briefly, the margin of appreciation is a doctrine developed by the ECtHR which recognises that individual countries are in a better position to decide the necessity of an interference for a particular social need. The circumstances of the pressing social need will differ in each country and the ECtHR does not see its role as creating a uniform standard although it does reserve the right to conduct its own fact-finding process in respect of the necessity (Harris *et al.*, 2009: 350). The implications of this will be discussed below in respect of obscenity where it is perhaps particularly important.

Justifying criminalisation

It was noted earlier that apart from the justifications put forward by Congress it is not easy to find legislative reasoning behind the criminalisation of virtual child pornography. In terms of a rational justification for criminalising this material the most notable are the arguments of the US Attorney General in *Ashcroft v Free Speech Coalition* 122 S.Ct. 1389 (2002). In essence four reasons were put forward:

- The images could be used to groom children for abuse.
- The material might 'whet [offenders'] own sexual appetites'.

- The existence of virtual child pornography makes it difficult to eliminate the market for child pornography through real children.
- Virtual child pornography makes it difficult to prosecute those who produce material using real children.

It is interesting that apart from the grooming point these reasons are realistically not the same as those put forward in the UK consultation.

Grooming

The first point raised is that of grooming and, as noted above, this is something that was raised in both the UK and United States. The term grooming has entered modern parlance although, like the term 'paedophile' it appears to have two definitions; a clinical definition and a societal definition. The term 'grooming' tends to be used by the legislatures to discuss the position whereby a child is befriended (typically via ICT) for a sexual purpose. Clinicians disapprove of this term as grooming can mean different things and also because it may detract from the issue that the majority of child sex offences take place within a familial environment (Gillespie, 2004: 586). They also worry that the term has begun to be used in a lay sense to mean the solicitation of a child over the internet (Gillespie, 2004: 587) which is certainly not true.

There has long been an argument that child pornography can be used as part of a desensitising process whereby the material is shown to children or even left so that the child discovers it accidentally (Renold and Creighton, 2003: 34) in order to normalise sexual activity (Taylor and Quayle, 2003: 23). Given that we know that some children will appear compliant in the child pornography and even appear to enjoy it (Lanning, 2005) the premise of the grooming argument is based on the fact that it encourages children to believe that sexual activity is both normal and enjoyable.

In *Ashcroft* the US Attorney General advanced an argument that had been rehearsed previously that virtual child pornography may be more potent in the grooming process because the images can be manipulated easier to show children enjoying them and/or their favourite characters can be shown to be engaging in sexual activity. The US Supreme Court in *Ashcroft* was unimpressed with this argument:

> There are many things innocent in themselves, however, such as cartoons, video games, and candy, that might be used for immoral purposes, yet we would not expect those to be prohibited because they can be misused.
>
> (122 S.Ct. 1389 at 1402)

This must be correct: it is not known how much grooming behaviour involves the showing of child pornography (either real or virtual) to children and how much is through other forms of behaviour. Anecdotal evidence would appear to suggest that more grooming takes place by befriending the child and gradually sexual-ising the conversation rather than through the display of pictures. That said, it is clear that some offenders do show child pornography to children (an early example of this is presented by Tate, 1990: 118–119) and it is certainly conceivable that some offenders will show children virtual child pornography.

However is the fact that this behaviour exists a reason to criminalise virtual child pornography? The US Supreme Court noted that a better approach would be to tackle those who attempt to solicit children (*Ashcroft*, p. 1402) and this would seem the more appropriate mechanism. Given that anything can be used as part of the solicitation process then the more appropriate response would be to crimi-nalise that approach or steps within it. This approach would certainly seem to be taken in England and Wales (irrespective of the fact that grooming was cited in the consultation on virtual child pornography).

Whilst the offence under s. 15, Sexual Offences Act 2003 is frequently cited as 'the' grooming offence it is, in fact, only one of a number of offences that have, at their heart, the intention to tackle solicitation/grooming. In the context of virtual child pornography the offence under s. 12, Sexual Offences Act 2003 would be relevant. This criminalises the situation where an adult, for the purposes of sexual gratification, causes the child to, *inter alia*, look at an image of a person engaged in sexual activity. The definition of 'image' is defined extremely widely as 'a moving or still image and includes an image produced for any means and, where the context permits, a three-dimensional image' (s. 79(4), SOA 2003). Setting aside the potential for this to include holograms it is quite clear that it could cover non-photographic forms of pornography. This is strengthened by s. 79(5) which states that references to a person includes an imaginary person, which must include cartoons or computer-generated images.

It had been questioned whether s. 12 would be effective where a person showed images to a child at the early ages of the grooming cycle because of the require-ment that it was for the purposes of sexual gratification (Gillespie, 2006; Ost, 2004) but in *R v Abdullahi* [2007] 1 WLR 225 the Court of Appeal rejected this argument. The court held that there was nothing within the Act which implied a temporal restriction and therefore so long as the showing was for the purposes of sexual gratification (including later on) then this criterion was satisfied (p. 229).

Given the construction adopted in *Abdullahi* and of the meaning of 'image' within the SOA 2003 it would seem that the criminal law already caters for those who show images to children. The fact that it does must cast doubt on the justifi-cation of criminalising the possession of child pornography since the possible harms caused by the showing of images would be caught by existing laws.

Whetting of 'appetite'

The second justification for criminalising virtual child pornography has been framed, somewhat inappropriately, as the fact that it might 'whet' a sex offender's appetite. This was explained in *Ashcroft* as meaning that the material may encourage them to engage in illegal conduct (122 S.Ct. 1389 at 1403). The link between child pornography and contact offending was discussed in Chapter 2 but some aspects of the discussion should be put in context here.

The argument is based on the premise that some will use virtual child pornography to obtain sexual gratification which will then lead them to committing contact offending. There does appear some limited evidence that virtual child pornography can act as a stimulant for the purposes of sexual gratification (Paul and Linz, 2008) although this research was focused on 'barely legal' pornography (i.e. adults posing as teenagers) rather than virtual images of younger children. However the research was clearly based on stimulation and the authors were very clear that there was no evidence to suggest that there was any greater likelihood that individuals would act on this stimulation (Paul and Linz, 2008: 35).

Another important study in this context is the extent to which child pornography, including virtual child pornography, can be considered evidence of cognitive distortion. There is evidence to suggest that the use of child pornography is a valid indicator as to whether a person is a paedophile (Seto *et al.*, 2006). This study demonstrated that those in possession of child pornography were more likely to be classed as paedophiles than even those who had contact offended (Seto *et al.*, 2006: 613). However the implications of this study need to be understood. The purpose of the study was to identify whether someone met the clinical definition of paedophilia. The study did not address the prevalence of future offending.

Does the result of Seto *et al.* justify criminalisation on the basis of 'whetting' the appetite of sex offenders? No. Paedophilia is not illegal, it is a recognised psychiatric disorder (DSM-IV-TR 302.2 and see Seto, 2008). All that Seto's evidence demonstrates is that those who are in possession of child pornography may have this psychiatric disorder. Even if it is used by paedophiles for stimulation the criminalisation of such material would simply be criminalising the thoughts of the individual. In the absence of a link to harm – either in its primary or secondary sense – then it would be difficult to justify the criminalisation of virtual child pornography on this basis alone. Indeed, in *Ashcroft* the US Supreme Court stated:

> First Amendment freedoms are most in danger when the government seeks to control thought or to justify its laws for that impermissible end. The right to think is the beginning of freedom, and speech must be protected from the government because speech is the beginning of thought.
>
> (122 S.Ct. 1389 at 1403)

Perhaps the argument could be presented in a different way so as to find the necessary harm. Rather than examine whether virtual child pornography whets the appetite for contact offending could it be argued that it whets the appetite for real child pornography? Given that child pornography involving a real child is both illegal and harmful could a ban on virtual child pornography be justified on the basis that it may cause offenders to look at child pornography? It would seem that there are two difficulties with making this argument. The first is that there is not, to the best of the author's knowledge, any study that examines whether offenders who access child pornography began with looking at virtual child pornography. Accordingly any link is unproven and without evidence of a link it would be difficult to justify interfering with the freedom of speech/expression.

The second problem with this argument is that there is some evidence to suggest that offenders have begun their offending history by accessing adult pornography (Taylor and Quayle, 2003: 71; Sheldon and Howitt, 2007: 100). Whilst there is some debate about whether this is true or whether it is offenders minimising their behaviour (Sheehan and Sullivan, 2010: 161) there would appear some evidence to support this contention, at least in part. Whilst some continue to argue against the availability of pornography (in part because of the graphic nature of material available on the internet) there has, in recent years, been no serious attempt to criminalise (adult) pornography. This being the case it would be difficult to justify criminalising virtual child pornography on the basis of whetting offenders' appetites without criminalising adult pornography (see also Levy, 2002: 323).

Elimination of the market

The third argument put forward in *Ashcroft* is that the criminalisation of virtual child pornography is necessary to ensure that the market for real child pornography is eliminated. The US Attorney General suggested that as virtual child pornography is almost indistinguishable from real child pornography it is traded in the same way and is an inherent part of the market for child pornography.

The US Supreme Court rejected this quite circumspectly by stating:

> The hypothesis is somewhat implausible. If virtual images were identical to illegal child pornography, the illegal images would be driven from the market by the indistinguishable substitutes.
>
> (122 S.Ct. 1389 at 1404)

Levy adopts a similar argument suggesting that if the material is indistinguishable but legal that pornographers would abandon the production of child pornography rather than risk criminal sanction (Levy, 2002: 320). The difficulty with this argument however is that it is easily stated but no evidence was adduced by either the Supreme Court or Levy to justify it.

Whilst virtual child pornography may well, in many cases, be indistinguishable from real child pornography a significant quantity of it is not at this level and there are lower-grade computer-generated images of abuse together with cartoons, etc. The argument that (legal) virtual child pornography would (contrary to what the government asserted) actually assist in the elimination of the market for real child pornography is premised on the basis that offenders gain equal stimulation from virtual and real child pornography. No studies exist to demonstrate that this supposition is correct although offender studies do seem to focus on the sexual interest of offenders to real children (see, for example, Seto *et al.*, 2010: 176) so is it certain that this logic applies? It would seem conceivable that (at least) some offenders gain sexual gratification from the knowledge that real children are shown involved in sexual activity.

However does the fact that the US Supreme Court and Levy are unsupported when making their counter-argument mean that the government was correct in their submission? The answer must be no. The issue is, in essence, very similar to the issue of the material 'whetting' the appetite of offenders discussed above. It was noted that there is no evidence that would suggest that offenders progress from virtual child pornography through to real child pornography. So whilst there is no evidence to suggest that pornographers will rely solely on virtual child pornography to escape criminal liability there is similarly no evidence to suggest that virtual child pornography has any causal connection to the market for real child pornography. Whilst it is quite possible, and indeed even likely, that offenders will be stimulated by both virtual and real child pornography the banning of virtual child pornography could only be justified on these grounds if it could be shown that it caused offenders to access real child pornography (and the subsequent harm that this entails). In the absence of such evidence then the justification cannot, it is submitted, be used.

Difficult to prosecute

The fourth justification put forward by the US government was that images are so realistic that it causes difficulty for the prosecution in that experts may not be able to tell the difference between real or computer-generated images (122 S.Ct. 1389 at 1404). No evidence was adduced by the government to show that this difficulty exists and Levy argues that 'it is not very difficult' for experts to distinguish between real or virtual images (Levy, 2002: 320) although he does not adduce any evidence either. That said, it is conceded that the fact that virtual child pornography is lawful and real child pornography is not may mean that the police and prosecutors may have to forensically examine images to decide their legality but this is not the same as saying that it is not possible to differentiate between them.

It is unlikely that even if evidence of difficulty was presented to the Supreme Court they would have altered their decision on this point. The Supreme Court notes that, in essence, the government was stating that protected speech could be banned in order to ban unprotected speech which would, in essence, turn the First Amendment upside down. It is difficult to argue against this conclusion: whilst the freedom of speech/expression is not absolute, exceptions to it must be justified on a specific and individual basis.

Found alongside real material

It will be remembered that one of the responses to the UK consultation on crimi-nalising the possession of virtual material was that it could be justified because it was found alongside real material. It is submitted that this is not sufficient reason. It will be remembered from Chapter 2 that many types of material are used by sex offenders and it is not uncommon to find a variety of material alongside real child pornography. In so far as it may cause difficulties to the police to differentiate between the material this was discussed above. The only other construction is that it should be criminalised because it is of interest to child sex offenders. This is analogous to the argument about it whetting an offender's sexual appetite and this was discounted above.

Reinforces negative opinions of children

A response to the UK consultation was that it was possible to justify criminalisation on the basis that it can reinforce negative views and feelings towards children This is perhaps an amalgamation of many of the arguments cited above but interestingly Levy argues that this is one of the few ways that by itself criminalisation can be justified. Having reviewed the feminist critique of the legalisation of pornography he concludes:

> [T]here are strong reasons to believe that virtual child pornography is one more piece in a set of interlocking societal relations and practices which harm women.
>
> (Levy, 2002: 323)

Others have similarly applied feminist arguments to justify the criminalisation of images (Harrison, 2006) but the difficulty with this approach is that the same logic can apply to adult pornography (something that Levy acknowledges). That being the case it is submitted that this cannot justify the criminalisation of virtual child pornography itself; if this justification is taken to mean that legislative action can be taken then it is submitted that it must apply to all those forms of pornography identified within the feminist critique (see, in particular, the works of MacKinnon but see Adler, 2001b for a rebuttal on this).

Morals

It can be seen from the preceding sections that there would appear to be an absence of proof that virtual child pornography causes harm to children. Of the justifications put forward none currently seem to be able to demonstrate the appropriate nexus of harm required by many jurisdictions to warrant a justified interference with the freedom of speech/expression. The argument that virtual child pornography sexualises and objectifies children is perhaps the most established but this remains a controversial argument based primarily on feminist jurisprudence. If that justification is to be used then it must also logically cover adult pornography too where feminists such as MacKinnon argue it is about harmful sexual action against women. It is unlikely such action will be forthcoming.

Until evidence of harm is forthcoming (and it is generally conceded that the courts, particularly the US Supreme Court would re-examine their decisions if evidence of a likelihood of harm was to be found) then it would appear that the only justification for criminalising virtual child pornography is based on morality. In some jurisdictions this is insufficient to criminalise virtual child pornography *per se* and so it must be tied to existing notions of immorality, most notably obscenity. This is particularly true of America where the response of Congress to *Ashcroft* was to introduce the Prosecutorial Remedies and other Tools to end the Exploitation of Children Today Act 2003 (a 'unique' name for legislation that appears to have been chosen to produce the acronym PROTECT Act) which, *inter alia*, invokes obscenity law to criminalise certain virtual child pornography (Adler, 2007: 708).

Obscenity is also at the heart of the decision of the UK government to criminalise the possession of computer-generated images of abuse in the Coroners and Justice Act 2009. The UK government noted expressly that there was no evidence of harm (MoJ, 2008: 8) but nevertheless thought that criminalising material that would be covered by the Obscene Publications Act 1959 can be justified. Accordingly the decision must be premised squarely on obscenity and, therefore, morality.

The provisions of the Obscene Publications Act 1959 and Coroners and Justice Act 2009 will be discussed in Chapter 7, but can morality justify an interference with the respective human rights? In America it was noted earlier that obscene material is considered to be outside the protection of the First Amendment (*Roth v United States* 77 S.Ct. 1304 (1957)) and therefore federal and state law can criminalise obscene articles. However an interesting issue is whether the mere possession of obscene articles can be criminalised.

It is commonly thought that simple possession of obscene material is a protected right (although under the Fourth Amendment (privacy of an individual's own home) rather than through freedom of speech) and therefore cannot be criminalised (see *Stanley v Georgia* 89 S.Ct. 1243 (1969); *US v 1,200-foot Reels of Super-8 mm Film* 93 S.Ct. 2665 (1973)). Notwithstanding this, US federal law purports to criminalise mere possession of virtual child pornography (18 USC §1466A) although at least one decision considers this unconstitutional (*US v Handley* 564 F. Supp. 2d 996 (2008)) although on different grounds (but see pp. 1000–1001 which indicated albeit *in obiter* that the rule in *Stanley* would apply to this material). The challenge in *Handley* was based on the argument that 18 USC §1466A is premised on the basis that the material is obscenity *per se* whereas the District Court held that the test for obscenity must be one for a jury applying community standards (p. 1006 f.).

If the decision in *Handley* is affirmed then this will not strike down the criminalisation of virtual child pornography: it simply requires that the material is classed as obscene as applied by community standards. As with the UK therefore it would seem that obscenity – which must be a moral judgment – is key to its criminalisation. However *Handley* gives support to the suggestion that mere possession is not justified (although the appellant in *Handley* was charged with importing the material (the importation occurring through downloading material from the internet) and the District Court held that this was not unconstitutional: see p. 1001 meaning that downloading virtual child pornography by the internet may be culpable).

What is the position under the ECHR? It was noted earlier that the protection of morals is considered a pressing social need under Article 10(2) so as to allow Member States to justify an interference with a right under Article 10(1). Previously reference was made to the fact that the ECtHR allows for a margin of appreciation to be extended to Member States and this is clear from its decisions relating to obscenity.

Perhaps the leading case in this area is *Handyside v UK* (1976) 1 EHRR 737. This concerned a publication known as the 'Little Red Schoolbook' that was published as intended to be read by children. It contained a number of different topics and was designed as a 'help' book whereby a person would read topics of interest to them rather than read it as a whole. The book contained references to disapproval of adults, drugs and sex. Whilst it had been published in a number of countries in the Council of Europe and indeed in some parts of the UK without criminal sanctions, the publisher had been convicted of obscenity in London after a campaign by several members of the media. The publisher petitioned the ECtHR holding that his conviction was an unjustified interference with his rights under Article 10.

The UK government conceded that Article 10(1) was engaged but argued that Article 10(2) applied as they sought to criminalise it for the protection of morals. The ECtHR, as already noted, took account of the fact that there is no uniform definition of morality, but they also placed great emphasis on the fact that the book was intended to be read by children (p. 755) and it noted that certain sections of the book were advocating promiscuous behaviour (p. 756). The ECtHR considered the proportionality of the measure and noted that an edited version of the book (which did not contain the references to sex) was allowed to circulate freely (p. 758) and therefore confirmed that the domestic countries had acted proportionally.

A key part of the decision in *Handyside* concerned the degree to which the ECtHR was prepared to defer to the national court's understanding of the pressing social need (Harris *et al.*, 2009: 11 f.). The ECtHR clearly finds that Member States are ordinarily in a better position to decide the pressing social need at the heart of Article 10(2). In *Müller v Switzerland* (1998) 13 EHRR 212, a case that concerned obscenity, the ECtHR noted that there was no uniform standard for decency and that it would differ between the countries. The ECtHR specifically rejected a suggestion that a uniform definition could be adopted across the Council of Europe.

In both *Handyside* and *Müller* there was concern that children may have had access to the material (and indeed in *Handyside* the publication was directed towards children). This could have had a significant impact on the pressing social need as it is commonly believed that children may be more readily corrupted. However in *Otto-Preminger-Institut v Austria* (1994) 19 EHRR 34 the ECtHR adopted a similar approach where there was no risk of children seeing the material. The case concerned a film considered blasphemous by many but the Institute was careful not to hold an open screening, warned potential viewers of the content of the film and also introduced a minimum age restriction. Despite this the ECtHR, upholding a ban, stated that the national State was better placed to decide whether the religious beliefs of their citizens would be attacked. The decision has been criticised as being overly deferential to State interests and unreasonable in deciding that the anticipated outrage of a local community (who would have not seen the film had they chosen not to do so) outbalanced artistic freedom (Harris *et al.*, 2009: 460).

Applying *Handyside, Müller* and *Otto-Preminger* it is highly likely that a state decision to criminalise obscene virtual child pornography would be considered a legitimate interference with Article 10. It is highly likely that the ECtHR would defer to Member States on what constitutes obscenity and over the need to protect morals through the use of the criminal law. What of the fact that the *Coroners and Justice Act 2009* will criminalise simple possession? It will be remembered that in the United States it would seem that simple possession of obscenity is unconstitutional. Could a similar approach be adopted by the ECHR?

As with America it is likely that any challenge would be based on privacy (Article 8, ECHR) since this, in essence, protects the right of an individual to pursue his life without undue interference by the State (see, for example, *Kroon v Netherlands* (1994) 19 EHRR 263). However Article 8 is a qualified right and Article 8(2) specifically lists as a pressing social need the protection of morals. Given the decisions in *Handyside, Müller* and *Otto-Preminger* it is likely that the ECtHR would accept the social need to criminalise mere possession. This leaves the issue of proportionality. To an extent the margin of appreciation makes it more likely that the ECtHR would defer to the national court's test of necessity but it has been noted that the Court reserves the right to consider the matter afresh.

Some have argued that simple possession is disproportionate (Williams, 2004: 254) but there is no decision from the ECtHR to support this argument and arguably the decisions discussed immediately above suggest that they are more likely to uphold the Member State's finding that morality requires protection. This is supported by the comments of the ECtHR in *Norris v Ireland* (1991) 13 EHRR 186 where it referred to *Handyside* and *Müller*, stating that whilst they related to Article 10 and not Article 8, the court 'sees no cause to apply different criteria in the context of Article 8' (p. 199). Given the abhorrence that society has to child pornography it is submitted that it is likely the ECtHR would accept that criminalising even mere possession would be proportionate to a pressing social need. Of course this is contrary to what liberalism teaches (particularly that derived from John Stuart Mill) and it remains controversial to many who believe that pornography, even abhorrent pornography, can be banned only when it causes harm or where it can be shown to be a matter of something other than community preference or taste (and the comments of Dworkin 1966: 1002 f. remain relevant to this argument), but it would seem the most likely current result if a challenge were brought under either Articles 8 or 10.

Chapter 6

Offences relating to indecent photographs of children

Chapter 2 considered the justification for the criminalisation of child pornography and Chapter 3 introduced the Protection of Children Act 1978 (PoCA 1978) and examined the definitions contained in that Act for an indecent photograph of children. The purpose of this chapter is to consider what offences exist in respect of indecent photographs of children. Other chapters will consider how the law in England and Wales deals with non-photographic representations of children.

This chapter will examine the law as it is currently defined and thus, not withstanding my conclusion at the end of Chapter 2 that it would be appropriate to move away from focusing on the image towards an understanding of offender behaviour, bringing with it the ability to depart from the subjective test, this chapter will examine the law in the current definition of indecency.

Making, taking and dissemination

As has been noted already, the principal law on the creation and dissemination of images is to be found in s. 1, Protection of Children Act 1978. This creates a number of different crimes, as set out in s. 1(1):

> It is an offence for a person –
>
> (a) to take, or permit to be taken, or to make, any indecent photograph or pseudo-photograph of a child; or
> (b) to distribute or show such indecent photograph or pseudo-photographs; or
> (c) to have in his possession such indecent photographs or pseudo-photographs, with a view to their being distributed or shown by himself or others; or
> (d) to publish or cause to be published any advertisement likely to be understood to be conveying that the advertiser distributes or shows such indecent photographs or pseudo-photographs, or intends to do so.

The essence of s. 1(1) is that 14 separate offences are created since there are seven methods of breaching s. 1(1) and each can be committed in respect of either a photograph or pseudo-photograph. For ease of writing I will simply refer to a photograph and not a photograph or pseudo-photograph but references and arguments should be taken to apply equally to both.

Taking or making an indecent photograph of a child

The first two ways of breaching s. 1(1) are to take or make an indecent photograph. Neither term is defined in the Act although 'take' is a word of ordinary usage and its definition is unlikely to pose any real challenge. Quite clearly in this context it means the person who takes (or, in the case of a film, records) the indecent photograph. What of 'make'? The term make was not originally included within the Protection of Children Act 1978 but was inserted as part of the reforms introduced by the Criminal Justice and Public Order Act 1994. The genesis of the amendment was quite clearly the belief that modern technology was posing difficulties for the application of the law as drafted.

The term 'make' also has an ordinary meaning and the *Oxford English Dictionary* defines the verb 'make' as being 'to bring into existence by construction or elaboration'. Bringing into existence must include the creation of a copy. So, for example, photocopying an image or, in the context of ICT, scanning an original photograph so that an electronic copy is then created, could both be said to be examples of making.

When the term 'make' is used in the context of creation it is uncontroversial and is undoubtedly comparable to the term 'take'. Both terms mean the creation of an image that did not otherwise exist, or a copy thereof. However the term 'make' was given a wider definition in the case of *R v Bowden* [2000] QB 88. Here, the appellant was charged with 12 counts of making an indecent photograph of a child, the agreed facts of the matter being that he deliberately downloaded a number of indecent photographs of young boys to his computer. At the Court of Appeal he argued a number of points. The first was that he argued that the wording of s. 1, PoCA 1978 did not refer to making an indecent photograph of a child but rather to making a pseudo-photograph of a child. He also argued that even if this were not the case, the term 'make' must mean the creation of an image and would not cover, for example, the downloading of an image that had already been created.

Turning to the first argument. Section 1(1)(a), PoCA 1978 *at that time* stated it was an offence 'to take, or permit to be taken, or to make any indecent photograph or pseudo-photograph of a child'. Counsel for the appellant argued that the section should be interpreted as meaning the verb 'to take' should apply to photographs and that the verb 'to make' should apply to pseudo-photographs as this was the natural way to describe the creation of a computer-generated or manipulated image (p. 94). The Court of Appeal rejected this argument out of hand noting that the plain language of the Act clearly stated that the verb 'to make' applied equally to either a photograph or pseudo-photograph.

In terms of the meaning of the term 'to make' the Court of Appeal placed reliance on the arguments of counsel for the prosecution:

[PoCA 1978] is not only concerned with the original creation of images, but also their proliferation. Photographs or pseudo-photographs found on the internet may have originated from outside the United Kingdom; to download or print them within the jurisdiction is to create new material which hitherto may not have existed therein.

(p. 95, per Michael Crimp)

The Court of Appeal was clear that the downloading of an image led to an image being made, that being the file that is now contained on the offender's hard disc and thus s. 1 was infringed. The logic of this decision was then taken further in the conjoined appeal of *R v Smith; R v Jayson* [2003] 1 Cr App R 13. The appellant Smith had opened an email that had attached to it an indecent photograph of a child. Whilst the majority of his arguments related to the *mens rea* of the offence (and will be discussed below) he sought to argue that the offence of making an indecent photograph of a child could not occur where the computer automatically created a copy of the image in the cache or other temporary folder (p. 218). The court rejected this argument noting that it was simply a natural extension to the ruling in *Bowden* and that a file had been created.

The more interesting issue was raised in respect of the appellant Jayson. He had been convicted of seven counts of making an indecent photograph of a child. The facts of the case were that it had been clear that the appellant had been viewing hardcore child pornography on his computer screen. Whilst he did not download any of the images, they had been automatically stored in his cache (p. 220). Counsel for the appellant sought to argue that although s. 7(4)(b), PoCA 1978 stated that a photograph included 'data ... capable of conversion to a photograph' this must mean that the material is capable of being retrieved. The image in the cache was not capable of being retrieved other than by the computer. The Court of Appeal rejected this argument and noted that nothing in the legislation required the material to be stored capable of being retrieved, merely that the data should be capable of being converted into a photograph (p. 222). Clearly this was the case here since the purpose of the cache allowed for the photograph to be subsequently displayed.

The second argument advanced by the appellant was that some of the photographs were not stored in the cache but were simply displayed on the screen and that this meant they existed solely in the random access memory (RAM) of the computer. The Court of Appeal rejected this argument in quite stark comments:

In our view, the act of voluntarily downloading an indecent image from a web page on to a computer screen is an act of making a photograph or pseudo-photograph ... By downloading the image, the operator is creating or causing the image to exist on the computer screen. The image may remain on the screen for a second or for a much longer period. Whether its creation amounts to an act of making cannot be determined by the length of time that the image remains on the screen.

(p. 222)

This is of significant relevance to situations where, for example, material is stored virtually (discussed below) and the cache is disabled. Assuming in such circumstances that a person is observed accessing an indecent photograph of a child – and observation would seem to be the only way of proving the case in those circumstances since the disablement of a cache may mean a forensic examination would not assist (save where the URLs are recoverable) – then they could still be convicted of the offence of making.

The decision in *Jayson* in this respect appears to contradict part of the decision of the Divisional Court in an earlier case of *Atkins v DPP* [2000] 1 WLR 1427. This case primarily concerned the *mens rea* of the offence and will be discussed further below. However the appellant in that matter had downloaded a number of indecent photographs of a child into a specific folder. In the cache of the computer were a number of other images that had been produced when the offender had viewed the images but had not downloaded them. The Divisional Court in *Atkins* rejected a submission by counsel for the Crown that the appellant had also made those images. Counsel argued that it should be irrelevant that he did not know the images were being stored in the cache but the Divisional Court rejected this saying that this would create an absolute offence and would be wrong (p. 1438). In *Jayson* there was no doubt that the defendant knew how a cache operated and to this extent it could be argued that this amounts to a material difference although the Court of Appeal in *Jayson* appears to state it did not ([2003] 1 Cr App R 13 at p. 222).

The premise of the decision of the Court of Appeal in *Jayson* was that deliberately calling up an image *on to the screen* amounted to making (p. 222). There was no doubt that Atkins had done this. Whereas Atkins was prosecuted on the basis that the files in the cache amounted to an indecent photograph of a child, it would seem that post-*Jayson* the more appropriate prosecution would be to use the files in the cache as *evidence* that the defendant had viewed an indecent photograph of a child on the screen. If this viewing was done deliberately then it would seem that the offence is made out.

The essence of the decisions in *Bowden* and *Smith; Jayson* therefore is that someone who deliberately views indecent photographs of a child on screen or downloads them is guilty of the offence of making an indecent photograph of a child. From a literal point of view it can be argued that the decision in *Bowden* is correct. A file now exists on a computer that did not exist prior to the offender's activity. It does not matter whether the image is in a folder selected by the offender or (as in *Jayson*) the cache. In either situation a file has come into existence. Whilst counsel for the Crown was correct in *Bowden* to argue that the image may never have been found in the jurisdiction before, it is submitted that this is irrelevant. It is the fact that the file did not exist on the computer that is relevant and, from a literal stance, the decision is therefore correct.

Bowden, and its subsequent extensions, are somewhat controversial notwithstanding that they are literally correct. The controversy is best summed up by Ormerod:

... it is arguable that such broad interpretation extends the offence beyond what is absolutely necessary given the existence of the offence of mere possession under s. 160 of the Criminal Justice Act 1988.

(Ormerod, 2000: 383)

Whilst the decision in *Bowden* was undoubtedly technically correct, the essential question that is raised is whether it was necessary. It will be seen below that the offence of possession could arguably have covered the situation just as easily (subject now to a discussion on a difficulty that arises where an image has been deleted: see *R v Porter* [2006] 1 WLR 2633 discussed below). Ormerod questions whether the storing of an image on a computer is 'equivalent to one who moves an ordinary photograph from one desk drawer to another in which case the section 1 offence ought not to apply' (Ormerod, 2000: 383). Of course it was noted in Chapter 2 that the process of collecting and sorting a collection could be considered an indicator of seriousness but this does not take away from Ormerod's point since a collector could just as easily sort physical photocopies by placing them into, for example, albums.

Akdeniz is critical of the decision in *Bowden*. In the case itself counsel for the appellant sought to admit material from *Hansard* to show that Parliament had intended the verb 'to make' to be restricted to pseudo-photographs. The Court of Appeal argued that the test encapsulated in *Pepper v Hart* [1993] AC 593 was not satisfied ([2000] QB 88 at 95) and realistically this is correct. However that is perhaps more an indictment of the decision in *Pepper v Hart* than the decision in *Bowden*. The freedom academia brings not to be tied down by *Pepper v Hart* allowed Akdeniz to argue, quite plausibly, that counsel was almost certainly correct (Akdeniz, 2008: 50). Certainly a perusal of Hansard during the passage of the 1994 legislation would seem to suggest that Parliament was concerned with the creation of computer-generated or computer-manipulated images of abuse. Nothing noted in Hansard would appear to suggest that Parliament had ever intended the downloading of material to be covered by the offence of making.

It will be seen below that the possession offence is certainly a capable and effective offence. Since the reforms introduced by the Criminal Justice and Court Services Act 2000 the offence is punishable by a maximum of five years' imprisonment. It will be seen from Chapter 10 that, for the purposes of sentencing, an offender who downloads material will be treated as though in possession of material (i.e. sentenced as though the maximum sentence is five years' imprisonment). The logic of this is undoubtedly based on harm: it is difficult to suggest that the harm caused by a person downloading material is any different to the harm caused by a person possessing it. Arguably this is the salient point. It could be argued that *Bowden* was a pragmatic decision. At the time that *Bowden* was made the penalty for possession was only six months' imprisonment whereas the penalty for making was three years. By 2000 the advent of the internet had ensured that the offences were being detected more frequently and the level of material recovered was more significant. It could be argued that *Bowden* was a policy decision in that it was the recognition that accepting it amounted to possession that would not have allowed courts to pass an appropriate sentence. Arguably the decision reinforces the criticism levelled earlier that the law may focus on the wrong issue. If the action of the offender was considered culpable then the decision reached in *Bowden* would be unnecessary. In terms of activities, the downloading of material must be considered to be possession. A person is deliberately choosing to store material and this is, realistically, no different to them storing photographs in an album or a drawer. What of *Jayson*? This is an interesting decision in that it suggests that deliberately viewing indecent photographs on the internet amounts to a criminal offence. It will be remembered from Chapter 2 that this could be justified, indeed the justification for criminalising the possession of material must apply equally to those who deliberately view it (the justification arising primarily from the issue of secondary victimisation). Should this realistically be classified as making however? It cannot be said to be possession – since, depending on the status of the cache, nothing is in possession – but this is a fiction necessary for the law as it is currently stated. Realistically if the law focused on the action of the offender then there is no reason why the law could not prohibit the viewing of a photograph rather than relying on the fiction that an image is made.

Mens rea

Section 1, PoCA 1978 is silent as to the issue of *mens rea* but it is well known that the courts dislike offences of strict liability and will allow them only where it can be shown that this was clearly the intention of Parliament (Ormerod, 2009: 156). The question of *mens rea* was raised for the first time in the case of *Atkins v DPP* [2000] 1 WLR 1427. The appellant was a lecturer in English at the University of Bristol. He had access to two computers for his post; a computer based in his office and also a shared departmental computer. An administrator was concerned about the website history displayed on the departmental computer and, upon examination, a number of indecent photographs of children were found in the cache. The appellant's computer in his office was also found and a number of indecent photographs were also found in that cache along with a directory that had been created by the appellant where a number of images had been downloaded.

The appellant was charged with 10 counts of possession of indecent photographs of children and 10 counts of making an indecent photograph of children, these 20 counts relating to the images found in the cache. A further 14 counts of making an indecent photograph of a child were charged in respect of the images that the appellant had deliberately downloaded. At the trial of first instance, the stipendiary magistrate acquitted the appellant of all charges in respect of making on the basis that copying an image (by, for example, downloading) did not amount to making. He was, however, convicted of the 10 counts of possession in respect of the images in the cache.

Both the DPP and the defendant appealed to the Divisional Court. Whilst most of the decision is relevant to the issue of possession (including an argument by the appellant that he had a legitimate reason for the photographs) and will be discussed below, parts of the case also relate to making. The Divisional Court allowed the appeal by the DPP in respect of the making charges on the basis of the ruling in *Bowden* but this is simply an application of the *actus reus* principles discussed above. However the Divisional Court considered the issue of *mens rea*, something that the Court of Appeal in *Bowden* had not. Counsel for the DPP had suggested that the offence under s. 1(a) should be construed as an offence of strict liability: the very act of causing a file to come into existence was sufficient to show that an indecent photograph of a child had been made ([2000] 1 WLR 1427 at 1438). However Simon Brown LJ, giving the judgment of the court, stated:

> I would unhesitatingly reject this submission … To construe it as creating an absolute offence in the sense contended for by the prosecutor, i.e. to encompass also the unintentional making of copies, in my judgment would go altogether too far … In short it is my conclusion that, whilst 'making' includes intentional copying … it does not include unintentional copying.
>
> (p. 1438)

The case demonstrated comprehensively that s. 1 required *mens rea*, with the requirement being that an offender acted deliberately; in essence requiring intention. The matter was revisited in *R v Smith; R v Jayson* [2003] 1 Cr App R 13. It will be remembered that in *Smith* the appellant had opened an email attachment that contained an indecent photograph of a child. The appellant argued that the email was unsolicited (p. 217) although the Court of Appeal disagreed with this and noted that the offender had been in discussion with another offender about such images and had arguably also sent images himself (pp. 218–219). The Court of Appeal held:

> We entirely accept that a person is not guilty of an offence of 'making' … if before he opens the attachment he is unaware that it contains or is likely to contain an indecent image.
>
> (p. 217)

The inclusion of the words 'likely to contain' would suggest that the requirement to act deliberately is not enough and that there must be knowledge, or even foresight, of the consequences of that action. The requirement for foresight can be justified in this context since it would be difficult to prove that a person will ever definitely know for certain the contents of an email prior to its opening whereas they could know that it is likely (not, it is submitted, merely *possible*) to contain an indecent photograph of a child.

What of the calling of an image to the screen? It will be remembered in *Jayson* that the Court of Appeal had ruled that the 'voluntary downloading [of] an indecent image from a web page on to a computer screen is an act of making a photograph' (p. 222). 'Voluntary' in this context must simply be another way of expressing the requirement that the offender must act deliberately. Whilst a person deliberately calling an image to the screen is likely to know its contents, the Court of Appeal was prepared to acknowledge foresight may exist here and they concluded:

> In our judgment, [the] *mens rea* is that the act of making should be a deliberate and intentional act with knowledge that the image made is, or is likely to be an indecent photograph or pseudo-photograph of a child.
>
> (p. 222, per Dyson LJ)

Pop-ups

So far what has been discussed is a person who has deliberately sought indecent photographs of children. A recent case however calls into question what the position would be where an indecent photograph of a child is made through an automatic 'pop-up' program.

It is trite to state that the internet is a popular tool for the proliferation of pornography in all its forms. The advent of the internet and, in particular, broadband has revolutionised the pornography industry turning it into one of the most commercially viable e-businesses (Lane, 2000). A considerable amount of adult pornography is available free on the internet but most of this (save for that which is accessible through, for example, peer-to-peer networks) acts as a method of encouraging users to pay for longer and higher quality material. A number of different strategies are used as part of this encouragement, including displaying thumbnails of images contained within the site and previews of material, including hard-core video clips. A common tactic is the use of 'pop-ups'. Pop-ups are a ubiquitous part of online life, so much so that a number of commercial programs are available to prevent their operation. They are now to be found on all types of websites, including newspapers. They are used as an advertising gimmick and are used to promote the latest film release, an online game or even a new book. However their origin probably lies in the pornography industry where their use remains prolific.

A typical pop-up in a pornography site could be an advertisement for a particular web page or it could as easily be an entire new window, displaying a different website, each with a series of 'thumbnails' of pictures that can be obtained on the site. Of course a difficulty with a pop-up is that the user has no control over its existence. Depending on the settings of the cache, the images contained in the pop-up will automatically be downloaded into the cache. There is also, of course, no guarantee that the images will be lawful, especially when the website that is being accessed is based outside of the United Kingdom.

What should the position be of someone who finds indecent photographs of children through a pop-up? To an extent it would seem relatively simple. *Smith; Jayson* states that a person must do a deliberate act knowing that an indecent photograph of a child will be obtained or is likely to be obtained. It could be argued that a pop-up is not a deliberate act. If an offender subsequently 'clicks' on to a thumbnail or downloads the image that has 'popped up' then this would be different: they have done a second, deliberate act and so they can, and indeed should, be culpable for this.

What of the situation where a user simply closes the pop-up even though the image is then stored in the cache? It may seem that the answer should be that the person is not culpable because of the absence of an initial deliberate act but the decision in *R v Harrison* [2008] 1 Cr App R 29 would appear to cast doubt on this assertion.

The appeal in *Harrison* is slightly confusing because the offender was charged with possession rather than making but the prosecution conceded, for no obvious reason, that they would have to prove that he had made the photographs in order to be guilty of possession. It is not known why the prosecution sought to make this concession or, indeed, why they even charged possession rather than making. One possible reason for the concession is that the appellant, no doubt going for the 'father of the year' award, attempted to suggest that it was his son who was responsible for the images rather than himself. However this does not explain why possession was charged in the first place (as this would simply require proof that the offender was knowingly in control of the images) and *Harrison* could be considered a perfect illustration of the absurdity caused by the current definitions of the law. If, as was discussed above, the law concentrated on the activities of the person rather than the image, then an offence of viewing or downloading could have been charged instead, making the position clearer.

The appellant agreed that he had accessed lawful (adult) pornography sites although he disagreed (contrary to what the prosecution contended) that he was aware that illegal material could be displayed automatically through a 'pop-up' and thus stored in the cache ([2008] 1 Cr App R 29 at p. 390). In what was described by the Court of Appeal as an 'attractive submission' (p. 391) counsel for the appellant argued that where an image is created by an automatic pop-up program it is the creators of the webpage rather than the user who has 'made' the image (p. 392). This was emphatically rejected by the Court of Appeal. Factual causation remains satisfied; but for the offender accessing the pornographic website the pop-up would not have activated and the file (in the cache) would not be made.

That part of the decision is, in effect, a relatively simple application of the *actus reus* principle set out in *Bowden*. Addressing the mental issue, the Court of Appeal continued that in this context the test is does the jury know:

> ... not only [that] the appellant knew about automatic 'pop up' activity when he accessed adult pornographic sites, but that he knew in accessing certain sites that there was a likelihood that these 'pop ups' would be illegal images.
> (p. 392, per Cranston J)

It is submitted that this is problematic and an extension too far. It was noted that in *Smith; Jayson* the Court of Appeal, for the first time, decided that knowledge was not required, simple likelihood would suffice. In terms of the activities in *Smith* this can be justified. The defendant made a conscious decision to open an e-mail attachment. There is likely to be circumstantial evidence which would guide the choice of an offender in doing so (e.g. who the email is from, what the subject of the email is, whether he has previously sought indecent photographs of children, etc.). The same is arguably true of *Jayson*. Where a person is calling an image to the screen it is likely that it will be from either a thumbnail (in which case the user can see what he is to load) or a URL which may (although it is conceded that it will not always) give some clue as to what the image is likely to be (e.g. the name of the file: there are phrases that are used to indicate an image is child pornography).

The same cannot be said of a pop-up, however. The user has no control over whether an illegal image pops up and can do nothing to prevent it (many sites spend a considerable amount of money developing technological solutions to evade pop-up blockers). The overall purpose of the offender is, presumably, to seek out lawful pornography. Should an offender who is seeking to do something lawful be penalised where an illegal image is automatically loaded without him being able to do anything about it? A mere likelihood is a low standard to require. Given that there is no global consensus on the age of consent or the definition of child pornography there must always be the possibility that a person accessing adult images could be subject to a pop-up displaying images of individuals that would be considered children in England and Wales, not least because of the way that websites are linked together. An offender may be looking at a site that certifies the age of those portrayed on its sites but this does not guarantee that it will not include a pop-up link with a site that does not.

It was noted above that there was confusion between possession and making in *Harrison* and this may be sufficient to render the decision *obiter*. It is submitted that the courts should be slow to follow this ruling and it would be better to require proof that an offender intended to access child pornography or was reckless as to whether he would so obtain. Mere likelihood cannot be equated to recklessness and the fact that the making is outside the control of the user alters, it is submitted, the basis of liability. To reinforce the point made at the start of this section, *Harrison* can be seen as additional evidence for the fact that the law is concentrating on the wrong issue. The law should focus on the actions of the offender rather than the acquisition of a photograph. If it did so then it would criminalise those who deliberately view child pornography rather than those who may come across it unintentionally when looking for adult pornography.

Defences

When initially drafted there were no defences to s. 1(1)(a). This was certainly a conscious decision by Parliament since there is clear evidence from Hansard that attempts were made to include a defence within it (see Hansard, HL Deb, vol. 394, col. 325, 28 June 1978). Parliament ultimately decided, however, to leave cases where there may have been a legitimate reason for the making or taking to the discretion of the DPP.

The Sexual Offences Act 2003 introduced two new partial defences to s. 1(1)(a). These were set out in two new sections; s. 1A (which refers to an exception where the parties are married or in an enduring family relationship) and s. 1B (which refers to exceptions for law enforcement agencies). Section 1A deals specifically with those adolescents between the ages of 16 and 18 and so this defence will be considered in Chapter 8 where it can be placed into context.

Section 1B(1) states:

> In proceedings for an offence under section 1(1)(a) of making an indecent photograph or pseudo-photograph of a child, the defendant is not guilty of the offence if he proves that –
>
> (a) it was necessary for him to make the photograph or pseudo-photograph for the purposes of the prevention, detection or investigation of crime, or for the purposes of criminal proceedings, in any part of the world;
> (b) at the time of the offence charged he was a member of the Security Service or the Secret Intelligence Service, and it was necessary for him to make the photograph or pseudo-photograph for the exercise of any functions of that Service; or
> (c) at the time of the offence charged he was a member of GCHQ, and it was necessary for him to make the photograph or pseudo-photograph for the exercise of any of the functions of GCHQ.

Whilst this would appear to be a relatively restricted defence it is, in fact, reasonably wide. Paragraphs (b) and (c) are notable because it provides recognition that child pornography is a global phenomenon in which organised criminal gangs are starting to be interested. The production of child pornography is also linked to the commercial trafficking of children. Whilst the intelligence services (the Security Service (a.k.a. MI5), Secret Intelligence Service (a.k.a. MI6) and GCHQ) are primarily focused on terrorism, they do have an increasingly important role in tackling child sexual exploitation. The defence under s. 1B expressly recognises this.

It should be noted that the defence requires not only that the defendant is a member of the relevant agency but that it was *necessary* for him to make the photograph or pseudo-photograph. Necessity is a term that is used elsewhere in the law and it has been held that it means something more than simply desirable (*R v Halloren* [2004] 2 Cr App R (S) 57) and this is perhaps particularly relevant in the context of child pornography where, as was discussed in Chapter 2, the proliferation of material can cause real harm to a child. The necessity test also ensures that it is only where a legitimate operation is undertaken that the defence applies and so an officer who acts on a frolic of his own will not be protected.

The principal provision within s. 1B is that contained within paragraph (a) which relates to the prevention, detection or investigation of a criminal offence or for the purposes of criminal proceedings. This is a wide provision and one that does not simply cover law enforcement officers but could also encompass a number of other organisations, including the Internet Watch Foundation, child protection organisations and even private companies. Whilst it is relatively easy to think of situations where a law enforcement officer or prosecutor will be required to make a photograph, what of private industry? Let us take the following example:

> D works in a bank where he has access to a computer. X believes that she has seen D accessing pornographic pictures on a computer and she reports this fact to Y, a HR person. Y asks Z, a network administrator, to examine D's network space. Z finds indecent photographs of children on the space. He makes a virtual copy of the network space and reports the matter to the police.

In this situation Z has undoubtedly 'made' an image but it would be inappropriate for him to face criminal liability for doing so. Z needed to make the image to investigate the suspicions. Similarly child protection professionals could be involved in the making of images:

> X, aged fifteen, sends Y, who works for the NSPCC, an email that she received and which she is worried about. In the email she says that a boy from her class has sent it to her and that it is a pornographic image of a child.

If Y opens the email then, according to *R v Smith* [2003] 1 Cr App R 13 she will have made an indecent photograph of a child. Clearly in the circumstances above, however, Y will need to open the email so that she can see what the image is and take the appropriate steps.

The defence (including paragraphs (b) and (c) discussed above) imposes a reverse legal burden on to the defendant – he must prove (to the civil standard) that he comes within the defence. The Association of Chief Police Officers and the Crown Prosecution Service produced a memorandum of understanding (ACPO/CPS, 2004) that set out the circumstances in which they would treat an offender as coming within the defence. The memorandum provides an indication of the circumstances when the police would not ordinarily investigate the matter or when the CPS would not proceed with a prosecution. The memorandum is not designed to cover those situations where police officers or prosecutors themselves make indecent photographs but rather it is designed for outside agencies that may encounter indecent photographs of children (e.g. the example set in the bank above). It should be noted that the circumstances set out in the memorandum are not the only ones where the defence will apply; the memorandum itself has no legal force and it is ultimately for the jury to decide whether the defence applies. If the circumstances in the memorandum are satisfied then ordinarily there will be no prosecution but even if a prosecution is brought, a person can still claim the defence.

The defence contained within s. 1B is unobjectionable and perfectly legitimate. It could be questioned whether it was strictly necessary however. A prosecution under s. 1 can only be brought with the consent of the DPP (s. 1(3), PoCA 1978). Where the making has occurred as part of a legitimate criminal investigation it is inconceivable that the DPP would ever give his consent. In Chapter 3 it was suggested that s. 1(3) was not necessarily an effective protection and the creation of s. 1B does seem to provide some support to this argument. It can be seriously questioned whether s. 1(3) affords, as has been claimed, legitimate protection to a parent who inadvertently takes an indecent photograph of their child when it was thought that the same discretion was not sufficient to protect law enforcement officers. If anything, therefore, s. 1B reinforces the need to protect parents and others who take legitimate photographs, either through a defence or, as suggested in the last chapter, through a refocusing of the criminal law.

Distributing or showing images

The next two methods of breaching s. 1 are to distribute or show an indecent photograph of a child (s. 1(1)(b), PoCA 1978). A further method is to possess the images 'with a view to their being distributed or shown by himself or others' (s. 1(1)(c), PoCA 1978). Given the meaning of 'possession' will be explored in full below it makes sense for this offence to also be considered here since the emphasis is on the distribution or showing.

Perhaps the easiest of the offences to discuss is that of showing. In *R v ET* [1999] Crim LR 749 the Court of Appeal ruled that showing meant displaying the photographs to another. The offence in *ET* was actually one under s. 1(1)(c) in that the offender had a cine film in his possession but there was no proof that he intended to show it to anyone other than himself. Of course where the film is electronic rather than physical then following *Jayson* – discussed above – it is quite possible that by calling the film up on to the screen he will now be guilty of making (s. 1(1)(a)) when viewing the image. This could be important where, for example, the film is on a DVD being watched on the computer. Such reasoning would appear contrary to the reasoning in *ET* and also contradict the possession offence (as previously noted) and is further support for a rationalisation of the offence.

Distribution is perhaps at its easiest when X deliberately sends Y an indecent photograph of a child. For the reasons set out in Chapter 2 this should be considered a criminal offence and indeed some have argued that it is serious offending behaviour in that it increases the number of people who have seen the photograph and, accordingly, can be said to increase the secondary victimisation of children. The advances in technology has meant that distribution is perhaps now easier than it was prior to the development of the internet and there is evidence that the number of prosecutions in respect of distribution is now increasing (Akdeniz, 2008: 45).

Distribution is not however always as simple as X sending Y an image. Interestingly the Protection of Children Act 1978 itself recognises this by the provision of s. 1(2) which states:

For the purposes of this Act, a person is to be regarded as distributing an indecent photograph if he parts with possession of it to, or exposes or offers it for acquisition by, another person.

Accordingly it is not simply the actual passing of a photograph that amounts to distribution, making it available to somebody will also amount to distribution. The Court of Appeal has, albeit *in dicta*, suggested that this form of distribution would be a separate form of the offence under paragraph (b) (*R v Goldman* [2001] EWCA Crim 1684 at [20]).

The use of s. 1(2) to define distribution as including the offer of a supply does, however, mean that there is a considerable overlap with s. 1(1)(c), that of having possession of the photographs with a view to their being shown or distributed. It is this offence that has been examined more frequently by the higher courts. A notable case in this regards was *R v Fellows and Arnold* [1997] 1 Cr App R 244. The first appellant in this case operated a computer archive that contained porno-graphic material, including indecent photographs of children. Access to the archive was by password and he provided passwords to certain individuals (including the second appellant) who could either download or upload images into the archive (the second appellant was convicted of distributing images by uploading images into the archive).

The first appellant was convicted of possessing indecent photographs of children with a view to them being shown or distributed. The basis of the conviction was that by supplying passwords to people this allowed them to access the archive where they could then download images. Whilst the majority of the grounds of appeal concerned the validity of treating files as a photograph (which was discussed in Chapter 3), the appellant also questioned whether the showing or distribution was present. Counsel for the appellant sought to argue that the first appellant was passive: he permitted others to have access to the archive rather than taking any positive action to distribute or show them (p. 255). The Court of Appeal ruled that the appel-lant had acted positively: he had taken steps to create the archive and to allow for others to access it through the provision of a password. The password was only given by the appellant and only after communication. The judge at first instance (Owen J) had suggested that this was analogous to providing a key to a library where pictures were displayed and that this would amount to showing (p. 249) and the Court of Appeal agreed with this ruling (p. 255).

Whilst this is perhaps true, it does demonstrate the overlap that exists between paragraphs (b) and (c). Given that Fellows operated the archive and freely allowed persons to download images from the archive he could as easily have been convicted of distribution under paragraph (b) on the basis that the archive must amount to the exposure of indecent photographs for the acquisition by another (s. 1(2)). Indeed, arguably it would have been easier to prove this and it would have not required the Court of Appeal to be troubled with the issue of whether active or passive participation was required. It perhaps reinforces the suggestion that the current laws are not drafted particularly coherently.

The Court of Appeal in *Fellows* did not have to consider the meaning of the words 'with a view to' contained in s. 1(1)(c) since it was obvious what his intention was. This issue was raised however in the later case of *R v Dooley* [2006] 1 WLR 775. The appellant used the peer-to-peer network KaZaA. Peer-to-peer networks operate on the basis that each user has a 'My shared folder' which all users on the network can access. If you copy material from someone else's folder it will be placed in your 'My shared folder' (and thus accessible to everyone) until moved out of the folder into an (unshared) folder. The appellant's computer was seized and several thousand indecent photographs of children were found on his computer, of which six were contained in the 'My shared folder'. He was convicted of possessing those six images with a view to them being distributed or shown but the appellant argued that the mere fact that the images were contained in the folder was not sufficient and that the Crown had to prove that one of the defendant's reasons for leaving the images in the folder was to enable others to access it (p. 778). Counsel for the Crown did not depart from that submission but suggested that oblique intention could be used, so that if it was inevitable that the image could be seen by others then this would suffice.

The Court of Appeal stated that the judge was right to draw a distinction between 'with a view to' and 'with the intention of' suggesting that they were two different concepts and that the former bears a wider definition than the latter. The court also approved the suggestion that the legislation did not require the distribution or showing to be the sole, or even primary, reason so long as at least one of his reasons for leaving the images there was to allow others to access them (p. 779). The court held that foresight was not sufficient, noting:

> One can envisage circumstances where a person foresees X as a likely consequence of doing Y, but does not do Y with a view to X. To take a far fetched example, a general may foresee the likelihood of his soldiers being killed in battle, but he surely does not send his troops into battle with a view to their being killed.
>
> (p. 779)

This must be correct but as Ormerod notes, this does make the offence much harder to establish (Ormerod, 2006: 546). In many instances it may not be possible to ever prove that a person foresaw that someone may be able to access the material rather than intended this to happen. *Dooley* may need to be treated with some caution. Ormerod argues that evidence of how KaZaA works must provide cogent evidence that one of the reasons behind not immediately moving images from a folder is to allow others to access the images (Ormerod, 2006: 546 this is an argument later supported by Rook and Ward, 2008: 143). This must be correct: if a person does not want to distribute images to others then they could be moved out of the folder. This logic was applied in the case of *Peebles v HM Advocate* (2007) JC 93, a Scottish case before the High Court of Justiciary (Appeal Court). The facts were broadly similar to those in *Dooley*. Counsel for the appellant sought to argue that there was no *mens rea* but the Lord Justice Clerk stated:

On the evidence the appellant had positively enabled the file-sharing function in the Kazaa programme, the jury were entitled to infer that one of his reasons for doing so was to allow others to have access to the files and therefore to conclude that he held the files with a view to their being distributed or shown by himself.

(pp. 99–100)

It is submitted that this is correct and it is for the police and prosecutors to obtain evidence of the knowledge of an offender's use of peer-to-peer software as this could be crucial for a successful prosecution.

Mens rea

It was noted above that it was decided in *Atkins* that s. 1(1)(a) did not create an offence of strict liability. In terms of s. 1(1)(c) *Dooley* decided the meaning of 'with a view to' and accordingly *mens rea* is required for that offence. What of s. 1(1)(b)? In *R v Price* [2006] EWCA Crim 3363 the Court of Appeal ruled that paragraph (b) creates an offence of strict liability, albeit one subject to a defence.

In *Price* the appellant was a schoolteacher. He was convicted of various offences relating to indecent photographs of children, including four counts of distributing an indecent photograph of a child. Another teacher at the same school as the appellant had asked him for a CD that she could burn material on to. The appellant gave her a CD and when she (eventually) went to burn some files on to it she noticed that there were a number of pornographic films on it, including several that contained indecent images of children. The appellant denied putting the material on the CD although he conceded that he must have passed the CD to the other teacher. He appealed, contending that it was not sufficient that the prosecution had to prove only that he handed over a disc containing indecent photographs of children; he argued that the prosecution should prove that he knew the disc contained indecent photographs of children.

Counsel for the prosecution argued that distribution was a strict liability offence subject to the defences contained within s. 1(4) which require the defendant to prove that he had a legitimate reason for the distribution (s. 1(4)(a)) or had not seen the photographs and did not know, or have cause to suspect, that they were indecent (s. 1(4)(b)). The Court of Appeal agreed, noting that if the prosecution had to prove that the defendant knew that the photographs that were being passed were of indecent photographs of children then there would be no room for the defence under s. 1(4)(b) (see [2006] EWCA Crim 3363 at [25]). Clearly this must be correct. Parliament must have intended the defence to prove that he did not know that the media distributed contained indecent photographs of children, which means, by necessity, that the prosecution need only prove that D distributed either a photograph or media containing an indecent photograph of a child. It should be noted that the prosecution bear the burden of showing that distribution did occur (including by using s. 1(2) by proving that D exposed or offered the photographs for acquisition) and that the distributed material was *in fact* an indecent photograph of a child. Accordingly the prosecution must prove the age, that it is a photograph and that it is indecent (the three issues discussed in Chapter 3). However once they have proved those elements then it is for the defendant to prove that he had not seen the photographs and did not know, or have any reason to suspect, that the images were of children. It is quite clear that this is a legal burden (*R v Collier* [2005] 1 WLR 843 and see Gillespie, 2005) but there is no reason why it should not be imposed in the circumstances.

Inciting distribution

Whilst it may seem that s. 1, PoCA 1978 covers most behaviours, the use of inchoate liability has increased their use, particularly in respect of incitement. One of the earliest decisions where incitement was used in this context was *Goldman* [2001] EWCA Crim 1684. The appellant wrote a letter to a company based in Amsterdam who had advertised the sale of pornographic videotapes including some that appeared to indicate they were child pornography and which also allowed customers to request a special tape, including banned material. The letter from the appellant asked the firm to provide a videotape involving 'very young (7 to thirteen – or slightly older if they appear childlike), pretty and (preferably) slim girls ...' (at [7]). The videotape was never supplied but the authorities became aware of the existence of the letter and he was charged with inciting the distribution of an indecent photograph of a child.

At trial, the appellant sought to argue that since he was responding to an advertisement to supply images the subsequent request for a videotape could not amount to an incitement to distribute. The trial judge rejected this (at [11]) and the appellant changed his plea to guilty and appealed to the Court of Appeal. Counsel for the appellant sought to argue that advertising photographs amounts to a criminal offence under s. 1(1)(d), PoCA 1978 (discussed below) and also distribution under s. 1(1)(b) since, as a result of s. 1(2), they have offered the photographs for acquisition. Counsel further argued that this meant distribution was a continuing offence and there was accordingly no incitement. The Court of Appeal disagreed noting that whilst offering material for exposure does amount to distribution, the actual sending of a videotape to another was a separate act of distribution (at [20]). They further held that incitement encompasses encouragement, persuasion or inducement (at [21]) and sending payment for a videotape must equate to persuasion or inducement (at [23]).

Goldman was unusual in that it involved a letter requesting the delivery of tangible photographs. The technological revolution has meant that such transactions would now be relatively rare. However the use of incitement appears to have survived advances in technology. Operation Ore was perhaps one of the largest police operations ever to be conducted by police forces in the United Kingdom. Ore was the British part of the global operation that began when the US Postal Inspection Service arrested Thomas and Janice Reedy who operated Landslide Productions. This was a vast commercial organisation and US law enforcement agents identified all the subscribers to the site. They parcelled this intelligence up and sent it to law enforcement agencies in each country.

In the UK the National Crime Squad (now subsumed within the Serious and Organised Crime Agency) was the 'lead' for intelligence and the US material was unpacked and sent to each police force for action. Chapter 12 will discuss some of the issues raised by the police operation but it should be noted here that it was an operation that lasted a long time. This meant that when officers attended some addresses the computer had been disposed of and there was, in some instances, no evidence of indecent photographs of children on their new computer (the name of the originating website (Landslide Productions) had been leaked and reported by the press which means it is conceivable that some people disposed of their computer fearing that they would be on the Operation Ore 'list').

The CPS decided that where there was evidence that a person had paid a subscription for Landslide Productions then they would attempt to use the law of incitement (as it then was) to find culpability. It should be noted here that this has proven to be an extremely controversial decision, with some suggesting that innocent people have been the subject of law enforcement interventions as a result of inadequate forensic examination or credit card fraud (something discussed in Chapter 12).

The first case to use incitement was *R (on behalf of O'Shea) v City of Coventry Magistrates' Court* [2004] EWHC 905 (Admin). The claimant was charged with three counts of inciting the distribution of indecent photographs of children based on evidence of his credit card transactions that he had been using Landslide Productions and actively sought child pornography images. He was committed to the Crown Court for trial but sought to challenge the committal on the basis, *inter alia*, that no offence had been committed. Counsel for the claimant noted that all transactions on Landslide were fully automated. A person would enter their credit card details and an automated payment system would process the credit card payment and provide the access codes to the site. Counsel argued therefore that no person had been incited which would be fatal to the prosecution case as the prosecution must prove an actual person was incited.

The Divisional Court accepted that it was 'trite law' that a machine could not be incited (at [32]) but they did not accept that no person was, in fact, incited in this case:

> However, the business operation of Landslide was operated by human beings … The computers were used to facilitate the business, and I accept the submission of the Crown that for the purposes of the committal, it is irrelevant to say that it was only the computer which was encouraged to commit the crime. The fact of the matter is that those lying behind it … were operating a business. By subscribing through the means of the computer, the claimant was, in my judgment, at least for the purposes of a prima facie case, established as inciting someone, namely those lying behind the onus of the company, to commit the offence.

(at [38])

The distinction drawn by the Divisional Court has not been received without critical commentary. Ormerod has stated that 'the court's acceptance of the broad proposition that there can be an incitement because there is a business behind the computer has the potential to undermine the clear acknowledgement that there must be "another" who is the incitee' (Ormerod, 2004: 950). Ormerod's argument is more powerful because he does not necessarily believe the decision is wrong, merely that the mental gymnastics performed by the court may be. He notes that there was sufficient evidence to show that the owners of Landslide produced bi-weekly updates to the site and accordingly this could be evidence to show that they were being influenced by the communications of individuals, including the claimant in this case (Ormerod, 2004: 951). As Ormerod notes, there is no need to show that the incitee was actually encouraged by the communication: merely that the encouragement (which applying *Goldman* would be the payment) was communicated.

Stating that there is someone who is 'behind' the business is problematic. What is the position where X, the creator of the site, ceases to update it? For example, X creates a site that allows individuals to pay for access to it and which displays (and allows users to download) indecent images of children. As with Landslide the payment system is fully automated. Whilst X created the site and posted the images on it, the site is not updated as X has moved on to other websites. The computer program running X's website will still process payment and X receives the money. In these circumstances can it really be said that D, who uses his credit card to access the website, has incited X? It is difficult to see how, since X will not know of D's existence. Is there a person 'behind' the company as intimated in *O'Shea*? It is difficult to see how there is. Whilst X created the site he is no longer doing anything with it other than receiving money. Incitement requires there be encouragement to commit an offence. Here X is, it is submitted, no longer consciously distributing images. They are being distributed in that they are being offered for acquisition (s. 1(2), PoCA 1978) but it is difficult to see how the payment is inciting X to distribute these rather than it being the computer that is being incited, something that as the Divisional Court accepted would not amount to incitement under the law.

O'Shea could, of course, be considered a public policy decision. The courts may have decided that they required a solution to the problem identified in *O'Shea* and they decided to extend incitement in this way. The difficulty is that this has led to the situation that Ormerod identified: it confuses the general law of incitement. The general rule of incitement is too important a concept in criminal law for it to be blurred by the practicalities of one situation. In reality the decision is a further example of the incoherence of the law relating to indecent photographs of children. Had the law, amongst other things, criminalised the *purchase* or the *obtaining* of indecent photographs of children then the stretching of the law required by *O'Shea* would never have been necessary and incitement could be restricted to those situations where a person is directly involved.

An issue that was not addressed specifically in either *Goldman* or *O'Shea* was the issue of jurisdiction. In both cases the businesses were based abroad (Holland

and the United States respectively). Any distribution would therefore have taken place outside of the jurisdiction so was there incitement? This issue was raised in the case of *R v C* [2006] EWCA Crim 2132 (also reported under the name *R v Tompkins* [2006] All ER (D) 433).

The defendant C was charged with inciting the distribution of indecent photographs of children after the police had evidence to show that he had used his credit card to access the websites operated by Landslide Productions. At trial, the Crown Court judge ruled that an incitement to commit a crime abroad is not indictable in this country unless the substantive crime is one which could be tried in this country (at [7]). The judge held that since Landslide Productions was based in the United States the distribution occurred there and accordingly no indictment could be raised here for that offence and thus there was no incitement. The prosecution appealed under s. 58, Criminal Justice Act 2003 contending that the judge was wrong in law.

The Crown argued that where the encouragement is to commit an offence within this jurisdiction then the courts have the power to try an offender in England and Wales even though the incitee is outside of the jurisdiction. Counsel drew support for his contention from *Goldman* and *O'Shea* although such support would be in the negative in that they simply demonstrate that jurisdictional issues were not raised there which implies that jurisdiction is not problematic but the support cannot go beyond mere implication. More support was drawn from the case of *R v Waddon* (2000, unreported) which concerned the Obscene Publications Act 1959. The Court of Appeal in that case agreed with a concession by counsel for the appellant that publication (for the purposes of that Act) takes place when the images are accessed within the territory of England and Wales (at [12]). The effect of this is that material that is hosted abroad could, if accessed by someone in England and Wales, be considered published for the purposes of the 1959 Act.

Counsel for the Crown in *C* argued that the logic of *Waldon* could be applied in the context of indecent photographs of children and argued that this meant that if images were sent from a website abroad to a computer in England and Wales this amounted to distribution ([2006] EWCA Crim 2132 at [20]). Of course this is not technically what happens: there is no sending of the images, it is simply that a user in this country accesses the images from the website and then chooses to download them. However the logic is correct in that *Waldon* would state that the images are published in this country meaning that they are being offered for supply in this country and applying s. 1(2), PoCA 1978 it can be said that they are therefore being distributed within this country meaning incitement would apply. Counsel for the defence, faced with this argument, conceded the point but the Court of Appeal felt it necessary to state that the Crown's argument was correct (at [23]) although the concession must mean that this is *obiter*. Once again however the issue could have been more easily resolved if the legislation examined the action of the offender and was not focused on the photograph. If the legislation criminalised the purchase or acquisition of indecent photographs of children the jurisdiction problem would not have been raised since the act of acquisition would have taken place in England and Wales.

Incitement as a common-law offence has now been repealed and replaced by the provisions of Part 2 of the Serious Crimes Act 2007 which has been described as over-broad, over-complicated and convoluted (Ormerod and Fortson, 2009). The offence of incitement is replaced with three offences broadly relating to causing or encouraging an offender to commit a crime. Whilst it is not strictly necessary to go into the detail of these offences for the purposes of this chapter it is certainly likely that the SCA 2007 will be used in the same context as above. It is likely that supplying payment details for access to a pornographic website or responding to an advertisement would be considered an act that is capable of encouraging or assisting the commission of a criminal offence (distribution) and the incitor will be intending to encourage that offence to be breached (s. 44(1), SCA 2007). Whilst a person is not to be taken as intending the offence to be breached by reason of foresight alone (s. 44(2), SCA 2007) proving intent in this context is unlikely to be difficult since the supply of payment must be considered the direct intent for access to be given or the material to be distributed. Section 47(2) states that 'it is sufficient to prove that he intended to encourage or assist the doing of an act which would amount to the commission of that offence' and clearly paying for access to indecent photographs (or otherwise soliciting the distribution of them) would satisfy this requirement.

The stretching of the language required in *O'Shea* may not be necessary under the SCA 2007. Whilst 'encourage' must relate to a person (the dictionary definition of encourage being 'give support, confidence, or hope to' (*Concise Oxford English Dictionary*)), it is difficult to see how a computer could be encouraged. The language of the SCA 2007 is encourage or *assist*. Depending on how this is construed it could be argued that providing payment details has assisted in the distribution of the material since if it were not for the payment, the distribution would not have occurred. If this logic is not adopted then it is highly likely that the courts would adopt the creative reasoning of *O'Shea* and decide that the person 'behind' the company was encouraged but this will almost certainly suffer from the same difficulties as discussed above; something a more rational set of offences would minimise.

Possession

When PoCA 1978 proceeded through Parliament there had been no intention to produce an offence of simple possession: i.e. where a person possessed indecent photographs of children for their own use. Possession was criminalised where there was an intention to distribute or show them (s. 1(1)(c), PoCA 1978 discussed above) but in the absence of such an intent then possession was lawful.

In the 1980s there was concern that not criminalising possession was a mistake and the matter began to be raised in Parliament. Eventually it was decided to legislate and it is clear that this decision was based on the premise of the market-reduction argument:

> We believe that people will be less willing to buy or keep this material if they know that they put themselves at risk of a criminal conviction, and the penalties, especially the public shame, that may follow. This should reduce the market for what is a vile product.
>
> (Hansard, HL Deb, 22 July 1988, vol. 499, col. 1699, per Earl Ferrers)

The prediction that the market would be reduced has proved sadly wrong, principally as a result of the technological revolution, with the advent of the internet meaning that the amount of material grew exponentially (Taylor and Quayle, 2003: 43).

The market-reduction argument was also cited as a way of ensuring that the harm to children would be reduced in that children would not be procured to appear in the photographs if there were a reduced market for them (Hansard, HC Deb, 28 June 1988, vol. 135, col. 305, per Geoffrey Dickens MP). Of course not everyone agrees with this argument. Not every member of the legislature was in favour of extending criminalisation to possession, with some noting that there was no proof that it would make children safe (Hansard, HL Deb, 22 July 1998, vol. 499, col. 1673, per Lord Monson) and there was also the suggestion that it could pose a risk of harm as it would prevent those with a sexual interest in children seeking a 'release' through the use of photographs (ibid.). This is a controversial issue and one that was discussed in Chapter 2 when dealing with the issue of contact offending, and it will be remembered that there is no evidence to support this argument.

The reasons for criminalising possession were discussed in Chapter 2 and it is not necessary to rehearse them here. It is interesting to note that there was relatively little discussion about the propriety of criminalising possession when the matter proceeded through Parliament, it being an issue that largely attracted cross-party support.

Possession is criminalised by s. 160, Criminal Justice Act 1988 (CJA), which is a relatively simple offence:

(1) Subject to section 160A, it is an offence for a person to have any indecent photograph or pseudo-photograph of a child in his possession.

The reason for its simplicity is that s. 160 is, in essence, a 'daughter provision' in that the definitions of 'photograph', 'pseudo-photograph' and 'child' are expressly the same as that within PoCA 1978 (s. 160(4) CJA 1988). The meaning of 'indecent' is also expressly the same and it has been noted already that this has meant that following the decision in *Bowden* [2001] QB 88 there is an overlap between s. 1, PoCA 1978 and s. 160, CJA 1988. The overlap is arguably even more significant in practice since it is not uncommon for prosecutors to charge s. 160 as a 'catch-all' provision where the entire collection is alleged to be in possession (Card *et al.*, 2008: 189). Following *Thompson* [2004] 2 Cr App R 16 it was stated that if this process was to be adopted then there should be a count on the indictment for each of the sentencing levels.

Meaning of possession

As with many of the terms in PoCA 1978, the CJA 1988 did not define what is meant by the term 'possession'. Clearly Parliament had in mind the situation where a person has physical custody of a photograph but technological changes have forced the courts to consider whether something wider is needed. *Bowden* did not really address the issue since by deciding that downloading amounted to creation it failed to address the issue of electronic possession. Similarly in *Fellows* [1997] 1 Cr App R 244 the appellant did not contest that he had possession of the material although he did question whether he possessed it for the purposes relevant under s. 1(1)(c), PoCA 1978.

The principal case that discusses the meaning of possession is that of *Porter* [2006] 1 WLR 2633. The appellant was convicted of 17 offences relating to indecent photographs of children. 15 offences related to the making of indecent photographs of children (the making being downloading applying *Bowden*) and two counts of possession. The first possession count related to 40 movies that contained indecent images of children and the second possession count related to 3,575 indecent photographs of children. Of the 40 movies, seven had been placed in the recycle bin which had then been emptied, the remaining 37 had not been downloaded but were recoverable from the cache.

The position in respect of the still photographs was more complex. 2,500 were thumbnails that were automatically created by the appellant using ACDSee, a computer-based photograph program. The original photographs had been deleted but the thumbnails which were automatically created could be recovered through specialist forensic techniques. The remaining still photographs had been deleted in the sense they had been placed in a recycle bin which had then been emptied.

The effect of this is that there were 33 movie files in the appellant's cache which could easily have been recovered and which the appellant conceded he could recover. The remaining moving files and all of the still photographs were only recovered as a result of forensic software which the defendant did not have access to. Whilst some commercial software would allow recovery of some of the images there was no evidence that the appellant had this software or had ever used it.

The prosecution argued that all they had to prove was that a person is guilty of an offence if he is in possession of a computer and indecent photographs of children capable of being viewed are recoverable from it ([2006] 1 WLR 2633 at 2637 at [10]). On that basis the Crown conceded that the stills produced by the ACDSee program were not in his possession in that he was not able to view them without specialist forensic software. Counsel for the appellant argued that a person should only be guilty of possession if the images were 'readily accessible to the accused for viewing at the time when they are said to be possessed' (p. 2637 at [9]). In support of this argument he suggested that a person who was in possession of them and had attempted to divest himself of the photographs through deleting them should no longer be considered to be in possession of them.

The Court of Appeal began by noting that the term possession had frequently caused trouble in the past in other contexts (p. 2637 at [13]). They held that defining possession in the way suggested by the Crown would be unreasonable (p. 2638 at [17]). They noted that some of the images on the disc could be recovered only by a program supplied with the authorisation of the government of the United States, and they held that it would be unreasonable to suggest that such images remained in his possession. The court held that the test of possession was whether a person had 'custody or control' of the images and said:

> In the ... case of deleted computer images, if a person cannot retrieve or gain access to an image, in our view he no longer has custody or control of it. He has put it beyond his reach just as does a person who destroys or otherwise gets rid of a hard copy photograph.
>
> (p. 2639 at [21])

A consequence of this approach is that the technological knowledge of the defendant will be important with the Court of Appeal stating that whether a photograph is in an offender's control will be a question of fact (p. 2640 at [22]).

Porter could be considered to be a relatively simple case. It would seem unobjectionable to state that where an offender is no longer able to access an image, he should not be considered to be in possession of it. Interestingly the Court of Appeal noted that the decision itself was perhaps unnecessary since had the prosecution brought the case on the basis that he was in possession of them prior to deleting them then this issue would not have arisen (p. 2637 at [12]). That said, there can be difficulties in proving this, not least because it would have to be shown that the offender did have possession and control at that time. The appellant in *Porter* conceded that he had deleted the images which is evidence that he was in possession and control of them at the time he chose to delete them but in *R v Rowe* [2008] EWCA Crim 2712 the Court of Appeal quashed the conviction of an offender who made no such assertion and who had been convicted of possession irrespective of the fact that the photographs had been deleted.

The Court of Appeal is correct to say that possession charges could have been brought under the circumstances outlined above but the easier approach where it is known that a person has downloaded the image is to charge s. 1, PoCA 1978 (using *Bowden*) and not possession. Traditionally possession has been used to encompass the whole of the collection since a person can only be sentenced for that which he is convicted of or pleads guilty to (*R v Canavan* [1998] 1 WLR 604 but now see s. 17, Domestic Violence, Crime and Victims Act 2004 although scepticism remains about its use (see Archbold, 2010: 1–142)).

Porter would appear further evidence of the paradox created by *Bowden*. Two people who do identical behaviour (download an indecent image of a child and then delete it) could be treated very differently depending on prosecutorial policy. Where a person is charged under s. 1, PoCA 1978 there is no defence whereas a person charged under s. 160, CJA 1988 will escape liability because it is no longer in their possession. This is a position that is difficult to justify and rationalisation of the law must be required.

Ormerod questions whether the concept of 'custody or control' is necessarily wise in the context of computers (Ormerod, 2006: 750) and he questions whether a more appropriate definition would be based on accessibility (Ormerod, 2006: 751). This is an interesting question when one considers the increased use of virtual storage, i.e. websites or FTP programs that allow users to store files on an internet-connected server and access them wherever. Virtual storage became popular in the context of photographs but ISPs such as BT (through their 'Digital Vault' program) promoted virtual storage as a way of ensuring that important files could never be lost if a computer broke. The files do not have to be stored within the jurisdiction and in many circumstances they will not be. What is the position where a person stores indecent photographs of children on a virtual storage program? Can it really be said that these images are within their 'custody or control'? It would be difficult to say that they are in their custody since the photographs are expressly not stored on the user's computer. Indeed, if Freenet (or equivalent) is used then the user will probably not even know where the files are held. What of control? It could be argued that they are since the user will have a password that will allow him or her to access the files and to delete them, copy them, forward them, etc. However is this enough for control? If the host decided to delete all the files then there would be nothing the user could do about this, so do they truly have control? Applying Ormerod's access test instead this would perhaps solve this difficulty since a person in the circumstances can be said to have access to them (until they are deleted by the host) and so it is perhaps more appropriate to say that they are in possession of them.

Mental element

In *Atkins v DPP* [2000] 1 WLR 1427 the Divisional Court was clear that a defendant must knowingly possess an indecent image of a child. In the context of *Porter* this would mean that unless a person was aware that the images remained on his computer even after he had deleted them then he should be acquitted (Ormerod, 2006: 750). In most situations this will be unproblematic since it is submitted that most people realise that simply pressing the 'delete' button does not delete a folder (until the user 'empties' the recycle bin) but this does mean that the defendant's computer skills become increasingly important in deciding the culpability of a person rather than the action they took.

Defences

Section 160 is subject to a number of defences. As with s. 1(1)(a), PoCA 1978 the Sexual Offences Act 2003 created a new defence (s. 160A) to cater for those situations where a person is in possession of a picture of a 16 or 17 year-old and this will be addressed in Chapter 9 as it primarily relates to those of a similar age. However s. 160(2) contains three defences in their own right:

   (a) that he had a legitimate reason for having the photograph or pseudo-photograph in his possession; or

   (b) that he had not himself seen the photograph or pseudo-photograph and did not know, nor had any cause to suspect, it to be indecent; or

   (c) that the photograph or pseudo-photograph was sent to him without any prior request made by him or on his behalf and did not keep it for an unreasonable time.

Before examining the specific defences it is worth pausing to note that the defences impose a reverse burden of proof: i.e. it is for the defendant to prove (rather than the prosecution to disprove) the existence of the defence (*Collier* [2005] 1 WLR 843 and for a discussion on this see Gillespie, 2005b). It is also worth noting the difficulty of *Bowden* one final time. Given the fact that the creation of a file (including a temporary one) is an act of making within the meaning of s. 1(1)(a), PoCA 1978 the actual usefulness of these defences is perhaps more questionable in the era of modern technology. Few people these days will have hard copies of indecent images of children and it is more likely that they will exist in electronic form. Since calling the image up to the screen is also an act of making (*Smith; Jayson*) then this may mean that few would be charged with possession rather than making. Of course where the making was for a legitimate purpose it is unlikely that the prosecution test would be satisfied but it should be noted, once again, that the implication of these cases is that the prosecution could choose to charge an offence to which there are few defences rather than the offence of possession where a defence may be put forward. Arguably this is thwarting the will of Parliament (who presumably decided in 1988 that a person who is in simple possession of an indecent photograph of a child should have a defence in certain circumstances) and is further proof for the need to rationalise the laws.

Legitimate reason

The first defence that can be claimed is that a person has a legitimate reason for possessing the indecent images. There will be many people who have a reason to possess images, most notably law enforcement agencies and those tasked with the investigation of child pornography. Given the wide definition that can be given to 'indecent' (discussed in Chapter 3) it is likely that certain teaching materials could, for example, amount to an indecent photograph of a child (particularly in the fields of medicine or social work). Whether a person has a legitimate reason must be a matter of fact for the jury although it is likely that a judge would be able to decide whether, as a matter of law, the explanation put forward by the defendant is *capable* of being a legitimate reason.

    The issue of academic research has proved to be popular in the context of what amounts to a legitimate reason. In *Atkins v DPP* [2000] 1 WLR 1427 the appellant, a lecturer in English, sought to argue that he possessed the images because he was researching the issue of child pornography. The Divisional Court did not have to rule on the propriety of this because the court at first instance had found that he was not engaged in 'honest and straightforward research into child pornography' (p. 1435). The Divisional Court did however concede that academic research could provide a legitimate reason and suggested that:

> The central question where the defence is legitimate research will be whether the defendant is essentially a person of unhealthy interests in possession of indecent photographs in the pretence of undertaking research, or by contrast a genuine researcher with no alternative but to have this sort of unpleasant material in his possession.
>
> (p. 1435)

That said, the Court of Appeal in *Wrigley* (2000, unreported) casts doubt on whether the distinction is necessarily as clear. In *Wrigley* the appellant had been convicted of one count of distributing indecent photographs of children and one count of possession of indecent photographs of children. He attempted to argue that he had a legitimate reason for distributing and possessing the images, namely academic research. He suggested that he was attempting to undertake a pilot project to assess whether there was enough material on this topic to read for a Ph.D. programme (at [9] of the judgment). The Court of Appeal noted that evidentially there were difficulties with advancing such a submission, not least the fact that he had not discussed the possibility of any programme with a tutor and after his release a number of tutors had advised him to disclose his material to the police, something he refused to do. Indeed, during his first police interview he said that he was interested in children although he denied being sexually attracted to them and did not mention academic research at all.

To an extent therefore it can be said that *Wrigley*, like *Atkins*, was a situation where the evidence simply did not demonstrate that legitimate research was being undertaken and that the two cases do not conflict. However the Court of Appeal implicitly approved a direction by the trial judge that was subtly different from that in *Atkins*:

> There is another little complication to all of this, because … if you conclude that the defendant had, as it were, a secret purpose of gratifying his own sexual curiosity in addition to a legitimate reason for doing what he did then he is still entitled to rely on the statutory defence … the statutory defence of a legitimate reason overrides and, as it were, suppresses any coexistent motive that he may have had to gratify his own sexual curiosity.
>
> (at [14])

The Court of Appeal stated that it was common ground that this was a correct judicial direction but it must be questioned whether it is. In *Atkins* the Divisional Court suggested that only where it is legitimate research for a legitimate, rather than unhealthy, interest would the defence arise yet the Court of Appeal in *Wrigley* is suggesting that so long as the research has legitimate academic merit then it would not matter if the defendant was doing the research because he has a sexual interest in children. The comments of the Divisional Court and Court of Appeal were both undoubtedly *obiter* and thus neither are strictly binding. It is submitted that the decision of the Divisional Court in *Atkins* is to be preferred. The defence of legitimate reason should be construed narrowly as the default position of the law is that possession of these photographs should not be permitted. It is conceded that there will be situations, including academic research, where possession of the material is necessary but the justification for the use of the material must be tested by the courts.

The Divisional Court in *Atkins* stated that courts should be sceptical of any suggestion that the possession of indecent images was necessary for academic research and this would seem correct. It is not enough that child pornography may be a subject of interest: the possession of illegal material can only be justified where it is necessary. In construing whether the research is legitimate the jury should look at the circumstances of the research. In *Wrigley* this would include the absence of any discussion with academics and in *Atkins* the fact that he was an English academic rather than, for example, an academic within the fields of policing, psychology or forensics must be relevant. Whilst previous research history must be relevant it cannot be conclusively so since a person must start somewhere. Also issues about transparency, security and ethical clearance must, it is submitted, be factors that can be taken into account by a tribunal of fact in deciding whether it was legitimate research.

There is some evidence that juries and criminal justice agencies are showing some scepticism when 'research' is raised. The celebrities Peter Townsend and Christopher Langham both sought to argue that they were engaged in research when they downloaded indecent images (Townsend claiming he was researching his autobiography and Langham seeking to argue it was necessary for a comedy programme) and in neither situation was the claim successful, in part because even on the facts that they put forward (in Townsend's case to the police as he was not tried but simply given a formal police caution) it is unlikely that it could be said that it was necessary for the images to be accessed.

Had not seen the photographs

The second defence is contained within s. 160(2)(b) and provides a defence where 'he had not himself seen the photograph … and did not know, nor had any cause to suspect, it to be indecent'. A literal reading of this defence would place the emphasis on indecency and not whether he knew or suspected the material to be of children. This would potentially create unfairness given that the simple possession of indecent material of adults is not a criminal offence.

Perhaps surprisingly this issue was not raised until the case of *Collier* [2005] 1 WLR 843. The police entered the appellant's house and seized a number of video tapes and CD-ROMs that contained adult pornography. Along with the adult pornography the video tapes also showed trailers for another movie that featured children engaging in sexual behaviour. The CD-ROMs principally contained images of adult pornography but did include four images of children in sexually explicit poses. He was charged with 11 counts of possessing an indecent photograph of a child and pleaded guilty when the judge at first instance stated that the defence applied only where he had no reason to suspect that the material on the videos or CD-ROMs was indecent. Given that the appellant had ordered pornography this would be impossible to argue.

The matter proceeded to the Court of Appeal where he sought to argue, *inter alia*, that the defence applied not to whether a person knew, or had reason to suspect, that any of the material was indecent but that it was an indecent photograph *of a child*. The Court of Appeal was clear that this must be correct and that it would be wrong to convict someone who had not seen photographs and did not know that they related to children (p. 848).

The decision of the Court of Appeal must be correct. The defence is not an easy one to prove (and *Collier* confirmed that there is a legal burden on the defence). The defence must prove that the material had not been seen. It is not enough that he has seen the material and believed that they were of children: the issue of age would appear to be one of strict liability (see Ormerod, 2004: 1041 who questions whether that should be correct). Accordingly a person who has a pornographic DVD and who watches it and decides the actors are aged over 18 will be guilty of possession under s. 160 if the prosecution can prove that he is wrong and that the actors are under the age of 18 (the issue of proving age was discussed in Chapter 3). In essence limiting the defence requires people in possession of pornography to be careful as to the type of material they hold.

However it would be taking the law too far to say that someone who orders pornography and who has not yet watched it would also be guilty of possessing indecent photographs of children if, unbeknown to him, the material featured children. The possession of adult pornography is lawful and a person should not be at risk of offending child pornography laws by ordering adult pornography. That said, it is important to note the extent of the defence noted above.

It was noted at the beginning of this chapter that *Smith* [2003] 1 Cr App R 13 had considered the *mens rea* for s. 1 and noted that the prosecution need to prove that the offender knew that the image was of an indecent photograph of a child or was likely to be such a photograph (at [19] of the judgment). In *Collier* [2005] 1 WLR 843 the Court of Appeal noted that for the reasons set out above this could not apply to s. 160 offences and that '... it follows (very ironically) that the prosecution have a heavier burden in the absence of a statutory defence' (p. 849 at [30]). This must be correct: under s. 1 the prosecution must prove this additional knowledge whereas for s. 160 it would appear that the prosecution need only prove that they knowingly possessed *something* that later turned out to be an indecent photograph of a child (*Atkins* [2000] 1 WLR 1427 and see Akdeniz, 2007: 279) but they do not need to prove that the defendant knew that this *something* was an indecent photograph of a child: the defence must prove that they *did not know* that it was an indecent photograph. Given that s. 1 is punishable by a higher sentence (10 years compared to five years) the propriety of this conclusion is perhaps more justified but given the ruling in *Bowden* has meant the same conduct could infringe either offence, this does raise interesting questions about which charge to bring. An offence under s. 160 would appear easier to prove (given the *mens rea* lacks this additional knowledge requirement) but where the images have been deleted this raises an obstacle (*Porter*, discussed above).

Unsolicited material

The final defence is contained in s. 160(2)(c) and states that a person has a defence if 'the photograph … was sent to him without any prior request made by him or on his behalf and he did not keep it for an unreasonable time'. There have been no reported cases that have yet examined this provision although it is inconceivable that what amounts to a 'reasonable time' will be a question of fact for the jury and will depend on the individual circumstances of the case.

One issue that has not yet been resolved is what the meaning of unsolicited is. Does this mean that the material has to be unsolicited or the indecent photographs of children have to be unsolicited? Let us take an example based on the facts of *Collier* albeit with a subtle change.

> D orders a DVD of what he believes is adult pornography. When he watches the movie he finds a scene that he believes may feature those under the age of 18. He decides to dispose of the DVD but the police arrest him before he does so.

In the example above the defence under s. 160(2)(b) cannot apply as he has now seen the material and it will be remembered that defence is premised on not seeing the material. Would the defence under s. 160(2)(c) apply? It could be argued that the material was not unsolicited since he ordered the material. Unsolicited ordinarily means that it was sent without request and this would appear not to be the case. However he did not solicit indecent photographs of children, he solicited adult pornography. It could be argued therefore that where a person does not know that material he has ordered contains indecent photographs of children this should be construed as being unsolicited.

Save where s. 160(2)(b) applies it would seem that the prosecution have to prove that the defendant knowingly possesses indecent photographs of children or which he knows is likely to contain indecent photographs of children (*Atkins*). Once the DVD has been viewed then the prosecution would be able to prove this as the suspect will know (or suspect) that it contains indecent images of children. If s. 160(2)(c) does not apply then the only acceptable position once the material has been viewed is to part with possession of it immediately. However is that realistic? Is it not possible that someone who sees an indecent image of a child for the first time will panic? Faced with the stories of what happens to those who access child pornography (discussed in Chapter 1) it is quite possible that they will be frightened and not sure of how to safely part with possession (for example, placing it in the rubbish bin may not suffice). It is submitted that this was the very reason why s. 160(2)(c) was enacted: as recognition that a person's immediate reaction may not be to dispose of the material. Accordingly s. 160(2)(c) should apply in circumstances where an offender did not know that he was receiving indecent photographs of children, even where he was soliciting indecent material (of adults).

Pop-ups

Akdeniz has suggested that in the context of the internet, pop-up photographs could be considered to be unsolicited (Akdeniz, 2007: 280). Pop-up photographs were mentioned previously in respect of s. 1, PoCA 1978 and it would seem correct that they could be considered unsolicited in that the user has no control over which photographs pop-up or indeed what their content is. If Akdeniz is correct how would the image be disposed of? Simply closing the window would not be enough: the image is still within the cache and in *Porter* [2006] 1 WLR 2633 the Court of Appeal held that images in the cache are still capable of being in possession. It would seem therefore, at the very least, that a user should 'empty' the cache or use an eraser program although, as will be seen in Chapter 10, the use of an eraser program can be considered an aggravating feature for sentencing. Whilst it is clearly appropriate that where an offender seeks to avoid detection through the use of an eraser/shredder program he is punished for this, the law should support a person who wishes to divest himself of material he did not wish to receive in the first place.

The issue of pop-ups does, of course, once again raise the incoherence produced by *Bowden*. If Akdeniz is correct then someone who downloads an indecent photograph of a child unintentionally via a pop-up and who deletes the image promptly will be not guilty of an offence under s. 160, CJA 1988. However applying *Harrison* [2008] 1 Cr App R 29 a person charged with an offence under s. 1, PoCA 1978 would have no defence where the same conduct was charged as making an indecent photograph of a child rather than simple possession. Such a position is, it is submitted, intolerable and demonstrates the pressing need for change.

Abuse of children through pornography

The third statute to examine is that of the *Sexual Offences Act 2003*. Whilst this statute has been considered already in the context of the amendments it made to the Protection of Children Act 1978 and Criminal Justice Act 1988 – most notably in respect of the defences – it also introduced three new specific offences relating to indecent photographs of children.

At the outset it is worth pausing to note a change in terminology. Whilst, as has been seen, both the 1978 and 1988 legislation disavowed the term 'child pornography' in favour of 'indecent photographs of children' the 2003 Act did not adopt this approach. Indeed, the three offences relate, *inter alia*, to the 'involvement of a child in pornography'. This is as close as one can get to the term 'child pornography' without actually using that phrase. Given the legislation then specifically relates the phrase to indecent images of children (s. 51(1), SOA 2003) it can be questioned what the purpose of using 'involvement in pornography is'.

The three offences under the SOA 2003 are:

- Causing or inciting a child to become involved in pornography (s. 49).
- Controlling a child involved in pornography (s. 50).
- Arranging or facilitating the involvement in pornography (s. 51).

The three offences are interlinked and each is punishable by a maximum sentence of 14 years' imprisonment, four years higher than an offence under s. 1, PoCA 1978.

It is submitted that the original purpose of these offences was very different from those which have appeared under the SOA 2003. The origin of the offences was, like a considerable amount of the SOA 2003, the review of sexual offences conducted by the Home Office in 2000 and published as *Setting the Boundaries* (Home Office, 2000).

In *Setting the Boundaries* the issue of the sexual exploitation of children was considered and the review decided that any offences designed to tackle this should not be restricted to simply child prostitution but should also cover other forms of exploitation, including the making of pornography for gain (Home Office, 2000: 114). The review was very careful to state that they thought offences should relate to the exploitation of children *for gain* (which was not restricted simply to money) and thought that where a child was to be exploited for the purposes of sexual gratification other offences would apply (Home Office, 2000: 114). The review accordingly recommended a series of offences which are, broadly speaking, contained within the SOA 2003 (Home Office, 2000: 115). The emphasis of the offences was clearly on the sexual exploitation of children and the review noted that the emphasis should be on the 'use of the child rather than the taking of pictures' (Home Office, 2000: 115).

The proposals by the review were eminently sensible. It would be easy to conclude that the offences under PoCA 1978 were more directly applicable to those situations where an offender created or disseminated an indecent photograph of a child for primarily sexual purposes. Of course PoCA 1978 was not premised on this basis and certainly ss. 1(1)(d) and 1(2) would appear to indicate that commercial exploitation was considered to be within the remit. The proposals in *Setting the Boundaries* could have marked a redefining of the offences, though with PoCA 1978 being used where there was sexual gratification and the new offences being used where the motive was primarily commercial. However this was not done. Sections 48–50 also apply to offences relating to child prostitution and whilst the definition of prostitution given in the Act specifically refers to gain (ss. 51(2–3) SOA 2003) no element of gain was introduced in respect of pornography, with the simple premise being that it should be construed as meaning an indecent image of a child (s. 51(1), SOA 2003).

The consequences of this approach is to introduce a further overlap in offences relating to child pornography. It was noted in the earlier sections of this chapter that there was considerable overlap in the offences within PoCA 1978 and, following *Bowden*, overlap between PoCA 1978 and the CJA 1988 but the SOA 2003 introduces a further layer. It is submitted that the vast majority of behaviour that would be within ss. 48–50 of the SOA 2003 could have been dealt with under PoCA 1978 by using inchoate liability.

For example, s. 48 of the SOA 2003 prohibits, *inter alia*, inciting a child to become involved in pornography. Given that pornography includes the production of an indecent photograph of a child, this would mean that s. 48 applies where D asks V, aged fifteen, to pose naked for a photograph. Undoubtedly this is incitement (which was discussed above) for V to become involved in pornography through the production of a nude photograph of herself. Section 48 is punishable by a maximum sentence of 14 years' imprisonment (s. 48(2)(b), SOA 2003) yet the offence of actually taking the photograph is punishable only by 10 years' imprisonment (s. 6(2), PoCA 1978). It is thus more serious to ask a child to pose for a photograph than it is to actually take the photograph.

If the context had been commercial child pornography then s. 48 would arguably make more sense. The commercial sexual exploitation of a child has been likened to modern-day slavery and this is undoubtedly true. People are making considerable financial gains from treating children as a commodity. Inciting a child to become involved in commercial child pornography would be serious and putting the child at significant physical and emotional harm.

Applying ss. 48–50 to commercial situations could allow the participants in a commercial enterprise to be criminalised. Section 50 criminalises, *inter alia*, the facilitation of a child in pornography. Given the involvement in pornography means the recording of an indecent image then this would mean that a person who allows a room to be used for the photographs to be recorded could be construed as facilitating the approach. Similarly the person who duplicates the images recorded – transferring the film on to DVD or mass-duplicating the DVDs – could be said to be facilitating the recording of the images and thus within s. 50. Quite rightly these people should be considered to be part of the exploitative process. Given the definition of involvement in pornography – the recording of an image – it is less clear whether the person who sells the material could be said to be within the meaning of s. 50. This would presumably depend on how widely 'facilitates' is defined. It could be argued that in a commercial enterprise the images are only recorded because they are to be ultimately distributed in which case it can be said that it is facilitation as it creates a demand for further pictures to be recorded. The alternative argument would focus on the literal meaning of words and suggest that the dissemination of images would be separate to the recording of the images and thus outside of s. 50. Of course where the image is a photograph or pseudo-photograph then it would unquestionably amount to distribution for the purposes of PoCA 1978.

Chapter 7

Non-photograph-based
child pornography

Chapter 2 discussed the definition of child pornography and it noted that whilst image-based child pornography is perhaps the most prolific, there are a number of different types including text, sound files and, as discussed in Chapter 5, cartoons and virtual child pornography. This chapter will examine how English law criminalises these forms of pornography. It is divided into two parts. The first examines the issue of obscenity and the second part examines the new provisions of the Coroners and Justice Act 2009 which focuses on the possession of, *inter alia*, virtual child pornography.

Obscenity

The first issue to examine is that of obscenity. The legislation concerning indecent photographs is unique in that it tackles the creation, dissemination and possession of indecent rather than obscene material. For the reasons discussed in Chapters 2–4 it is justified to criminalise material that is indecent but the legislation applies only to photographs and pseudo-photographs. Where the material is another type – text, sound, drawings or cartoons, etc. – then the only recourse is the general rules relating to obscenity. Cartoons, drawings and virtual child pornography are in a slightly different position in that their publication or dissemination is dealt with under the obscenity legislation whereas their possession is dealt with under the Coroners and Justice Act 2009.

The limits of this chapter should be understood at the very beginning. This chapter will not discuss the general law of obscenity which applies to conduct much wider than child pornography. Indeed, there is technically no requirement that material considered to be obscene is sexual and can include other depictions (in *John Calder (Publications) Ltd v Powell* [1965] 1 QB 509 the matter concerned a book which included graphic depiction of drug taking). However whilst some of the principles discussed in this chapter can be applied more broadly, the examination here will be restricted to forms of child pornography. For these purposes three categories will be examined; text, sound and non-photographic images (which, for simplicity will be referred to as 'images'). This material was summarised in Chapter 2.

Basic framework

Two offences are contained within s. 2(1), Obscene Publications Act 1959 (although modified by the Obscene Publications Act 1964). These are the publishing of an obscene article and the possession of an obscene article for publication for gain. The former is the more usual offence. Several elements of both offences are commonly defined, the most relevant being; 'obscene', 'article' and 'publication'.

Obscene

The first, and the most significant, aspect to define is that of 'obscene'. It will be remembered from Chapter 3 that the term 'indecent' is defined by reference to the term 'obscene' (*R v Stanford* [1972] 2 QB 391) but the converse is not true for the OPA 1959. The OPA 1959 provides a statutory definition of 'obscene' and the courts have been quite clear that this, rather than any other definition, must be given to jurors (*R v Anderson* [1972] 1 QB 304). The statutory definition is put forward in s. 1(1), OPA 1959:

> For the purposes of this Act an article shall be deemed to be obscene if its effect or (where the article comprises two or more distinct items) the effect of any one of its items is, if taken as a whole, such as to tend to deprave and corrupt persons who are likely, having regard to all relevant circumstances, to read, see or hear the matter contained or embodied in it.

The key test therefore is the statutory test of 'deprave and corrupt' although these terms have caused significant difficulties throughout the history of the obscenity law (Robertson, 1979). Perhaps the most significant definition was provided by Byrne J in *R v Penguin Books Ltd* [1961] Crim LR 176 which was the infamous *Lady Chatterley's Lover* case. The judge said:

> 'To deprave' means to make morally bad or morally worse; to pervert; to debase. 'To corrupt' means to render morally unsound or rotten; to ruin a good quality; to defile...
>
> (p. 177)

It is a matter of fact for the jury to decide whether the material is capable of doing this and in *R v Elliot* [1996] 1 Cr App R 432 the Court of Appeal was clear that the test was not whether it was disgusting, offensive or shocking but solely whether it would deprave or corrupt a reader (p. 434). This is important in the context of virtual child pornography: it is not enough that a person accessing such images would be shocked or disgusted by them, they must be corrupted or depraved by seeing them.

Of course the key question then becomes who must be depraved and corrupted? Where the publication is to a restricted number of people then clearly it would be the recipients. Where however the publication is at large the question becomes more problematic. In *R v Calder & Boyars Ltd* [1969] 1 QB 151 the Court of Appeal stated that a significant proportion of the intended readership should be depraved or corrupted but this was doubted in *R v Whyte* [1972] AC 849 where the House of Lords held that this was probably only appropriate in the circumstances of that case. In *R v Perrin* [2002] EWCA Crim 747, a case that concerned obscenity on the internet, the Court of Appeal confirmed that the statement in *Calder* was fact-specific and was relevant in those particular circumstances where a large number of copies of a book had been in circulation (at [25]).

In *Perrin* the court noted that the issue of proportion must depend on the audience and who has access to the material (at [26]) and concluded:

> Where, as in the present case, there is and can be no suggestion that publica-tion is for the public good and the provisions of the 1964 Act are not in issue we see no reason why the task of the jury should be complicated by a direc-tion that the effect of the article must be such as to tend to deprave and corrupt a significant proportion, or more than a negligible number of likely viewers … it is much better … for the jury to be directed simply in accordance with the words of the statute.
>
> (at [30])

The words of the Act state the matter is obscene if it tends to deprave and corrupt persons 'who are likely, having regard to all relevant circumstances, to read, see or hear the matter ...' (s. 1(1), OPA 1959). As noted above the Court of Appeal suggested that the test will depend on the type of audience and it is notable that in *Perrin* itself the appellant was convicted only in respect of material that was avail-able freely, including potentially to children. The prosecution arose out of images gathered by a police officer who accessed a website. There was an age verification system that ensured that only those who provided credit card details were able to access the vast majority of the site but there was some material that was freely available as a 'preview' and which could be seen before the age verification portal. The jury convicted the appellant only in respect of the image that was found before the age verification system, i.e. something that children could access. The Court of Appeal approved of this distinction and whilst they accepted that some viewers will not be corrupted by obscene material (discussed below) the position is different where material is made available to any viewer. In particular the court noted that a jury can take all the circumstances of the publication into account and they noted that this included the fact that internet-savvy young people would be able to freely access the images that were found on the preview pages (at [22]).

The circumstances of the publication would seem important in respect of publi-cation by the internet. *Perrin* confirms that availability by young people is an important factor and this can also be seen by the first-instance trial of Darryn Walker. Mr Walker was charged under the OPA 1959 for publishing a blog which described the kidnap, sexual torture and murder of the members of the pop group Girls Aloud (see 'Civil servant in court over Girls Aloud "porn blog"', *Times*, 3 October 2008). The prosecution was advanced on the basis that the blog was easily available to people on the internet, including children and young people (a significant proportion of the band's audience). However the prosecution was abandoned when expert evidence was adduced by the defence that this was not true and that it would be relatively difficult to access the material without specifically knowing of its existence.

Whilst some have suggested that the prosecution was doomed to fail because prosecuting the written word under the OPA 1959 is almost impossible (Hughes, 2009) the decision to stop the prosecution does not support such a contention. Whilst it is true to state that after the *Oz* and *Inside Linda Lovelace* trials (discussed in Travis, 2000) the prosecution of literary works would be extremely difficult, it does not follow that, for example, paedophilic literature will necessarily be accepted. Instead the decision to halt the trial would appear to be consistent with the principle identified in *Perrin* that all the circumstances of the likely audience must be taken into account. If expert evidence suggests that it is unlikely that young people would see the material then it is perhaps more difficult to suggest that this sort of material would deprave and corrupt individuals. Similar logic could apply to virtual child pornography and text-based depictions. Depending on their content they may be unpleasant or disgusting but they may not, by themselves, be depraving or corrupting to adults. That said, of course, many depictions could well meet the deprave or corrupt test even when children are unlikely to come across them. However this does raise a further interesting question. What happens where the publication is to those who have a sexual interest in this material?

In *R v Clayton and Halsey* [1963] 1 QB 163 the only persons who saw the material were police officers assigned to the Obscene Publications Squad of the Metropolitan Police. The appellants were convicted of publishing obscene material (by selling the material to the police officers) but their conviction was quashed because the officers accepted in evidence that they had seen thousands of similar photographs and would not be depraved or corrupted by the images contained within the book purchased. The Court of Appeal stated that where the publication was to specific persons then the OPA 1959 was clear that it was the effect on *those persons* that was relevant not the possible effect on future customers (p. 167). The court went further and rejected the argument that material could be so inherently obscene that anyone, including an experienced or scientific viewer, must be susceptible to some form of corruption (p. 168) and emphasised that it is the effect on the actual person that is relevant.

Could this be applied to those with a sexual interest in children being sent child pornography? The simple answer is no because the key is that in *Clayton* it was said that the material would have no effect on the police officers but this is unlikely to be the case with those with a sexual interest in children. If they view (or, in the context of sound, listen to) material for the purposes of sexual gratification then liability should still arise since it has been held that a person can be depraved or corrupted more than once (*R v Calder & Boyars Ltd* [1969] 1 QB 151; *R v Barker* [1962] 1 WLR 349 esp. at p. 352). Certainly this would seem the most likely application where child pornography is being shared amongst those with a sexual interest in children; given the definition of 'to corrupt' includes making someone morally unsound then it is quite possible that some child pornography material will meet this threshold.

Article

The OPA 1959 applies to obscene articles. Section 1(2), OPA 1959 defines 'article':

> In this Act ... 'article' means any description or article containing or embodying matter to be read or looked at or both, any sound record, and any film or other record of a picture or pictures.

This is an extremely broad definition but does not expressly cover electronic media which is hardly surprising given it was passed in 1959. In Attorney General's Reference (No. 5 of 1980) (1981) 72 Cr App R 71 the Court of Appeal held that a video tape would be included within an article and in *R v Fellows; R v Arnold* [1997] 1 Cr App R 244 the Court of Appeal held that electronic data would also be included within the meaning of s. 1(2) (see p. 252). The court was clear that Parliament intended, when passing s. 1(2), to cover any product that was capable of containing pictures, the written word or sounds. In any event the Criminal Justice and Public Order Act 1994 expressly contemplated electronic data (when it amended s. 1(3), OPA 1959 to include the transmission of data).

Publication

Both offences within s. 2(1), OPA 1959 require either publication or possession for publication. Section 1(3), OPA 1959 defines publication as someone who:

(a) distributes, circulates, sells, lets on hire, gives, or lends it, or who offers it for sale or for letting on hire; or
(b) in the case of an article containing or embodying matter to be looked at or a record, shows, plays or project it, or, where the matter is data stored electronically, transmits that data.

Sections 1(4)–1(6) also define publication as including obscene material in a programme to be broadcast but that is not directly relevant to this chapter and will not be discussed. Section 1(3)(a) covers most forms of dissemination in *R v Barker* [1962] 1 WLR 349 it was suggested that s. 1(3) establishes three distinct groups:

... in one group, comprising the words 'sells, lets on hire, gives or lends', publication is to an individual; in the second group, comprising the words 'distributes, circulates' publication is on a wider scale involving more than one person; in the third group a mere offer for sale or letting on hire constitutes publication.

(p. 351 per Ashworth J)

The logic of *Barker* would appear correct and this has a direct impact, as discussed above, on the obscenity question. Whilst s. 1(3)(a) contemplates, as Ashworth J notes, not only actual distribution but also the mere offering of material, it should be noted that this applies only where it is offered for sale or let. Thus if, for example, two persons are talking in a chat room and A offers to send B an image constituting virtual child pornography for free this would not come within the definition of publishing in s. 1(3).

Section 1(3)(b) is particularly important in the context of visual depictions of child pornography and includes the showing or displaying of the material. Perhaps more significantly is the fact that it includes the transmission of electronic data that constitutes an obscene article.

In many situations it will not be difficult to prove publication: in respect of child pornography it will be where A sells material to B or where A emails B the material. However the internet obviously allows for distribution to be conducted in other ways. What is the position where A, for example, produces a website that hosts child pornography or he hosts it in a 'shared' folder on a peer-to-peer network?

In *R v Waddon* (2000, unreported) the Court of Appeal considered a website that hosted obscene material. The police accessed the site (which required a membership subscription to be paid) and, once access had been granted, a police officer was able to print various obscene articles. The website was based in America but the Court of Appeal ruled that:

... there can be publication on a web site abroad, when images are there uploaded; and there can be further publication when those images are downloaded elsewhere.

(at [12] per Rose LJ)

The effect of this is that where A, the owner of a website, allows users to download images contained on the site there is publication for the purposes of the OPA 1959. It should be clear who is committing the offence. It is not the person who downloads the image who is guilty but the person who hosts the website. There is clearly no difficulty with the proposition that uploading images amounts to distribution. At its basic premise, uploading involves the transmission of data (the images, text or HTML coding) from a computer to the servers where the webpage is itself stored. This would clearly meet the definition under s. 1(3)(b). What of downloading data? Where is the publication? Downloading involves receiving data from the server where the material is hosted on to the computer used by the user. Thus data must be sent – for it to be received – but it is not from the user that originally posts the material but from the server hosting the material.

In *Waddon* this was unproblematic because the appellant was the director of the company that owned and operated the website. Therefore it could be said that he controlled the material on the server and was therefore responsible for the data being sent when a user downloaded it. Similar principles were applied in *R v Perrin* [2002] EWCA Crim 747 where the appellant conceded that he was the majority shareholder of a company that hosted the material and therefore he conceded that he had published the material (at [5]).

Both *Waddon* and *Perrin* involved commercial organisations but not all material is commercial and some will involve circulation within a small number of people with an interest in this material. Let us take the following example:

> X posts an obscene computer-generated image of a child on to an FTP site that is hosted by Y and which has a number of members, all of whom have a sexual interest in children. Z downloads the image that X posted.

The liability of X for publication here would seem to be solely on the basis of the uploading (the transmission of data from his computer to the FTP site) and not on the actions of Z. Whilst X has clearly transmitted data, he is not responsible for the site and thus he did not transmit the data that Z downloaded; that was sent from the servers operated by Y.

Y will also be liable for the publication of obscene child pornography applying the ruling in *Waddon*. Whilst Y did not post the original data, he is responsible for the FTP site from which the data was transmitted to Z. Accordingly it can be said that he comes within the provisions of s. 1(3)(b). This logic would appear to be confirmed by the decisions in *R v Fellows; R v Arnold* [1997] 1 Cr App R 244 where it was held that allowing users to see photographs hosted on a computer amounted to, *inter alia*, the showing, playing or projecting of those images (p. 256).

An interesting point in respect of Y's liability is what happens if he does not own the site but merely operates it in an administrative capacity. There are a number of 'hosting' websites available that allow anyone to create a sharing site or a discussion board (which would allow users to attach or swap files). Y could therefore be responsible for the board (e.g. deciding who has access, who is allowed to share files, etc.) but not actually physically own the obscene articles (the owner would instead be those who own the servers on which the material is electronically stored). If Y does not own the server then it could be argued that Y has not transmitted the data: any transmission has been made from the server (owned by the third party) and not by Y himself.

Establishing liability for Y may be based on the fact that he has showed, played or displayed the material. In *R v Fellows; R v Arnold* [1997] 1 Cr App R 244 the appellant *Fellows* created a file-sharing system on the computers of Birmingham University and allowed certain persons (including *Arnold*) access to the material stored in the archive. He was convicted, *inter alia*, of publishing obscene material. *Fellows* did not own the servers and so it cannot be said that he transmitted the data but his conviction was based on the premise that the data stored on the archive was shown, played or projected by him to those who gained access to the archive (p. 256). Certainly there is nothing in law that suggests that it is only the owner who must show, play or project an article: any number of persons could do this. As Y is providing access to the website it is possible that it could be argued that he has shown, played or projected the material that is seen on the website applying the logic of *Fellows*.

One issue that was not discussed in *Fellows* is what happens where the image is not actually displayed until after the transmission? Whilst it is easy to see showing, playing or projection where A visits a website and sees a picture or hears a sound that is found on that website, it is perhaps less easy to see this where instead the image or sound is simply stored as a file and the user downloads that file without ever opening its contents. The inclusion of the words 'transmits data' within s. 1(3)(b) would appear to have been included to cater for situations where text, a picture or sound is not seen or heard on the actual site but is instead transmitted in its electronic file state. If that is the case then it would seem that the only recourse is to use transmission although this may mean that third parties (such as Y in the example above) who do not actually transmit data but simply facilitate their transfer may not be guilty.

Where a third party does own the servers on which the material is hosted, what is their liability? In the vast majority of situations it is submitted that there will be no liability since it is a defence for a publisher to say that he had not examined the article and had no reasonable cause to suspect its publication would render him liable for prosecution under the OPA 1959 (s. 2(5), OPA 1959). As the hosting websites will undoubtedly host many thousands of sites it is unlikely they will be able to view the material on each.

Z will bear no liability under the OPA 1959 since he has not transmitted data. Whilst he received data this is not a criminal offence under the OPA 1959 and neither is simple possession. Of course where the image was requested then this may amount to an offence under Part 2 of the Serious Crimes Act 2007 but in all other circumstances it would appear that Z would not commit an offence.

Of course the position becomes even more complicated by the fact that the internet is a truly global resource. It is possible, and indeed extremely likely, that the material will be hosted outside of the United Kingdom but accessible by those within England and Wales. This was true of both *Waddon* and *Perrin* and in both cases the Court of Appeal was untroubled by this, in part because the finding that distribution can take place where material is downloaded meant that publication took place in England and Wales. The decision of the Court of Appeal in *Perrin* to follow the ruling in *Waddon* has been criticised as ignoring the fact that the comments in *Waddon* were *obiter dictum* (Hirst, 2003: 190). Hirst believes that neither *Waddon* nor *Perrin* concentrated on the wording of s. 1(3)(b) and, in particular, that publication does not suggest that 'the act of publication occurs where the transmission is received' (Hirst, 2003: 190). If the wording of s. 1(3)(b) is examined then these criticisms may be justified. Section 1(3)(b) includes the *transmitting* of data but what does that mean? The *Oxford English Dictionary* defines the verb 'to transmit':

> To cause (a thing) to pass, go, or be conveyed to another person, place or thing; to send across an intervening space; to convey, transfer.

If transmission means simply the sending of information (in this context, from computer A to computer B) then the criticism of Hirst is valid. The sending has taken place from outside the jurisdiction and the OPA 1959 does not mention receiving and so the courts would have no jurisdiction. The alternative construction however – and the one implicit within *Waddon* – is that transmission means more than just sending. The dictionary definition also refers to the conveying of information *to* a person or thing. This could be taken to mean that transmission encompasses both the sending *and* receiving of data. If that construction is used then at least some part of the *actus reus* takes place within the territory of England and Wales which would allow for jurisdiction to be secured. However it is undoubtedly placing a strain on the construction since, in essence, this would imply that where a signal (or equivalent) is sent but not received it would not have been transmitted.

Hirst criticises the ruling in *Waddon* as imposing English criminal law on foreigners who host material abroad (Hirst, 2003: 190). Certainly the construction of *Waddon* and *Perrin* undoubtedly widens the territorial application of the criminal law. For example:

> X is a citizen of the United States who operates a website that hosts obscene material that is (lawfully) hosted in the United States but which is accessible in the UK by a person with access to the internet. X comes to the UK on holiday.

Waddon and *Perrin* would mean that X could be arrested when he enters England because he has published obscene material in the UK even though his business may not have marketed or sought customers in the UK. Criminal law is not alone in taking this approach as the libel laws in England and Wales also apply to foreign articles that are readable in England; something that is extremely contentious in the era of the internet (see, for example; Eardley, 2006; Melville-Brown, 2009). Indeed, the use of the libel laws in this way has led some jurisdictions to question whether they will allow judgments of English courts to be executed in their state (Balin *et al.*, 2009). Could the same apply to criminal prosecutions under the OPA 1959? So far there has been no suggestion, not least because the UK is not alone in extending their territory in this way (perhaps the most notable comparable example is the US approach to online gambling (Zekos, 2007)). However the fact that other countries do this does not detract from the criticism of Hirst that this is arguably extending territoriality beyond that which was commonly accepted.

The offences

As noted already there are technically two offences contained within the OPA 1959 (the second being inserted by s. 1(1), OPA 1964). The first offence is to publish, whether for gain or not, an obscene article. The second offence is to possess an obscene article for publication for gain (whether gain to himself or to another).

The first offence is the simpler of the two:

> ...any person who, whether for gain or not, publishes an obscene article ... shall be liable [for an offence].
>
> (s. 2(1), OPA 1959)

The offence is triable either way and is punishable by a maximum sentence of five years' imprisonment. The particular aspects of this offence were discussed in the definitional aspect above and little more has to be said. The wording of s. 2(1) should be noted in that where actual publication is being alleged it is not necessary to prove that it is for gain.

Has an obscene article for publication

The second offence is also contained within s. 2(1), OPA 1959:

> ...any person ... who has an obscene article for publication for gain (whether gain to himself or gain to another) shall [commit an offence].

As with the other offence under s. 2(1) the offence is triable either way and punishable by a maximum sentence of five years' imprisonment. Section 1(2), Obscene Publications Act 1964 states:

> ...a person shall be deemed to have an article for publication for gain if with a view to such publication he has the article in his ownership, possession or control.

This is slightly wider than the definition of 'possession' (in that s. 1(2) envisages the owner of an article to 'have' an article even if he is not in possession of it) although for the purposes of this chapter it will be more usual for a person to be in possession. Two mental elements exist in respect of this offence. The first is that the possession must be for gain, meaning that there must be the intention to publish the article.

The biggest difference between this second offence and the first is that this time the fact is that it must be for gain. Section 1(5), OPA 1964 defines publication for gain as including where the gain is to be accrued 'by way of consideration for the publication or in any other way' which is extremely broad. Quite clearly where there is financial remuneration this will come within the meaning but what of situations where the 'gain' would be for other articles? There is no reason why this should be excluded from the definition since it is, it is submitted, a gain 'in any other way' and a swap should amount to a gain in that the person is seeking to accrue something he does not already have (the material). This is potentially significant in respect of situations where offenders meet to share or swap obscene material that they have in their possession or control.

Peer-to-peer networks

The phrasing of the OPA 1959 raises issues in respect of peer-to-peer networks and these should be considered here. The first is in respect of the person who has obscene material and who is allowing a person to access it. Under what circumstances can it be said that such persons have a view to publishing it? It is submitted that in this context the logic of *R v Dooley* [2006] 1 WLR 775 is also likely to apply to an offence under the OPA 1959: i.e. a person need not have possession of an article solely for the intention of publishing it to be guilty of the offence.

An interesting question that follows from this, given the definition in s. 1(2), OPA 1964, is what the liability of the operators of an FTP/discussion board site would be. It will be remembered from the example given in p. 156 above that it is possible that a person who operates an FTP/discussion board site but does not actually own or control the servers on which obscene material is hosted may not be liable for their publication when people post obscene material to those sites. However the wording of s. 1(2) which includes exercising control and not just possession or ownership of the images may mean that those who operate the sites – and decide who should be allowed to access the material – may be guilty of having an obscene article with a view to it being published. A defence exists where the person has not seen the material and had no reasonable cause to suspect that it could come within the OPA 1959 (s. 1(3)(a), OPA 1964) but this is unlikely to apply to those who operate a website for those with a sexual interest in children, etc. Where a person exercises control of the board through, for example, allowing users to join, deciding whether files are able to be posted, downloaded or transferred then it is submitted that they may come within the definition of s. 1(2). However in order to show liability for this offence under s. 1(2), OPA 1959 it will be necessary to show 'for gain'. Given that many of these websites are non-commercial this may be hinder a prosecution.

The second issue in respect of peer-to-peer networks relate to those who access the files hosted by the network. Rowbottom, 2006 argues that those who download material from a host computer are publishing them (p. 104). This argument is based on two aspects. The first is that they have published the data by transmitting it, and the second argument is based on the premise of distributing it.

Dealing with transmission first, it is difficult to see how this applies. It has been noted above that this is doubtful since downloading data involves the user *receiving* data rather than sending it. Transmission is not defined in the Act but its dictionary definition was discussed above and it is submitted that it is highly unlikely that downloading the material would amount to transmission which would suggest the sending of information and even if receipt is encompassed (see the discussion on p. 158 above) it would still be necessary for the publisher to have sent the material: something that has not occurred here.

The second basis is on distribution. The term distributes is not itself defined in the Act and so alternative definitions need to be examined. In the context of child pornography it may be useful to consider how it is defined in the Protection of Children Act 1978. It will be remembered from Chapter 4 that s. 1(2), PoCA 1978 states:

> . . . a person is to be regarded as distributing . . . if he parts with possession of it, or exposes or offers it for acquisition by, another person.

This definition places the emphasis not on the person who acquires the image but rather the person who sends or exposes the image for transfer. What of the dictionary definition? The *Oxford English Dictionary* defines the verb 'to distribute' as:

> To deal out or bestow in portions or shares among a number of recipients; to allot or apportion as his share to each person of a number.

This supports the definition provided in PoCA 1978 and suggests that distribution is committed by the person who sends the image rather than the person who receives it. Whilst it is true to state that a person who accesses a peer-to-peer system initiates the transfer of the particular file, it remains, in essence, a request and the 'host' person can decide who he will allow access to those files. Accordingly it is submitted that a person who accesses a file on a peer-to-peer network is not distributing the material and accordingly is not guilty of publishing the material.

Defences

There are a number of defences to a prosecution under the OPA 1959. One defence – that a person had not seen the material – has already been discussed above but s. 4, OPA 1959 provides for a further defence: that the publication is for the public good. The grounds are that the publication is justified in the interests of 'science, literature, art or learning, or of other objects of general concern' (s. 4(1), OPA 1959). Subsection (1) does not apply to a picture film or soundtrack (the latter meaning a sound recording designed for playing with a moving picture film (s. 4(5)) but such material is justified on the grounds that it is in the interests of 'drama, opera, ballet or any other art, or of literature or learning' (s. 4(1A), OPA 1959).

Expert evidence as to the merits of the public good is expressly permitted (s. 4(2), OPA 1959) either in support or to negate the defence. Accordingly there has been some concern that obscenity trials turn into a battle of the experts.

To some degree it may be thought that the defence of public good would have little to do with child pornography but provisions in other countries have demonstrated that this is far from true. Whilst it may be difficult to argue that image-based child pornography has any artistic merit this may, presumably, depend on the circumstances. It is known that the depiction of adolescent sexual activities is to be found in art throughout history (Kleinhans, 2004; Travis, 2000) and thus some forms of depiction may lead to the defence being attempted. This may be particularly true in respect of cartoons which form part of the Manga/Hentai genre. Manga cartoons, including sexually explicit cartoons, are arguably part of the Japanese culture and many would argue that they form an art form (see Ito, 2005; Kinsella, 2000, and Zanghellini, 2009). Expert evidence can almost certainly be called to say that Manga is an art form and thus the jury would be faced with the decision as to whether the publication of Hentai is for the public good. A jury should consider the possible public good against the depravation and corruption that may be caused by its publication (*R v Calder and Boyars* [1969] 1 QB 151) but it is less than clear how they are supposed to reach a proper conclusion in this form.

A somewhat unique feature of image-based child pornography will be the fact that the new offence of possession under the Coroners and Justice Act 2009 (see below) does not contain a defence of public merit. Thus if X sends Y an obscene picture of a child that experts agree is of artistic merit, a slightly absurd position could be created whereby X is acquitted of distributing (publishing) the picture but Y is convicted of possessing it. There is something unjust about such a position and it will be interesting to see whether the courts 'read in' a defence of public merit either within the definition of obscenity or to comply with Articles 8 or 10 of the ECHR (although, as was noted in Chapter 6, there is a strong argument that prohibition of the material on the basis of morals is justified).

The position in respect of text is perhaps even more uncertain as what constitutes literary merit is perhaps even more open. It has been suggested that since the trials relating to the Marquis de Sade prosecution of text-based material would be extremely rare (Edwards, 2000; Travis, 2000). Certainly the mere description of sexual activity with a child is not devoid of literary merit else Nabokov's *Lolita* would be criminalised. It may be thought that it is possible to differentiate between self-penned works and literary works such as *Lolita* but it is worth remembering that in the Canadian case of *R v Sharpe (No. 2)* 2002 BCSC 423 the defendant was able to produce numerous experts to testify as to the literary merits of his self-penned text stories describing various sexual activities involving children, including sadomasochism (para. 39 f.).

The difficulty in rebutting expert evidence of public good does mean that prosecutions under the OPA 1959 are somewhat rare (Edwards, 1998 and there is no evidence to suggest that the picture has changed very much since). The prosecution bears a high burden on providing the case and, combined with the fact that there is some doubt whether the OPA 1959 tackles the appropriate people in the online era (i.e. the doubt over whether a person downloading material is caught by the provisions) it has been suggested that this is one of the reasons why the government has turned to the criminalisation of obscene material (Rowbottom, 2006). Certainly in the context of child pornography 2009 marked a significant change in the way that non-photographic visual depictions of child pornography is dealt with under the criminal law. The Coroners and Justice Act 2009 introduces an offence of simple possession, a landmark change from the position under the OPA 1959.

Coroners and Justice Act 2009

Chapter 5 noted that the Coroners and Justice Act 2009 (CJA 2009) criminalised the possession of prohibited images of children. This section will critique the new provisions and consider how they may be used. It will be remembered from the previous chapter that the government premised the rationale for these offences on the basis of harm and the Human Rights Joint Committee, in their Eighth Report, doubted whether in the absence of evidence to support this that the crimes would be necessary and proportionate (see, in particularly 1.175 and 1.178). Liberty raised similar concerns and noted that whilst legitimate and proportionate legal restrictions on pornography can be justified this tends to be where harm can be shown (Liberty, 2009: 21). Chapter 5 doubted whether evidence of harm exists but also concluded that, somewhat controversially, it is likely that the criminalisation of the possession of this material may be justified for the protection of morals, especially given the margin of appreciation adopted by the European Court of Human Rights.

This section will therefore operate on the premise that the provisions of the CJA 2009 are likely to be considered compliant with the ECHR by domestic courts and the ECtHR. The text will concentrate on how the provisions are likely to be construed and used. An interesting point to begin with is an argument of Liberty:

> [W]e fear that the ... offence could ... detract attention from those who cause genuine hurt. It would, for example, be tragic if the creation of an offence aimed at private cartoons and drawings reduced the police resources available to tackle real child pornography ...
>
> (Liberty, 2009: 21)

The issue of policing will be discussed in Chapter 12 but this is certainly a pertinent point. The police have only limited resources and it is known that harm to children is caused by child pornography (both in its primary and secondary sense) and accordingly it is to be hoped that the emphasis of the police and other law enforcement agencies remains on this crime. The government argued that material within the CJA 2009 is often found alongside real child pornography (see the Explanatory Notes to the then Bill). If this is so then these laws could apply to such material but it is perhaps more questionable whether the laws should be used to target those who do not have real child pornography or against whom intelligence does not suggest that they pose a danger to children.

Definitions

The first issue to consider is the definition of a prohibited image used for the new offence. Section 62(2) states:

> A prohibited image is an image which –
>
> (a) is pornographic;
> (b) falls within subsection (6); and
> (c) is grossly offensive, disgusting, or otherwise of an obscene character.

This therefore forms the basic definition but a number of issues need to be further defined, in particular:

- The meaning of 'an image'.
- The meaning of 'pornographic'.
- The content within subsection 6.
- The meaning of 'grossly offensive, disgusting or otherwise of an obscene character'.

An image

The first issue to consider therefore is what constitutes 'an image'. Section 65 states:

> (2) 'Image' includes –
>
>   (a) a moving or still image (produced by any means); or
>   (b) data (stored by any means) which is capable of conversion into an image within paragraph (a).
>
> (3) 'Image' does not include an indecent photograph, or indecent pseudo-photograph, of a child.

Subsections (2) and (3) need to be read together. The purpose of s. 65(3) is, presumably, to ensure that where a person has a photograph or pseudo-photograph in his possession proceedings are brought under s. 160, Criminal Justice Act 1988 instead. Section 65(4) cross-references the definition of indecent photograph and indecent pseudo-photograph to the legislation under the Protection of Children Act 1978. There is no difficulty where the image is a photograph and s. 65(3) is important in this regard in preventing a prosecution being brought against a crime that is considered less serious than possession of an indecent photograph of a child (see below for a discussion of sentence). However more problematic is perhaps the reference to pseudo-photograph.

By stating that an image does not include a pseudo-photograph of a child this must, it is submitted, be a defence to the offence under s. 62(1) that the image is, in fact, a pseudo-photograph. Indeed, since s. 65(3) is part of the definition of the offence, it would follow not only is it a defence but that the prosecution will bear the burden of proving to its ordinary standard that the relevant image is *not* a pseudo-photograph. It was said in Parliament that the definition of a pseudo-photograph is readily understood (see the proceedings of the Public Bill Committee, Session 2008–2009, col. 489) but it was seen from Chapter 3 that this is not necessarily correct. There have been few cases on the meaning of a pseudo-photograph and it is submitted that it may not be readily understandable what the difference between the two are.

A pseudo-photograph is an image 'whether made by computer graphics or other-wise howsoever, which appears to be a photograph' (s. 7(7), Protection of Children Act 1978). The express reference to being made by a computer-graphics program means that virtual child pornography was being contemplated. Whilst therefore material that is clearly not a photograph – i.e. drawings or cartoons – will not come within this definition and can therefore only be included within the CJA 2009 provi-sions, the position with computer-generated images is less straightforward. It must presumably be a question of fact as to whether an image appears to be a photograph or not, and this will presumably entail the jury considering the quality of the image. The uncertainty of what precisely a pseudo-photograph is will presumably mean that prosecutors will have to be careful when they come to framing an indictment.

Apart from the possible conflict with pseudo-photographs the definition of image is relatively uncontroversial. It would seem to apply to any visual depiction and will include, therefore, a drawing or cartoon. It will not cover a tracing of an indecent photograph as it will be remembered that this is in itself an indecent photograph of a child (s. 7(4A) PoCA 1978 discussed in Chapter 3). Paragraph (b), which includes data (stored by any means) is directly comparable to s. 7(4), PoCA 1978 and is clearly designed to apply in the same way. There is no reason why this should cause any conflict.

Pornographic

The next issue is that s. 62(2)(a) requires the image to be pornographic. This is itself defined in s. 63(3):

> An image is 'pornographic' if it is of such a nature that it must reasonably be assumed to have been produced solely or principally for the purpose of sexual arousal.

It was noted in the preceding section that the law of obscenity did not require that the material was sexual but the same is not necessarily true here. That said, the wording of the provision must be considered carefully. It does not require that the material is sexual, it requires that it is produced for the purpose of sexual arousal and therefore this will include scenes of violence where it is for a sexual purpose. The wording is similar to that used for the offence of possession of extreme pornography (s. 63, Criminal Justice and Immigration Act 2008). Writing on these provisions, Rowbottom, 2006 questioned whether for an offence of possession the intention of the maker should be relevant (p. 103). This is an interesting question since it could be argued that it is more relevant to ask whether the possessor is keeping the material for the purposes of sexual arousal rather than whether it was produced for that purpose. The difficulty of such an approach, however, is that this could lead to different results for the same material (in that some will find it sexually gratifying and others will not) which would be unproblematic if the justification was the prevention of harm (and sufficient evidence could be shown to find this) but it is less appropriate where the justification is moral since, presumably, the same image would be morally repugnant irrespective of whether an offender uses it for the purposes of sexual gratification.

The explanatory notes accompanying the Act state that it will be for the jury to decide whether an image is pornographic (para. 364) which must be correct but it is silent as to whether expert witness testimony can be called. It will be remembered from Chapter 3 that expert evidence is not admissible in prosecutions for indecent photographs of children either as to age or indecency. However it was noted above that expert evidence is admissible in obscenity prosecutions, although the general rule is that expert evidence cannot be used to assist in deciding whether a matter is obscene (*R v Calder & Boyars Ltd* [1969] 1 QB 151) as distinct from assisting in whether there is a defence of 'public good'. On that basis it may seem more likely that expert evidence will not be admissible (since s. 4(2), OPA 1959 expressly provides for expert evidence in relation to the defences whereas the CJA 2009 is silent as to expert testimony) but the courts have allowed expert evidence to be used in exceptional cases for the 'deprave and corrupt' test (*DPP v A&BC Chewing Gum Ltd* [1968] 1 QB 159).

Expert evidence is usually admissible where something is outside of the jury's own knowledge and experience (Choo, 2006). In respect of virtual child pornography it is quite likely that in many instances the jury will be readily able to decide whether something has been produced solely, or principally, for the purpose of sexual arousal but this will not always be the case. Where it is a single image then the context is likely to be highly relevant but what of the position where there are a number of images? Section 62(4) states:

> Where ... an image forms part of a series of images, the question whether the image is [pornographic] is to be determined by reference to –
>
> (a)   the image itself; and
> (b)   (if the series of images is such as to be capable of providing a context for the image) the context in which it occurs in the series of images.

The section then continues with a rather strangely worded subsection (5):

So, for example, where –

(a) an image forms an integral part of a narrative constituted by a series of images; and

(b) having regard to those images as a whole, they are not of such a nature that they must reasonably be assumed to have been produced solely or principally for the purpose of sexual arousal;

the image may, by virtue of being part of that narrative, be found not to be pornographic, even though it might have been found to be pornographic if taken by itself.

In essence subsections (4) and (5) are stating that where there is more than one image in the item then the question of whether it is produced solely or principally for the purpose of sexual arousal is to be considered by reference to both the image and any context it is within. Subsection (5) specifically contemplates the situation whereby an image by itself might be considered pornographic but will not be when the sequence as a whole is considered. This is the opposite position that is adopted in respect of indecent photographs where it has been held that the individual image is relevant (see *R v Murray* [2004] EWCA Crim 2211).

What will form part of a sequence? It was noted in Chapters 2 and 3 that a considerable amount of indecent photographs of children are, in fact, stills from a movie. It is quite possible that the same is true of virtual child pornography. Where, for example, a person has twenty stills from the same movie then this would meet the test of subsection (4) of being a series of images. Accordingly a defendant may seek to argue that the sequence as a whole and not just an individual image must be relevant.

The second, and perhaps more likely, situation where a sequence will be developed is in respect of comics. It is clear from the proceedings of Parliament that one of the intentions of the government in introducing the CJA 2009 provisions was to criminalise certain types of Anime (those most notably known as Manga or Hentai) (see Parliamentary Debates, House of Commons, Official Report, Public Bill Committee, Coroners and Justice Bill, twelfth sitting, Tuesday 3 March 2009, at col. 487). Certainly some forms of Anime, including comic books, do show the sexual abuse, rape or torture of persons depicted as children, often very young children. (An interesting overview of different types of Manga can be seen from Perper and Cornog, 2002.) However the question that will have to be asked of the jury is whether the comic book as a whole was produced for the sole or primary purpose of sexual arousal. If the purpose is something else – for example violence or the subjugation of children – then it is not clear that the test under subsection (3) will be satisfied irrespective of the fact that a single image within the whole context may be highly sexualised.

Should expert evidence be admissible here? If a jury is looking at a series, including a context, then should they, for example, receive expert evidence in respect of the cultural impact or origins of Manga? As there is no defence of artistic merit (cf the position in respect of obscenity but note classified works are exempt (s. 63, CJA 2009 discussed below)) this may be relevant to whether the work is pornographic or not. Such an approach would, however, lengthen any trial.

Subsection (6)

Even if an image is pornographic it must fall within s. 62(6) which states:

> An image falls within this subsection if it –
>
> (a) is an image which focuses solely or principally on a child's genitals or anal region; or
> (b) portrays any of the acts mentioned in subsection (7).

Subsection (7) states:

> Those acts are –
>
> (a) the performance by a person of an act of intercourse or oral sex with or in the presence of a child;
> (b) an act of masturbation by, of, involving or in the presence of a child;
> (c) an act which involves the penetration of the vagina or anus of a child with a part of a person's body or with anything else;
> (d) an act of penetration, in the presence of a child, of the vagina or anus of a person with a part of the person's body or with anything else;
> (e) the performance by a child of an act of intercourse or oral sex with an animal (whether dead or alive or imaginary);
> (f) the performance by a person of an act of intercourse or oral sex with an animal (whether dead or alive or imaginary) in the presence of a child.

Setting aside the acts described in subsection (7) for a moment, the first issue to note is that of 'child'. The emphasis on this offence is prohibited images of a child but what does this mean? Section 65(5) states a child means a person under the age of 18 and subsection (6) states:

> Where an image shows a person the image it to be treated as an image of a child if –
>
> (a) the impression conveyed by the image is that the person shown is a child; or
> (b) the predominant impression conveyed is that the person shown is a child despite the fact that some of the physical characteristics shown are not those of a child.

Given that these provisions will apply, *inter alia*, to cartoons and computer-generated images it is perhaps surprising that 'person' is not defined more fully since some imagery involves mythical creatures such as fairies, etc. (see, for example, Zanghellini, 2009: 164 who presents an example of 'a fairy tale' in Japanese Yaoi Manga cartoons). Section 65(7) states 'references to an image of a person include references to an image of an imaginary person' which clearly means that it is not necessary that the person is identifiable but would this include imaginary creatures? The dictionary definition of person is 'a human being regarded as an individual' (*Concise Oxford English Dictionary*) which may exclude mythical creatures such as fairies, etc. If a more interpretative stance is taken however then s. 65(6)(b) could be used since the predominant impression will be that it is a child but some of the physical characteristics (e.g. wings(!)) are not those of a child. Certainly if a literal interpretation was to be given to 'person' this could exempt a considerable body of work. However if fairies, etc. are to be covered does this not move the material further away from any nexus of harm since the legislation would, in essence, be criminalising the sexual representation of mythical creatures, which could seem somewhat unusual.

Another difficulty that will undoubtedly be raised is how one ages a cartoon? Where realistic computer-generated images are being produced it may be possible to identify an approximate age; this is less easy with cartoons, especially Manga derivatives where frequently the representations are of a generic cartoon type that bears little resemblance to any identifiable ethnicity. To take an example of a genre that perhaps many are familiar with—Pokemon—how does one age the characters depicted there? For example in the Anime series there is a character known as Misty, a redheaded female. There are no clues given as to her age although she is clearly represented as being post-pubertal. The age must be a question of fact but how do a jury decide the age of a cartoon character? As a definitional aspect the jury must be sure beyond all reasonable doubt that the person represented is under 18. In respect of indecent photographs of children it is clear that expert evidence as to age is not permitted (*R v Land* [1988] 1 Cr App R 301) but will the same be true of this legislation? Whilst it is perhaps not unreasonable to suggest that jurors may be able to age children from their normal experience, the same may not be true of cartoon characters.

Assuming that an age can be ascertained then it is clear from ss. 62(6)–(7) that the image must focus on the genitalia or anal region of the child or portray a sex act listed within subsection (7). There is little difficulty with the acts listed and it covers most sexual activity that would be illegal if it involved a real child. It should be noted that even where the act is within subsection (7) the definition of 'pornographic' must be satisfied and, in particular, this may mean in the context of a cartoon that the series of images is pornographic. This may be relevant where, for example, sexual penetration is shown as a depiction of violence rather than sex.

Grossly offensive, etc.

The final requirement of the definition is contained within s. 62(2)(c), that the image must be 'grossly offensive, disgusting or otherwise of an obscene character'. This section demonstrates that the material must be obscene and not merely indecent. Accordingly a different threshold to the indecent photographs legislation is being used. The terms are relatively straightforward and the test for obscenity is largely understood. Given that 'obscene' is not defined in the Act it is most likely that the common-law definition will be used, i.e. making reference to contemporary standards of decency (see, for example, *R v Stamford* [1972] 2 QB 391).

Exempted material

Some Anime have been certified for release to the public and s. 63 provides an exception where the material has been classified. The exception applies to 'an image which forms part of a series of images contained in a recording of the whole or part of a classified work' (s. 63(2)) and being classified means under the procedures of the Video Recordings Act 1984. It applies to material that is contained on a 'disc, tape or other device capable of storing data ...' (s. 63(7)). This is broadly defined so as to ensure that, for example, material that has been downloaded from the internet will be included.

Where the material is completely classified then there is little difficulty but the more complicated issue is where a still or clip of a classified work is taken from the work. Subsection (3) states that an image is not subject to the exclusion if:

(a) it is contained in a recording of an extract from a classified work; and
(b) it is of such a nature that it must reasonably be assumed to have been extracted (whether with or without other images) solely or principally for the purpose of sexual arousal.

This provision stops people from taking a clip of a classified film out of context and is perhaps similar to the ruling in *R v Murray* [2004] EWCA Crim 2211. However there is arguably a significant difference. The footage in *Murray* had been manipulated so that it concentrated specifically on the genitals of the child. The decision in *Murray* was less to do with its origins and more to do with the fact that the appellant had created a new image. It also involved a real child and accordingly the harm nexus is arguably clearer. The position here however is less clear. If it is manipulation in the same way as in *Murray* then this may be justified but, as will be seen, the section contemplates that an excerpt of a classified film may be classed as prohibited. If D copies five seconds of a classified film (and assuming that it shows footage within the meaning of s. 62) it would seem that the exemption may not apply, yet the footage appears in the original footage. In the absence of any harm nexus it is difficult to see why an excerpt should be criminalised yet a full film should not.

That said, the effect of s. 63(3) would appear to draw the distinction in the way discussed. The test under s. 63(3)(b) is expanded upon in subsections (4) and (5):

(4) Where an extracted image is one of a series of images contained in the recording, the question whether the image is of such a nature as is mentioned in subsection (3)(b) is to be determined by reference to –

    (a) the image itself; and

    (b) (if the series of images is such as to be capable of providing a context for the image) the context in which it occurs in the series of images; and

section 62(5) applies in connection with determining that question as it applied in connection with determining whether an image is pornographic.

(5) In determining for the purposes of this section whether a recording is a recording of the whole or part of a classified work, any alteration attributable to –

    (a) a defect caused for technical reasons or by inadvertence on the part of any person; or

    (b) the inclusion in the recording of any extraneous material (such as advertisements) is to be disregarded.

These sections, like so many modern pieces of legislation, are unlikely to win a 'plain English' award. Taking subsection (5) first it would seem that the purpose of this section is to ensure that an innocent alteration is not criminalised. It is quite possible that an entire classified work is not recorded because of a technical fault or, as the explanatory notes suggest, a person setting the timer wrong (para. 374). Clearly a person should not be liable under these circumstances. Proving this could raise some interesting issues however. Presumably the length and type of material recorded will be relevant. So, for example, if the only bit recorded was sexually explicit it may be more difficult to suggest that this was the product of a technical fault. The Act is not at all clear who bears the burden of proving that the footage is excluded. Section 63(1) states that 'Section 61(1) does not apply to excluded images' which suggests that it is part of the definition meaning that the prosecution would bear the burden of disproving the technical fault. Certainly nothing within s. 63 would appear to suggest a burden on the defence since nowhere is language such as, 'if it is proved' or 'it is a defence to show'. Disproving a technical fault to the prosecution standard could be challenging in many instances.

If we return to subsection (4) it would appear that its purpose is to provide a test of whether the images in possession have been extracted from the classified work for the purpose of sexual arousal. In effect it mirrors the test contained in s. 62(4) and means reference should be made not only to the image that would seem to infringe s. 62(1) but also any other images that accompany it. Where it is decided that the recording at issue was extracted from a classified film for the purposes of sexual gratification then the exemption under s. 63(1) will not apply and an offender will be liable under s. 62(1).

The offence

Section 62(1) states, 'it is an offence for a person to be in possession of a prohibited image of a child'. Accordingly s. 62(1) is a relatively simple offence although, as will be seen, the simplicity of the provision does mask some potentially difficult issues in terms of how the offence will operate in practice.

Section 62 is silent as to *mens rea* but it would seem inevitable that a mental element is required. It was noted in Chapter 6 that the courts have been quite clear that a person must knowingly possess an indecent photograph (*Atkins v DPP* [2000] 2 Cr App R 248) and it is inevitable that the same principles would apply here.

The term 'possession' is not defined although this is perhaps not surprising since it is not defined for the purposes of indecent photographs of children either (see the wording of s. 160, Criminal Justice Act 1988). Quite clearly it will be possible to 'read over' much of the case law as regards the possession of indecent photographs to these provisions. It is obvious that the provisions are based on s. 160 and accordingly similar principles will apply. This being the case possession will be defined as having custody or control of the images.

An important distinction between the CJA 2009 and the indecent photographs legislation is that there is no equivalent offence to making a prohibited image. It will be remembered from Chapter 6 that the decision in *R v Bowden* [2001] QB 88 has had a significant impact on the way the law operates, especially where the law of possession is problematic. Two issues are likely to be the most problematic; those involving deleted or cached images and those where the offender is viewing rather than downloading them.

Deleted or cached files

It will be recalled from Chapter 6 that many prosecutions relating to indecent photographs of children concern photographs that have been forensically recovered. Chapter 6 discussed the circumstances when this is possible and it will be remembered that broadly speaking it exists in two circumstances; where files have been marked for deletion (but have not been physically erased from the hard disc surface) or when they have been (automatically) stored in the cache.

In *R v Porter* [2006] 1 WLR 2633 it was held that because a person could not ordinarily access the files in the unallocated parts of the hard disc, they could not be said to be in custody or control of the images and were therefore not in possession of them. Possession must be a continuing offence (Card *et al.*, 2008: 189) and in *Porter* the court noted that the prosecution could have chosen to charge possession at the time of deletion (p. 2637). This is similar to the rules of some other countries and it will be seen in Chapter 8 that in some states deleting an image can be construed as a person exercising custody and control over it. The difficulty with this approach however, is that it would be necessary to show that D possessed the images at the time of the deletion and not somebody else. That said, more than one person can be in possession of an item and so it is not necessary, for example, to show that D downloaded the images (cf the position as regards 'making' an indecent photograph of a child). However the mental element identified in *Atkins* is required so it would be necessary to show that D, who exercises custody or control of the computer, was aware of the existence of the files even if he claims they were downloaded by someone else. Where this could not be shown then a person would be entitled to an acquittal.

The second issue is where images are contained within the cache. In *Porter* the Court of Appeal stated that it was a matter of fact whether a person is in possession of images ([2006] 1 WLR 2633 at 2640) and this will take into account their technical knowledge. Unlike deleted files that will ordinarily require sophisticated knowledge or a specialist program to access the images, the cache is ordinarily accessible by anyone simply by opening the appropriate folder or looking into the 'history' page of the web browser. Accordingly it is perhaps more likely that where an image is recovered from the cache that a person could be said to be in custody and control of that image (since it is readily accessible and can be moved or copied). However, as noted above, the defendant must *knowingly* possess these images and proving this may be difficult. For example, the cache would automatically download every image on a webpage irrespective of whether a user has seen it or not. This can be important where a webpage is long and requires a user to scroll down to see all the contents. The cache would save images that the user may not have even seen if he did not scroll down. For this reason prosecutions will often not charge thumbnail images and only those where evidence shows the thumbnails have been 'clicked' and access sought to the larger image. This is because the clicking must act as proof of knowledge of that image.

Viewing

The second issue where the current offence may cause some difficulties is in respect of viewing material. Section 62(1) is very clear that a person must be in possession of the prohibited images but what happens where the person is looking at images online without downloading them? Where they are static images then it is quite likely that the images will be placed in the cache and, as noted above, it is possible that a person may be deemed in possession of these subject to the mental element being satisfied. What of those situations where the images are not recorded in the cache (as some browsers allow users to disable the cache), where the defendant does not have control of the cache (e.g. when he is in a cyber-cafe) or where the material is a moving image that is streamed (which would not be recorded in the cache)?

If no image is saved on the computer then there is nothing to be in possession of. With indecent photographs of children the intentional viewing of an image can amount to 'making' (s. 1(1)(a), Protection of Children Act 1978 and see *R v Smith; R v Jayson* [2003] 1 Cr App R 13). The logic of the court in *Jayson* was that calling an image on to the screen, even for a short period of time, meant that a new (copy) of the image was created and displayed. However s. 62(1) does not criminalise the making of an image, it concerns only the possession of it. Can it be said that a person who views an image is in possession of it? If, as would seem clear, the test is custody and control it would seem that the answer must be no. Where a person does not download the image it cannot be said that he has custody of the image: the image remains on the server of the person who has uploaded it.

In *R v Daniels* 2004 NLCA 73, a Canadian case, it was held that viewing images may amount to possession but this was in a slightly different context. There the offender had selected a number of images and he had the decision whether to download them or abandon the downloading process. The court held that this amounted to control and there is some logic to this. However the key here was that the person had chosen to start the downloading process and had he not pressed 'skip' the image would have automatically downloaded. This showed a degree of control but it must still be questioned whether a person in this position has custody of the images. In any event this rule does not apply to situations where a person simply looks at an image (including streamed footage) since in those circumstances it cannot be said that a person is exercising control.

It was noted in Chapter 5 that many were opposed to the creation of this offence and, applying their logic, the criminalisation of mere viewing would be an additional interference that would be unjustified. However if the justification for the offence is, as noted in Chapter 5, based on morality it could be questioned whether viewing images is as morally wrong as possessing them. Certainly where the images are on the internet the difference between possession and viewing is perhaps moot. If a person looks at an image on site X every day is this any different to if he possessed image X? It could be argued that it is, since ultimately if the site is removed then D can no longer see the image (unlike if he possessed it) but whilst the site is there he can view it as many times as he wishes. Similarly with the advent of virtual storage devices the boundaries between possession and viewing are becoming blurred. If the files are stored on an FTP or virtual storage device is he in possession of them? Whilst he undoubtedly has control of the images (in that he can access them, share them or delete them) it is more questionable whether he has custody of them because the owner of the site that hosts the storage could shut the site down without any notice to the users.

Creation

It is worth pausing to discuss the issue of creation. Whilst s. 62(1) deals with the possession of material and the OPA deals with its publication what about those who create the materials? Where the materials are created with the intention of publishing them then the OPA will deal with this as the person would be in possession of them with a view to publication (s. 2(1), OPA 1959). Where they have been created by a person for their own purposes and without any intention to disseminate them then this will not come within the OPA 1959. If a person creates an image then he must, by implication, also be in possession of it and thus a person will commit the offence under s. 62(1). It will be interesting to see how the courts or the Sentencing Council approach such conduct and, in particular, whether it is classed as more serious. Whilst creation of child pornography is ordinarily considered more serious than mere possession (SGC, 2007: 109) will the same be true here where the legislation does not differentiate between the conduct and where there is no intention to disseminate them?

Penalty

Section 66, CJA 2009 details the penalty for the offence under s. 62(1). The offence is triable either way and the maximum sentence is three years' imprisonment when tried on indictment (s. 66(2)(b)) or 12 months' imprisonment when tried summarily in England and Wales (s. 66(2)(a) when read in conjunction with s. 66(3)(a)). This penalty is less than that for possession of an indecent photograph of a child (s. 160(2A), Criminal Justice Act 1988) although this is justified by the fact that no real child is portrayed (although see the argument in Chapter 5 where it was noted that the CJA 2009 may apply where a real child is portrayed in which case it could be argued three years is insufficient). Three years was presumably also chosen because the maximum sentence under the OPA 1959 is five years' imprisonment (s. 2(1)(b), OPA 1959) and the simple possession of obscene material must be considered less serious than their publication.

A person convicted under s. 62(1) will be subject to the notification requirements under Part 2, Sexual Offences Act 2003 only where they receive a sentence of at least two years' imprisonment (Sch. 3, para. 35A, SOA 2003). Given that the maximum sentence is three years' imprisonment and an offender pleading guilty will receive a discount of up to one-third (SGC, 2007b) it is submitted that it is likely that the notification requirements will apply to this offence only in exceptional cases. Potentially this could be useful in showing the proportionality of the requirements if they are subject to challenge under Articles 8 or 10 of the European Convention on Human Rights (the success of which was doubted in Chapter 6).

Chapter 8

Other approaches to criminalising child pornography

Chapter 6 detailed how the law in England and Wales criminalises photograph-based forms of child pornography and Chapter 7 examined how other forms of visual imagery is criminalised. The purpose of this chapter is to provide an equivalent to Chapter 4 by examining what offences other jurisdictions have in respect of child pornography. This will allow a comparison to be made between the laws and allow the reader to consider if there are alternative means of criminalising child pornography.

United States

The first jurisdiction to examine is that of the United States. It will be recalled from Chapter 4 that this involves an examination of the federal legal system, and the trigger for when federal jurisdiction applies will be examined momentarily. The offences are largely contained within 18 USC §2252A but the production of child pornography is dealt with in 18 USC §2251. As in Chapter 4, the complexity of the provisions means that they are not reproduced verbatim.

Federal jurisdiction

Federal law applies where it can be shown that it is an international or interstate matter or that the conduct took place on federal land (e.g. indigenous Indian land, US armed forces territory, etc.). This is reflected in the language of §2251 and §2252A where they require the conduct to take place through the mail, interstate or foreign commerce or within the special maritime and territorial jurisdiction or federal property. That said, the requirement for foreign commerce has been interpreted liberally and so, for example, in *US v Schene* 543 F.3d 627 (2008) the defendant was convicted of the possession of child pornography produced using materials that had been mailed, shipped or transported in interstate or foreign commerce (18 USC §2252A(a)(5)(B)). The foreign element was satisfied because it was shown that the hard drive, on which the images were stored, was manufactured in Singapore. The court, following the decisions of the Seventh and Ninth Circuits held that child pornography is produced when it is downloaded or copied to a disc (discussed further below) (p. 638). Applying that logic it held that this meant that the child pornography was made using material from foreign commerce in that the disc was made abroad (p. 639).

Where the internet is used then proof of interstate or a foreign element is perhaps easier to show. Web servers are hosted in different locations around the country and indeed the world, and if it can be proven that a person's email or browser was connected to a server outside of the State the person resides in then this element would be satisfied too (see, for example, *US v Rayl* 270 F.3d 709 (2001) at p. 715). In *US v Hornaday* 392 F.3d 1306 (2004) the Eleventh Circuit went further saying 'the internet is an instrumentality of interstate commerce' (p. 1311) implying that the use of the internet is almost automatic proof of interstate or commercial elements. The consequence of this is that, in essence, the use of the internet will ensure that the activities of a person can be brought under either state or federal law. The exact jurisdictional preference between state and federal authorities is not particularly clear, extremely complicated and certainly beyond the scope of this book. For the purposes of this chapter it will be taken as read that the use of the internet will ordinarily involve an interstate matter.

It should be noted that 18 USC §2252A also refers in a number of places to the use of the mail. The US postal service is operated at a federal level and thus the use of the mail system will also ensure that the matter can be a federal matter. This is important where, for example, an offender is not using the internet but is, instead, purchasing or disseminating child pornography material using the postal service.

As each of the offences contained within 18 USC §2252A requires federal jurisdiction to be secured the issue of jurisdiction will not be discussed in more depth below. An assumption will be made, instead, that each of the issues discussed above will be done in such a way as to engage the federal jurisdiction.

The offences that appear to be prescribed under federal law are:

- Production.
- Mailing or transporting.
- Receiving or distributing.
- Reproducing or advertising, promoting or soliciting.
- Selling or possessing with intent to sell.
- Possessing or accessing.

Each of these will be examined in turn. There are also a number of defences and these will be examined afterwards.

Production

There are two offences relating to production that are of relevance; production of child pornography and producing an image of child pornography that is an adapted image of an identifiable manner. These will be considered separately.

PRODUCING CHILD PORNOGRAPHY

Producing child pornography is, unlike the other offences that are to be examined, contained within a separate section of the penal code, 18 USC §2251. The section actually creates four offences. The first (18 USC §2251(a)) tackles those who use, persuade, induce, incites or coerces any minor to engage in, or assist in engaging in sexually explicit conduct for the purpose of producing any visual depiction of such conduct or for the purposes of transmitting a live depiction of such conduct. The interstate/foreign commerce requirements are contained within (a) but as noted above these are easily answerable.

It is notable that 18 USC §2251(a) includes not only the recording of the conduct but also live broadcast. The issue of live streaming was not discussed in great depth in Chapters 2–7 of this book, in part because in England and Wales it is likely that such conduct would be dealt with as a separate form of liability, either as complicity to a substantive sex offence, facilitating the commission of a sex offence (s. 14, SOA 2003) or the facilitation of child pornography (ss. 48–50, SOA 2003). It is clearly an important provision since it is known that many sex sites now stream (or 'broadcast') live sexual activity and there is some evidence to suggest that this also occurs in respect of the sexual abuse of a child (Wortley and Smallbone, 2006) and this should be considered a serious matter that leads to both the direct and indirect sexual exploitation or abuse of a child.

The second offence (18 USC §2251(b)) tackles those who are a parent, guardian or other person who has control over a minor that allows their child to be used to commission an offence under paragraph (a). The essence of paragraph (b) is that the parent, etc. does not need to be involved in the actual production of the footage, but merely knowingly permitting the minor to engage in sexually explicit conduct for the use of it to be recorded or broadcast is culpable. Again it is submitted that there is little difficulty in criminalising such conduct since a parent or guardian has a duty to safeguard their child.

Nevertheless whilst there are strong public policy reasons for criminalising this behaviour – and certainly a parent who knowingly allows their child to be used in the production of child pornography must be considered to be complicit in their exploitation or abuse – it does raise questions about the liability of parents of an adolescent. What of the situation where a parent suspects that his 16 year-old daughter may be masturbating in front of a webcam when talking to her 17 year-old boyfriend on line? The footage is likely to amount to sexually explicit conduct but can the parent actually prevent it? The requirement under the section is that the parent 'knowingly' permits their child to engage in explicit sexual conduct and this implies more than mere suspicion but what happens if they do know (the parent accidentally walked in on a previous conversation, etc.)? A parent is unlikely to be able to stop such conduct – whilst removing webcams was, at one point, perhaps easy to do now they are built into many laptop computers and monitors and, in any event, are extremely cheap. Are they supposed to report their daughter to the police in order to ensure that they themselves are not liable? Of course such a person may be protected through prosecutorial discretion but it does raise the point that an issue that seems obviously correct – criminalising those parents who knowingly allow their child to be abused for the purposes of child sexual exploitation – could have unintended circumstances.

The third offence (18 USC §2251(c)) adopts an extraterritorial stance to the production of child pornography so long as either the person who produces it intends to transport the material to the United States or the material is transported. The meaning of transported will be discussed below but it does raise the question about whether this provision would apply where the material is accessible by persons within the US jurisdiction, i.e. a person within US jurisdiction accesses the material online. The statute does not expressly refer to the use of computers (cf the use of this term in 18 USC §2252A) but it does refer to 'any means' which must include computers. The issue of jurisdiction is considered in more detail during Chapter 11.

The fourth and final offence (18 USC §2251(d)) criminalises those who make, print or publish any notice or advertisement offering to receive, exchange, buy, distribute or reproduce any child pornography or advertises, etc. the participation of any sexually explicit conduct by or with any minor for the purposes of producing child pornography. Again this is largely uncontroversial and is seeking to tackle those who will be complicit with the production and dissemination of child pornography.

PRODUCING CHILD PORNOGRAPHY FROM AN ADAPTED IMAGE

18 USC §2252A(a)(7) criminalises 'knowingly produces with intent to distribute, or distributes, by any means . . . child pornography that is an adapted or modified depiction of an identifiable minor'. It is perhaps interesting that this is contained within 18 USC §2252A in that production of child pornography itself is contained within 18 USC §2251. The key difference between the production offences is the fact that this is the production of material from an 'adapted or modified depiction of an identifiable minor'.

The term 'identifiable minor' was discussed in Chapter 4 and it will be remembered that it is not necessary to prove the actual identity of the child, merely that it is identifiable as a real child (18 USC §2256(9)). By adaptation or modification the legislation is clearly seeking to tackle the morphing of images or those images where a child is placed within a pornographic context. Whilst there may be no direct abuse suffered by a child in these circumstances, clearly there can be exploitation where the child is recognisable, and psychological harm and distress could be caused to the child, especially where the image portrays the child engaging in sexual behaviour that did not happen.

Mailing or transporting

This is contained within 18 USC §2252A(a)(1) which makes it an offence to knowingly mail or transport child pornography. The term 'mails' is not defined although clearly this is a reference to the postal service and would include, therefore, situations where a person sends child pornography through the postal system.

The term 'transport' is not defined either but clearly it must relate to the sending of child pornography. The paragraph expressly includes the use of a computer to transport child pornography and thus it has been questioned whether the sending of child pornography through email amounts to transportation. In *US v Kiderlen* 569 F.3d 358 the Eighth Circuit held that 'transports' is satisfied by transmission by email (p. 368) and this must be correct given how email works. Where a picture is attached to an email then a copy of that image is sent from computer X to computer Y and this is arguably no different to a situation whereby D duplicates an image and sends it through the post. In this context the decision of the Fifth Circuit in *US v Goff* 155 Fed.Appx.773 (2005) is interesting. The appellant was convicted of transporting child pornography through email and he sought to argue that there was no proof since the original images were not located on his hard drive. The Court of Appeals rejected this argument noting that there was no requirement under the statute for this: it sufficed that the prosecution could prove that an email originating from the appellant's account transported an image to another person (p. 775). In other words if the email is recovered at the destination then it is irrelevant that the original image cannot be located on the originator's computer (subject, of course, to a situation where the defendant is alleging his email has been compromised). Again this must be in line with the ordinary understanding of the term transporting.

The term 'transporting' implies that it is the defendant who is sending material and in *US v Mohrbacher* 182 F.3d 1041 (1999) the Ninth Circuit held that a person who downloaded images from the internet was not guilty of transporting them (p. 1050). From the point of view of the technicalities of downloading it could have been argued that the user has transported the material that he chooses to deliberately download, but realistically it would be more appropriate to suggest that the host computer is the one who has transported them. The defendant who selects them has undoubtedly solicited the images but, as will be seen, reliance on transportation is not required as receiving child pornography is also an offence.

Receiving or distributing

18 USC §2252A(a)(2) criminalises the receipt or distribution of child pornography. The offence is relatively complicated in that §2252A(a)(2)(A) refers to child pornography and §2252A(a)(2)(B) refers to material that contains child pornography. It could be questioned what the difference is but it is likely that the latter includes, for example, books that contain a single image that could be constituted as child pornography. The terms 'receiving' and 'distributing' are not defined. Whilst it may be thought that each of the terms are readily understood there has been some quite significant and interesting case law that has assessed the meaning of these terms.

It was noted above that sending an email containing child pornography amounts to its transportation, but it must also presumably amount to its distribution. To an extent it can be argued that it is a matter of prosecutorial discretion as to whether to indict transportation or distribution. However distribution has been construed much wider than this. In *US v McVey* 290 F.3d 1279 (2002) the Eleventh Circuit held that somebody who posted child pornography online making it available to others to see had distributed the material. In other jurisdictions this is dealt with by other verbs but if distribution is construed as making material available to others (which would accord with its ordinary meaning) then *McVey* is correct.

The concept of making images available is at the heart of the decision in *US v Christy* 65 MJ 657 (2007) where the Army Court of Criminal Appeals was asked to rule on the use of peer-to-peer technology. The appellant downloaded child pornography using a peer-to-peer network and left the downloaded images in his 'shared' folder. The appellant accepted that he knew how a peer-to-peer system operated and that he could have moved the images into another folder which would have prevented other users from accessing them (p. 663). The appellant stated that he had no doubt that other users had accessed the files and downloaded them and on that basis the court found no difficulty in upholding his conviction of distribution. The court implied that it is not necessary for someone to have actually downloaded a file to secure a conviction on that basis and certainly that would seem to be consistent with the decision in *McVey*. It will be remembered from Chapter 6 that in England and Wales the decision of *R v Dooley* [2006] 1 WLR 775 required the prosecution to prove that at least one of his reasons for keeping material in the 'shared' folder was the intention to distribute the material. The decision in *Christy* addressed this point and noted that the mental requirement for §2252A is knowledge which the court expressly noted is a lesser requirement than intent (65 MJ 657 at p. 662). A particular emphasis was placed in the case on whether the offender knew how peer-to-peer systems operate and, in particular, the fact that to load the software on to the computer requires a user to acknowledge that other users can access the material (p. 664). Accordingly purpose appears to be less significant than knowledge that somebody *could* access child pornography even if they have not in fact done so.

Receiving child pornography is obviously a separate issue and it should be noted at the outset that a mental element is required. The Code is quite clear and a person must *knowingly* receive child pornography. Therefore where material is sent unsolicited then no liability will arise. Clearly receiving child pornography can arise following a request for it but it need not and the decision of the Ninth Circuit in *US v Mohrbacher* 182 F.3d 1041 (1999) is interesting in this context. The court held that a person who downloads an image from the internet is guilty of receiving child pornography. Whilst this is technically correct (in that the data that creates the file has been received by the host computer and put together to form child pornography) it does create a slight paradox because, as will be seen, simple possession is also an offence under §2252A.

To an extent the position in America would appear to duplicate the position in England and Wales following *R v Bowden* [2001] QB 88 as discussed in Chapter 8. The same conduct (downloading) is capable of amounting to a criminal offence under two different provisions. This was expressly confirmed by the Ninth Circuit in *US v Olander* 572 F.3d 764 (2009) where the court said:

> There is little to distinguish possession from receipt. If one receives child pornography, one necessarily possesses it, at least for a short time . . . Indeed, in many cases, the relative culpability may be higher for possession, given that a defendant can destroy or discard the pornography, thereby ceasing to possess it, while no action can erase the fact of the receipt that led to the possession.
>
> (p. 769)

As with the position in England and Wales, the different offences are punished in different ways, with receipt attracting a higher penalty than mere possession (see §2252A(b)(1) cf §2252A(b)(2): receipt is punishable by imprisonment of not less than five years' imprisonment and no more than 20 years and possession by imprisonment of not more than 10 years). If, as the Ninth Circuit suggests, there is no difference between them then why should the punishment differ? In *Olander* the court opined (*in dicta*) that the punishment may be higher because it is not necessary to have received material to be in possession of it (p. 769). The difficulty with this argument is that they then suggest that the creator of material will not have received it, but it would be unusual to suggest that the creator of material should receive a lesser sentence given that their proximity to the primary abuse or exploitation of the child is that much closer (especially when it is recalled that since *Ashcroft* the material must involve a real child).

In any event *Olander*, and related decisions, appear to suggest that American law, as with the position in England and Wales, has created a system whereby there is duplication between the offences. It was suggested in Chapter 4 that downloading is akin to possessing material and should be treated accordingly. The same logic would seem to apply to the position in America and it would be better for the law to be clarified so as to permit only one charge to be brought where material is downloaded from the internet.

Until such clarification is reached then prosecutors have a discretion as to what to charge an offender with. In *US v Bobb* 577 F.3d 1366 (2009) the Eleventh Circuit held that it was not possible to charge a person with two separate offences for the same conduct but they expressly upheld charges of receipt and possession when they were framed so as to refer to different time periods. They noted:

> [The appellant's] convictions and sentenced were based on two distinct offenses, occurring on two different dates, and proscribed by two different statutes. Count I of the indictment charged Bobb with taking 'receipt' of child pornography on November 12, 2004, while Count II charged Bobb with

having 'possession' of child pornography in August 2005. The evidence . . .
proved [he] received child pornography on November 12 . . . by downloading
the seven zip files . . . and, in August 2005, he possessed 6,000 additional
images. Accordingly, the record shows that the indictment charged Bobb
with two separate offenses, and the Government introduced evidence to
convict him of those distinct offenses.

(p. 1375)

Whilst this is undoubtedly technically correct it does not answer the difficulty of
overlap. Where the images were all downloaded it must be questioned whether it
is appropriate to charge two different offences for what is, in essence, the same
conduct. For the reasons given above it is submitted that it would be more appropriate for the law to treat the downloading of child pornography as possession
save where there is evidence to show that the person later did something with that
material (e.g. distribute or place it in a 'shared' folder, etc).

DISSEMINATING MATERIAL TO A MINOR

A separate, but linked, offence is that contained within 18 USC §2252A(a)(6) which
prohibits the distribution, offering, sending or providing of child pornography to a
minor.

This is an interesting provision and is one that is dealt with in different ways by
other jurisdictions. For example, in England and Wales the Protection of Children
Act 1978 does not differentiate between the showing or distribution of material to
either adults or children although, as will be seen from Chapter 10, it would be
considered a serious aggravating factor for sentence. Whilst there is an offence
under s. 12, Sexual Offences Act 2003 to, *inter alia*, show sexual material to a
child this does not differentiate between showing adult or child pornography to
the child.

These offences are, in essence, tackling the concern that material could be used
to 'groom' children for contact abuse. This was discussed in passing during
Chapter 2. The behaviour will not be discussed in depth here since it is questionable whether it is realistically an offence relating to child pornography *per se* or
rather the attempt by an offender to solicit a child for the purposes of sexual
gratification. Accordingly it is submitted that the offence is better examined in
relation to the grooming and solicitation of a minor.

Reproducing or advertising, promoting or soliciting

18 USC §2252A(a)(3) creates an additional two offences. The first (§2252A(a)(3)
(A)) criminalises a person who reproduces child pornography for distribution
through the mail or any interstate or foreign commerce system. This is a relatively
simple offence and although 'reproduces' is not defined in the legislation it is a
word of ordinary usage and so should not cause too many difficulties.

The second offence (§2252A(a)(3)(B)) is actually a series of offences and covers someone who knowingly:

> advertises, promotes, presents, distributes or solicits ... any material or purported material in a manner that reflects the belief, or that it is intended to cause another to believe, that the material or purported material is, or contains –
>
> (i) an obscene visual depiction of a minor engaging in sexually explicit conduct; or
> (ii) a visual depiction of an actual minor engaging in sexually explicit conduct.

It is notable that a wider definition of materials is given in sub-paragraph (i) although this is probably acceptable since it is expressly using the (higher) standard of obscenity rather than the lesser standard of, for example, lasciviousness.

The terms themselves are relatively simple to define and are unlikely to cause any difficulties of construction. In *US v Williams* 128 S.Ct. 1830 (2008) the Supreme Court said of this paragraph:

> Generally speaking §2252A(a)(3)(B) prohibits offers to provide and requests to obtain child pornography. The statute does not require the actual existence of child pornography ... Rather than targeting the underlying material, this statute bans the collateral speech that introduces such material into the child pornography distribution network. Thus, an internet user who solicits child pornography from an undercover agent violates the statute, even if the officer possesses no child pornography. Likewise, a person who advertises virtual child pornography as depicting actual children also falls within the reach of the statute.
>
> (pp. 1838–1839)

It can be seen therefore that this provision differs from the other parts of §2252A in that no material need ever exist or indeed amount to child pornography. It seeks to tackle those situations where people either solicit child pornography from others or where they state that they can supply material that amounts to child pornography. It is obviously an important provision especially in the context of the internet (and so-called 'sting' operations, something discussed in Chapter 12).

The Supreme Court noted that nothing within §2252A(a)(3)(B) required there to be a commercial element to any transaction, (p. 1840) something that is obviously crucial since much of the distribution that takes place over the internet is not thought to be commercially motivated (although there is some evidence that this is perhaps changing; see IWF, 2010) and paragraph (B) is designed to include, for example, requests or offers to supply material between those persons with a sexual interest in such material. The Supreme Court concludes that 'offers to provide or requests to obtain child pornography are categorically excluded from the First Amendment' (p. 1842) which is an important statement. By upholding this provision the Supreme Court has approved the attempt by Congress to criminalise not only those who are involved in the production and dissemination of child pornography but also those who seek to engage in this behaviour. Soliciting or offering material widens the cycle of harm caused by child pornography (both in terms of primary and secondary harm) and it should be legitimate to criminalise such activities.

Selling or possessing with intent to sell

18 USC §2252A(a)(4) creates two offences relating to the selling of child pornography or possessing child pornography with intent to sell it. 18 USC §2252A(a)(4) (A) criminalises the selling (or possession with intent) in the special maritime and territorial jurisdiction or on any land or building under the control of the US federal government or on Indian land (which is under federal protection). 18 USC §2252A(a)(4)(B) criminalises the selling (or possession with intent) of material that has been mailed or transported relating to interstate or foreign commerce or which has been produced with materials so gathered. The meaning of the production of interstate or foreign commerce was discussed at the beginning and it was noted that this has been given a wide meaning, particularly in respect of computer components. The effect of this is that a person who sells (or possesses with intent to sell) material via the internet or by computer is likely to breach this offence.

The terms used in this provision are readily understood with the only difficulty being the extent of possession; something that is discussed below. It is noticeable that the legislation uses the term 'with intent' which would suggest an extra mental requirement. The section requires that a person knowingly sells or possesses with intent which would suggest that a person must knowingly sell child pornography or knowingly possess it. If the latter, then the person must possess it with the intention of selling it. It will be remembered that in *US v Christy* 65 MJ 657 (2007) the court held that knowledge was a lesser mental element than intention and thus a higher standard must be required in respect of the reason for the possession. There has, to the author's knowledge, been no reported cases on this paragraph and accordingly it is not known whether the federal courts will adopt the logic of the Court of Appeal of England and Wales in *R v Dooley* [2006] 1 WLR 775 by finding that the ulterior intent is satisfied if a reason (not necessarily *the* reason) for possession was to sell the material. It is submitted that such logic would be appropriate in the circumstances set out in §2252A(a)(4).

Possession or accessing

18 USC §2252A(a)(5) introduces two offences. §2252A(a)(5)(A) criminalises those who in the special maritime and territorial jurisdiction of the United States

or a place under the control of the federal government knowingly possesses or knowingly accesses with intent to view any 'book, magazine, periodical, film, videotape, computer disk, or any other material that contains an image of child pornography'. §2252A(a)(5)(B) criminalises those who knowingly possess or knowingly access with intent to view any material that contains child pornography that has been mailed, shipped or produced using any interstate or foreign commerce issue. The manner in which jurisdiction is secured, particularly in respect of the internet, has been discussed already and this obviously applies here. §2252A(a)(5) in effect creates two offences; that of simple possession and knowingly accessing child pornography with intent to view it.

SIMPLE POSSESSION

The first offence is therefore that of simple possession. The term 'possession' is not defined in the Code and the term has been the subject of some discussion by the courts. One of the most important cases governing possession is *US v Tucker* 305 F.3d 1193 (2002) where the Tenth Circuit used the dictionary meaning of the term holding that it meant, 'the holding or having something (material or immaterial) as one's own, or in one's control' (p. 1204). This would suggest that at the heart of the concept of possession is the idea of having the material in one's custody or control. It is not necessary to prove that a person has exclusive possession of material so long as the tribunal of fact has evidence before it that a person had the material in his possession (*US v Schene* 543 F.3d 627 (2008)).

The concept of control means that it is not necessary to show that a person has actual custody of the images. In *US v Romm* 455 F.3d 990 (2006) the Ninth Circuit upheld a conviction where a person demonstrated his control by deliberately enlarging images on a screen previously displayed as a thumbnail and also by downloading them to his computer for a short period of time prior to deletion. The decision in *Romm* has also been considered to be authority for the proposition that deleting images is asserting control of them (*US v Shiver* 305 Fed. Appx. 640). Obviously not every deletion will amount to the assertion of control since it could be a concerted effort to divest one of unwanted child pornography but in *Shiver* the Eleventh Circuit upheld a conviction for the possession of child pornography where an offender accessed his internet cache and manually deleted the images contained therein.

Shiver is an interesting case as it demonstrates one of the approaches taken by the federal courts concerning possessing images in a cache. In *US v Tucker* 305 F.3d 1193 the Tenth Circuit upheld a conviction for a person who viewed child pornography on the internet and who knew that the images he viewed would be stored automatically in the computer cache (p. 1204). This approach bears striking similarities to the approach adopted by the courts in England and Wales in *Atkins v DPP* [2000] 1 WLR 1427 where an awareness of how a cache operated was considered to be sufficient to show possession.

What of the situation where a person does not know of the existence of the cache? Following the logic of *Shiver* and *Tucker* a person cannot be knowingly in possession of images they are not aware of. In *US v Stulock* 308 F.3d 922 the Eighth Circuit noted:

> . . . one cannot be guilty of possession for simply having viewed an image on a web site, thereby causing the image to be automatically stored on the browser's cache, without having purposely saved or downloaded the image.
>
> (p. 925)

It will be seen below that such behaviour no longer escapes criminal liability but the possession point must hold true: the mental element of knowledge would require an appreciation that the images are being stored (even if automatically).

The analysis above concerned the mental element of possession: a person must know that the images are being stored in the cache. What of the situation where a person has knowledge but does not have control? Can there still be possession? In *US v Navrestad* 66 MJ 262 (2008) the appellant engaged in sexual conversations with a number of persons whilst at an internet cafe on an army base, including someone he thought was a 15 year-old boy but who was, in fact, an undercover police officer. He also accessed a number of images contained within a virtual storage device (i.e. a space on the internet where users could store files in a manner akin to a hard drive). Some of the files within the virtual storage devices amounted to child pornography and the appellant viewed these at the internet cafe. He was convicted of possessing child pornography but he appealed arguing, *inter alia*, that he was not in control of the images.

There was no doubt that the appellant was deliberately viewing child pornography and he may have been aware that these images were recorded in the cache but was there control? The court noted that the appellant had no access to the cache (something common in internet cafes) and indeed had no ability to even download the images to a portable storage device (p. 267). The court found that this was a significant distinguishing factor from cases such as *Tucker* in that those cases referred to the cache on the person's own computer (p. 268). If a person cannot access the cache then it would be irrelevant even if the person knows that the images are being automatically stored because the control aspect of possession is not satisfied.

In Chapter 6 it will be remembered that in England and Wales the Court of Appeal in *R v Porter* [2006] 1 WLR 2633 decided that a person cannot be in possession of images that have been deleted and are not accessible without forensic software. What is the position under US federal law? *Navrestad* would suggest that the answer should be that they are not in possession because, applying the logic in *Porter*, a person cannot be in control of images they cannot access. That said, there has been no specific case, to the best of the author's knowledge, that has addressed this issue specifically and the federal courts appear more concerned about how the images got there in the first place rather than whether they could be accessed at the time of arrest. So, for example, in *US v Toschiaddi* (2009, unreported) the US Navy–Marine Corps Court of Criminal Appeals upheld a conviction for knowingly possessing material where the appellant was the only person who had access to the computer and had access to the passwords on the machine. Given that receiving child pornography is a criminal offence (see the discussion above) then this would suggest that deleted material may not be in possession but could be evidence of either the receipt or accessing of child pornography.

ACCESSING

It was noted above that in *US v Stulock* 308 F.3d 922 the Eighth Circuit held that a person could not be guilty of possession through merely viewing websites. However Congress in 2008 amended the law and, as noted at the beginning of this section, an alternative to simple possession contained in §2252A(a)(5) is that of knowingly accessing child pornography with an intent to view it. The effect of this is that viewing can now amount to a criminal offence. The implications of this is perhaps best summarised by the Eleventh Circuit in their decision in *US v Shiver* 305 Fed. Appx 640 (discussed above). After discussing whether a person is in possession of images in the cache, the court notes the Congressional amendment and states:

> This amendment has essentially settled the question in this case of whether a defendant must exercise control or dominion over an image for purposes of §2252A(a)(5)(B). Under the statute's present language, control appears unnecessary, so long as an individual knowingly accesses the illicit images.
>
> (p. 642)

In other words §2252A(a)(5) will now criminalise those who deliberately view child pornography on the internet. The extent of the provision should be qualified by the mental element however. There are two mental elements to satisfy. The first is that a person knowingly accesses child pornography and this must mean that they are aware that it is child pornography material that they are accessing. The second is that they have an intention to view that material. Whilst ordinarily this would not be problematic to prove, it would provide an exemption where the person is accessing child pornography for other purposes (for example, a network administrator who accesses files on the network to delete them or to forward them to law enforcement individuals). It was noted above that construing possession has caused the courts a degree of difficulty but basing a prosecution on access rather than possession may allow some of these difficulties to be circumvented.

Defences

Few defences exist under federal law for offences relating to child pornography. In many instances the defendant simply seeks to challenge the production of evidence or the assertions of the prosecution (particularly over whether the material is of children, is of sexually explicit conduct or is done knowingly). Similarly a number of challenges to the constitutionality of the provisions has been recorded but these are not defences *per se*. No specific defence exists on the face of 18 USC §2251 (production of child pornography) but 18 USC §2252A does contain a small number of defences on the face of the legislation.

Mistake of age (production)

As noted already, 18 USC §2251 does not contain any specific defences but some defendants have sought to argue that they should not be liable where they do not know the age of the child or claim to think that the subject was above the age of 18. In *US v Pilego* 578 F.3d 938 (2009) the Eighth Circuit held that a person who produced child pornography could not raise a mistake of age as an affirmative defence. The appellant had been convicted of producing child pornography when he recorded a sexual encounter he had with a 14 year-old boy. He sought to argue that he was not aware of the age of the child and that he should be allowed to raise this as a defence and to do otherwise would breach his constitutional rights under the First Amendment. The Eighth Circuit however held that the offence was equivalent to statutory rape offences and that it was widely accepted that the presumption of *mens rea* could be displaced for those offences. The court also held that a person producing pornography should be required to ascertain the age of children portrayed and that it was not unreasonable to require this of them (p. 944).

Similar reasoning was adopted by the Fourth Circuit in *US v Malloy* 568 F.3d 166 (2009). The court considered the First Amendment and noted that since producers of pornography are required to verify the age of those depicted and because child pornography is ordinarily outside of the First Amendment, the absence of an affirmative defence did not contravene the US Constitution.

Age (§2252A)

18 USC §2252A(c) creates an affirmative defence that applies to all conduct discussed above except conduct under §2252A(a)(3)(A) (the advertisement, promotion, distribution or soliciting of material) and §2252A(a)(5) (possession). The affirmative defence applies:

(1)

    (A) the alleged child pornography was produced using an actual person or persons engaging in sexually explicit conduct; and

    (B) each such person was an adult at the time the material was produced; or

(2) the alleged child pornography was not produced using any actual minor or minors.

The defence under subsection (2) does not apply to material that involves child pornography as described in §2256(8)(C). This type of material was defined in Chapter 4 but it will be remembered that it is, in essence, non-photographic images of identifiable children. It may be questioned whether this is, in reality, a defence since it has been noted already that the prosecution have to prove that the pornography involves real minors. However it was also noted that ultimately it is a question of fact whether a person is a child and whether the material involves a real child and accordingly the jury can reach its conclusion by its own judgment on the material presented before it, with assistance from expert witnesses. A jury may conclude that the material is of a real minor but §2252A(c) directs the acquittal of the offender where he can prove that despite this evidence the material did not involve the use of a real minor. Realistically this is probably only provable when the defendant knows the victim and can prove his or her age at the time the material was made, something that may not be easy to prove.

Innocent possession

18 USC §2252A(d) creates a defence to the offence of simple possession. It applies where the defendant:

(1) possessed less than three images of child pornography; and
(2) promptly and in good faith, and without retaining or allowing any person, other than a law enforcement agency, to access any image or copy thereof –

   (A) took reasonable steps to destroy each such image; or
   (B) reported the matter to a law enforcement agency and afforded that agency access to each such image.

This is a relatively restricted defence in that an offender must not have more than three images. Presumably the number three was chosen because it was thought that a person would not have unintentionally accessed this type of material if it were found in greater numbers. The use of the internet and possible pop-up applications perhaps casts doubt on this but it should be remembered that true unsolicited child pornography – whether sent by email, mail or produced automatically by pop-up mechanisms – will not be culpable save where the prosecution can prove that a person *knowingly* downloaded or received the images. Where, therefore, a person argues that he is in receipt of 50 unsolicited images §2252A(d) will be of no assistance but the defendant should be entitled to an acquittal if the prosecution are unable to prove that they were accessed, etc. knowingly.

The defence under §2252A(d) could apply where a person downloads material that, at the time, he believes is of adult pornography but subsequently decides (or discovers) that the subject is actually of a minor. Under these circumstances the offender should try to divest himself of the possession of the images by, for example, reporting the matter to a law enforcement agency or deleting the images. It will be remembered that a deleted image will not necessarily be erased from the machine but where an offender does not have specialist software that allows the access of such material then deleting the image (and emptying the recycle bin) is likely to be considered a reasonable step. Of course where a person has downloaded more than three images in those circumstances then the defence will not apply. As possession is a continuing offence, the person will be deemed to be in possession of them when he discovers their real age and where there are more than three images then sub-section (d) will not assist. That said, it is likely that prosecutorial discretion would mean it is unlikely a person under those circumstances would be charged where he took steps to delete the images or report them to a law enforcement agency.

Canada

The second jurisdiction to examine is that of Canada. It will be remembered from Chapter 4 that the law relating to child pornography in Canada is set out in s. 163.1 of the Criminal Code and four separate offences are created:

- Making child pornography.
- Distributing child pornography.
- Possession of child pornography.
- Accessing child pornography.

As with the United States, each of these will be examined in turn.

Making child pornography

The first offence is that contained within s. 163.1(2) and criminalises those who 'make, prints, publishes or possesses for the purpose of publication' any child pornography. The offence is punishable by a minimum sentence of one year imprisonment and a maximum of 10 years.

The term 'making' is not defined but it is submitted that it means the creation or duplication of images. Few cases have discussed the meaning of making but an important case in this context is *R v Horvat* (2006, unreported). The defendant was charged, *inter alia*, with one count of making child pornography, the particulars being that he copied child pornography on to a DVD, CD and a memory card. Counsel for the defence sought to argue that where the copying was for his own use, then this should be treated as possession and not making. Lack J, in the Superior Court of Justice, rejected this submission and stated that it was a matter of simple construction:

> Before the process, the data did not exist in that medium. After, the data on the disk or DVD or memory card can be used in different ways than it could have been if left on the hard drive.

This must be correct and thus the duplication of material must amount to the making of child pornography but does this reliance on technical processes mean that downloading images will also be considered making child pornography? It will be remembered from Chapter 6 that the courts in England and Wales adopt this approach (*R v Bowden* [2000] 1 QB 88). Certainly applying the logic of *Horvat* it could apply but there is no evidence that such a construction has been applied in Canada. An argument against this approach would be that it would unduly interfere with s. 163.1(4.1) which is concerned with accessing child pornography although most cases of computer downloading appear to treat the matter as one of possession. Certainly for the reasons given in Chapter 4 there is no reason to advocate the adoption of such an approach and it would be better for s. 163.1(2) to be restricted to the creation or duplication of images.

In most situations the child pornography made will be adduced to the court as part of the prosecution evidence but there is nothing within s. 163.1(2) that requires this. *R v CM* 2009 MBPC 35 was a slightly unusual case in that no photograph was adduced and the tribunal of fact was called upon to decide whether a photograph had, in fact, been taken. The complainant in the matter was a 6 year-old-girl who alleged that she was posed by the defendant who then took pictures of her. No photographs were adduced but the judge was satisfied that the conduct had occurred and he convicted him of the offence.

Distributing child pornography

The second offence is contained within s. 163.1(3) and criminalises anyone who 'transmits, makes available, distributes, sells, advertises, imports, exports or possesses for the purpose of transmission, making available, distribution, sale, advertising or exportation any child pornography'. As with s. 163.1(2) the offence is punishable by a minimum term of one year imprisonment and a maximum of 10 years.

Many of the words in s. 163.1(3) are straightforward and it is clear that the offence is designed to tackle the dissemination of child pornography. Reference to transmission and making available were inserted by later legislation to strengthen the law as regards computer-based child pornography (Curry, 2005: 156). It is this latter phrase – 'making available' – that has been considered by the courts. Whilst in many circumstances it will be relatively clear that a person has made information available (as in where, for example, a person hosts a bulletin board where child pornography can be downloaded); in other cases it will be less straightforward, particularly where a user uses a peer-to-peer program.

One of the first cases to discuss the use of peer-to-peer programs was *R v Johannson* 2008 SKQB 451. The appellant was detected by a police member of an internet child exploitation unit who identified that he could obtain child pornography from the defendant's use of the Gnutella file-sharing network. When arrested, the defendant's computer was found to include the 'LimeWire' file-sharing program. A forensic examination of the computer could not show any evidence of person-to-person distribution but the initial alert had demonstrated that some child pornography was capable of being downloaded by others who viewed the material in his own shared folder. The defendant stated that he was not aware that he could make material available by using the LimeWire program (at [19]) but the judge ultimately rejected this, in part because of the technical awareness of the defendant and the fact that LimeWire itself made clear it was a file-sharing program.

The important feature of the judgment, however, was the judge's ruling that the offence under s. 163.1(3) does have *mens rea* in that the accused must have the intention to make child pornography available to others (at [34]). Gabrielson J continued by noting that intention should include the 'normal inference that one intends the natural consequence of one's actions' (applying the earlier decision in *R v Missions* (2005) 196 CCC (3d) 253). The judge was clear that the natural consequence of the use of the file-sharing program and, in particular, the failure to move images to a non-sharing folder was a natural consequence and could be inferred as intention. This can be contrasted with the approach of the English courts where they have held that oblique intention is not appropriate in such circumstances (*R v Dooley* [2006] 1 WLR 775 discussed in Chapter 6) and that proof that at least one of the purposes of leaving files in a 'my shared' folder is required before a person can be convicted of the equivalent offence.

That said, the difference in approach may not be that significant. In *R v Dittrich* (2008), unreported, the defendant was charged with making available child pornography through the use of the LimeWire program. Whilst there was evidence to suggest that somebody had made child pornography images available, when the accused's computer was seized there was no material that could be made available because he had deleted it from the shared folder. Jenkins J, acquitting the defendant, noted that file-sharing programs are lawful and therefore the mere use of them could not amount to the offence of making available without proof that the accused used it 'for the purpose of sharing child pornography with others' (at [17]).

The principal difference between *Johannson* and *Dittrich* is the fact that images had been removed from the shared folder and perhaps also that in *Johannson* the defendant denied that he knew how LimeWire operated (which the judge believed was false testimony). *Dittrich* does not directly deny that oblique intent can be used although reference to purpose does appear to imply a requirement for direct intent. Realistically however the decision in *Dittrich* can be explained on the basis that the Crown could not prove who used the computer at the time when the child pornography was available for share (at [19]: more than one person had access to the machine) and thus it was not possible to prove that the defendant, who had removed the images from the shared folder, intended to make them available.

The final point to note about this section is the use of the term 'imports' in the context of computer-based child pornography. It will be remembered from Chapter 6 that there is a debate as to whether downloading child pornography from another jurisdiction would amount to the offence of importing it. In Canada the answer to this appears to be 'yes' as the Newfoundland and Labrador Court of

Appeal sustained a conviction for importing child pornography where a person paid a subscription fee which allowed him to access a computer 'bulletin board' hosted in another jurisdiction from which he could download child pornography (see *R v Daniels* 2004 NLCA 73 discussed further below).

Possession

Section 163.1(4) creates an offence of simple possession. It will be remembered that both sections 163.1(2) and 163.1(3) provided for an offence of possession with ulterior intent, but this provision is one of simple possession. The offence is punishable by a maximum term of imprisonment of five years.

The term possession is not defined within s. 163.1 but it is defined earlier in the Code. Section 4(3)(a) of the Code states:

A person has anything in possession when he has it in his personal possession or knowingly:

(i)   has it in the actual possession or custody of another person; or
(ii) has it in any place, whether or not that place belongs to or is occupied by him, for the use or benefit of himself or of another person

This is considered to create two forms of possession; actual possession and constructive possession. Actual possession was discussed in *R v York* (2005) 193 CCC (3d) 331 as meaning s. 4(3)(a)(i):

Personal possession is established where an accused person exercises physical control over a prohibited object with full knowledge of its character, however brief the contact may be, and where there is some evidence to show the accused person took custody of the object willingly with intent to deal with it in some prohibited manner.

In the context of child pornography therefore it is not enough that a person has possession of, for example, a computer containing images that amount to child pornography; the offender must know that the images are present. Thus Canadian law, as with most other jurisdictions, requires *mens rea*.

Constructive possession is contained within s. 4(3)(a)(ii) and this does not require physical custody of the material.

In this situation, control is constructive and it arises from the person having or putting the things at a place for his use or for the use of another person.
(*R v Morelli* 2008 SKCA 62 at [34])

In the context of child pornography this could include, for example, storing CDs, DVDs or memory sticks in a safe deposit box or passing it on to someone else for safe keeping. Clearly the use of constructive possession in this context ensures that someone cannot evade liability through passing material to others (although this does, perhaps, raise questions as to the distinction between constructive possession and distribution: is the latter when it is intended that the recipient will 'use' the material rather than passively keep it?).

In many instances proving possession will not be problematic. Where a person is the sole person with access to a machine, the fact that child pornography is contained on the machine and has been viewed is likely to be sufficient to prove guilt. The link between possession and control does mean that sometimes actions other than keeping material can show possession. In *R v Chalk* 2007 ONCA 815 the appellant had been convicted of possessing child pornography. The child pornography was found on a family computer to which each member of the family had access. The appellant had admitted to downloading adult pornography and watching it, sometimes with his girlfriend. The appellant had been arrested on an unrelated matter concerning the daughter of his girlfriend and when he spoke to his girlfriend after his arrest he asked her to delete all of his files from the computer before the police looked at the computer (at [6]). The girlfriend was curious as to what files were on the computer and discovered child pornography, which she subsequently reported to the police.

The appellant accepted that he knew there was child pornography on the computer but he denied that he was the one who downloaded it (although he could not say who had downloaded it). The trial judge convicted the appellant of possessing child pornography on the basis that he was aware of the existence of the child pornography and exercised control over it by instructing it to be deleted. The Court of Appeal of Ontario upheld the conviction stating that the defendant did not ask for the files to be deleted because he did not want them, but rather because he did not want the authorities to be aware that there was child pornography material on the computer (at [26]). By asking for the files to be deleted the appellant provided evidence that he was knowingly in possession of illicit material. Whilst the court accepted that sometimes a person will know that he has control over material but will not be criminally liable (at [25]) such cases are ordinarily restricted to situations where a person takes possession with the intention of either destroying the material or reporting it to the authorities. In this case it was clear that the appellant had an ulterior motive for the files being deleted (his desire to ensure that the authorities were not aware of their existence) and accordingly this exception did not apply and he demonstrated sufficient control over the material to demonstrate possession.

Whilst it would ordinarily be possible to adduce the material to prove possession it would seem that this is not always necessary nor, indeed, does it necessarily need to be shown that a person had the actual material rather than mere access to it. In *R v Daniels* 2004 NLCA 73 the appellant paid a fee to a site which allowed him to download images. Records indicated that he downloaded 13 files, eight of which were child pornography files and a further five child pornography files appeared to have been requested but aborted before transfer. None of the images were found on the appellant's computer and he argued that this was because he had pressed 'skip file', a function available on his software, that aborted the download process. His conviction for possession and importing were sustained on the basis that he had the constructive possession of the images. It will be remembered above that with constructive possession a person need not be in actual physical control of the images, indeed s. 4(3)(ii) states 'has it in any place . . . for the use or benefit of himself'. Welsh JA, giving the judgment of the court, stated that constructive requirement consisted of three elements:

• Knowledge of the item.
• Intention or consent to have possession of the item.
• Control over the item. (At [9].)

There was no doubt that the appellant had knowledge of the items as the files were clearly described as material containing child pornography. Similarly by ordering the material it was clear that the mental element was satisfied with the appellant clearly intending to possess the material, the only issue was whether he exercised control. Welsh JA stated he did:

> . . . once the downloading had begun, absent some computer malfunction, Daniels had complete control in deciding how much of the image would be displayed on the computer screen. To be in possession of child pornography, it is not necessary for the individual to have viewed the material. For example, a person may obtain pornographic material in an envelope, but without viewing it, either place it in a drawer or dispose of it in the garbage. It is the element of control, including deciding what will be done with the material, that is essential to possession.
>
> (at [12])

The judge noted that the position of the eight images ordered could be contrasted with the five images aborted in that with the former they would have been delivered but for his actions: i.e. they showed him in control, whereas with the five aborted images they would not have been delivered (at [14]).

To an extent *Daniels* could be considered to be a surprising case in that it appears authority for the proposition that ordering material online can amount to possession even where the material is never, in fact, delivered. In some jurisdictions the behaviour in *Daniels* may have been resolved through the law of attempt but this is clearly not the position in Canada. In the context of constructive possession it does make sense in that he clearly had control over the material he ordered even though physical possession was elsewhere. It does leave the question however of what the distinction is between the offences of possession and accessing. The case of *Daniels* also raises the question about the difference between possession and importing, although this is perhaps more readily understood since, in many jurisdictions, counts on an indictment are charged as representative of the behaviour, and possession is sometimes used as a catchall.

A somewhat problematic case is that of *R v Garbett* 2008 ONCJ 97. The defendant was charged, *inter alia*, with the possession of 48 images that constituted child pornography. Forty-six of these images were found on the hard disc of the defendant's computer, which only he had access to. All 46 images were recoverable only with the use of ENCASE, a specialist forensic software program. Thirty of the images were partial recoveries and the police forensic officer testified that he was not able to say whether the file had been accessed in the six months before the computer was seized. This was important because the prosecution had decided to proceed summarily, meaning that there was a limitation period of six months. Of the remaining 16 images, it was possible to state when they had been created or accessed but where the date and time was one of creation, the expert witness testified, it was not possible to say whether the offender knew that the image was being downloaded or whether it was an automatic function of the browser.

The judge ruled that at the time the computer was seized it was not possible to show that the defendant had control over the images and that as the expert prosecution witness had stated he could not be sure the offender either possessed the images within six months or was aware of the existence of the images; the defendant had to be acquitted of those charges.

It has been remarked that there are two readings of this case (Benedet, 2008). The first is that it is simply an example of the prosecution failing to prove their case. Had they not chosen to proceed summarily then the limitation period would not have been an issue. Also, the police had not discussed the defendant's knowledge in sufficient detail and this contributed to a failure to prove *mens rea*. The second reading is that the decision does make prosecuting child pornography more difficult as it could be read as deciding that it is not sufficient to prove that images were found on a computer that the defendant had sole access to, and who admits to accessing child pornography.

Garbett, at least in part, appears similar to the ruling of the English Court of Appeal in *R v Porter* [2006] 1 WLR 2633. Deleted images that can only be accessed by specialist forensic computer software cannot be considered to be in the control or possession of an offender. That is relatively uncontroversial. The time limitation point undoubtedly caused difficulties in this case. The question unanswered by this case concerns the *mens rea* of the offence. MacDonnell J stated:

> If a person exploring the internet were to come across child pornography, recognize its criminal character and then either delete it or exit out of the web site displaying it, the combination of the person's power of the image, the exercise of that power to delete it, and the knowledge of the character of the image would not necessarily constitute a possession giving rise to criminal liability.

(at [47])

This, it is submitted, goes to the issue of the automatic downloading of an image. MacDonnell J appears to be saying that where there is unintentional access then the automatic downloading of an image should not amount to possession. Where, however, the person did not do this then arguably possession may be satisfied. The prosecution must adduce evidence to show that the offender deliberately sought child pornography or was aware that child pornography could exist. It will be remembered from Chapter 6 that English law places its emphasis on the defendant knowing how a cache operated (*Smith; Jayson* [2003] 1 Cr App R 13 and *R v Harrison* [2008] 1 Cr App R 29). Perhaps if Garbett had been asked whether he knew that images he viewed on line would be automatically downloaded by his browser (which, in this day and age is likely) then the prosecution could have succeeded. This line of reasoning would appear to gather some support from the case *R v Braudy* [2009] OJ No. 347 where the Ontario Supreme Court of Justice stated that whilst the possibility of inadvertent web browsing and pop-ups does exist, a court should not place too much emphasis on this, in part because awareness on the part of the user that the material may be present on what he is browsing will suffice (at [54]). The earlier case of *R v Jenner* (2005) 195 CCC (3d) also emphasised the fact that exculpatory theories require evidence for support. In *Garbett* arguably the prosecution did the defence's work by raising potential exculpatory defences but without adducing evidence to contradict them. If the Crown shows that a user is aware that child pornography is present and addresses the issue of automatic downloads then it would seem that a prosecution is more likely to succeed.

Accessing

The fourth offence is that contained within s. 163.1(4.1), which was a later addition to the Criminal Code. This section criminalises those who 'access' child pornography. The offence is punishable by a maximum sentence of five years' imprisonment, i.e. the equivalent of possession. Section 163.1(4.2) defines 'access' for the purposes of this part of the Code as:

> . . . a person accesses child pornography who knowingly causes child pornography to be viewed by, or transmitted to, himself or herself.

The inclusion of transmission is perhaps surprising (as this is a verb used in the distribution offence) but the key here is that it must be to himself. Accordingly where a defendant was to log on to a bulletin board and download an image of child pornography it would seem that this would amount to an offence of accessing child pornography.

Accessing child pornography will also clearly cover those situations where a person browses the internet looking for child pornography but who does not download them. It was noted in Chapter 6 that in *R v Jayson* [2003] 1 Cr App R 13 this was controversially dealt with in England and Wales through the offence of making. The Canadian treatment of a specific offence related to possession must be the preferred option. It is notable that s. 163.1(4.2) makes clear that a mental element is required: the person must knowingly access child pornography and this must mean that the person is deliberately seeking access to child pornography. Where the material is displayed accidentally then no liability can arise although presumably if a person, once alerted to the existence of child pornography, continues to browse it that person could be guilty of the offence at that point.

The biggest issue with the offence of accessing is perhaps understanding its distinction to possession. It will be recalled from the earlier discussion that cases such as *Daniels* 2004 NLCA 73 demonstrate that a person can be guilty of possession even when no photograph is in their physical custody. The behaviour in *Daniels* (browsing a file-transfer program and selecting images to download) is perhaps better suited to the offence of accessing child pornography although, that said, it is possible that where the site merely describes a photograph rather than displaying it that it could not come within the offence of accessing as the user does not 'cause child pornography to be viewed'. That said, in *R v Carsewell* 2009 ONCJ 297 Dawson J, in the Ontario Court of Justice, stated:

> I have come to the conclusion . . . that a person who is accessing child pornography on a web site is in possession of the child pornography at the time they are viewing it. They have control over it at that point, they have possession of it on their screen, and they are able to view it, download it, or store it at that point in time.
>
> (at [398])

Given this statement it would seem that there is a considerable overlap between the offences of accessing and possession. Given the conclusion of Dawson J and the broad definition of possession outlined above it could be questioned whether there is a need for the offence of accessing and whether it would be preferable, therefore, to simply charge possession in circumstances where a person is deliberately viewing child pornography on the screen.

Defences

A number of defences exist to the child pornography laws in Canada. Some of these defences are set out in the Criminal Code itself and others are set out within case law, most prominently the two 'exceptions' (which must be *de facto* defences) identified in *Sharpe* 2001 2 SCC 2.

Age

The first defence is that contained within s. 163.1(5) and it states:

> It is not a defence to a charge under subsection (2) in respect of a visual representation that the accused believed that a person shown in the representation

that is alleged to constitute child pornography was or was depicted as being under eighteen years of age or more unless the accused took all reasonable steps to ascertain the age of that person and took all reasonable steps to ensure that, where the person was eighteen years of age or more, the representation did not depict that person as being under the age of eighteen years.

This is quite a convoluted statement but, in essence, means that a mistake of age must be based on reasonable grounds. Interestingly the defence appears to apply only to subsection (2) which concerns the making of child pornography. The defence makes clear that the defendant must take all reasonable steps to ascertain that the person depicted in the visual representation is aged 18 or over *and* that the representation does not depict the person as being under the age of 18. The issue of age depiction was discussed in Chapter 4 and it was noted that a literal interpretation would seem to include 'dress-down pornography' irrespective of whether it was obvious the person depicted was aged 18 or over, but that the Canadian courts had held that the preferred construction of the section was to adopt an objective approach to the question of age (see, for example, *R v Garbett* 2008 ONCJ 97).

Section 163.1(5) refers only to the offence of making: what is the position in respect of the distribution or possession of child pornography? In *R v Geisel* (2000, unreported) Giesbrecht PJ was asked to consider whether a defence existed for someone who possessed child pornography but who took reasonable steps to ascertain that the child was above the relevant age (in that case, 14). The learned judge did not decide the point directly because he found that the defendant and had not taken reasonable steps to ascertain the age (at [106]) but the judge implied that no defence would exist under these circumstances.

Public good

Section 163.1(6) includes a catch-all public defence. It states:

No person shall be convicted of an offence under this section if the act that is alleged to constitute the offence:

(a) has a legitimate purpose related to the administration of justice or to science, medicine, education or art; and
(b) does not pose an undue risk of harm to persons under the age of eighteen years.

This is an interesting provision because it has been heavily amended from the original text of s. 163.1 whereby the defence used to say:

Where the accused is charged with an offence ... the court shall find the accused not guilty if the representation or written material that is alleged to constitute child pornography has artistic merit, or an educational, scientific or medical purpose.

Thus it can be seen that the original wording talked about artistic *merit* whereas it now states that it has a legitimate purpose related, *inter alia*, to art. In *R v Paintings, Drawings and Photographic Slides of Paintings* [1995] OJ 1045 McCombs J, sitting in the Ontario Supreme Court, had to rule upon the original wording of the defence. The learned judge held that the wording clearly differentiated between educational, scientific or medical purpose on the one hand and artistic merit on the other (at [81]). The judge held that artistic merit must mean that it must 'potentially provide something of value to the viewer' (at [86]) before ultimately concluding that 'the legal meaning of the artistic merit defence includes a consideration of standards of community tolerance based on the risk of harm to children' (at [189]).

In *R v Sharpe* 2001 SCC 2 the Chief Justice of Canada, McLachlin CJC, disagreed with the ruling of McCombe J. The Chief Justice argued that whilst artistic merit could be taken to mean that it must have some objective merit, this carried with it the risk that poor, inept or artists at the beginning of their career may not be entitled to plead the defence (at [62]). The Chief Justice preferred the argument that artistic merit meant possessing the quality of art (at [63]) and held 'I am not persuaded that we should read a community standards qualification into the defence' (at [65]).

Since *Sharpe* the defence has clearly been amended and it is not clear what difference, if at all, this change of wording makes. The emphasis is clearly now on whether there is an artistic purpose rather than artistic merit but this perhaps does not add much to the equation. Presumably it will mean that where it can be shown that the person making, distributing or possessing child pornography did so for the purposes of sexual gratification then the defence will not apply, irrespective of whether it could be construed by critics as art. However where it is not possible to show sexual gratification, will the change of wording realistically make any difference? Surely 'for the purpose of art' will be construed to include those people who claim that they have produced representations of child pornography to challenge the views of society in respect of this behaviour? In the *R v Paintings* case, the art was described in detail and included paintings that brought with it impressions that a child had performed the act of fellatio on an adult. McCombs J, hearing evidence from artists, formed the view that 'the work as a whole is presented in a condemnatory manner that is not intended to celebrate the subject matter. In other words, the purpose of the work is not to condone child sexual abuse, but to lament the reality of it' ([1995] OJ 1045 at [45]). Would a different result be achieved under the new wording? Probably not.

In terms of the other purposes contained within s. 163.1(6) these are, to an extent, somewhat unproblematic and take account of the fact that a variety of professionals may need access to child pornography. It was noted in Chapter 4 that the law in England and Wales is relatively strict in the circumstances that a defence may apply. Indeed, whilst the defence of 'legitimate purpose' to the offence of possession may cover educational, scientific or medical purposes (discussed in *Atkins v DPP* [2000] 1 WLR 1427) it will be remembered that this defence does not, theoretically, avail those who download or show such material. The Canadian legislation goes further and expressly provides the defence to all offences relating to child pornography. In *R v Sharpe* 2001 SCC 2 the Supreme Court of Canada held that the defences should be interpreted liberally (at [69]) although McLachlin CJC did imply that any claim should be sceptically received when she noted that 'arguably few medical, educational and scientific works would fall within s. 163.1' (at [68]).

It should also be noted that the revised wording makes clear that the defence applies only where it does not pose 'an undue risk of harm to persons under the age of eighteen'. Quite what that means in practice has not yet been decided but it is presumably designed to tackle those situations where someone purports to make child pornography for a legitimate purpose but in doing so actually creates harm to the child through, for example, the proliferation of child pornography or by, for example, causing them to have harmful sexual relationships. It can be questioned whether paragraph (b) actually adds anything to situations other than art since it is difficult to see how a bona fide scientific, medical or educational project would pose such a risk of harm. The defence may, however, prevent an artist from filming two 13 year-olds having sex as a piece of 'living art'. It is likely that irrespective of what, if any, artistic merit is pleaded in such a situation the harm to the children in being enticed to have sexual intercourse below the age of consent would counteract the defence.

Australia

The third jurisdiction to examine is that of Australia. It will be remembered from Chapter 4 that this is a federal country consisting of six states and two self-governing territories. As with Chapter 4 it will be possible to examine how each jurisdiction criminalises actions relating to child pornography. It will be remembered from Chapter 4 that the Parliament of Western Australia is currently debating major changes in its law. In this section the law which is in force at the time of writing will be stated. Where there is the opportunity to do so however a commentary will be made on what impact the proposed changes may make to the law.

Most jurisdictions differentiate between the offences through their inclusion in discrete sections, however the Northern Territory is unique in that it is contained in a single section (s. 125B, Criminal Code Act). The offence has the marginal note of 'possession of child pornography' but it is then defined in subsection (1) as:

A person who possesses, distributes, produces, sells or offers or advertises for distribution or sale child abuse material . . .

All forms of behaviour are subject to the same penalty (a maximum of 10 years' imprisonment: see s. 125(1)(a)). As these terms are used by other jurisdictions within their offences they will be examined at that point.

The Australian Capital Territory adopts a similar approach although it separates out the offence of simple possession. A person who produces, publishes, offers or sells child pornography commits the offence of 'trading in child pornography' (s. 64A, Crimes Act 1900) whereas simple possession is dealt with under s. 65. The penalties differ with trading being punishable by a maximum sentence of 12 years' imprisonment (s. 64A(1)) and simple possession being punishable by a maximum sentence of five years' imprisonment (s. 65(1)). As with the Northern Territory, these terms will be considered below.

Production or making

The first category of offences to examine is that of the production or making of child pornography. Table 8.1 discusses whether each jurisdiction deals with either or both.

It can be seen that all jurisdictions other than Western Australia currently criminalise the production of child pornography (s. 60, Classification (Publications, Films and Computer Games) Enforcement Act 1996 criminalises the possession, possession with intent, sale or supply of child pornography). That said, it is an offence to copy child pornography where it is intended to sell or supply child pornography (s. 60(1)(a)). The Child Exploitation Material and Classification Legislation Amendment Bill, currently before Parliament, will alter this in that it is intended to amend the Criminal Code of the State to, *inter alia*, criminalise the production of child pornography (by inserting a new s. 218 into the Code).

It can be seen from Table 8.1 that the majority of Australian jurisdictions refer to the 'production' of child pornography. The term 'produces' is rarely defined but it is submitted that it is likely to mean to bring into existence. It could also

Table 8.1 Production or making

Jurisdiction	Producing	Making
Australian Capital Territory	✓	✗
Commonwealth	✓	✗
New South Wales	✓	✗
Northern Territory	✓	✗
Queensland	✓	✓
South Australia	✓	✗
Tasmania	✓	✗
Victoria	✓	✗
Western Australia	✗	✗

involve the duplication of material but what of downloading? In *R v Leonard (No. 3)* [2008] NSWDC 211 Berman SC DCJ commented, when passing sentence on an offender, that downloading material amounted to possession (at [16]). Whilst obviously not conclusive as it is only the District Court of one jurisdiction – and a comment made in a sentencing decision at that – it would seem to indicate that the principle used in England and Wales of treating downloading as the making of child pornography is not followed in Australia. Certainly a reading of other sentencing cases would suggest that downloading images is ordinarily dealt with through the offences of possession rather than the production of child pornography. It was noted in Chapter 6 that this is arguably the more appropriate manner to deal with downloading and as possession is punished appropriately in each of the Australian jurisdictions there is no real reason for downloading to be treated as production.

Distribution

The second offence to consider is that of the distribution of material. It can be seen from Table 8.2 that all the jurisdictions criminalise distribution in some form but in three jurisdictions the matter is subject to some caveats.

Australian Capital Territory

It will be remembered that the Australian Capital Territory uses a single offence to deal with actions other than simple possession (s. 64A, Crimes Act 1900). This refers to 'produces, publishes, offers or sells child pornography'. The term distributes is not expressly used and it could be questioned whether simple forms of distribution are necessarily covered by the legislation. Whilst 'offers' and 'sells' may cover a significant proportion of distribution it is not clear that it will cover all types of distribution. For example, if X asks Y to send him an

Table 8.2 Distribution

Jurisdiction	Distribution
Australian Capital Territory	✓[a]
Commonwealth	✓
New South Wales	✓
Northern Territory	✓
Queensland	✓
South Australia	✓
Tasmania	✓
Victoria	✓[a]
Western Australia	✓[a]

Note
a See text for further explanation.

image of a child and Y does so, has there been distribution? It may well depend on how X knows that Y has that image: if he has been told by Y that he does then this may amount to offering but it is not clear that this will cover all eventualities.

The other alternative is to use the term 'publishes'. Whilst this term is not defined in the Act or the Legislation Act 2001 it is a word of ordinary usage and the *Oxford English Dictionary* defines the verb as 'to make public'. Clearly therefore placing an image on the internet would be considered to be publishing but would the transmission of an image from one person to another? There is no reason why it should not and the dictionary further defines the verb 'publish' to mean 'to communicate to a person or persons' meaning that the sending of child pornography to another person should come within the term publishes.

State of Victoria

The State of Victoria primarily deals with offences relating to child pornography in the Crimes Act 1958 but that legislation does not, on the face of it, tackle the distribution of child pornography (with it merely tackling the production and possession of child pornography). However distribution is dealt with under separate legislation, the Classification (Publications, Films and Computer Games) (Enforcement) Act 1995. Section 57A of that offence provides for an offence of 'publishing or transmitting child pornography', this being defined as:

> A person who knowingly uses an online information service to publish or transmit, or make available for transmission, objectionable material that describes or depicts a person who is, or looks like, a minor engaging in sexual activity or depicted in an indecent sexual manner or context is guilty of [an offence].

Thus online distribution will be covered although it is notable that the definition of child pornography for the purposes of the 1995 Act is subtly different to that used in the Crimes Act 1958 (discussed in Chapter 4). The primary difference is the inclusion of the requirement that the child should be depicted in an 'indecent sexual manner' whereas under the Crimes Act 1958 the material includes any description or depiction of a minor engaging in sexual activity. In most situations this distinction is likely to be slight as most depictions of a minor engaging in sexual activity would probably meet the indecent test and so where distribution takes place online then this would amount to a criminal offence. Where distribution is not covered, of course, is where online communication technologies are not used (save where it is through the use of a carriage service when it amounts to Commonwealth law as the carriage service is a federal service and thus brings the matter within federal law). That said, it would seem the vast majority of distribution now takes place over the internet, other ICT or the mail and so any loophole is theoretical rather than practical.

Western Australia

Western Australia does not criminalise all forms of the distribution of child pornography. The current legislation is similar to that in the Australian Capital Territory in that only the sale or supply (or offer to sell or supply) child pornography is culpable (s. 60(1)(b), Classification (Publications, Films and Computer Games) Enforcement Act 1996). Arguably 'supply' is wide enough to cover most forms of distribution although it is not known whether the courts would currently require there to be a commercial element to this (in that it is prefaced by the word 'sells'). On a plain reading of the term there is no reason why it should and thus it may be that distribution is adequately covered.

The Child Exploitation Material and Classification Legislation Amendment Bill currently before the Western Australia Parliament will, if passed in its current form, clarify the position by introducing a specific offence of distributing child pornography (new s. 219 of the Criminal Code). This new offence will cover all forms of distribution including non-commercial transmission. It will be a significant improvement on the current position.

Other jurisdictions

The term 'distribution' (or 'dissemination' as it is called in New South Wales and South Australia) is frequently further defined. For example, the New South Wales legislation defines 'disseminate' as:

(a)   send, supply, exhibit, transmit or communicate it to another person; or
(b)   make it available for access by another person; or
(c)   enter into any agreement or arrangement to do so.

(s. 91H, Crimes Act 1900)

This definition makes it very clear that all forms of distribution will be covered by this legislation, including the making available of images. It is notable that distribution does not *have* to occur. The making available of material will be covered irrespective of whether anyone actually distributes the material and also by paragraph (c) which criminalises the making of an agreement to do so. Accordingly if D agrees to send an image that constitutes child pornography to Y then he will be guilty of dissemination irrespective of whether he does. Paragraph (c) could be important in the context of sting operations since it will not matter to the liability of D if Y is a police officer.

Making available

Related to the issue of distribution is that of making child pornography to others. It has been noted already that an issue of particular relevance in modern times is the use of websites of peer-to-peer program that allow people to access files on a host computer. In Chapter 6 the issue of peer-to-peer availability was noted and, in essence, this means that where a file is included within a 'shared' folder it is possible for others to access the material. Some jurisdictions in Australia have criminalised this. See Table 8.3.

The position in respect of 'making available' is slightly equivocal. Whilst a clear majority of jurisdictions do criminalise making child pornography available, the position in three jurisdictions; the Australian Capital Territory, the Northern Territory and Victoria must be discussed in more detail.

Western Australia currently does not criminalise making available child pornography but the Child Exploitation Material and Classification Legislation Amendment Bill currently before the Western Australia Parliament will, if passed in its current form, introduce such an offence by expressly stating that making child pornography available amounts to the offence of distribution (by inserting a new s. 219(1)(b) into the Criminal Code).

Australian Capital Territory and Northern Territory

The law in both the Australian Capital Territory and Northern Territory does not expressly mention making material available although they do both criminalise the offering of material (s. 64A, Crimes Act 1900 and s. 125C, Criminal Code Act respectively). Whilst this term is not defined it is quite possible that it would cover situations whereby a person makes material available to others. However the term 'offer' does suggest a more positive act than merely making material available: it suggests that a person is consciously deciding to provide material to another person rather than merely allowing anyone to access their files.

Victoria

In the State of Victoria the making available of child pornography is dealt with under the Classification (Publications, Films and Computer Games)(Enforcement) Act

Table 8.3 Making available

Jurisdiction	Making available
Australian Capital Territory	✗[a]
Commonwealth	✓
New South Wales	✓
Northern Territory	✗[a]
Queensland	✓
South Australia	✓
Tasmania	✓
Victoria	✓[a]
Western Australia	✗

Note
a See text for further explanation.

1995 (s. 57A). Accordingly it is restricted to material classed as child pornography under that Act (rather than the wider definition given under the Crimes Act 1958) and that to material which is made available through the use of an online communications system although that would certainly cater for peer-to-peer networks.

Mental requirement

Where making child pornography available does amount to a criminal offence then what is its mental requirement? It will be remembered that in the English case of *R v Dooley* [2006] 1 WLR 775 it was held that a person must have, as at least one of their purposes, the intention to disseminate material for them to be guilty of the offence of possession with intent to supply material. It could be argued that the offence of possession with intent differs to making material available, at least as regards the mental element. It will be remembered from Chapter 4 that certainly the English Court of Appeal questioned whether oblique intent applies to the offence of possession with intent. In *R v Molloy* [2008] SASC 352 Kelly J, in the South Australian Court of Criminal Appeal, said of the mental element for making material available:

> One of the critical issues for the jury's determination . . . [is] whether the prosecution have proved beyond reasonable doubt that the appellant intended to make the child pornography material found on his computer available to others, or at the very least, that he had the knowledge that he was making available child pornography material or he was reckless with respect to the fact that he was making available material which constituted child pornography.
>
> (at [43])

This demonstrates that there is a mental element but that it is arguably less stringent than that required in England and Wales in that intention or recklessness will suffice. In *R v Salsone, ex parte the Attorney General of Queensland* [2008] QCA 220 the Court of Appeal of Queensland were concerned with the equivalent offence. The defendant was charged with making child pornography available when he downloaded material but kept it in his 'shared folder' (i.e. equivalent facts to *Dooley*). The police, when interviewing him, adduced responses from him to show that he was technically proficient and that he was aware how the peer-to-peer system worked. The court noted:

> . . . it is an offence to make child exploitation material available for access by someone, even if the material is not actually 'distributed' in the ordinary sense of that word. [The defendant's] admission that it was possible for other LimeWire users to access images from the Limewire folder and downloaded them, one at a time, was sufficient to constitute the offence of distributing child exploitation material.
>
> (at [11])

This would suggest that the knowledge of how the system works is sufficient as a mental element even if there is no positive intent to make the material available.

Possession

All jurisdictions criminalise the simple possession of child pornography and thus it is not necessary to produce a table. In most jurisdictions it attracts a lesser penalty than that which is involved in the production or dissemination of the material but this is not true in the Northern Territory where, as noted at the beginning of this section, all activities are under the same offence.

Most jurisdictions do not define the term possession although some do. Queensland refers to it as:

> having under control in any place whatever, whether for the use or benefit of the person of whom the term is used or of another person, and although another person has the actual possession or custody of the thing in question.
>
> (s. 1 of the Criminal Code)

Thus possession would appear to be related to the issue of custody and control, concepts that were also found in England and Wales and Canada. Should possession have a mental element to it? Some jurisdictions address this issue expressly whereas others are silent. Possession of child pornography in Tasmania requires a person to be in possession and that he 'knows, or ought to have known, that the material is child exploitation material' (s. 130C, Criminal Code Act 1924). The inclusion of 'ought to have known' widens the mental element beyond mere knowledge and includes situations where a person could reasonably be expected to have known that the material was child pornography.

New South Wales adopts a slightly different approach stating that a person will be deemed to have possession who:

(a) has any property in his or her custody; or
(b) knowingly has any property in the custody of another person; or
(c) knowingly has any such property in a house, building, lodging, apartment, field, or other place, whether belonging to or occupied by himself or herself or not, and whether such property is there had or placed for his or her own use, or the use of another.

> (s. 7, Crimes Act 1900)

Thus the mental element of knowledge is only required in respect of situations where a person does not have the property in their custody. This is presumably because the concept of custody requires a person to be aware that they have property in their possession. Of course the New South Wales legislation (as with most other jurisdiction save for Queensland and the Northern Territory discussed above) is silent as to whether there is a double fault element: the first in respect of knowledge that they have material in their possession and the second that the material amounts to child pornography. The most important case in this area is *He Kaw Teh v R* [1985] HCA 43 which did not, in fact, refer to child pornography at all. The case concerned drugs offences and a question as to the meaning of possession was raised. The High Court of Australia ruled:

> A person cannot . . . possess something when he is unaware of its existence or presence. But he will, since possession is used in its barest sense, possess something if he has custody or control of the things itself or of the receptacle or place in which it is to be found provided that he knows of its presence. He need not know what it is (other than to the necessary extent to know of its presence) nor its qualities. Thus a person will possess narcotic goods if he has, to his knowledge, custody or control of something which is in fact a narcotic substance, even if its packaging prevents him from knowing what it is and even if he does not know its quality as a narcotic substance.
>
> (at [31] per Gibbs CJ)

It has been accepted in at least the Supreme Court of New South Wales that *He Kaw Teh* can be read across into laws relating to child pornography (see *Clark v R* [2008] NSWCCA 122) and certainly there seems no reason why it should not (save in those jurisdictions where the mental element is addressed more specifically). The second part of the extract of the judgment of Chief Justice Gibbs above also answers the question about the possible second mental element for child pornography. If the same reasoning is to be applied – and it is suggested that it should – then it would seem that it is only necessary to prove that a person is in possession of material that turns out to be child pornography not that it is necessary that they know it is child pornography. If this is correct then it would seem that the position in Australia mirrors that in England and Wales (see *R v Collier* [2005] 1 WLR 843 and the discussion in Chapter 6) rather than the position in Canada where it is necessary to prove knowledge of the character of the material (*R v York* (2005) 193 CCC (3d) 331), i.e. knowledge that it was child pornography.

Reverse burden

It was noted earlier that the Northern Territory adopts a single offence that criminalises all actions in respect of child pornography. An interesting provision within the offence is that the legislation itself creates a presumption in respect of possession.

> In respect of a charge against a person of having committed an offence against this section, proof that child abuse material was at the material time in or on a place of which the person was:
>
> (a)   the occupier; or
> (b)   concerned in the management or control;

is evidence that the child abuse material was then in the person's possession unless it is shown that the person then neither knew nor had reason to suspect that the child abuse material was in or on that place.

(s. 125B(3), Criminal Code Act)

This clearly creates a reverse burden of proof although this will only apply where the prosecution can prove (to the required standard) that material was found, that the material was 'child abuse material' within the meaning of that Act (discussed above) and that the defendant was either the occupier of the place where it was found or that he was concerned in its management or control. That said, this is an interesting proposition since it will not be easy for a defendant to disprove the allegation, especially since he needs to prove that he could not reasonably *have* known that it was child abuse material.

Deleted images

It was noted in Chapter 6 and in other parts of this chapter, that a particular issue that arises in respect of child pornography is where the material is either stored in the computer's cache or where the material has been deleted and later recovered forensically. In respect of material stored in the cache this was addressed, albeit indirectly, by the Supreme Court of New South Wales in *DPP v Kear* [2006] NSWSC 1145. The defendant had been charged with possession of child pornography in respect of 5,000 thumbnail and 247 larger images of children found in his internet cache. The defendant admitted paying for access to a child pornography website but denied ever downloading any images. There was no evidence to suggest that the defendant knew how the cache worked (at [8]) and faced with this evidence the prosecution conceded (and the court implicitly approves) that possession would not be possible under such circumstances (at [9]) since the defendant cannot be said to know of their existence (thus failing to satisfy the first limb of the possession tests). In essence this is comparable to the decision of the Divisional Court of England and Wales in *Atkins v DPP* [2000] Cr App R 248.

Similar logic obviously applies in respect of images that are recovered forensically after deletion. The Supreme Court of New South Wales was called upon to consider this issue in *Clark v R* [2008] NSWCCA 122. The accused was charged with possession of a substantial quantity of child pornography. Some of the files were contained within the temporary internet cache and some were recovered forensically after they had been deleted. In respect of the images within the cache the Supreme Court simply adopted the same logic as in *Kear*. However as regards the deleted images they expressly considered the English case of *R v Porter* [2006] EWCA Crim 560 which, it will be remembered from Chapter 6, decided that a person could not be said to be in possession of images that they have lost control over: i.e. images that they could no longer access. In *Clark* Barr J stated:

No doubt some users of computers are highly expert in the art and realise that data which have been 'deleted' may remain in whole or in part upon the hard drive and may by employing suitable means, be identified and retrieved. No doubt many other users of computers believe that the word 'deleted' means what it says. Such persons, wishing to rid themselves forever of material on their computers, believe that by following the deletion procedure they have achieved exactly that end.

(at [227])

The judge then continued:

The [judge] was obliged to ask himself whether the accused knew that the data reproduced . . . existed on the hard drive at the date of search and, if so, whether he knew how to retrieve them.

(at [246])

Thus the Australian courts appear to have adopted the same approach to the possession of deleted images as the courts in England and Wales. Of course it should be stressed that this ruling is limited to a charge of possession and, even then, at the time of the search. It was noted in Chapter 6 that a possible work-around to *Porter* would be to charge possession prior to deletion although this would be subject to any limitation period and also proof that the person did possess the material at that time (and that it was not someone else). Accordingly where it could be proven that the accused possessed images prior to deletion (by adducing forensic evidence of the downloading or accessing of images) then it may be possible to convict a person on that basis (subject to any defences discussed below).

Accessing

The final offence to consider is that of accessing. It is notable that in *DPP v Kear* [2006] NSWSC 1145 the accused admitted to deliberately accessing child pornography websites but was acquitted of possession of those images on the basis that he did not know they were automatically saved to his cache. Some Australian jurisdictions have altered the law to provide for liability through accessing child pornography which must, for example, include browsing the internet. Table 8.4 details which offences currently expressly criminalise assessing.

It can be seen that currently only a minority of jurisdictions in Australia have adopted this approach, with it currently being restricted to the Commonwealth and the States of Tasmania and South Australia. Each of these jurisdictions require that a person intentionally accesses child pornography. Tasmania is perhaps the simplest provision in that it provides for a person 'who, with intent to access child exploitation material, accesses child exploitation material is guilty of a crime' (s. 130D, Criminal Code Act 1924). This must mean that the person must

Table 8.4 Accessing

Jurisdiction	Accessing
Australian Capital Territory	✗
Commonwealth	✓
New South Wales	✗
Northern Territory	✗
Queensland	✗
South Australia	✓
Tasmania	✓
Victoria	✗
Western Australia	✗

intentionally access material that amounts to child pornography, i.e. the person is aware that the material being accessed is child pornography.

The South Australian law criminalises someone who 'intending to obtain access to child pornography, obtains access to child pornography or takes a step towards obtaining access to child pornography' (s. 63A(1)(b), Criminal Law Consolidation Act 1935). This must mean that the mental element is the same as in Tasmania but it is notable that access need not take place (although in the other jurisdictions this may be dealt with by an attempt). Accordingly where X seeks to access a particular website that he knows has child pornography hosted on it but the site for whatever fails to load then he has still committed the crime.

The Commonwealth law differs in that it splits the mental element. It provides that a person must intentionally access material but be merely reckless as to whether that material amounts to child pornography: s. 479.19(2)(b), Criminal Code Act 1995). This is certainly wider than either the law in Tasmania or South Australia and would cover situations where, for example, a person accesses teenage pornography without checking whether the age of the person depicted was, or appeared to be, over the age of 16 (the relevant age for Commonwealth law).

It has been noted that not every jurisdiction in Australia creates an offence of accessing child pornography and it is perhaps interesting to note that the Child Exploitation Material and Classification Legislation Amendment Bill currently before the Western Australia Parliament will not introduce such an offence. It is not clear why this is the case but presumably the Bill's authors believe that accessing can be dealt with through the offence of possession. However it was noted in Chapter 2 that there are circumstances when accessing child pornography could be considered as problematic as possessing child pornography and yet not come within the legal meaning of that term. It will be for the courts to decide whether possession can cover facilities such as cloud storage.

Defences

The final issue to consider is the defences that apply to the various offences. Most jurisdictions expressly include a number of defences within their provisions. Table 8.5 lists how the various jurisdictions deal with defences.

It can be seen that South Australia lists only one defence (that of unsolicited material, see s. 63A(2), Criminal Law Consolidation Act 1935). The Australian Capital Territory also lists only one (s. 65(3), Crimes Act 1900):

> It is a defence to a prosecution for an offence against this section if the defendant proves that the defendant had no reasonable grounds for suspecting that the pornography concerned was child pornography.

Given that the prosecution bear the burden of proving the elements of the definition set out in Chapter 4, it can be questioned whether this is truly a defence. Realistically it will be comparatively rare for this to be pleaded as it is more likely that the prosecution would need to prove that the defendant is aware of the material. It may conceivably be of relevance in respect of the offender's understanding of age, i.e. whether the offender had reasonable grounds to believe that the person depicted was over the age of 16 (the age of a 'child' for the purposes of child pornography). If they did then the defence must come into play as the defendant can prove that he was not aware that this was *child* pornography rather than adult pornography.

Law enforcement

All but three jurisdictions expressly cater for a defence for law enforcement. The equivalent offence was considered in Chapter 6 for England and Wales. The

Table 8.5 Defences

Jurisdiction	LE	PB	C	UM	YPD
Australian Capital Territory[a]	✗	✗	✗	✗	✗
Commonwealth	✓	✓	✗	✗	✗
New South Wales	✓	✓	✓	✓	✗
Northern Territory	✓	✗	✓	✗	✗
Queensland	✗[a]	✓	✓	✗	✗
South Australia	✗	✗	✗	✓	✗
Tasmania	✓	✓	✓	✓	✓
Victoria	✓	✓[a]	✓	✗	✓
Western Australia	✓	✓	✓	✓	✗

Notes: *LE* Law enforcement. *PB* Public benefit (including artistic merit). *C* Material has been classified. *UM* Unsolicited Material. *YPD* Young person's defence.
a See text for further details.

defence applies only where it is necessary to the conduct of the investigation or prosecution of law enforcement and very little needs to be said on this as it is obviously an appropriate defence.

The State of Queensland does not expressly mention law enforcement as a defence but it does have a defence of public benefit (s. 228E(2)(a), Criminal Code Act) and also to institutions that have been provided with an exemption (s. 228E(3)). It is highly likely that law enforcement activities would be brought within either definition. As noted above, the legislation of South Australia and the Australian Capital Territory do not contain defences but presumably in these jurisdictions the matter would simply rely on prosecutorial discretion. A prosecutor will not proceed where a law enforcement officer (or equivalent) is required to download, make or possess images for the purposes of investigating or prosecuting of crime.

Public benefit

The Commonwealth legislation provides for a defence where something is for a public benefit (s. 474.21(1), Criminal Code Act 1995) although the legislation is clear that it must not extend beyond that necessary for the public benefit. The term public benefit is then defined to include situations where it is necessary to enforce the law, the administration of justice or conducting 'scientific, medical or educational research'. The issue of the enforcement and prosecution of the law was dealt with above which leaves the science, medicine and education. The Commonwealth legislation is unique in that it requires such research to have ministerial approval (s. 474.21, Criminal Code Act). All other jurisdictions (other than South Australia and the Australian Capital Territory as discussed previously) contain exemptions for scientific, medical or educational research but they do not require political authorisation. The legislation does not make clear whether the exemption is a question of law or fact although it is submitted that it is most likely to be a question of fact. As with the position in England and Wales (see *Atkins v DPP* [2000] Cr App R 248) it is submitted that it is likely only bona fide research will be exempt.

The States of Victoria, Western Australia, New South Wales, Queensland and Tasmania all have a defence for artistic merit (at least in respect of possession). In none of these pieces of legislation is the term artistic merit defined nor is it explained whether it is a matter of law or fact. The difficulty of using words such as 'artistic merit' was discussed in the context of Canadian law. The issue of artistic merit must also raise questions as to whether the use of expert evidence is admissible when deciding whether material has artistic merit.

Most jurisdictions qualify the defence of artistic merit in some way. For example, in Queensland the use of the material must be reasonable in the circum-stances (s. 228E(2)(b), Criminal Code Act) and presumably this is to ensure that people cannot rely on artistic exemptions where the material is harmful to a child. A similar approach is adopted by New South Wales where the defence must be placed in the context of the circumstances in which it was produced or intended to be used (s. 91H(4)(c), Crimes Act 1900). In Victoria the defence of artistic merit is qualified by stating that it does not apply where the prosecution rely on the fact that the child is actually (as distinct from appearing to be) under the age of 18 (s. 70(3), Crimes Act 1958).

Chapter 2 discussed the tension that undoubtedly exists between art and child pornography and the Australian legislation (unlike the position in England and Wales) is obviously seeking to address this in part. That said, it is quite clear that art should not be used as an excuse where a child has been actually harmed or exploited and the qualification of this defence is to be welcomed.

Classification

Most jurisdictions provide for a defence where it can be shown that material has been granted a certificate by a relevant censorship body. Clearly this is an appropriate defence; it would be inconsistent for the law to on the one hand decide that it can be produced or distributed but on the other hand decide it could not be accessed or possessed. A similar defence also exists for those who undertake the classification, as clearly those who exercise this responsibility should not be criminalised for the possession of such material when it was given to them for that purpose.

Unsolicited material

Western Australia, New South Wales, South Australia and Tasmania all have a defence in respect of unsolicited material. All premise the defence on the premise that the material was sent unsolicited and that once the defendant became aware of its existence, they took reasonable steps to remove it. This is comparable to the defence in England and Wales contained within s. 160(2)(c), Criminal Justice Act 1988. As with the position in England and Wales it is not clear whether the material has to be unsolicited or whether it is child pornography that must be unsolicited. So, for example, where A orders a DVD of what he believes is adult pornography but a DVD of child pornography is sent instead, can A still plead the defence? It would seem logical to say that the answer should be 'yes'. What are reasonable steps to delete the material will depend on the circumstances of each case and, when computers are involved, will presumably include the technical proficiency of the offender (since if he is aware how to 'undelete' images then simple deletion will presumably not suffice).

Young person's defence

The State of Victoria has two defences that could amount to a 'young person's defence'. These are contained within paragraphs (d) and (e) of s. 70(2), Crimes Act 1958 and state:

    (d) that the defendant made the film or took the photograph or was given the film or photograph by the minor and that, at the time of making, taking or being given the film or photograph, the defendant was not more than two years older than the minor was or appeared to be; or

    (e) that the minor or one of the minors depicted in the film or photograph is the defendant.

Clearly paragraph (d) is dealing with those situations where the defendant and the subject of the photograph was in a relationship and decided to take photographs of themselves. That said, paragraph (d) does not expressly refer to consent (cf the position in England and Wales: s. 160A, Criminal Justice Act 1988). Could it therefore apply to D, a 15 year-old boy, who surreptitiously takes a photograph of V, his 14 year-old girlfriend, when she takes a shower at his house? V is not aware of the photograph but paragraph (d) does not indicate that she needs to be: the requirements would seem to be met in that he took the photograph and at the time of the taking he was not more than two years older than the minor. It would seem somewhat unusual to provide for a defence in these circumstances although the wider principle of removing adolescents from criminal justice interventions is perhaps more desirable and this will be explored more fully in Chapter 9.

The State of Tasmania also provides for a young person's defence:

> It is . . . a defence . . . to prove that the material which is the subject of the charge depicts sexual activity between the accused person and a person under the age of eighteen years that is not an unlawful sexual act.
>
>   (s. 130E(2), Criminal Code Act 1924)

This defence is extremely similar to one of the exceptions identified by the Canadian Supreme Court in *R v Sharpe* 2001 SCC 2 and will be discussed in greater depth in Chapter 9, where an analysis of the legal and policy implications of adolescents becoming involved in child pornography will be discussed.

Chapter 9

Young people and child pornography

So far much of the discussion that has taken place is premised on the basis that an adult has been accessing or producing child pornography: it has been noted at the heart of the justification for criminalising child pornography that it amounts to the abuse or exploitation of a child. However whilst it would seem that the 'typical' defendant in a child pornography case will be an adult, it is clear that minors are also involved in child pornography. For clarity, this chapter will not be discussing the fact that some children depicted in child pornography would appear to be compliant (see Lanning, 2005, for a useful discussion on this) as the children depicted in there have been conditioned, groomed or coerced into such participation. Rather this chapter is concerned with those who consciously and deliberately seek to become involved with child pornography.

This is an area that has received little academic attention (Quayle and Taylor, 2006) in part because there has been no systematic review of this area (Gillespie, 2008: 112). Whilst some studies have identified that children access pornography in general (Livingstone and Haddon, 2009; Ybarra and Mitchell, 2005) few have considered the specific issue of adolescents accessing child pornography (an exception being Moultrie, 2006, discussed below). Whilst some of the literature demonstrates that children unintentionally access pornography it is also clear that some minors deliberately seek access to adult pornography (Livingstone and Hodden, 2009: 16) and it would seem (perhaps unsurprisingly) that this is more likely to be boys (Quayle *et al.*, 2008: 60). Whilst there is some evidence to suggest that there may be harm suffered by exposure to pornography (Ybarra and Mitchell, 2005) others have noted that male adolescents have sought out pornography as part of their sexual development for many years (Ybarra and Mitchell, 2005: 484).

Separate to the literature that exists in respect of the accessing of adult pornography there is some evidence to suggest that adolescents are also complicit in child pornography. A key New Zealand study showed that those under the age of 20 accounted for a quarter of detected persons accessing child pornography (Carr, 2004: 2). Whilst the latest data shows a slight decrease the detection of adolescents accessing child pornography remains statistically significant (Sullivan, 2007: 3). Recently attention has been paid to the issue of adolescents being involved in the production of child pornography, particularly so-called 'self-exploitation' images (see, for example, Leary, 2007; Humbach, 2009; Parker, 2009).

This chapter will consider how we should respond to minors being deliberately involved in child pornography and also detail the response of the legal system. It will be necessary to draw a distinction between the production of child pornography and accessing child pornography since it is submitted that these raise separate issues.

Production

The first issue to discuss is the production of child pornography. For clarity it will be remembered that the premise of this chapter is based on minors (i.e. those under the age of 18) deliberately choosing to produce child pornography. There are a variety of documented forms of adolescent production of child pornography but they would seem to fall into four principal categories:

- *Sexting*. This will be defined below but is, in essence, the situation where a person takes a sexually explicit photograph of themself using ICT (usually a camera-equipped mobile telephone) and passes it to one or more persons.
- *Recording of sexual activity*. This is where two adolescents record themselves participating in sexual activity, including sexual intercourse.
- *Commercial activity*. The situation where a person decides to obtain money or other tangible goods as a result of self-generated child pornography.
- *Harassment*. Where a minor produces child pornography for the purposes of harassing or bullying a person.

All four forms will interlink to an extent although it should be noted that of the four forms, only the final one (harassment) will be considered non-consensual *per se*. That is not to say that there may be questions about consent in some of the other categories (most notably the second category) but the fourth is an example when it is highly unlikely that the person portrayed in the material will have consented to being recorded. This has specific implications and these will be discussed below. A second distinction can be drawn between these categories; that being only the third category will automatically involve production for commercial reasons, in the other categories the production will ordinarily not be for the intention of making money. That is not to say that there is not a commercial element in the other categories since the nature of the dissemination of child pornography could mean that material that was produced for private use is quickly used for commercial reasons by people other than those who created it (for an example see Quayle and Taylor, 2006: 125).

Identifying the behaviour

Whilst it is submitted that there are different categories of adolescent production, the (legal) consequences of production is similar. Accordingly this section of the chapter will be structured by identifying the different forms of behaviour (i.e. the categories discussed above) before then discussing the legal and policy implications of this behaviour as a whole.

Sexting and recording activity

Whilst these constitute two separate categories of behaviour they will be considered together since, as will be seen, they raise similar issues.

'Sexting' is a term that has been developed by the media. It would appear that it was first coined by the UK press (Parker, 2009: 1) but it is one that has quickly gained acceptance throughout the world. The term is considered to encompass sexually explicit text and images created and disseminated by camera-equipped mobile telephones (Parker, 2009; Humbach, 2009: 3). Whilst it is a relatively recent phenomenon and clearly applies to both adults and children it would seem that teenagers have quickly taken to using mobile technology for these purposes. Quayle and Taylor hypothesise that this may have something to do with the ubiquitous possession of mobile telephones by the teenage population (Quayle and Taylor, 2006: 124) but also because increased accessibility of pornography on the internet has led to the situation whereby attitudes to sexually explicit material has changed. They report one 16 year-old boy who stated, 'Pornography is just part of the culture now. It's almost like it's not even, like, porn' (Quayle and Taylor, 2006: 125). The consequences of exposure to pornography will be discussed elsewhere but its ease of access and popularity of viewing appears to have almost normalised it and, as evident by this quote, some sexual depictions are considered by some adolescents to be routine and not pornographic.

Whilst this is an emerging issue, it is clear from press reports that sexting is, whilst perhaps not necessarily routine, not extraordinary either. A US survey suggested that almost one in five US teenagers admitted to taking nude or semi-nude pictures of themselves and sending them to others (Humbach, 2009: 2).

Whilst sexting is largely used to discuss the proliferation of material sent by mobile telephone it would seem equally appropriate for it to apply to internet-based material. It is known that some adolescents will send sexually explicit pictures or footage of themselves either by email or through posting it on a social networking site or even disseminating live footage by sitting in front of a webcam (Quayle and Taylor, 2006: 125; Leary, 2007: 5).

It is not clear why teenagers are exhibiting this behaviour: some have suggested that the risk of sexually transmitted diseases mean that many middle-class adolescents are eschewing sexual intercourse and instead engaging in masturbation, oral sex or the production of pornography (Quayle et al., 2008: 70, citing Uecker, Angotti and Regnerus, also see Quayle and Taylor, 2006: 126, who note that the growth of this sexualised behaviour is in contrast to the reduction in adolescent pregnancy, birth and abortion rates). Without an understanding of why adolescents are exhibiting this behaviour it is not immediately clear whether they fully understand the consequences of their actions although there appears some evidence (albeit anecdotal) to suggest that they do not (Brady, 2007: 632).

The second category, it will be remembered, is self-recording. This is directly related to sexting but is separate because, it is submitted, of the purpose of the production. It is clear that some adolescents, in a relationship, are recording themselves having sexual intercourse or sexual activity with each other. It is perhaps not surprising that this is happening since it is known that many adults do the same thing – indeed nearly every month there is an incident whereby a well known celebrity 'suffers' from the embarrassment of a sex tape being released (with suspicions that some tapes have been released deliberately) – and there is a considerable market on the internet for 'amateur' pornography (Lane, 2000). Certainly there are a number of sites that purport to host material posted by its viewers showing couples engaging in sexual activity and some sites have developed a 'YouTube' type system whereby posts can be uploaded easily (whilst YouTube itself is proactive in taking down sexually explicit material that is posted).

Self-generated material is undoubtedly problematic (Quayle *et al.*, 2008) in that it can be easily misused. As many teenagers have discovered a 'sexting' message sent to one person can easily be sent to others and, quite quickly, a network of people known to the person portrayed (e.g. a school) can have seen the image, causing distress to the person. Similarly an emailed image or self-recorded footage can be easily disseminated and it has been noted, for example, that a number of so-called 'revenge' web sites exist where users are encouraged to post sexually explicit material of previous boy or girlfriends (Quayle *et al.*, 2008: 64) and there is some evidence to suggest that adolescents are using these sites. That said, there appears to be denial from many of the adolescents that are exhibiting this behaviour, believing that the negative consequences will not happen to them (Quayle *et al.*, 2008: 66). There is an undoubted paradox that is created in relation to adolescent use of ICT. Many adolescents are extremely proficient at using ICT and they increasingly do not differentiate between the online and offline worlds yet at the same time they appear naive as to the consequences. A parallel could perhaps be drawn to social networking sites where media reports suggested that their profiles were causing some applicants to be rejected for jobs (Bloxham, 2010); presumably even more likely where the behaviour is sexual.

Commercial activity

The third category was commercial activity. It should be noted at the outset that the term 'commercial activity' is being defined broadly and it is meant as the production of child pornography for the purposes of receiving money or other material benefit. With sexting and the recording of sexual activity it would seem that the production was undertaken either for social or sexual purposes. The overriding purpose in the behaviour discussed in this section is to receive money or goods.

There are a number of sub-strands to this category but the advent of digital technology, particularly webcams and camera-phones, appears to have revolutionised this area. Perhaps the significant distinction is between 'small-scale' activity and 'large-scale' activity although it would appear that the latter may develop out of the former.

The advent of webcams led to new opportunities for people to self-exploit themselves. Probably the first person to exploit this potential was Jennifer Ringley who, in 1996, created 'Jennicam'. (Whilst some argue that 'Jennicam' was not the first footage of its type, it certainly appears to have been the most successful.) 'Jennicam' showed Jennifer Rigley undertaking her daily life allowing people to 'log on' to the site to see what she is doing. Most of the time the footage merely showed her working at the computer, sleeping or studying (Lane, 2001: 253) but it did occasionally show nudity and many logged on to the site in the hope of seeing this although Rigley herself argued that this was not the purpose of the site (White, 2003: 14).

Regardless of what the overall purpose of 'Jennicam' was, many quickly realised that money could be made from appearing before a webcam, and the term 'camgirl' (or 'camboy') was coined to describe those who would appear nude or semi-nude in front of a webcam for financial or material purposes (White, 2003: 15). There appear to be two varieties to the camgirl phenomenon. The first, like 'Jennicam', operates on the basis that a person will pay to see footage. The growth of online payment systems (such as PayPal) which provide for instantaneous payment to be received by a person mean that this is perhaps easier than at any time before. The second type is based on the premise of a 'wish list' whereby a person creates a list of desired goods at an online retailer and persons who like what they see will purchase the gift. This phenomenon appears similar to the Japanese phenomenon of 'compensated dating' whereby sexual activity is given in return for a gift (Udagawa, 2007).

Whilst much of the camgirl material is by adults it became clear that adolescents were also taking advantage of this phenomenon although, at least initially, it quite often showed them posing in a bra or bikini and the footage was, in essence, no different to what would be seen on a beach (Rowan, 2002). However it became quite clear that adolescents would quickly go further than this, perhaps understanding the popularity of teenage sexuality. An early report demonstrates that adolescents certainly appeared to understand this with one 15 year-old girl who called her site 'Underage Piece of Ass' (Emmett, 2001). Certainly there is also some evidence to suggest that adolescents understand that there is a need to show nudity or semi-nudity to get people's attention and thus receive financial rewards (Rowan, 2002: 16). In many instances there is a complete lack of understanding about the implications of posting such material, with some adolescents stating they thought the behaviour was 'safe' (Mieszkowski, 2001) despite the fact that there are some reports of people being approached offline after posting content.

Whilst it would seem that in many instances the 'camgirl' phenomenon remains localised there are occasional instances of escalation. Perhaps the most notable of these was the case of Justin Berry (discussed in Eichenwald, 2005). Justin was a teenage Californian who set up a webcam looking for friends. He began talking to a number of adults and one offered him $50 to sit in front of his webcam with his shirt off. The requests became more explicit but as they did so the amount of money being offered increased too. Eventually Justin created a subscription site that also charged for 'private performances' which would include Justin having sexual intercourse with prostitutes. Eventually the site got out of control and Justin became a drug addict before reaching a plea bargain with federal prosecutors whereby he would not be charged with child pornography offences in return for co-operation in respect of tracking and identifying those who subscribed to his site.

The story of Justin Berry is extreme and it is not suggested that all 'camgirls' and 'camboys' will end up in his predicament but there is some evidence to suggest that there is escalation in what they are prepared to show in order to continue to receive money (Bocij, 2004). Whilst it is unlikely many adolescents would go to the extremes that Justin did, it would seem that there is a degree of progression with some moving, for example, from gifts to money-making sites.

Harassment

The fourth category identified was harassment. It is necessary to be clear what is meant in this section. It has been seen already that some of the self-generated child pornography will ultimately be used for harassment and this is undoubtedly a danger of this material. Those problems were discussed above and will be considered below in respect of solutions but in this section the material is produced *with the intention* of it being used for harassment.

It is trite to say that whilst ICT has brought about many social benefits it also brings with it dangers, child pornography being one of these. An interesting issue in terms of ICT use is the extent to which adolescents have used ICT to facilitate pre-existing problematic behaviour, a good example of which is bullying. The term 'cyberbullying' has been coined to cover those situations where ICT has been used to facilitate the bullying or harassment of others (O'Connell *et al.*, 2004: 2). Whilst this will sometimes involve harassing or bullying people not known personally to the child (other than in an online environment) there appears to be evidence that it sometimes also acts as an additional dimension to offline bullying (Gillespie, 2006).

Whilst cyberbullying can take place in a variety of different ways there is some evidence to suggest that adolescents are reporting the belief that they have been the unwilling subject of a photograph, including photographs of themselves in states of partial or total undress (NCH, 2005: 2). These images will not infrequently be recorded at school, for example in the changing rooms (Li, 2007). The images are then circulated via mobile telephone or, in some extreme cases, 'outing' sites have been created whereby the pictures are posted online either on a webpage or a social networking site (Bamford, 2004). The consequences of this behaviour are significant. In terms of harm the victims can suffer significant psychological distress and there have been isolated examples of suicide arising out of cyberbullying. Where sexually explicit photographs form part of the cyberbullying the child is also likely to suffer the secondary victimisation of knowing that their image is being used by some for the purposes of sexual gratification (Palmer, 2005). There is also the risk of contact harm. Some incidents of cyberbullying have involved the posting of sexually explicit material online together with contact details. Sex offenders have then sought to contact the victims (Bamford, 2004). Potentially there is the difficulty that some offenders may take advantage of a victim's distress to help groom a child for abuse by befriending them online before then abusing them.

As with other forms of adolescent-generated child pornography there appears no recognition of the risks by those who post the material. Indeed, because the purpose of the incident is to cause harassment and, according to some literature, to cause hurt and distress to the victims (Vandebosch and van Cleemput, 2008: 501) it can be questioned whether the perpetrators even care about the consequences of their actions.

Responses to production

Clearly the production of child pornography in these circumstances is of real concern. There appears to be a complete lack of understanding on the part of adolescents as to the consequences of what they have done. In a paper contributing to the Third World Congress against Child Sexual Exploitation it was noted that 'the young person . . . lacks control on many levels – legal, cultural, normative, technological – over the artefacts after they have been created' (Quayle *et al.*, 2008: 71 citing Heverly). Thus even if the adolescent purports to exercise control over the actual production of the image they do not necessarily realise that they cannot control what happens to the image post-production and how readily it can escalate out of control.

There will be a number of responses to adolescent production of child pornography but the distinction here will be between legal (meaning a formal criminal justice) intervention and non-legal interventions (meaning in this context education or therapy).

Non-legal interventions

It was seen from the preceding section that adolescents do not appear to understand the implications of their behaviour. It is interesting that this should be the case since, at least with self-generated material, there has been a number of high-profile incidents where celebrity sex tapes have been released and so the potential for this to happen is well known. Perhaps the difficulty is more to do with their perception of any harm or damage that could be caused. The release of the celebrity sex tapes have, generally speaking, been without any real repercussions and with some (e.g. Paris Hilton) there was arguably a positive rather than negative effect in terms of a career. The same will not be true of adolescents but do they necessarily appreciate this? The quote from a 16 year-old boy will be remembered: 'Pornography is just part of the culture now. It's almost like it's not even, like, porn' (Quayle and Taylor, 2006: 125). If pornography is becoming normalised then there is the risk that they do not necessarily consider the release of material to be problematic or embarrassing although that is likely to change as the circulation increases. Similarly they may not understand the risk of solicitation that disclosure of sexually explicit material may bring (Quayle et al., 2008: 70). A programme of education can be put in place so that adolescents understand the risks. This should not just be when an adolescent is detected producing child pornography but in general so as to attempt to reduce the production of self-generated material.

What of those adolescents who have produced child pornography or been involved in child pornography? It may be necessary to produce a therapeutic response to some, especially those who have exhibited problematic sexual behaviour (Longo, 2004; Quayle, 2007). A therapeutic response can be initiated within a child protection framework, allowing adolescents to understand the risk that they have put themselves (and others) in.

Legal responses: England and Wales

In many countries the law does not differentiate between adolescent or adult perpetrators of child pornography offences, meaning that an adolescent who produces child pornography could be guilty of a serious sexual offence. A good example of this is England and Wales where, contrary to contact offending where specific legislation exists in respect of juveniles (s. 13, Sexual Offences Act 2003), the law in respect of child pornography refers to a *person* and not to an *adult*. Accordingly a child who deliberately takes an indecent image of a child (including themselves) is prima facie guilty of a sex offence punishable by up to 10 years' imprisonment.

The criminalisation of child pornography has long been argued as a necessary part of the protection of children from the exploitation and abuse caused by child pornography but it must be seriously questioned whether it was ever intended to apply to adolescents who produce explicit material of themselves. That said, there are examples of criminal justice agencies using the legislation to investigate, and in some cases prosecute, adolescents. Within the United Kingdom there has (so far) been relative restraint but there have been some stories that suggest formal investigations have, at least, taken place. Two cases are of note. The first was in 2005 when six schoolgirls took topless photographs of each other and posted them on the internet. Whilst it would appear that no prosecution was eventually brought, at least one of the girls was arrested and questioned on suspicion of taking indecent photographs of children. The second case concerned a 16 year-old international footballer who, when aged 15, recorded a friend having sex with a 14 year-old girl and then sent the footage to others. This boy was prosecuted but the court decided not to impose a punishment. However a note of caution should be raised here. Proceedings in the Youth Courts are rarely reported and disposals other than by prosecution (e.g. a reprimand, final warning or conditional caution) would not be reported at all. Given central statistics do not differentiate between adult and child offenders, it cannot be known for certain that other prosecutions or formal interventions have not occurred.

It was noted at the beginning of this section that, technically at least, an adolescent who takes an indecent photograph of a child is liable for an offence under the Protection of Children Act 1978. It will be remembered from Chapter 6 that the Sexual Offences Act 2003 raised the age at which a person is considered to be a 'child' for the purposes of child pornography from the age of 16 to 18. It will also be remembered that this undoubtedly creates a paradox whereby a person of 17 can have sexual intercourse but cannot take a picture of herself naked. The Sexual Offences Act 2003 showed some sop to this by producing a defence although, as will be seen, this is confusing and problematic.

The defence, created by s. 45, Sexual Offences Act 2003, is to be found in the Protection of Children Act 1978 as s. 1A. It provides:

(1) This section applies where in proceedings for an offence under section 1(1)(a) of taking or making an indecent photograph of a child, or for an offence under section 1(1)(b) or (c) relating to an indecent photograph of a child, the defendant proves that the photograph was of the child aged sixteen or over, and that at the time of the offence charged the child and he –

    (a) were married or civil partners of each other; or
    (b) lived together as partners in an enduring family relationship.

(2) Subsections (5) and (6) also apply where, in proceedings for an offence under section 1(1)(b) or (c) relating to an indecent photograph of a child, the defendant proves that the photograph was of the child aged sixteen or over, and that at the time when he obtained it the child and he –

    (a) were married or civil partners of each other; or
    (b) lived together as partners in an enduring family relationship

(3) This section applies whether the photograph showed the child alone or with the defendant, but not if it showed any other person.

(4) In the case of an offence under section 1(1)(a), if sufficient evidence is adduced to raise an issue as to whether the child consented to the photograph being taken or made, or as to whether the defendant reasonably believed that the child so consented, the defendant is not guilty of the offence unless it is proved that the child did not so consent and that the defendant did not reasonably believe that the child so consented.

(5) In the case of an offence under section 1(1)(b), the defendant is not guilty of an offence unless it is proved that the showing or distributing was to a person other than the child.

(6)   In the case of an offence under section 1(1)(c), if sufficient evidence is adduced to raise an issue both –

(a)   as to whether the child consented to the photograph being in the defendant's possession, or as to whether the defendant reasonably believed that the child so consented; and

(b)   as to whether the defendant had the photograph in his possession with a view to its being distributed or shown to anyone other than the child;

the defendant is not guilty of the offence unless it is proved either that the child did not so consent and that the defendant did not reasonably believe that the child so consented, or that the defendant had the photograph in his possession with a view to its being distributed or shown to a person other than the child.

The defence is problematic in a number of ways. The first is in terms of policy. If, as the government contends, a child under the age of 18 is insufficiently mature to make a decision as to whether to consent to the behaviour (discussed above) then it would seem paradoxical to make consent an inherent part of the test and yet s. 1A(4) states that a defendant is to be acquitted unless the prosecution can prove, to the requisite standard of proof, that the child did not consent. This does, at least, provide recognition for the fact that a defence should only exist to consensual behaviour but it is difficult to understand why some children – irrespective of their individual maturity – are deemed sufficiently mature to make the decision and others are not.

The defence applies only to children aged 16 or 17 and thus above the age of consent. No defence exists in respect of a child below that age. This, as will be seen, mirrors the position in many other legal systems, and is at least comparable to the position in respect of contact offending. The principal difficulty with this defence, however, is the absurd restriction as to the number of 16 and 17 year-olds it applies to. The defence applies only to those who are married, in a (formal) civil partnership (i.e. a same-sex partnership formalised under the Civil Partnership Act 2004) or who live together in an 'enduring family relationship'. When a defence was first mooted it was based on consent and not relationship (Gillespie, 2004) but Parliament tightened it considerably. The then Parliamentary Under-Secretary of State stated that it was designed to 'protect the privacy of a marital or enduring relationship' (Gillespie, 2004: 364) and so it was presumably based on the fear that raising the age of a child to 18 could infringe Article 8 and/or 12 of the European Convention on Human Rights.

The term 'enduring family relationship' is not defined and is not easily understood. Presumably given the premise put forward by the Parliamentary Under-Secretary, it is a relationship analogous to marriage or a civil relationship but how is this to be judged? The requirement that the parties live together is also problematic and perhaps demonstrates a naive view of teenage relationships. It also creates a potentially absurd situation whereby two 17 year-olds who live together but only met three months ago may be protected by a defence but two 17 year-olds who have been in a relationship since the age of 13 and who are engaged to be married will not. The logic of this distinction is, it is submitted, flawed.

Section 1A(3) states that the defence exists only where the photograph shows the child alone or with the defendant but not with anyone else. To an extent this can be said to be a (reasonable) attempt to prevent the exploitation of others. So, for example, if a person has a picture of herself with an ex-boyfriend this picture could not be given to the new boyfriend. Where both subjects of the photograph are shown in an indecent pose then this is justified but what of the situation where only one is indecent? Does the same justification apply? A more problematic example could be where, for example, a picture shows A, a 17 year-old girl, at a nudist beach. Let us assume that she is naked and posed in such a way that would make it an indecent photograph. If in the background of the picture any other persons are shown (which is quite possible on a beach) then the defence does not apply irrespective of whether the persons are identifiable. Whilst the law states that the defendant may be shown, what does this mean in the context of a photograph that depicts three-way sexual intercourse? At the age of 16 this would be perfectly lawful but if A, a 17 year-old girl wanted to photograph herself having sex with two other persons then this will be illegal.

Evidentially there are also difficulties with this defence as it appears to include a mixture of both legal and evidential burdens on the defence (something unnecessary to discuss in this section but see Gillespie, 2005b) and it is extremely difficult to see how this defence could be readily explained to a jury.

The defence is, it is submitted, absurdly written and was introduced because of Parliament's desire not to interfere with the privacy of the marital bedroom. However it is a paternalistic defence that shows no recognition for the realities of teenage sexuality. Whilst it may be unwise for adolescents to photograph themselves, it is contradictory to say that it is acceptable for some to do so but dangerous for others. It is also absurd that two 17 year-old children can have sexual intercourse with each other but are liable for a custodial sentence of up to 10 years' imprisonment if they photograph each other instead.

Legal responses: other jurisdictions

It was noted that in England and Wales the criminal justice agencies have, so far as we know, been slow to use the criminal law as a response to adolescent production of child pornography. In other countries this is not the case, particularly America where evidence suggests that not only are adolescents prosecuted for self-generated material, some prosecutors are deliberately resorting to prosecutions to send a warning to adolescents (Humbach, 2009). The propriety of using criminal prosecutions in this way has been considered in detail in two state cases before (separate) courts of appeal. The first case of note is *Vezzoni v State* (2005, unreported) before the Washington Court of Appeals. The appellant was in a relationship with a girl called TN when they were both 16 years old. After having sexual intercourse the appellant asked if he could take pictures of her and she agreed. A week later the relationship broke up. Some three months later the appellant developed the pictures and showed them to several classmates. He was charged and convicted of one count of dealing in child pornography and one count of possessing child pornography.

The appellant sought to challenge his conviction on the basis that it infringed his privacy. The Court of Appeals firmly rejected the appeal and noted, for example, that the State had to protect children, including from themselves. The court noted that there had been a number of cases before the US Supreme Court that noted that the right to privacy and free speech were not absolute and that child pornography laws were not unconstitutional. The court also rejected an argument that the statute was not intended to cover adolescents, noting that the legislation specifically did not differentiate between age and therefore adolescent behaviour was firmly within the provisions.

The second case is *AH v Florida* 949 So.2d 234 (2007) which was heard in the District Court of the State of Florida. The appellant here was a 16 year-old female who was charged alongside JGW, her 17 year-old boyfriend. They took pictures of themselves naked and engaged in sexual performance and AH emailed one of these photographs to JGW. The District Court refused to quash the charges, again premising their decision on the basis of harm. The majority stated:

> . . . this Court recognises a compelling state interest in protecting children from sexual exploitation, particularly the form of sexual exploitation involved in this case.
>
> (p. 236)

The court does not explain what the exploitation in this case was and so it is presumably the exploitation inherent in child pornography. However as noted earlier in this book this is ordinarily premised on the basis of the abuse a child suffers or the exploitation of the image. It is not clear that in this case there was any exploitation *per se*. The image was taken by AH and was not circulated to anyone other than JGW. Can this really be said to be exploitative? Advocates of setting the age at 18 would answer that the answer is 'yes' but even if it is accepted that it is possible to self-exploit in this manner it is less than clear that this should be enforced by the criminal law. The court appeared concerned about the future harm that could be caused if the photograph was to be released and based their decision, in part, on a highly dubious proposition:

> Minors who are involved in a sexual relationship, unlike adults who may be involved in a mature committed relationship, have no reasonable expectation that their relationship will continue and that the photographs will not be shared with others intentionally or unintentionally.
>
> (p. 237)

No evidence is given for this proposition and it is submitted that it is highly questionable that adults can reasonably expect their relationship to continue. The court ultimately decided the point on maturity:

> These children are not mature enough to make rational decisions concerning all the possible negative implications of producing these videos.
>
> (p. 239)

Given that JGW was already 17 at the time of the trial it is less than clear that he, for example, would be any more mature in the matter of months until his eighteenth birthday and no evidence was given as to the maturity of AH. The court simply seems to adopt the logic of the legislators in deciding that at the age of 18 a child somehow achieves instant maturity, something that is not, it is submitted, true.

It should be noted that not every state in America adopts the same approach and some states (most notably, Arkansas, Utah and Ohio) have altered the law to specifically deal with adolescent production (Parker, 2009: 5). The alteration is in terms of penalty. If Utah is taken as an example, the distribution of child pornography is transformed from a third-degree felony for a person aged 18 or over (Utah Code 76-10-1204(4)(a)) to a class A misdemeanour for a person aged 16 or 17 and a class B misdemeanour for a person under 16. This is a significant change but still potentially criminalises those who produce child pornography. Vermont has adopted a different approach. Parker argues that they have decriminalised sexting (Parker, 2009: 6–7) although a closer analysis of the legislation shows that, when it comes in force, sending an indecent visualisation of him or herself to another person remains a criminal matter (13 VSA 64§2802b(a)(1)) but that a minor who has not been referred for the matter previously shall not be prosecuted (13 VSA 64§2802b(a)(2)) and even if they are prosecuted they should not be subject to the sex offender notification requirements. This is an innovative move by the Vermont legislature and at the time of writing it appears no other state has followed this move.

What of other countries? It will be recalled from Chapter 8 that Canada and some states of Australia provide for defences in respect of adolescent production of child pornography. The Canadian defence arises from the decision of the Supreme Court in *R v Sharpe* 2001 SCC 2. This case was discussed earlier but it will be remembered it was a constitutional challenge to Canada's child pornography laws. McLachlan CJC stated:

> The second class of materials [exempted] concerns privately created visual recordings of lawful sexual activity made by or depicting the person in possession and intended only for private use. Sexually explicit photographs taken by a teenager of him- or herself, and kept entirely private, would fall within this class of materials. Another example would be a teenaged couple's private photographs of themselves engaged in lawful sexual activity.
>
> (at [76])

The justification for this exemption was based on the fact that it implicates the values of self-fulfilment and self-actualisation which are important factors for the freedom of expression.

The exemption is similar to the defence adopted in England and Wales (but without the absurdity of the prescribed relationships) in that it applies to those above the age of consent. Accordingly it will not be of assistance to those below the age of consent who photograph themselves. At the time of *Sharpe* this was the age of 14 but it is now 16 and so the exception will apply only to those aged 16 or 17. It is clear that it applies only to privately created and held material (see the Chief Justice's remarks at para. [118]) and so commercial production or the production of material where it was intended to distribute the material widely would not come within the exception.

On the face of *Sharpe* there is no requirement that all parties to the filming consent to it although it is perhaps implicit within it. Certainly it is submitted that this must be an inherent part of any defence as to do otherwise must inevitably raise questions about exploitation. *Sharpe* appeared to suggest that the exemption applied to s. 163.1 of the Code, i.e. all child pornography offences. Again this would be logical as it should apply to the production (taking) of child pornography and also its possession and distribution. An interesting decision in this context is *R v Dabrowski* 2007 ONCA 619 where the Court of Appeal for Ontario decided that private possession was not restricted to the actual person depicted in the photograph or who took it.

The appellant in *Dabrowski* was charged with the possession and distribution of child pornography. He had been in a sexual relationship with a 14 year-old girl (at the time when the age of consent was 14) and this had included videotaping themselves engaged in sexual activity. He gave the videotape to a third party (a friend of his) for 'safe keeping'. His conviction for possession and distribution was quashed on the basis that the exception in *Sharpe* should not be taken to mean exclusive possession and could include the distribution of the material to others depending on the circumstances (at [29]). The court noted that to hold otherwise would mean that the material could not, for example, be held in a safety deposit box or given to a lawyer or trusted person. That said, the court did acknowledge that distribution could mean that there is a loss of privacy and they implied that this should be the test: stating questions as to the level of control maintained, whether others viewed the material and the purpose of why the material was distributed will all be relevant (at [30]). Whilst the court was perhaps right to note that exclusive possession would mean, for example, that holding material in a safety deposit box would breach the provisions, it is submitted that a court should be slow to accept that the distribution of material outside of those who are depicted in the video is permissible. Whilst a safety deposit box or lawyer may be appropriate (depending on the circumstances) the distribution of material to someone who could view it or further distribute it would not be justified.

Canada is not alone in deciding to exempt adolescents from certain forms of production, with two of the Australian states also providing defences. The State of Tasmania provides a defence very similar to those already discussed:

It is . . . a defence . . . to prove that the material which is the subject of the charge depicts sexual activity between the accused person and a person under the age of eighteen years that is not an unlawful sexual act.

(s. 130E(2), Criminal Code Act 1924)

The reliance on it depicting lawful sexual activity means that, as with the Canadian defence, it will apply to those aged 16 or 17. The State of Victoria adopts quite a radically different model. Two defences are created, these are contained within paragraphs (d) and (e) of s. 70(2), Crimes Act 1958 and state:

(d) that the defendant made the film or took the photograph or was given the film or photograph by the minor and that, at the time of making, taking or being given the film or photograph, the defendant was not more than two years older than the minor was or appeared to be; or

(e) that the minor or one of the minors depicted in the film or photograph is the defendant.

Clearly paragraph (d) is dealing with those situations where the defendant and the subject of the photograph was in a relationship and decided to take photographs of themselves. It is notable that, as with the Canadian exemption (and unlike the position in England and Wales), there is no express mention of consent. It is to be hoped that the courts construe the defence to apply only where the minor is aware of the recording since otherwise it allows for the exploitation of a minor. Unlike the other defences that have been noted in this section, the law in Victoria does not appear to have a minimum age and so it would seem to apply to a 15 year-old boy and his 14 year-old girlfriend. Most other jurisdictions have restricted the defence to the recording of lawful sexual activity (meaning those above the age of consent) and to this extent this defence is wider. Paragraph (e) clearly covers self-generated 'sexting'. Again there appears no minimum age for this defence.

How to respond to adolescent production

No single response discussed above would appear suitable to all forms of adolescent child pornography production, in part because of course the circumstances will change. A balance needs to be drawn between protecting children (including from themselves) and punishing those who harm other adolescents.

It was noted at the beginning of this chapter that it was submitted there were four forms of adolescent production. Of these arguably three involve prima facie consensual behaviour, with one (harassment) being non-consensual. It is submitted that the justification for criminalising non-consensual behaviour is perhaps higher than for consensual behaviour but it should still not be used automatically. There are other alternatives (such as educational initiatives, social contract-based solutions (e.g. Acceptable Behaviour Contracts or Antisocial Behaviour Orders) or school-based punishments (Gillespie, 2006: 135)) and these may be appropriate.

There will be circumstances when the harassment is so serious that the criminal law must be used. A more interesting question – although one realistically outside the remit of this book – is whether child pornography laws should be used or criminal offences relating to harassment (see Gillespie, 2006 for a discussion on this). Is the production of child pornography here the primary motive for the criminal conduct or, more likely, is it the harassment? As noted above, a breach of child pornography laws carries with it significant implications, not least the fact that an offender is considered to be a sex offender. Should this apply where there is no clear sexual motivation (as distinct from the intent to cause harassment or distress) and where the production of child pornography is, in essence, incidental to the overall criminal activity?

What of the situations where the behaviour is consensual? Traditionally the presence of a commercial motivation would be considered a significant aggravating feature (SGC, 2007: 111) but should the same be said of adolescents seeking to exploit themselves for financial gain? A parallel could perhaps be drawn to the position in relation to child prostitution. Whilst it is often said that prostitution is not illegal, this is far from true with, amongst other things, soliciting being subject to the criminal law (see Gillespie, 2007). Prostitutes, including child prostitutes, have been the subject of a criminal law intervention for many years (Ayre and Barrett, 2000). In 2000 the government launched a policy document entitled *Safeguarding Child Involved in Prostitution*, one of the purposes of which was to create a presumption against the prosecution of children under the age of 18 who were involved in prostitution. That is not to say that prosecutions cannot happen – indeed controversially the guidance specifically states that they can (Phoenix, 2002) – but rather that the clear presumption is that they should be treated as victims of sexual exploitation first.

Perhaps the same approach could be adopted to commercial self-exploitation. The law should consider adolescents who undertake this behaviour to be children in need and not potential defendants. However if this approach is to be taken then there must be clarity over what we mean by a child. The nature of child pornography is that it is quite possible that a person will not be detected until they are no longer a child (indeed in the example of Justin Berry, discussed above, he was not detected by the authorities until he was an adult (Eichenwald, 2005)). This should not mean that they are treated as an adult and prosecuted: rather the presumption against criminalisation should exist in respect of all material created when the person was a minor.

There may be circumstances when a prosecution would be appropriate and this could include situations where, for example, a youth has begun to commercially exploit other adolescents. Whilst a person exploiting another will frequently be considered worthy of prosecution it becomes perhaps more complicated where that person is an adolescent. Do they understand the harm and exploitation they are facilitating? Are they victims themselves (i.e. facilitating the exploitation on behalf of another)? These are all factors that must be taken into account but it is submitted that a criminal justice intervention cannot be ruled out in these circumstances.

This leaves the first two categories: sexting and self-recorded images. It will be remembered that these appear to be the largest categories of self-generated material. The harm caused by the *production* (as distinct to its distribution) is limited to those recorded. It is, of course, conceivable that a subject was not aware that their sexual activity was being recorded (the use of hidden cameras is not uncommon in the field of the production of child pornography). Where this is the case then this must be classified as non-consensual recording. Where the parties are aware of the recording and have consented to this (rather than merely acquiesced to it which would suggest an absence of consent) then this could be construed as consensual behaviour. Solo self-generated material (e.g. sexting) must, by its very nature, be classified as consensual.

An absence of consent makes it more likely that a criminal justice intervention should be required. The surreptitious recording of a sexual act without a person's consent is a significant interference with the autonomy of that individual and would, in any event, amount to a criminal offence (the offence of voyeurism: s. 67, Sexual Offences Act 2003, see especially s. 67(3)). Should it amount to an offence under the child pornography laws? Arguably yes: an adolescent should be aware that recording without permission is wrong and, as has been discussed already in this book, the footage can be easily misused which could cause significant harm to the other party. Of course it will always be a matter of prosecutorial discretion as to whether a prosecution should be brought but non-consensual recording should be capable of being prosecuted.

What of consensual production? A distinction probably has to be drawn between activity by those under 16 and those under 18. It will be remembered from Chapters 2 and 3 that the age of a child for the purposes of child pornography is now 18 and that the author believes that the age of consent is more appropriate. Those chapters discussed the various difficulties that disparity between ages has caused but the most significant of them is that two persons aged 16 or 17 can have sexual intercourse with each other but cannot take a sexualised photograph of one another. The arguments for criminalising this are, it is submitted, unconvincing and certainly their prosecution would seem disproportionate.

The exception created by the Canadian Supreme Court in *R v Sharpe* 2001 SCC 2 could act as an appropriate model to decriminalise consensual activity by adolescents over the age of consent. It seems unlikely that any government would reduce the age of a child so in order to ensure that there is not the paradox created by the disparity in ages it should recognise the exception put forward in *Sharpe*. In this way adolescents at the age of consent are not penalised for behaviour that could be less sexualised than sexual intercourse (e.g. a topless photograph). Even if they are recording pornographic videos (e.g. recording themselves having sexual intercourse) the so-called maturity argument does not, it is submitted, justify criminalisation. As discussed in Chapter 2 having sexual intercourse carries with it permanent risks and so if the law states that a person is old enough to make the decision as to whether to have sexual intercourse it should also recognise that (s)he is old enough to make a sexualised recording.

That said, the limits of *Sharpe* should be recognised. The Supreme Court did not state that adolescents over the age of consent should be exempt from the law. It stated that they should not be liable for the production and possession of the images; not distribution (save where it is between the people featured in the footage). It does not provide exemption to someone who distributes the footage to his or her friends or who later posts the material on to the internet. The distribution or showing of images to third parties must be considered to be an act of exploitation and one that could cause severe embarrassment to the subject and, if posted on the internet, could result in harm. The implications of this distribution or showing would, it is submitted, justify a prosecution in appropriate cases because the harm nexus has been altered. Where the material is possessed, shown or distributed only between the subjects then any harm caused is, it is submitted, potential rather than actual. It is the *risk* of harm that concerns people, not any actual harm that has been caused. Where the distribution goes beyond the subject then harm can begin to be caused, beginning with feelings of hurt or embarrassment and, potentially, the risk of harm through solicitation or the realisation that strangers are using the image for sexual gratification.

Perhaps this is what separates out *AH v State* 949 So. 2d 234 (2007) from *Vezzoni v State* (2005) in that in the latter case the photograph was not developed until after they had broken up and the defendant showed the photographs to several classmates. In *AH*, however, the only distribution took place between AH and JGW (the boyfriend). Padovano J, who provided the dissenting judgment in *AH*, thought that anticipated harm was not sufficient and noted the original intentions of the parties:

> The critical point in this case is that the child intended to keep the photographs private. She did not attempt to exploit anyone or to embarrass anyone.
>
> (949 So.2d 234 (2007) at 240)

It is submitted that there was no direct harm or exploitation in *AH* whereas there was in *Vezzoni*. Any harm in *AH* was potential harm: the footage *might* have been distributed and it *might* have been seen by others but it was never intended for this to happen and it is equally conceivable that it would not have been circulated more widely. The court in *AH* appears to conflict two separate issues: the harm justifying the criminalisation of the initial production and the harm justifying the criminalisation of distribution. If it was to be shown or distributed to someone other than AH or JGW then the person distributing or showing it could be culpable for that.

What of the situation whereby the participants are under the age of consent? It would seem at first sight that they should be treated in the same way but there is a difficulty with this argument. The exception in *Sharpe* was premised quite clearly on the recording of *lawful sexual activities*. This premise illustrates the principal difficulty that would be caused by dealing with those under the age of consent in the same way; it would create a paradox. When the Sexual Offences Act 2003 was proceeding through Parliament there was considerable angst at the fact that it provided specifically for the criminalisation of adolescents (s. 13, Sexual Offences Act 2003). Some of the commentary was simply factually incorrect in that it suggested that, for the first time, adolescents were to be the subject of criminal law when, in fact, they always had (as the previous laws on indecent assault and unlawful sexual intercourse with a girl did not restrict the age of the defendant) but some were concerned that the new offence would make it more likely that an adolescent may be prosecuted (see, for example, Hansard, HL Deb, 17 June 2003, vol. 649, col. 683).

If sexual activity is illegal between minors then it would be paradoxical to state that an adolescent could take a sexualised photograph. If D cannot legally touch V's breasts, it would be improper for the law to say that he could photograph them. Thus criminalisation would seem inevitable so as to allow compatibility with existing sexual offences laws. However the mere fact that something is criminal does not mean that a person should be prosecuted for it: it has long been a rule in England and Wales that just because someone has breached the law does not mean they should be automatically prosecuted and the 'public interest test' in the Code for Crown Prosecutors demonstrates this. Despite s. 13 existing it is quite clear that not every sexual act between adolescents is prosecuted and the CPS will consider the nature of the activity and its consensual nature in deciding whether to prosecute. The same should apply to the production of child pornography by adolescents: a prosecution should only occur when it is clearly in the public interest to do so and sexting or consensual recording (without distribution) may not be.

There would appear some evidence to suggest that the police and CPS are adopting this approach since despite there being media reports as to adolescents being investigated, or even arrested, in relation to child pornography charges (Levy, 2005) there is no evidence to state that a prosecution has been brought. That said, the absence of any statistics mean that it would not be easily known whether prosecutions have been brought.

The existence of s. 13, SOA 2003 does raise one further point about the criminalisation of adolescents. If a child produces child pornography then they are liable for imprisonment for up to 10 years' imprisonment (s. 6(2), Protection of Children Act 1978). However where an adolescent has sexual intercourse with a child over the age of 13 (s)he is liable to a maximum sentence of five years' imprisonment (s. 13(2)(b), SOA 2003). Accordingly it is twice as serious for a 15 year-old boy to take a topless picture of his 15 year-old girlfriend as it is for him to have sexual intercourse with her. Clearly this cannot be right and if the criminalisation of adolescent sexual activity is to continue as a matter of legislative policy then offences under the Protection of Children Act 1978 should be brought within s. 13. Admittedly the courts are unlikely to impose a heavy sentence on an adolescent but the formal sentencing guidelines do differ between offences under PoCA 1978 and s. 13, SOA 2003.

The one area where there is parity is over the notification requirements. An adolescent convicted under either s. 13 or s. 1, PoCA 1978 will only be subject to the notification requirements where a custodial sentence of at least 12 months' imprisonment is imposed (paras 14 and 22 of Schedule 3, SOA 2003). It will hopefully be rare for a custodial sentence to be imposed and accordingly an adolescent is unlikely to be subject to the notification requirements (something that was of concern to Smith, 2008). However the notification requirements is only one aspect of the child protection framework and a conviction under either s. 13 or s. 1, PoCA 1978, would amount to a child sex offence and would show on, for example, an enhanced criminal records check. This could still be extremely disadvantageous to a child and would probably restrict their employment prospects. This only serves to reinforce the fact that a prosecution should only be brought in extreme circumstances (ordinarily where there is an absence of consent or where there has been distribution beyond the participants recorded).

Accessing child pornography

The first part of this chapter considered the position where adolescents produce child pornography, however this is unlikely to be the only contact an adolescent may have with child pornography. It has been noted that some adolescents deliberately seek out pornography (Longo, 2004: 47; Cameron et al., 2005) and it would be naive to suggest that they only seek adult pornography. Indeed, there is evidence from other countries, most notably New Zealand, that adolescents accessing child pornography was statistically relevant (Carr, 2004: 2), indeed the report noted that accessing by young people (defined as those under 20) comprised a quarter of identified offenders. This section of the chapter will discuss the implications of an adolescent accessing child pornography.

Unlike the position with the production of child pornography, it does not appear that the legislation in any of the countries that are examined in this book have altered their law to take account of adolescents who are accessing child pornography. Chapters 6 and 8 noted that in all countries the downloading of child pornography amounts to a serious offence and in many countries viewing child pornography is too. There appears slightly more evidence to suggest that adolescents involved in the accessing of child pornography are more likely to receive a formal criminal justice intervention than those involved in the production. In the absence of central statistics it is necessary to refer to circumstantial evidence and press reports but these do indicate that adolescents have been prosecuted for downloading child pornography (Moultrie, 2006; Gillespie, 2008). There also appears some evidence to show a rather worrying trend in that people aged 18 are being prosecuted for behaviour although it is unlikely that this behaviour began on their eighteenth birthday. Press reports of 18 year-olds being prosecuted for the offences (when they are formally an adult), whilst not frequent, are certainly noticeable. Perhaps the most significant example of an adult being prosecuted for adolescent offending is Attorney General's Reference (No. 8 of 2009) *(sub nom R v McCartney)* [2009] NICA 52.

The offender in this case pleaded guilty to 30 counts of making an indecent image of a child (the making being downloading following the ruling in *R v Bowden* [2000] 1 QB 88). The transcript is clear that:

> The offender was born on 20 February 1988. The offences relate to activities of the offender between 18 January 2004 when he was fifteen years and ten months and 4 April 2008 when he was twenty years and one month.
>
> (at [2])

Thus it is clear that he is prosecuted for behaviour undertaken whilst an adolescent. Counsel for the Attorney General suggested that 'there is a bright line at age eighteen at which the needs of retribution and deterrence take over' (at [14]). The suggestion that an adolescent may suddenly, on their eighteenth birthday, appear to recognise the harm that they are undertaking seems somewhat unusual and certainly does not appear to take account of any understanding of problematic adolescent sexual behaviour.

Whilst there are a number of reasons why adolescents may access child pornography it is submitted that a key issue is one identified by Longo:

> . . . an important indicator of sexual health for teenagers is the degree to which the sexual behaviour is in the service of developmentally, appropriate sexual needs as opposed to primarily nonsexual needs.
>
> (Longo *et al.*, cited in Quayle and Taylor, 2006: 120)

To an extent this can be varied slightly by reference to the development of sexually appropriate behaviour and those situations where inappropriate sexual development or interest has been identified. The internet allows adolescents to explore their sexuality in a way that was not possible until its advent (Quayle *et al.*, 2008: 71) but the exploration of sexuality is an inherent part of adolescent sexual development. Adolescents have been 'exploring their differences' for many years through playing 'doctors and nurses' and adolescent escapades to, for example, peek into changing rooms, etc. It is quite possible therefore that some form of accessing may not be a display of problematic behaviour (although Quayle, 2007 notes that a difficulty in this area is that there is a dearth of information about what constitutes 'normal sexual development' (p. 202)).

Why do adolescents access child pornography? In an important study in New Zealand it was noted that most young people who accessed material in that study were attempting to obtain 'age appropriate' material (Carr, 2004: 65), i.e. material that showed children close to their own age. To an extent this could be considered to be comparable to the behaviours exhibited above and whilst it is not to be condoned (because of the victimisation issues arising out of its production) it must be questioned whether, by itself, it can be construed as deviant or worthy of a criminal justice intervention.

However a more worrying trend that was also identified by Carr is that more than half of the adolescents identified in the study were actively trading material relating to children aged two to seven (Carr, 2004: 65). This is undoubtedly highly problematic given what is known about how the proliferation and dissemination of material contributes to the victimisation of children and, potentially, an increase in the material. It was not clear from Carr's study what the purpose of the distribution was and, for example, whether it was in order to obtain age-appropriate material or whether it was for more deviant purposes. Irrespective of the motivation it is a troubling trend and demonstrates a lack of appreciation of the situation by adolescents. Indeed, there is some evidence to suggest that adolescents who access the material see the children depicted as being sexual objects rather than as human beings and certainly not as victims of a serious sexual assault (Moultrie, 2006: 170 who reports an adolescent offender stating that the very young children shown in the images he had accessed were 'little machines' who 'were bred for it').

How should the law deal with an adolescent who is accessing child pornography? Quayle and Taylor make an important point when they note that the internet is largely unregulated (especially in respect of adult pornographic material) and that a child is suddenly able to gather vast amounts of material. They conclude that:

> rather than criminalising such activities in relation to the new technologies, we should see them as a child protection issue, both for the victims in child abuse images but also for those victimised by a largely unregulated environment.

> (Quayle and Taylor, 2006: 127)

This is perhaps an important point: technology has developed in such an extreme way that it is perhaps unsurprising that adolescents are being exposed to material that few would have seen some years ago. The internet includes extremely hard-core material, including depictions of rape (or simulated rape) and numerous fetishisms. Without a programme to assist adolescents in understanding this material it is perhaps not surprising that some will look towards deviant material; some no doubt as part of sexual experimentation and discovery (something that appears borne out by the research conducted by Carr, 2004 and Moultrie, 2006 who both noted that a significant proportion of adolescents who download child pornography indicate that they began by looking at hard-core (adult) pornography before seeking out child pornography). Quayle and Taylor postulate that these adolescents should be considered children in need of assistance rather than being labelled a sex offender.

In many instances it will be difficult to argue against the proposition that children are in need of protection but in others it will be necessary to formally intervene. It may be thought that distribution could be used as a dividing line in that the harm caused by distribution is arguably greater than possession (see the discussion in Chapter 2) but it will be remembered that the analysis of Carr, 2004 does not suggest that there is necessarily any greater harm posed by those adolescents. An additional complication is the issue of victimisation. It was noted above that Quayle and Taylor believe that adolescents who access child pornography can be considered victims but it would seem some are direct victims of sexual solicitations by others.

Moultrie found that this was an issue in the study that she undertook. She noted:

> Young people in this sample have undoubtedly been victimised, in that adults have sent them abuse images and communicated with them about the sexual abuse of younger children
>
> (Moultrie, 2006: 172)

Others support this conclusion, with some noting that some adults will send child pornography to adolescents as part of a process of desensitising the child to sexual activity (Palmer, 2004). A case that demonstrates the difficulty of this is reported by Quayle *et al.* who present the case of:

> . . . a thirteen-year-old boy introduced to adult pornography on line. He was encouraged to masturbate to this material and then, over time, introduced to illegal material of children being sexually abused. By the time the police arrested this young person . . . he was masturbating to images of very young children being buggered and raped.
>
> (Quayle *et al.*, 2008: 75)

Is this person an offender or a victim? Moultrie argues that the terms are unhelpful (Moultrie, 2006: 173) because of the complexity of understanding what they have done. Whilst some may be victims their behaviour is undoubtedly problematic and there would appear to be an element of voluntariness in respect of some of the behaviour, which may require a formal intervention. This difficulty is perhaps also noted in *R v McCartney* [2009] NICA 52, discussed above. It was clear from the transcript that the offender began to access child pornography following online meetings with adults who suggested images to access (at [7]). The Court of Appeal recognised that he had been 'corrupted' by the adults but seemed less prepared to understand the effects of this conditioning. For example, it concluded:

> [W]e entirely accept that even a corrupted offender must accept increasing culpability as he moves from adolescence to adulthood . . .
>
> (at [15])

Is it realistic to expect a person to understand their behaviour as they age? If a person has been groomed or corrupted to believe that such behaviour is normal should they be considered criminally culpable? It could be argued that it should be considered criminally culpable since adolescents do appear to minimise their involvement (Moultrie, 2006: 170) and at some point there should be recognition that their actions are illegal even if they (for whatever reason) believe that it is acceptable; and accordingly a deliberate course of conduct to circumvent the law may need criminal intervention. Perhaps it is ultimately an issue of sentencing and disposal. In *McCartney* the court decided that a custodial sentence should not be imposed (notwithstanding the fact that there was a very large number of images at all levels of classification: see [2009] NICA 52 at [8]) to reflect the corrupting influence.

Realistically the offending behaviour of an individual accessing child pornography will differ in each case. Quayle *et al.* note:

> It is apparent that we understand very little about how children become involved in accessing abusive images, the relationship of this to other sexually problematic behaviours and the developmental needs that this may be meeting.
>
> (Quayle *et al.*, 2008: 75)

Without such understanding it will not be possible to identify the circumstances when adolescent offenders should be the subject of criminal intervention. It would be easy to state that where they seek to access 'age appropriate' material then a non-criminal justice intervention should follow but the findings of Carr, 2004 and Moultrie, 2006 suggest that adolescents will frequently be in possession of other material. This, together with the findings that some may themselves be victims of exploitation by adults seeking to solicit them for sex, means that it can be difficult to understand when they have participated in culpable behaviour. It is submitted that the law should be slow to prosecute those under 18 save where there is clear evidence of deliberately deviant behaviour. However the mere fact that a person becomes 18 should not be used as an indication that it is right to prosecute someone, especially where the behaviour arises from the time when they were an adolescent.

Chapter 10

Sentencing

Until now, the focus of this book has been a discussion on how people commit a criminal offence by their actions relating to child pornography. In this chapter the issue of how they should be sentenced for their crime will be discussed. The focus of this chapter will be the sentencing guideline produced by the Sentencing Guidelines Council in England and Wales as this provides a series of important principles that can be tested. It is conceded that other countries also have developed sentencing guidelines, most notably the United States through the Federal Sentencing Guidelines, and some reference will be made to these. However focusing on the guideline in England and Wales will allow sentencing to be analysed in depth and this could allow general conclusions to be drawn.

This chapter is not intended to be a critical examination of the penology of sentencing, as it is simply not possible to do that in a book of this type and size. For that reason there will not be an examination of each type of sentence (e.g. the various community sentences or the purpose of imprisonment) or indeed the rationale or purpose behind sentencing. This is, admittedly, an interesting issue in the context of child pornography. (For example, should it be considered a derivative of child abuse or of obscenity? The rationale of sentencing probably differs between both.) However such a discussion would be a chapter in its own right.

The guideline

Whilst this chapter will use the focus of the Sentencing Guidelines Council definitive guideline, it will not discuss whether it is appropriate that a guideline exists as this is an issue that goes beyond the sentencing of child pornography (for an interesting discussion see Wasik, 2008). The chapter will not analyse whether the guideline itself is being followed consistently. It is extremely difficult to ascertain this, since, as will be seen, there are so many individual characteristics behind a sentencing decision. Hebenton *et al.* purported to demonstrate that the guideline was not being followed (Hebenton *et al.*, 2009) but it is submitted that their analysis does not demonstrate this. They focused on a small sample of cases that were found before the appellate courts and they focused simply on a small number of issues. Restricting an analysis to cases before the Court of Appeal is problematic since sentencing is ordinarily the province of the first-instance courts and the Court of Appeal selects those cases that will appear before it (as leave is granted). The sample is even more skewed because the prosecution can appeal against a lenient sentence only in respect of certain offences (those within ss. 35–36, CJA 1988). Offences relating to indecent photographs of children are not prescribed and so the sample of Hebenton *et al.* could only involve those cases where the defence believed the sentence was wrong and not the prosecution. Even where the Court of Appeal does select a case, it can only interfere with a sentence when the threshold is met, that being where the sentence is manifestly excessive (*R v Waddingham* (1983) 5 Cr App R (S) 66); accordingly the Court of Appeal upholding a sentence does not mean that the sentence was necessarily correct.

For these reasons an analysis of whether the guideline is being followed will not be carried out in this chapter. That is not to state that such research would be unimportant. The aim of Hebenton *et al.*'s research was worthy but such analysis would be complicated and will require resources and time beyond that which can be included within this book. This chapter will instead focus on why the components of the guideline exist and how they have been interpreted by the courts. Cases purporting to apply the guideline will be examined to see what conclusions can be drawn about how the guideline is being implemented but the qualification noted above should be noted: it is not intended to be an empirical analysis of whether the guideline is being followed.

Before discussing the guideline in depth it would be worth pausing to note how we arrived at this position and what the guideline is. It would appear that there is some confusion over what the guideline is. The current guideline is that issued by the SGC in 2007 as part of the definitive guideline on sexual offences (SGC, 2007). This replaced the earlier guidance that had been produced for the Court of Appeal.

It was the Court of Appeal itself who first decided to issue guidance on the sentencing of offences relating to child pornography. The first attempt was made in *R v Toomer et al.* [2001] 2 Cr App R (S) 8 where the Court of Appeal, for the first time, made 'observations' on the sentencing practice of courts when faced with offenders in respect of child pornography. The guidance was limited but there was a clear consensus that any commercial involvement raised the offence to one of significant seriousness (p. 34) as did the extent of any distribution. Interestingly the court held that 'the character of the defendant is an important factor' (p. 34) a remark that the SAP, SGC and Court of Appeal have suggested is no longer true although, as will be seen below, there is some evidence to suggest that the position in *Toomer* continues to exist.

In *R v Wild* [2002] 1 Cr App R (S) 37 the Court of Appeal sought the view of the SAP on how offenders who breach the Protection of Children Act 1978 should be sentenced (p. 161) and this invitation was taken up by the SAP who formulated a consultation paper and, eventually, advice to the Court of Appeal (which was broadly accepted in *R v Oliver et al.* [2003] 1 Cr App R 28; for a critique see Gillespie, 2003). This guidance continued until it was updated in 2007 when the

SGC produced a definitive guideline on sexual offences. Whilst these offences are not within the Sexual Offences Act 2003 the SGC took the opportunity to update and reissue the original advice (SGC, 2007: 109–114). The SGC stated that the guidance set out in *Oliver* largely remains accurate (SGC, 2007: 109) but some important amendments were made.

The original advice of the SAP, with which the Court of Appeal agreed, was that there were two factors of importance in deciding the correct sentence; the nature of the material and the offender's involvement with the material (SAP, 2002: 5). Additional factors would then become relevant, including a number of aggravating and mitigating factors, and the correct sentence could then be set. The SGC also followed this pattern and so it remains the most relevant method of setting the sentence.

In order to fully understand the guideline the various components of the guideline will be examined, beginning with the two key concepts – the nature of the material and the offender's involvement with the material.

Nature of the material

The first factor that was considered important is its nature. This was discussed extensively in Chapters 2–4 of this book and it was noted that offenders use a wide range of material. Chapters 3 and 4 discussed what threshold was used to criminalise child pornography and this will not be revisited as that relates to what is or is not illegal. However the SAP suggested that the nature of the material could also be used to determine how serious the offence is. They stated that seriousness could be based in terms of the degree of harm that is experienced by the child portrayed in the photograph (SAP, 2002: 6). Of course this proposition can be criticised in that a photograph is simply a snapshot in time: and a photograph that shows, for example, an adult touching the breast of a child does not mean that the child was not later penetrated by the adult. Indeed, a possible difficulty with linking harm and nature is the fact that many photographs are stills from a film (Taylor and Quayle, 2003: 39). Thus it is quite possible that D has a photograph of V that does not depict any penetrative sexual activity. If however that series is known and, later in the filming, the child was sexually penetrated then it must be seriously questioned whether D's photograph tells us anything about the harm suffered by the child. V has been sexually assaulted and the photograph D has is part of the chain of events that led to this harm. However it is an accepted rule of sentencing that a person can only be sentenced on the basis of what crime has taken place. It is quite possible that D did not realise there were/are other photographs in the same series and thus sentencing on the basis of the (eventual) harm would seem potentially unfair to that defendant.

The better approach to understanding the logic of the SAP is to note the purpose of the legislation. Whilst its ultimate aim was to protect children through the criminalisation of child pornography (McCarthy and Moodie, 1981) it was noted in Chapters 2–4 that, in essence, child pornography laws, including the Protection of

Children Act 1978, are derivatives of the obscenity legislation. Therefore, as a principle, the more 'severe' the 'pornography' is, the more grave the offence (an analogy could be drawn to the Obscene Publications Act 1959 and this principle was recently enunciated by the Court of Appeal in *R v Snowden* [2010] 1 Cr App R (S) 39 at p. 236). How does one decide the severity of pornography? The impact on the child *in that depiction* or the nature of the activity depicted is an appropriate way of doing this. The focus can only be on the image at issue and not what happened either earlier or later, because the focus of the law's attention is the image of the child.

It is not only England and Wales that believes the nature of the material is an important part of the sentencing process. The US federal sentencing guidelines, whilst not expressly using the term 'nature', does require a sentence to be aggravated where material portrays 'sadistic or masochistic conduct or other depictions of violence' (US *Federal Sentencing Guidelines Manual* §2G2(4)) and certainly this would be consistent with the position in England and Wales. Other countries also adopt a similar approach. Perhaps one of the more important recognitions of this can be found in the Supreme Court of Tasmania where in *DPP v Latham* [2009] TASSC 101 Porter J stated that the nature and content of the image was a key factor in setting the sentence (at [34]). The judge described this as 'including the age of the children and the gravity of the activity portrayed – in particular, the degree of obvious physical harm or fear or distress in the victim' (ibid.). Other jurisdictions in Australia have reached similar conclusions (see, for example, the comment of the New South Wales Court of Criminal Appeal in *R v Gent* [2005] NSWCCA 370 at [99]). Canada has also considered nature as extremely important. In *R v Hunt* 2002 ABCA 155 the fact that the images were 'graphic' was considered to be a key factor in the sentence. A clearer statement is to be found in *R v Kwok* (2007, unreported). In this case Molloy J, sitting in the Ontario Superior Court of Justice, was faced with an offender who had gathered in excess of 2,000 images including 60 video clips. The material was described as being sadistic in nature and including material relating to very young children, including babies (at [48]). The judge describes the nature of the material as being an 'extremely aggravating' factor (ibid.).

Where England and Wales does perhaps differ from other countries is in the systematic approach it takes to ascertaining the nature of material. The SAP looked to the COPINE scale for assistance. The COPINE scale will be remembered from Chapter 2 when it was used to demonstrate the breadth of material that is used by offenders. It was put together as a typology of paedophile picture collections and it was designed, in part, to assist law enforcement agencies by providing 'an objective means of judging the nature of collections' (Taylor *et al.*, 2001: 100). However it is also worth noting that it was intended to ignore legal definitions of child pornography and instead emphasise a psychological approach to the use of pictures (Taylor *et al.*, 2001: 99–100), and to this extent its use within a legal context is controversial. That said, the typology was based on victimhood and if a photograph is to be judged against what it depicts then using an adaptation of the COPINE scale could bring with it some advantages, notably the fact that ordinarily the impact on the victim will be more severe as the scale progresses.

Initially the SAP sought to include images between COPINE levels 2 through 10 into a five-point scale (SAP, 2002: 6) but, as noted in Chapter 3, the Court of Appeal rejected this approach and instead stated that the five-point scale should be adjusted so that levels 1 to 3 inclusive were excluded (*R v Oliver* [2003] 1 Cr App R 28 at p. 467). Although its five-point scale began with 'erotic posing' (which is COPINE level 5) a question mark existed over the place of COPINE level 4 (Gillespie, 2003). This confusion was further confused slightly when both the SAP and Court of Appeal in *Oliver* used slightly different terminology than that used in the COPINE scale. The original scale is presented in Table 10.1.

It was noted in Chapters 2 to 4 that the place of nudity is the subject of some debate and presumably this meant that images that showed mere nudity – where they were indecent – should be treated as a 'level 1' image although presumably at the less serious end of this.

A difficulty with the SAP definition was that by directly transplanting the COPINE scale into the five-point sentencing scale they missed one crucial issue that related to the role of an adult. COPINE level 7 images involve the penetration

Table 10.1 The COPINE scale and that used in *R. v Oliver* (2003)

Oliver scale	COPINE scale
1 Images depicting erotic posing with no sexual activity	5 Erotic posing (deliberately posed pictures of children in sexualised or provocative posing)
	6 Explicit erotic posing (emphasising genital areas of the child)
2 Sexual activity between children, or solo masturbation by a child	7 Explicit sexual activity (involves touching, mutual and self-masturbation, oral sex and intercourse by child, not involving an adult)
3 Non-penetrative sexual activity between adults and children	8 Assault (pictures of children being subjected to a sexual assault, involving digital touching, involving an adult)
4 Penetrative sexual activity between children and adult	9 Gross assault (grossly obscene pictures of sexual assault, involving penetrative sex, masturbation or oral sex involving an adult)
5 Sadism or bestiality	10 Sadistic/bestiality: (a) Pictures showing a child being tied, bound, beaten, whipped or otherwise subjected to something that implies pain, or (b) Pictures where an animal is involved in some form of sexual behaviour with a child

Notes: Oliver scale: [2003] 1 Cr App. R. 28 at p. 467. *COPINE scale:* Taylor et al., 2001: 101.

of a child without an adult being present and the SAP, without necessarily under-standing the logic of this, classified this as a 'level 2' image whilst deciding that non-penetrative sexual activity involving a child amounted to 'level 3'. The law, however, distinguished between penetrative and non-penetrative activity, perhaps most prominently after the Sexual Offences Act 2003 where, for example, forced fellatio is classed as rape (ss. 1 and 5, SOA 2003) and where penetrative activity with a child can carry a much higher maximum sentence than non-penetrative activity (cf s. 6(2) and s. 7(2), SOA 2003).

From a psychological perspective the absence of an adult from an image can be relevant in understanding why an offender has a particular image in his collection, but from a legal perspective it did have the appearance of a paradox in that penetrative activity between children was considered to be less serious than non-penetrative activity involving a child and yet that was not representative of the law of sexual offences. When the SGC reissued the guideline they accepted this point, at least in part, when they moved penetrative images to level 4. The revised classification is:

1   Images depicting erotic posing with no sexual activity.
2   Non-penetrative sexual activity between children, or solo masturbation by a child.
3   Non-penetrative sexual activity between adults and children.
4   Penetrative sexual activity involving a child or children, or both children and adults.
5   Sadism or penetration of, or by, an animal. (SGC, 2007: 109.)

The placement of penetrative activity as 'Level 4' is to be welcomed, as it does better reflect the realities of this behaviour but the revised scale does raise other issues. For example, the SGC states 'images depicting non-penetrative activity between children are generally less serious than images depicting non-penetrative activity between adults and children' (SGC, 2007: 109). This is presumably because it is thought that the impact of adult involvement means the activity is more serious. However when such matters were raised when the original COPINE typology was being put together the involvement of a child was recognised:

> ... although the offender may not be visible in the scene [i]n videos of this kind of material, it is not uncommon to hear the photographer giving instruc-tions to the child on what pose to take, to smile, and so on. Although not necessarily visible, the adult is present as the director of poses.
>
> (Taylor *et al.*, 2001: 104)

Chapter 9 discussed the concept of children being involved in the production of child pornography, but it would seem more likely that the majority of pictures depicting sexual activity between children or even solo sexual activity are insti-gated by an adult. This will be seen below in respect of those who have solicited children online and encouraged children to, for example, expose themselves on a webcam. Where the reality of the situation is that an adult is involved and has either enticed or coerced a child into sexual activity it must be questioned whether this is any less serious than when the adult itself has sexually assaulted the child and the shift to level 4 represents this.

The use of the COPINE scale has not been without criticism although some of this is arguably not the fault of the SAP and SGC. For example, Carr notes that an impact of the use of the COPINE scale is that criminal justice agencies are basing the prioritisation of resources on the basis of the SGC scale and downplaying the significance of those involved with level 1 images (Carr, 2004: 14). That the police, in particular, adopt this approach is perhaps understandable. The police perceive their role as the investigation of crime and it is in their interests to prior- itise suspects that will receive significant sentences. However as Carr notes, the difficulty with this approach is that there is no evidence to suggest that an offender who accesses level 1 images is any less dangerous than someone who accesses level 5 images (Carr, 2004: 15). Indeed, Carr argues that the converse may even be true, as a person is being sexually stimulated by scenarios that he is more likely to encounter. It has been stated that a problem with the criminal justice system in relation to child pornography is that it concentrates on the offender at the expense of the victim (Taylor and Quayle, 2003: 206). If Carr is correct in stating that the police are prioritising operations on the basis of the COPINE scale then this would, at one level, add weight to the argument by Taylor and Quayle, in that the police are potentially ignoring the risks that people who engage with level 1 material may pose to children. Is this the fault of the SGC scale though? Probably not. It was noted above that guidelines were being developed by the courts prior to the SAP being invited to provide guidance (most notably in *R v Toomer* [2001] 2 Cr App R (S) 8) and thus it is likely that some sort of categorisation would be adopted in any event. The police have limited resources and thus prioritisation is inevitable. How they prioritise is a matter for the police and not the sentencing council and the criticism should realistically not be transferred from the police to the SAP.

Other criticisms of the use of the scale are linked to the misunderstanding of the purpose of sentencing the offender as discussed below. So, for example, it has been stated that basing the sentence on the typology may not tell us anything about offender behaviour or their risk to children (Beech *et al.*, 2008: 221). Whilst this is undoubtedly true it was noted above that sentences for this type of offence are not based on what someone might do but rather on what they have done; i.e. accessed indecent photographs of children. Therefore the basis of sentence should be on how grave the access or photographs were although conceptions of risk are important in a secondary sense and this is discussed further below.

Although England and Wales are among the few countries to have adopted a derivative of the COPINE scale in such a formal way, some other jurisdictions have considered its applicability to their sentencing decisions. For example, in *R v Missions* 232 NSR (2d) 329 the Nova Scotia Court of Appeal approved of the use of the five-point *Oliver* scale and this was followed by the Territorial Court of Yukon in *R v VH* 2008 YKTC 21. However it has never been formally recognised and in many other cases the scale is not referred to and a general discussion of the nature of images is included. In the Australian Capital Territories the use of the scale in *Oliver* would appear to be more formalised. In *R v Silva* [2009] ACTSC 108 the Supreme Court of the ACT stated that 'the classification of pornographic material is commonly done by the [Australian Federal Police] for the prosecuting authorities using what is known as the Oliver scale' (at [6]) which is interesting as it would seem therefore that it is the police that have led to the scale being adopted rather than it being a decision of the judiciary to recognise it. Certainly by *R v Ashman* [2010] ACTSC 45 the Supreme Court had noted that 'in addressing the nature of the material, the approach has been taken to follow the seriousness set out by the United Kingdom Court of Appeal in *R v Oliver*' (at [9]) which suggests that the use of the scale is now accepted as standard practice, at least within the Australian Capital Territories. Other jurisdictions are perhaps less clear about whether they adopt the scale. For example, in New South Wales, the courts appear happy to refer to the general principles within *Oliver* (see, for example, *R v Gent* [2005] NSWCCA 370 and *Whiley v R* [2010] NSWCCA 53) but have not specifically referred to the five-point scale.

An interesting issue about where the COPINE/*Oliver* scale is being used in other jurisdictions is there does not appear to be recognition of the change made to the scale by the Sentencing Guidelines Council in their definitive guideline. It was noted earlier that perhaps one of the most prominent changes was the reclassification of penetrative sexual contact between children from level 2 to level 4. Where those jurisdictions are using the original *Oliver* scale then this flaw remains unchecked.

Extent of involvement

The second primary factor in deciding the sentence is to consider what the offender's involvement with the material is. What is meant by this? It would seem to mean the proximity of the offender to the actual abuse of the child. It was explained by the SAP thus:

> We ... referred to evidence that child abusers commonly use and are influenced by pornography. An offender convicted only of possessing child pornography clearly cannot be sentenced on the basis that he is an actual or potential child abuser, but those who produce or distribute the material do have a more direct responsibility for its eventual use, as well as for encouraging further production.
>
> (SAP, 2002: 5)

In addition to this the SAP stated that a commercial involvement would significantly aggravate an offence (SAP, 2002: 7).

Possession

The SAP's reference to the use of pornography by sex offenders is interesting but it should be noted that it is carefully phrased. It is not stating that there is evidence to show a link between the possession of child pornography and those same offenders committing contact abuse, instead the link is phrased in the opposite direction, that there is evidence to suggest that those who do sexually abuse a child may have been influenced by child pornography. The implication of this logic was discussed in Chapter 2. An obvious issue but one not mentioned by either the SAP or the SGC in its later guideline, is that where sexual abuse has been aggravated by the use of pornography a question must arise as to whether this should act as an aggravating factor for sentence. It would seem that the answer is that it generally is not considered as an aggravating factor. For example, it could be argued that consecutive sentences should be imposed in such circumstances to reflect the fact that the production of child pornography adds an extra element to the abuse that is suffered by the child. However it would appear that the default position is that consecutive sentences are not imposed and instead separate sentences are imposed, which are served concurrently. Does this adequately reflect the culmination of what the offender has done? It would seem not: the sentence is unlikely to be higher than a person would get for *either* making child pornography or the sexual abuse of a child. It is submitted that the harm inflicted is such that consecutive or part-consecutive sentences could be justified to reflect the totality of the conduct.

The SAP must, for reasons outlined at the beginning of this chapter, be correct to state that a person who possesses indecent photographs cannot be sentenced on the basis that they *might* then go on to abuse a child. That said, this is perhaps a simplistic statement as it will be seen that arguably this does happen when decisions are made not only about dangerousness (discussed below) but also because it does seem to influence the sentence imposed when aggravating and mitigating circumstances are considered (discussed further below). However as a general principle it would seem appropriate to state that a person who possesses indecent images should not be sentenced on the basis that he *might* be involved in the sexual abuse of a child. However this general rule must be subject to two limitations. The first is where an offender has already been convicted of the sexual abuse of a child. In such circumstances it could be said that the possession of child pornography demonstrates that he continues to pose a risk to children (see Chapter 8 for a discussion on this) and accordingly this must be a factor that is taken into account. The SAP accepted this logic and stated that such previous convictions must be an aggravating factor (SAP, 2002: 11). Whilst the same point was not made expressly by the SGC, this should be placed in the context of the fact that the guideline stated that a previous conviction for a sexual offence was a general aggravating feature for any sexual offence (SGC, 2007: 9) and thus it is submitted that the same position is adopted.

The second qualification of the general rule that a person convicted of possession should not ordinarily be sentenced as though he has abused a child is where he is closely connected to the actual abuse of a child. For example, X and Y talk on the internet. X offers to provide Y pictures of his 7 year-old daughter and Y replies 'yes, please'. It is entirely possible that Y would be sentenced only on the basis that he possessed the images (see the discussion on this below) since he has not necessarily caused or encouraged (viz. incited) the distribution of the images. However in the circumstances described in that example it cannot be said that Y is a simple possessor as his behaviour is proximate to the actual abuse of a child. Y would, it is submitted, realise that his acceptance of these photographs will encourage X to produce more photographs of his child and accordingly the offender should be sentenced accordingly.

Other offences

The quote of the SAP differentiated possession from the other offences, and the SAP continued with this distinction:

> We concluded that sentencing levels for those convicted of the more serious offences of making, showing or distributing images of children should reflect that responsibility.
>
> (SAP, 2002: 5)

The SAP note that in this context 'making' means the production of images, and in essence they conclude that the offences of the production and dissemination of indecent photographs should be considered automatically more serious than possession, owing to the proximity of the behaviour to the abuse of a child. It is submitted that this is correct and it was noted in Chapter 2 that the consequences of the production and dissemination of child pornography is that a child is harmed, both in a primary and secondary sense, and that the responsibility of an offender who produces or disseminates such photographs is not insignificant.

The second aspect of this proposition is that where the offender's proximity to the direct harm of a child is particularly close – where, for example, an offender is taking indecent photographs – then this should be reflected in the sentence. How this plays out in practice is discussed below where it will be seen, for example, that the use of the SAP/SGC scale is perhaps more controversial but as a general proposition it is clearly an appropriate statement.

It was noted earlier that the existence of a commercial element to the crime was considered to be a serious aggravating factor. However the meaning of commercial activity was not confined purely to a pecuniary sense:

> We suggested [in the consultation paper] . . . and again there was general agreement with our view, that the swapping of images should in itself be regarded as a commercial activity, because it fuelled the demand for material.
>
> (SAP, 2002: 7)

To an extent this was then implicitly qualified when the SAP referred to 'wide-scale distribution'. This qualification makes sense in the context of what was being said. It has been noted already that there is doubt as to the proportion of commercial child pornography available (although it is thought that it is beginning to now increase (IWF, 2010)). Restricting commercialisation to its pecuniary sense would be unfortunate and the SAP was correct to suggest that wide-scale dissemination can be imputed from the wide-scale dissemination of images as it is known that a considerable amount of indecent photographs are traded without payment through, for example, swapping images (Taylor and Quayle, 2003: 184 and Jenkins, 2001). Whilst, as a matter of policy this would appear an appropriate stance to take, there would appear to be some doubt as to whether the courts have followed this part of the guidance. Certainly it would seem clear that where there is a pecuniary commercial interest the courts regard this as a very serious aggravating factor, indeed agreeing that this is one of the most serious forms of the offence (see, for example, *R v Van Der Huure* [2008] EWCA Crim 1727 where a sentence of imprisonment for public protection was upheld on a Dutch citizen who ran a commercial child pornography company and who distributed DVDs from England). There would also appear to be an indication that the courts are prepared to accept that proven wide-scale dissemination is to be a serious aggravating factor (*R v Davenport* [2009] 2 Cr App R (S) 38). However a more difficult position is where there is *potential* wide-scale dissemination. Thus where, for example, an offender uses peer-to-peer software or posts a photograph to an FTP or website where it can be readily accessed. In each of these situations it is difficult to quantify the distribution. However should an offender be rewarded for the fact that it is not possible to show how many people have accessed the site? It is beyond the offender's control as to how many people access the material through peer-to-peer or a website and yet there appears some evidence that the courts have not taken this issue as seriously (see the comments of Rafferty J in *R v Barber* [2009] EWCA Crim 774 at [9] and see *R v Dooley* [2006] 1 WLR 775 discussed in Chapter 6). This is to be regretted. It is submitted that widespread dissemination should be construed as commercial trading and thus attract the more serious punishments and this must include situations where offenders put information into a domain where it is easily accessed and traded. This would appear analogous to a commercial release of material and should be treated as such.

Developing a 'hierarchy' of offences would appear to be common in many other jurisdictions. This is perhaps not surprising since it was noted in Chapter 8 that in most jurisdictions possession was considered less culpable than other types of behaviour. However it is worth noting that other jurisdictions believe that distribution is an important aggravating circumstance. The US federal guidelines consider distribution to be a significant aggravating factor (US Federal Sentencing Guideline Manual §2G2.2(3)), especially where it involves a pecuniary advantage being gained. In *DPP v Latham* [2009] TASSC 101 the Supreme Court of Tasmania explicitly agreed with comments of the author that noted distribution leads to repeated victimisation of the child (at [35]). Canada also treats distribution seriously and *R v Johannson* 2009 SKQB 12 is interesting because the Queen's Bench for Saskatchewan treated the use of peer-to-peer technology as an aggravating factor as it 'made the child pornography available worldwide' (at [16]). This is an important recognition of the fact that peer-to-peer technology can allow anyone to access material, allowing for much greater distribution then that which could occur if the distribution took place between named individuals. That said, not everybody agrees with this provision. Basbaum criticises a similar decision in the US saying it penalises a 'defendant [who] failed to disable the feature that automatically makes the user's images available to [other] users' (Basbaum, 2010: 1299). The difficulty with this argument is that it misrepresents what a defendant does. It presents the actions of the peer-to-peer user as an omission but it is not clear that this accurately depicts what is involved. The argument – as with that presented in *R v Dooley* [2006] 1 WLR 775 – is premised on the fact that a person does not know how peer-to-peer programs work and yet it is more likely that they do. If an offender does not wish to be considered a distributor – and thus not attract the aggravated sentence – then they should ensure that they are not allowing people to access their material. Distribution increases the victimisation of the victim and it is not unreasonable to hold that a person who has allowed access to images is guilty of an aggravated offence. An example of a ruling where similar reasoning was adopted by the courts is *R v Carson* [2008] QCA 268 where the Queensland Court of Appeal upheld as an aggravating factor the fact that an offender had not 'switched off' the distribution feature of his peer-to-peer software (at [23]).

Form of material

Two interesting issues arise in respect of the form of material and how these relate to the sentencing guidelines issued by the SGC and courts. The first relates to the question of whether movie/video clips should be treated differently to photographs, and the second relates to the place of pseudo-photographs within the sentencing framework.

Moving images

The first issue is that of movies. It has been noted several times in this book that the internet has revolutionised the way in which child pornography is produced, disseminated and possessed but the growth of broadband and fibre optic connections has also had an impact. It is now possible to send lengthy movies over internet connections in a relatively short period of time. At a commercial level, the (legitimate) paradigm of this is the growth of iTunes where TV episodes and even full-length movies can be purchased quickly and cheaply. The pornography industry has quickly identified the potential of this and many sites will allow users to download or stream (view live in a way similar to watching on the internet) high-definition broadcasts of adult pornography, and child pornographers have not been slow to use this technology.

How should movies be classed for the purpose of sentences? Theoretically a movie on a computer is a single file in the same way that a single photograph is. However in reality the two are very different. A movie could (and frequently is) be divided into literally thousands of indecent photograph 'stills'. Also some would argue the impact of a video is greater, in part because of the sound and the fact that one can predict what is about to happen. Whilst there is no published research on whether the impact is greater in respect of child pornography, anecdotally those who work with child pornography will frequently state that it is, particularly when sound is involved although there is no research, to the best of the author's knowledge, that addresses this issue.

Should a movie therefore be considered more serious than a simple photograph? It would seem clear that if, as was seen above, the seriousness of child pornography should be based, in part, on the presented impact on a victim, a movie should be classed by its most severe depiction. By this what is meant is that an image that portrays penetrative sexual activity with a child should be classed as 'level 4' material even if this is only a small proportion of its overall length. The SAP, Court of Appeal and (implicitly) the SGC believe that nature should be decided on victimisation and accordingly a child that suffers a penetrative assault should be considered to be the victim of a more serious offence than non-penetrative assaults, and the sentence for child pornography should reflect this.

A more difficult question is whether a movie should always be considered more serious than a photograph. Surprisingly the SAP and SGC have been silent as to this point and it does not, for example, feature in the list of aggravating circumstances when realistically it could be expected to. The Court of Appeal has not reached a considered conclusion on this issue. In *R v Gorringe* [2004] EWCA Crim 3152 the Court of Appeal held that movies should be treated differently:

> . . . we reflect that videos are in a different league to single images. It is not a case of there being just sixteen images [the defendant was found in possession of sixteen videos]. Every second of the two and a half hours of video involves a considerable number of individual images.
>
> (at [4])

The Court of Appeal was therefore concerned that videos were intrinsically different yet by 2006 the position had changed:

> [W]hilst a moving image will inevitably depict the particular activity in more graphic detail and for varying lengths of time, with accompanying sound, this does not mean that there is something intrinsic in a moving image which will inevitably merit a greater degree of censure or condemnation than a still image or a series of still images which depict the same activity.
>
> (*R v Somerset* [2006] EWCA Crim 2469 at [10])

Thus the Court of Appeal turned away from the suggestion that videos were more serious *per se*. From one point of view this is arguably correct in that if defendant A has a 10 minute video clip that shows a child being raped, is this any different to defendant B who has the same images but as a series of 100 still photographs? Does the fact that the image is moving and may possibly have sound (which, of course, is not strictly speaking relevant for the purposes of PoCA 1978) mean that it is fundamentally more serious? On another level however a difference already exists since, as will be seen below, quantity does have some relevance and if a video is not considered aggravation then an offender may be considered to be in possession of a single product (a video) at, for example, level 4 whereas another defendant could be in possession of the same material and yet as it is 100 still photographs he will be in possession of a large collection of level 4 images and this can have an impact on sentencing (discussed further below).

The most recent decision of the Court of Appeal in this regard is *R v Handley* [2009] EWCA Crim 1827 where the Court of Appeal stated that 'in our judgment indecent movies are not per se worse than a still photograph' (at [12]). To give the Court of Appeal some credit they then continued to state that 'whether they are will depend on the content of the movie' but this does not give much indication as to what should be considered relevant for the purposes of sentencing.

It is submitted that it is regrettable that the Court of Appeal has adopted an ambivalent stance to the issue of moving images, although (to be fair) this could be just clumsy expressionism in *Handley*. A movie, especially where it shows a sexual assault or rape, is intrinsically worse than a single image of the same scene. Does it affect the victimisation of the child? Perhaps not in its primary sense, in that as discussed above, a still photograph showing, for example, a level 2 image does not guarantee that the child was not later subject to a level 4 image, but it is submitted that the secondary victimisation may be greater: the impact on a victim knowing that an hour-long video of her being subject to an extended rape and sexual assault may be more impactive than the knowledge that indecent photographs are circu-lating. Even if this is not true, it is submitted that videos should be considered more serious because of the nature of the material. In *Somerset* the Court of Appeal stated, but then ignored, a crucial issue: a movie portrays the acts in more graphic detail. As discussed already child pornography laws are derivatives of obscenity laws and it is submitted that a more graphic depiction can be considered more obscene and therefore worthy of punishment (for a contemporary sentencing exercise under the obscenity legislation see *R v Snowden* [2010] 1 Cr App R (S) 39).

Some countries have decided that a moving image can be translated into a finite number of images. For example, the US federal guidelines state:

> Each video, video clip, movie or similar visual depiction shall be considered to have seventy-five images. If the length of the visual depiction is substan-tially more than five minutes, an upward departure may be warranted.
>
> (para. 4 of the commentary to §G2.2 of the
> *Federal Sentencing Guidelines*)

A difficulty with this approach is it is not clear why this approximation has been chosen. For example, a 'typical' frame rate for a movie is 24 frames per second; i.e. each one-second of a film can be separated into 24 stills. In this context a five-minute movie would comprise more than 75 photographs but it cannot be said that each frame will depict the sexual abuse or exploitation of a child. Also, it is perhaps a pragmatic choice since taking a literal stance would mean that a movie would translate into several thousand images but the vast majority will be essentially the same: it will take tens of images for a physical change to be noticeable. The fact that a movie may not show explicit activity for its full length and that many of the 'stills' will not be physically different means that it is difficult to equate movies with a specific number since that must be both representative of the conduct and fair to the defendant (who should be sentenced on the basis of what he actually possesses). The US federal guidelines are, in essence, a compromise in that they select as a somewhat arbitrary figure a relatively low equivalent count. That said, it will be seen that the quantity of images can result in a serious sentence uplift (US *Federal Sentencing Guidelines Manual* §2G2.2(7) discussed below) and the thresholds are sufficiently low that two-movie clips would lead to a significant increase in sentence.

It is submitted that it would not be appropriate to approximate a movie with a particular quantity of still images but instead their presence should be considered an aggravating factor that is taken into consideration when deciding the appropriate sentence. It is submitted that a movie is different to a still photograph and that it is inappropriate to treat them as the same: a movie portrays the abuse of a child in a more realistic manner and this should be reflected in the sentence.

Pseudo-photographs

The second issue raised is in respect of pseudo-photographs. The SAP noted that it was *possible* (my emphasis) for indecent photographs to be taken without abusing a child and stated that the possession of pseudo-photographs 'should be treated as being at the lowest level of seriousness, and that making such images is less serious than making photographic images of real children' (SAP, 2002: 9). This was followed by the Court of Appeal who stated:

> Possession . . . of artificially created pseudo-photographs and the making of such images, should generally be treated as being at a lower level of seriousness than possessing or making photographic images of real children.
>
> (*R v Oliver* [2003] 1 Cr App R 28 at p. 468)

Interestingly however the Court of Appeal did qualify their statement:

> . . . there may be exceptional cases in which the possession of a pseudo-photograph is as serious as the possession of a photograph of a real child: for

example where the pseudo-photograph provides a particularly grotesque image generally beyond the scope of a photograph.

(Ibid.)

This qualification was then later followed by the SGC (SGC, 2007: 109) although interestingly their guideline arguably goes further than mere possession but this will be discussed momentarily. The SAP noted that the proposal to treat pseudo-photographs differently was not supported by everyone (SAP, 2002: 9) and the Children's Charities' Coalition for Internet Safety (CHIS) (an organisation comprising the leading children's charities including the NSPCC, Barnado's and NCH) were particularly vociferous in their criticism. CHIS argued that this was, in essence, the SAP trying to change the law because Parliament, in passing the Criminal Justice and Public Order Act 1994 which introduced pseudo-photographs into PoCA 1978, did not differentiate between penalties (Carr, 2002: 1). Whilst it is correct to state that the Parliament did not prescribe a lesser penalty for pseudo-photographs this logic can only be taken so far. For example, Parliament has listed making, taking and distribution within the same offence (s. 1, PoCA 1978) and yet nobody has questioned that the sentence of a court should differentiate between these forms of behaviour. Parliament sets the maximum term of imprisonment but leaves it to the courts to decide how offending is placed within a scale cascading down from this maximum sentence.

CHIS also complained that the original SAP advice did not differentiate between pseudo-photographs within the level of material they depict (i.e. the nature of their material) and complained that someone who, for example, possesses sadistic pseudo-photographs should not be treated more leniently than someone who possesses a simple level 1 photograph (Carr, 2002: 2). As noted above the Court of Appeal has perhaps taken this on board by qualifying the statement of the SAP stating that 'particularly grotesque' images will not attract this lesser penalty ([2003] 1 Cr App R 28 at p. 468). However it is far from certain that 'grotesque' means a level 5 image not least because the Court of Appeal also stated that such images should go 'beyond the scope of a photograph' which many pseudo-photographs may not. It could be argued that Parliament, by including pseudo-photographs, intended that a person should be sentenced according to the gravity of what is being portrayed. Whilst a child will not have been abused in the production of a pseudo-photograph, it would seem appropriate to consider that pseudo-photographs will differ in their indecency and obscenity and that an offender should be sentenced according to the type of activity that is being portrayed. To this extent it is submitted that the criticism of CHIS is correct and that adopting the approach that all pseudo-photographs should be considered as less serious is inappropriate.

However a more significant criticism that can be levelled against the SAP/SGC and Court of Appeal statement is that it ignores the realities of some forms of pseudo-photographs. It was noted in Chapters 2, 3 and 6 that there are a number of different types of pseudo-photographs and that whilst some will not involve a child (e.g. where an image of a young-looking adult is manipulated by a graphics program) but others will (e.g. where a photograph of a child eating an ice cream is superimposed on to an adult pornographic image so as to make it look like the child is performing a sex act). The SAP/SGC and Court of Appeal guidelines do not differentiate between these two types of pseudo-photographs and yet they should be treated significantly differently. Whilst in neither situation has a child been abused, in the second example a child can still suffer harm. It is has been seen throughout this book that a child who is portrayed in an indecent photograph of a child can suffer secondary harm through the knowledge that people are obtaining deviant sexual gratification from their depiction and/or the fear that a child was a willing participant in sexual activity. There is no reason to suggest that the same will not be true of those depicted in pseudo-photographs (and indeed in *R v H* [2005] EWCA Crim 3037 discussed momentarily there was evidence to support this contention (at [7])).

Few cases have considered this point and so it is not clear whether the courts necessarily appreciate this distinction. The one notable case where this point was rehearsed, in part, was *R v H* [2005] EWCA Crim 3037 although this was an unusual case. The appellant was a school teacher and in that capacity he had photographed numerous pupils legitimately. However he had also downloaded large quantities of child pornography and he then produced pseudo-photographs by superimposing the pupils' faces on to the indecent photographs of the child. Counsel for the defence raised the SAP/*Oliver* point that these were simply pseudo-photographs but the Court of Appeal appeared somewhat unimpressed by this argument and stated that 'the judge would have been quite correct in saying that the offender was actively involved in the production of images at levels 4 and 5' (at [16]). Given the photographs themselves were innocent this must be recognition by the Court of Appeal that where a real child is involved then pseudo-photographs will not be considered the least serious form of the offence. This is to be welcomed and it is to be hoped that this logic will be followed by the courts in the future.

The final issue to consider before leaving the issue of pseudo-photographs is their applicability to other offences. The SAP were clear in their guideline that only the possession and creation of pseudo-photographs should be considered as less serious.

> We accept . . . that a pseudo-photograph and a real photograph may have an equally corrupting effect on the viewer, and that pseudo-photographs may be traded for commercial gain as if they were real. The distinction between real and pseudo-photographs will, therefore, be irrelevant in a case involving the showing or distribution of images to others.
>
> (SAP, 2002: 9)

The Court of Appeal in *Oliver* did not comment on this part and so it was not clear whether the SAP's statement was being accepted or not. This perhaps marked a difficulty with the initial system of sentencing guidelines in that the SAP was merely giving advice and it did not become formally law until the Court of Appeal ruled on the matter (it then forming part of *stare decisis*). As has already been noted, there have been few cases that have considered specifically the issue of pseudo-photographs and so it is not known how the courts would rule on this matter.

The SGC, when it came to reissuing (in a slightly amended form) the guideline did not draw any distinction and indeed dealt with the issue of pseudo-photographs very briefly. After presenting the (reformulated) five-point scale they moved on to general issues and stated, 'Pseudo-photographs should generally be treated as less serious than real images' (SGC, 2007: 109). It is not clear whether the SGC were intending to reformulate the advice given by the SAP but it is submitted that this statement by the SGC is very different to that which was formulated by the SAP. By stating that pseudo-photographs should be *generally* treated less seriously, this implies that this should be the rule regardless of the mode of conduct, i.e. showing and distribution included.

The SGC dealt with indecent photographs extremely briefly and thus there was no explanation why they contradicted the SAP guidance. The SAP produced a consultation paper prior to the SGC passing its definitive guideline (SAP, 2004). It does not seem from that paper that the SAP had intended to revisit their original statement, and it is notable that, for example, when they discuss the showing or distribution of images they refer to *both* photographs and pseudo-photographs (SAP, 2004: 11). Whilst the definitive guideline did not appear until almost three years later it would be strange if the Council decided to unilaterally alter this position without explaining why or expressly drawing attention to the alteration. It is submitted that it is more likely to be sloppy wording. That said, for the reasons set out above it may be appropriate to draw a distinction between those pseudo-photographs that depict a real child and those that do not. Some have questioned how this could be proven (CHIS, 2002: 3) but this may be resolvable with guidance. Certainly it is submitted that where it can be proven that real children are involved in their production (for example, in cases such as *H* [2005] EWCA Crim 3037) a court should take this into account when sentencing.

Aggravating factors

Whilst the nature of the material, an offender's involvement with it and, to some degree, its form will be the primary factors relating to the sentence it is clear that, as with most crimes, there will be both aggravating and mitigating circumstances. In this section an analysis will be made of the current factors and consideration given to whether alternative factors can also be included.

The SAP, in its original advice, concluded that the following factors should aggravate the sentence:

- Showing or distributing indecent photographs to a child.
- Substantial quantity of photographs.

- The manner in which a collection is organised.
- Public distribution.
- Where an offender has produced child pornography, whether the offender has abused a position of trust to produce the photographs. (SAP, 2002: 11–12.)

The Court of Appeal in *Oliver* largely accepted these factors but they also added an additional factor, that being the age of the child portrayed may also be an aggravating feature ([2003] 1 Cr App R 28 at p. 468). The SGC, in its definitive guideline, added additional factors although these were primarily aimed at the offence of taking images as they included the use of drugs or alcohol to facilitate the offence, a background of intimidation or threats to the victim (SGC, 2007: 114). The SGC also stated that 'financial or other gain' would be an aggravating factor although, to an extent, this has already been discussed in respect of an offender's involvement with the material.

Not all of these factors necessarily have to be discussed. For example, the first factor, the showing or distribution of photographs to a child is simply common sense. It has been noted that a concern over child pornography is that it could be used as part of a grooming process (Taylor and Quayle, 2003: 25) and it is certainly appropriate to consider that an offender who is showing indecent photographs of a child to another child should be subject to a higher sentence than would otherwise be given for showing or distribution. Linked to this is the notion that the distribution of images to public areas, for example, websites, etc. could also be an aggravating factor. Again this would appear to be relatively uncontroversial: distribution is a serious offence in its own right but where it can be distributed to a wide number of persons then it is appropriate that the sentence reflects this. It was noted above that there is some doubt as to the extent that this needs to be proved but as a point of principle it must be correct.

A factor that, as will be seen, is particularly controversial is the quantity of material. Although this is mentioned as an aggravating factor it is also used in respect of the thresholds themselves. As the two concepts are linked they will be discussed at the same time during the later parts of this chapter.

Organisation

Perhaps the first factor that requires discussion is the statement by the SAP that the manner in which a person has organised his collection could be an aggravating factor. The justification for this is that the SAP suggests it 'may indicate a more or less sophisticated approach to trading, or a higher level of personal interest in the material' (SAP, 2002: 12). The Court of Appeal in *Oliver* accepted this proposition without comment. The origins of this comment are almost certainly the statement by Taylor *et al.*, when they produced the COPINE scale, who stated that 'obsessional sorting or organising of the material is ... an indication of the offender's involvement with the pictures and the amount of time spent "off line" engaging with the material' (Taylor *et al.*, 2001: 106).

Other studies have examined whether the organisation of material may indicate the active use of such material. The categorisation can be extremely detailed and could involve, for example, an offender dividing the collection into a series of groupings, each depicting a type of activity or victim (Sheldon and Howitt, 2007: 105). It has been suggested that a consequence of this cataloguing is that an offender spends a considerable period of time viewing the photographs which may increase sexual arousal (Sheldon and Howitt, 2007: 106) and others have suggested that an offender can gain pleasure from the process of cataloguing his collection (Bjarkman, 2004 cited in Quayle *et al.*, 2006: 124).

By cataloguing the images the collection will become accessible and decisions can be made as to the extent to which any collection, or part of a collection, can be made available to others (Quayle *et al.*, 2006: 121). An important aspect of this can be that it increases the trading of images. It is known that many pictures form part of a 'series', where the same victim is portrayed, in part because a victim may be abused for several years. By cataloguing the images it is possible to seek to complete a series, and to trade pictures in order to gain the missing images (Taylor and Quayle, 2003: 161), including using material that a person would not ordinarily 'use' but would hold for trade to obtain pictures that were of interest (Sheldon and Howitt, 2007: 106). At the extreme end, it would appear that in order to complete a series or gain access to the catalogues of others some offenders would produce new material so as to have something to trade (Taylor and Quayle, 2003: 161 present an interview with 'ES' who started offending against his daughter so that he could trade material with others).

Given that it has been stated that the offender's involvement with indecent photographs is one of the primary factors governing sentence (discussed above) then it would seem appropriate to consider organisation as an aggravating factor since the evidence above demonstrates that this shows the offender is displaying a greater involvement with photographs even where they are distant from the actual production. Can this be justified? It is submitted that the answer is 'yes'. It has been shown throughout this book that there is a secondary victimisation inherent in indecent photographs and the cataloguing of the images is capable of aggravating this secondary impact. If the images are more readily viewed, or an offender can seek to complete a series of pictures showing the full degradation of the victim, or the images are more easily traded then this must have an impact on the secondary victimisation of the child and warrants an increased sentence.

Position of trust

An interesting issue that arises in respect of child pornography offences is the question of the relevance of a position of trust. In terms of general sex offences the breach of a position of trust is considered to be a significant factor (SGC, 2007: 9) and this is particularly true where it involves a child of the family (SGC, 2007: 10). This is for very understandable reasons and in terms of the creation of indecent photographs (taking or, depending on the circumstances, the making) the

SAP stated unequivocally that the breach of a position of trust should be considered an aggravating point (SAP, 2002: 12). Whilst the SGC does not mention a position of trust expressly it does, as noted above, appear as a general aggravating feature and so it must be implicitly accepted; although it is submitted that it would have been preferable if the SGC had expressly stated that a position of trust is an aggravating factor for the production of indecent photographs.

There would appear some evidence that the courts have followed this logic and certainly this would be expected. So, for example, in *R v JF* [2008] EWCA Crim 1942 the Court of Appeal considered the production of indecent photographs of a child by a grandfather of his granddaughter was an aggravating feature. Similarly in *R v M* [2008] EWCA Crim 3335 the fact that an uncle had produced indecent photographs of his neice, whom he was sexually obsessed with, was considered a significant aggravating factor even though the actual photographs produced were limited to Level One images. That said, the courts do not always appear to follow this logic. In *R v C* [2009] EWCA Crim 2253 the offender was convicted of, *inter alia*, the digital penetration and production of indecent photographs of his niece and the Court of Appeal appeared to accede to a submission by defence counsel that this did not involve an abuse of trust (at [12]). It is difficult to accept this argument: the offender only had access to the child because of his relationship to the child and it is submitted that this is an abuse of trust and should have been considered as such.

Positions of trust are not, of course, restricted to familial situations and the courts have adopted the similar logic in other situations that demonstrate an abuse of trust. In *R v H* [2005] EWCA Crim 3037, a case that has already been discussed, the fact that the offender was a teacher who had taken pictures of children at his school (which he then used to make pseudo-photographs) was considered relevant for sentence (at [17] although the Court of Appeal used the slightly strange formulation of 'the offender was involved in the production of images . . . including, for what it is worth, a process that involved a breach of trust'. It is submitted that this was unfortunate phrasing since the breach of trust should be 'worth' something). Perhaps a more clear-cut example is *R v McKain* [2007] EWCA Crim 1145 where a pastor took level one pictures of a 15 year-old boy who had baby-sat for the offender on occasion and whom he had caught smoking and watching pornography. The Court of Appeal noted that this was a breach of trust (at [10]) and also rejected the suggestion that his positive good character, i.e. his work as a pastor, should be taken into account (at [14]) which must be correct. It would be unusual for a court to, on the one hand, aggravate a sentence on account of his vocation and immediately afterwards mitigate the sentence for the exact same reason.

That a position of trust should be relevant when photographs are taken is perhaps uncontroversial and is simply an extension of the usual rule in sexual offences, especially since (as has been noted already in this book) the taking of photographs may involve both primary and secondary harm being caused to a child. Of perhaps more interest is whether a position of trust is relevant for other offences (e.g. possessing, showing or distributing indecent photographs). The first difficulty with deciding this would be ascertaining what amounts to a position of trust. Obviously this is easier in respect of the production of indecent photographs where the nexus that exists between offender and victim can be easily defined. Outside of these situations it is perhaps less easy a concept to define but it is submitted that it is tied to the notion of character. This is something that will be discussed again below in respect of personal mitigation, but should character be considered only a mitigating circumstance or in certain circumstances can it be said to be an aggravating factor?

An argument could no doubt be made that a person who has been given discrete authority over the public should be treated more harshly when they then breach the rules that they are paid to uphold. Of course the position is perhaps easier to justify when there is a direct link between the offence and their office (e.g. corruption, excessive force or a sexual assault committed whilst on duty). Where there is no direct link should the mere fact that a person holds a position of authority in society act as an aggravating factor?

In the context of indecent photographs it would seem that the courts adopt the approach of examining the circumstances of the offence rather than the position of the offender itself. In *R v Sackman* [2010] EWCA Crim 19 a Dutch naval officer working at NATO HQ in Northwood downloaded indecent photographs of children on to his work computer and from there he had sent them to his computer at home. The judge of first instance, with whom the Court of Appeal appeared to agree, held that the offender was 'guilty of an abuse of a responsible position of trust over a long period' (at [8]). What was the abuse of a position of trust? The offender was not, for example, likely to encounter children during his work for NATO so it must be the breach of trust implicit within his role as a NATO officer.

The same logic was not adopted in *R v Barker* [2002] EWCA Crim 1730, a pre-*Oliver* case: the Courts Martial Appeal Court quashed a sentence of dismissal with disgrace to one of simple dismissal for a Corporal in the Royal Military Police. The court saw no reason why the more significant penalty of dismissal with disgrace should be imposed even though they conceded that the guidance was that this should ordinarily be imposed for a sexual offence (at [5]). The offence took place whilst serving in Gibraltar although the images were downloaded to his personal computer. The court did not take into account the fact that he was a member of the Royal Military Police or that it occurred whilst he was serving.

The distinction between *Sackman* and *Barker* would seem to be where the offence took place. In *Sackman* the offender had used his work computer at NATO headquarters to access indecent photographs of children. In *Barker* although he was in Army accommodation he used his own computer to access the material and there is no evidence he did so whilst on duty. In reality it is perhaps this that marks the distinction and if there was evidence that he had used, for example, an Army computer then this could rightly be considered to be an aggravating feature.

Age

An interesting factor to discuss is the concept of age. In its original advice the SAP had stated that it did not think that age should be relevant:

> On balance we maintain our original view that the age of the child(ren) portrayed should not **in itself** [their emphasis] be taken to aggravate or miti- gate the seriousness of an offence, since it is very difficult to quantify the effect of age in terms of aggravation of the offence.
>
> (SAP, 2002: 13)

The Court of Appeal took a subtly different approach where they said that age *could* be a factor because 'assaults on babies or very young children attract particular repugnance' (*R v Oliver* [2003] 1 Cr App R 28 at 470). To an extent this is only a minor amendment since it relates to extremities and is also premised on the basis that a younger child may be caused physical harm in the production of the images (something also discussed by the SAP) but it is a subtle shift. By the time the SGC produced its definitive guideline the position had changed once again. Age becomes a relevant factor although it is perhaps moot as to whether or not it amounts to an aggravating and mitigating factor *per se*.

The SGC guideline follows the general approach adopted by the SOA 2003 which is to differentiate between the ages of children in respect of offences. Broadly speaking, the SOA 2003 creates three age bands; offences under those aged under 13, offences under those aged under 16 and offences under those aged under 18. The age of 18 applies to exploitative offences including, it will be remembered from Chapter 3, indecent photographs of children. The distinction between the under-13s and the under-16s was found, in at least one form, in the Sexual Offences Act 1956 (ss. 5 and 6) but the SOA 2003 formalised it across a series of offences. In the guideline on sexual offences the SGC has said that the sentence should be higher where the child is under 13 (SGC, 2007: 110) and reduced where the age of the child is 17 or 18 (ibid).

The courts have certainly followed the lead of *Oliver* and do appear to consider very young children to be an aggravating factor, not only for production but also for distribution and possession (*R v P* [2008] EWCA Crim 2714; *R v Davenport* [2009] 2 Cr App R (S) 28). Age is a common aggravating factor in many other jurisdictions, which perhaps supports the decision of the Court of Appeal (and later, the SGC) to consider it so. In *R v WAE* (2009, unreported) the Provincial Court of Newfoundland and Labrador followed the lead of the English Court of Appeal in *Oliver* by stating that the age of the child, particularly very young children, should be considered as aggravation (at p. 45 of the transcript). The Ontario Superior Court of Justice also placed significant emphasis on the age of the child, particularly young children, in *R v Kwok* (2007, unreported). In Australia a similar approach is taken with the New South Wales Court of Criminal Appeal considering age to be a relevant consideration (*R v Gent* [2005] NSWCCA 370 at [990]) and in America the US federal guidelines also mention age, although there the distinction is to pre-pubescent (*Federal Sentencing Guidelines Manual* §2G2.2(b)(2)).

Can it be justified to pass a more severe sentence because of the age of the child depicted? The SAP had originally rejected the idea of treating age as an aggravating factor because they believed that an older child could suffer just as much harm as a younger child (SAP, 2002: 13). This is undoubtedly true and in respect of secondary harm it may even be greater as an older child may be aware that they have been photographed whereas a younger child may not. However it has been noted that harm is not the sole basis on which a person is sentenced for these offences. There are other bases on which a person can be sentenced and it has been noted that one basis is that the more graphic an image the greater the sanctions that can be imposed (*R v Snowdon* [2010] 1 Cr App R (S) 39). As the Court of Appeal in *Oliver* noted there is (justified) revulsion when an offender accesses young material and this can be reflected in the sentence. A possible justification for doing this is that there is evidence that the age of children in images is becoming ever younger and more graphic (IWF, 2007). Whilst it has been noted that the primary harm is perhaps one step removed, there must be recognition that the production of indecent photographs of children will require children to be abused. If it is correct that the average age of children portrayed in the photographs is becoming younger this means that ever-younger children are being sexually abused. It is submitted that there is no reason why this cannot be reflected in a higher sentence.

Participation: a missing factor?

It has been seen that the courts will generally take account of the extent of the offender's involvement with indecent photographs of children, although questions have been raised in this chapter about whether the courts fully appreciate the offender's actions. An issue that is perhaps related to this but which has not been discussed is the extent to which an offender is involved with others. Clearly where there has been distribution then the courts will take note of the fact that an offender has passed material to others but should the courts go further and take account of the involvement of an offender in a collective?

The internet provides an opportunity for a virtual community or collective to be established. Communication may be text-based but it is clear that there is the opportunity to befriend people online and to enter discussions with them (see, perhaps most notably Rheingold, 1993). The communities can exist in a variety of different types of online medium, with the type of community differing depending on the technologies that it uses (Kollock and Smith, 1999). Sex offenders, including those with a sexual interest in children, have formed collectives for many years. Perhaps the most notable organisations in this field were NAMBLA (North American Man/Boy Love Association) in the United States and PIE

(Paedophile Information Exchange) in the United Kingdom. Whilst there were some members of the organisations that would act in a high-profile way, some activists lost their employment (O'Donnell and Milner, 2007: 10). As technology developed new opportunities arose for collectives to be created and they became increasingly more covert, in part because the law enforcement community began to take notice of their activities (see, for example, the discussion on the Dutch Paedophile Association in O'Donnell and Milner, 2007: 11). Those with a sexual interest in children began to realise that the internet provided an opportunity to meet like-minded individuals from across the world.

Some groups became extremely large and perhaps the most notable of these was the 'w0nderland club' which was an online collective that included members from 49 different countries in the world (O'Donnell and Milner, 2007: 39). Advances in technology, most notably peer-to-peer technologies, means that the groups can become increasingly difficult to detect and infiltrate (something discussed in more depth in Chapter 12). Online collectives would seem to be much more than a simple repository of images and Taylor and Quayle, presenting research on one collective, noted that participants were valued in a group for a number of factors, including their frequency of use and the duration of participation (Taylor and Quayle, 2003: 132). Participating in a collective can help normalise the offender's feelings and behaviours, with offenders stating that it made them feel like their actions were legitimate (Taylor and Quayle, 2003: 183). The collective became a social interaction for users (Jenkins, 2001: 106) and allows for security and technical advice to be given (Taylor and Quayle, 2003: 137) and the ability to complete a series of pictures (Jenkins, 2001: 103) and it would also appear that this would include offenders being encouraged to progress with their offending (Jenkins, 2001: 109), including by progressing on to contact abuse (Taylor and Quayle, 2003: 161 presenting the comments of 'ES'). Being a participant in a collective would appear to be an important feature of gaining access to large collections of material, including newly created and posted material (Taylor and Quayle, 2003: 160)

As participation can lead to an escalation of material and the legitimisation of deviant sexual practices it could be argued that it is a factor that should be taken into consideration, for example as an aggravating factor. It is not listed as a factor by either the SAP or SGC but it is not clear that they ever considered the issue. An argument against treating it as an aggravating factor is that having deviant sexual desires by itself is not illegal and ordinarily talking about these sexual desires is not illegal either (save where it amounts to a conspiracy because it is clear that two or more persons have agreed a course of conduct that involves the sexual abuse of a child). Why therefore should a sentence be aggravated because a person performed ostensibly lawful conduct even though it would be distasteful to many? An argument for considering it as an aggravating factor is that other factors are ostensibly lawful and yet they remain aggravating factors. In the context of indecent photographs the most obvious factor would be the use of software that 'wipes' the forensic footprint of a computer (Attorney General's Reference (No. 89 of 2004) [2004] EWCA Crim 3222 and *R v Constantine* [2009] EWCA Crim 2092).

Involvement with a collective could, it is submitted, be considered a factor that is relevant to their involvement with material. Even if the material is not obtained from the collective, their participation by discussing material, etc. can be considered to be involvement since the offenders are justifying their use of the material and attempting to normalise their behaviour (Taylor and Quayle, 2003: 132). This would seem to be as relevant as the organisation of material.

The courts do not appear to consider participation when setting the sentence. In *R v Davenport* [2009] 2 Cr App R (S) 38 an offender was sentenced to three years and six months' imprisonment for the making, distribution and possession of a large quantity of material, including the distribution of level 5 material (at p. 269). The court sentenced the offender on the basis that he had distributed images but, whilst they noted that he belonged to a 'a forum for people interested in child pornography' it did not appear that they believed that this was significant beyond the fact that it assisted in showing distribution. In *R v Sackman* [2010] EWCA Crim 19 the offender was a Dutch naval officer who was convicted of the making of indecent photographs. The court noted that he had participated in chat rooms and this included conversations that were being investigated by the police for offences relating to incitement (at [7]). The judge sentencing the offender considered his participation to be a matter of relevance in deciding whether to impose a sentence under the 'dangerousness' provisions of the CJA 2003 (at [15]). The Court of Appeal however decided that this would not justify dangerousness (which may well be appropriate given the criteria for those sentences – discussed later in this chapter) but it was not considered to be an aggravating factor either.

It would seem that the courts do not consider participation to be a relevant factor. In *R v Barber* [2009] EWCA Crim 774, discussed below, the fact that the distribution was restricted to a collective was even considered to be a mitigating factor by the Court of Appeal, something difficult to justify. The same approach is not adopted in other countries and the Ontario Court of Appeal in *R v F(DG)* 2010 Carswell Ont 146 has expressly considered the issue of participation to be a relevant factor for sentencing. The offender in this case pleaded guilty to a number of offences relating to the sexual abuse of children, including offences relating to child pornography and offences relating to substantive contact sex offences on his 4 year-old daughter. The offender was part of a collective that was based in an internet chat room (at [4]) and would regularly speak to offenders on the chat room about his deviant sexual interests and stated that he abused his own daughter 'after receiving active encouragement by his on-line peers' (at [8]). Of course this latter comment could simply be an example of displacement where the offender is seeking to blame others for his own behaviour, but it could equally be considered to be a truthful statement and that participating in the collective led him to create child pornography using his own daughter. The Supreme Court held that the use of the chat room to both talk about child pornography and to trade it was to be considered an aggravating feature (at [25]) and it is submitted that this is an appropriate response.

Our understanding of research into offender behaviour shows that offenders will use collectives and networks to share material, justify their behaviour and encourage each other's actions. Even where a person does not share material within the collective it is submitted that their active participation is likely to be seen as encouragement for others to share material or to abuse children. It is known that some members of a collective will produce child pornography to increase their status within a collective (Taylor and Quayle, 2003: 132) and therefore those within the collective are complicit with this production. It would seem appropriate therefore to recognise this by treating participation as an aggravating factor.

Mitigating factors

In the same way that there are aggravating factors there are factors that will mitigate sentence. Unlike with most of the aggravating factors, many of the mitigating factors are personal to the defendant himself. However it is still necessary to discuss these, albeit in a generic manner. The SAP in its initial advice suggested that few general mitigating factors would be relevant, mentioning only good character and a timely guilty plea (SAP, 2002: 13) and the Court of Appeal in *Oliver* accepted this ([2003] 1 Cr App R 28 at p. 470) but in the Definitive Sentencing Guideline produced by the SGC three further factors were added:

- A few images held solely for personal use.
- Images viewed but not stored.
- A few images held solely for personal use and it is established that the subject is aged sixteen or seventeen and that he or she was consenting. (SGC, 2007: 114.)

As with the aggravating circumstances it is not necessary to consider each of these in detail. The issue of quantity is to be discussed separately in any event as it is a factor that appears important in respect of the sentence that accrues. The final factor listed by the SGC – a few images of 16 and 17 year-olds held for personal use – will also not be discussed in depth but this is an important factor. In Chapter 6 it was noted that the SOA 2003, when raising the age of a 'child' to 18, introduced an extraordinarily complicated defence that is overly restrictive. The SGC is accepting this and noting that where a 16 or 17 year-old, who does not come within the defence, has consented to an offender having possession of the images this should, quite rightly, be considered a mitigating factor. Realistically it is also a factor that should be considered when the CPS decides whether to prosecute an offender in the first place.

Guilty plea

The first factor that should perhaps be discussed in detail is that of an early guilty plea. It has long been customary for the courts to consider an early guilty plea as

a mitigating factor (Ashworth, 2005: 163). The rule was gradually more formalised and placed on a statutory footing (initially under s. 48, Criminal Justice and
Public Order Act 1994) with the latest authority deriving from s. 144, Criminal
Justice Act 2003. The SGC guideline on sexual offences does not deal expressly
with a guilty plea as this is the subject of its own sentencing guideline (SGC,
2007b).

Section 144, CJA 2003 makes it clear that the stage at which a guilty plea is
given, and its circumstances, must be taken into account when deciding the level
of discount (s. 144(1), CJA 2003). The SGC formulated this into a 'sliding scale'
of discounts ranging from a full one-third discount where an offender pleads
guilty at the first reasonable opportunity to a discount of one-tenth where the trial
has begun (SGC, 2007b: 5). The rationale for treating a guilty plea after the
commencement of a trial is that some costs will still be saved. The usual justification for providing a more substantial discount for an early guilty plea is not only
the cost savings that can be involved where a trial need not be heard but also the
fact that it saves witnesses the inconvenience of having to testify (Ashworth,
2005). Where there is a victim this can be particularly traumatic and certainly this
could be true where, for example, the offence relates to the taking of an indecent
photograph of a child. In cases relating to indecent photographs of children there
is an additional factor which is the fact that it will prevent the jury needing to be
exposed to the photographs. It will be remembered from Chapter 3 that it is a
matter of fact for the jury whether a photograph is indecent or of a child.
Accordingly in a contested trial the jury must be shown the photographs regardless of how distressing or disturbing they may be.

Treating a guilty plea as a significant mitigating factor is not without criticism.
In some cases – and this could well be true of many cases relating to indecent
photographs of children – the defendant will have little choice but to plead guilty:
they will, in essence, have had no choice. For example, if an offender is found to
have a computer that he has sole access to and which contains 1,000 images of
pre-pubescent children at levels 3–5 it would be inconceivable that the offender
would have a defence (see Chapter 6). Material at levels 3–5 is highly likely to be
indecent and if the children are pre-pubescent there will be no doubt that they are
of a person under 18. Such a substantial quantity means it would be unlikely that,
for example, an offender could state that he had not downloaded the material
intentionally. Why therefore should he be awarded a significant discount for
sentence?

The SGC note that a defendant is fully entitled to put the prosecution to proof
(SGC, 2007b: 6). In the example above, therefore, they could quite properly test
the prosecution on whether the chain of evidence has remained complete and that
the forensic analysis was conducted properly. They could quite properly assess
whether the prosecution has satisfied each of the elements that they are required
to prove. If they decide to do this then some costs will be saved and so it has been
suggested that a reduced sentence should still be awarded to ensure that people
do not put the prosecution to (costly) proof when the case against them is

overwhelming. However the question is perhaps not whether any discount should be given but what level of discount should be given.

Prior to the discount for a guilty plea being placed on a statutory footing there was authority to suggest that an offender caught 'red-handed', i.e. an offender who had little choice but to plead guilty, could have the discount withheld (*R v Landy* (1995) 16 Cr App R (S) 908) although this was criticised by some academics (see, for example, Ashworth, 2000: 144). Whilst the legislation clearly requires a person to be given a discount, the SGC does recognise that 'the fact that the prosecution case is overwhelming without relying on admissions from the defendant may be a reason justifying departure from the guideline' (SGC, 2007b: 6). They then go on to suggest that any lesser reduction should be 20 per cent rather than the full one-third (ibid.) although presumably this is also subject to the principle of the 'sliding scale'.

The discount for a guilty plea raises interesting philosophical questions about its propriety, especially where an offender does not demonstrate remorse but is merely recognising the strength of the prosecution evidence. It has also been noted that it is arguably offensive from the point of view of placing pressure on defendants to plead guilty even where they believe themselves to be innocent because it can lead to a substantial reduction in lengthy sentences (Ashworth, 2005: 170). These are cases that are realistically outside the scope of this chapter but certainly there must be recognition that in a number of instances in relation to indecent photographs of children there can be significant doubt as to whether the guilty plea is accompanied by any remorse for their actions. The reality of the situation is that the economics of sentencing are such that a guilty plea will always be rewarded as the State has a pecuniary interest in avoiding trials. In respect of cases involving indecent photographs of children, there appears no evidence that the courts are departing from the general rule in these matters and certainly there is little evidence that they are, for example, applying a lower discount for 'red-handed' cases. This can be contrasted with, for example, Scotland where the same approach is not adopted. In *Brown v H.M. Advocate* [2010] HCJAC 24 an offender pleaded guilty to downloading 4,542 items relating to indecent photographs of children, including 759 video films and 3,747 still photographs (at [5]). The material related to girls aged between the ages of two and 13 and over 1,300 were at levels 4 and 5. The High Court of Justiciary stated:

> [I]n the circumstances of the present case where the question of a substantive defence has never been suggested, and the evidence can properly be described as conclusive, we are of the view that a discount of amounting to a full one third of the sentence, despite the early plea, was inappropriate
>
> (at [10])

Thus the starting point does not appear to be, as in England, that the maximum credit *should* be awarded but instead the court should consider whether there was any alternative for the defendant. The High Court of Justiciary was not saying that no discount should still be given, which recognises that a defendant is fully entitled to put the prosecution to proof, but it does perhaps note the reality of many of these cases and question whether a defendant that has no option but to recognise his offending behaviour should be rewarded by a generous discount.

Character

The second major mitigating factor is usually that of good character. This factor exists in two dimensions. The first is an absence of previous convictions and the second is worthy social contributions. Whilst they are, to an extent, often considered together they are based on slightly different justifications.

The first issue therefore is the absence of previous convictions. This has traditionally been recognised by the courts as a mitigating factor in some, but not all, crimes (Ashworth, 2005: 163). The reduction is based on the premise that a person may have an isolated lapse in ordinary judgment and therefore the fact that they are not a persistent offender can be taken into account. It was noted already above that previous criminal convictions can in fact aggravate a sentence but an absence of convictions need not act as a neutral factor; it could be a mitigating factor. That said, there is recognition that for some offences the absence of a previous conviction should mean very little. There are some crimes where 'human frailty' simply cannot be an excuse. The SAP, in its original guidance, questioned whether good character should be relevant for these offences although it did premise this by stating that a court would ordinarily take account of good character (SAP, 200: 13). In *Oliver* the Court of Appeal was perhaps a little more blunt and stated 'some, but not much, weight should be attached to good character' ([2003] 1 Cr App R 28 at 470). The SGC in its definitive guideline was silent on the matter but does state that the mitigating factors set out in *Oliver* remain relevant (SGC, 2007: 109) and so the position would seem to be that some credit should be given for good character but not much. This would appear to be the general position although in some cases it would seem that the issue is given more attention than others. So, for example, in *R v Biddulph* [2009] EWCA Crim 1776 the Court of Appeal stated that the offender's good character had not been taken into account sufficiently yet in *R v McKain* [2007] EWCA Crim 1145 the court stated:

> We must observe that matters such as prior good character, stress and the fact that court proceedings of this nature have devastating consequences for the offender and his family are hardly exceptional in this class of case.
>
> (at [14])

This is perhaps the statement closer to what was intended in *Oliver*. This is perhaps particularly true where the images have been built up over a considerable period of time. In these instances it would be difficult to argue that there has been a single lapse due to human frailty; it is a considerable period of offending that has just simply not been detected before now. For this reason it is submitted that the position in *Oliver* and *McKain* is arguably correct and previous good character should be considered as an additional but perhaps not key factor.

The second issue relating to character is that of worthy social contributions. It is clear that the courts have considered that good character does not only encompass the fact that a person has not been convicted of an offence but may also take into account contributions that one has made to society. Whilst they should be distinct the courts do have the tendency to combine the two and, when talking about character, make reference to character testimonies that people put forward and contributions made to society. Ashworth argues that social deeds should not be taken into account when deciding the sentence as it is an exercise in 'social accounting' (Ashworth, 2005: 173). In an earlier work he had suggested that the public were unlikely to be impressed by the fact that a person had been rewarded because of good deeds (Ashworth, 2000: 151). Whilst this may be true it would probably depend on the circumstances of the good deeds. Whilst they may be willing to accept a person who performs a feat of extraordinary courage (the paradigm perhaps being *R v Reid* (1982) 4 Cr App R (S) 280 where an offender awaiting sentence attempted to rescue three children from a blazing house), they may be less willing to accept a person being given a discount for having served as the mayor of a town (as happened in *R v Powell* [2001] 2 Cr. App. R (S) 30 albeit this was before the SAP issued its advice on child pornography).

Ashworth is undoubtedly correct to argue that character can act as an exercise in social accounting and it should be questioned whether the fact that a person has done even exemplary public service should act as mitigation. There is a tendency in such situations to focus on the offender as a person and not his actions. Perhaps an example of this is *R v Gardener* [2006] EWCA Crim 2439 which related to a regimental sergeant-major who had served operationally in Northern Ireland, the former Republic of Yugoslavia and the first Gulf War (at [7]). A considerable proportion of the judgment of the Court of Appeal is taken up with a discussion of his career in the army, including a statement that he was shortly to have been appointed to the most senior warrant officer position in the entire British army (at [9], although this appears to be a mistake by the Court of Appeal, as the RSM of the corps is the senior warrant officer of the corps but there are others in the army who rank as high). The court obviously found his career of importance and nothing in this section should be taken as detracting from his fine work: I fully support the armed services and believe the work that they do, on behalf of us, is vital and worthy of the highest respect. However should this lead to a (substantial) discount for an offence that is not connected in any way with his work? The judgment focused entirely on the offender and did not mention the fact that downloading indecent images of children is not victimless. The court concluded:

We cannot leave this case without emphasising how impressed we have been at all we have learnt about this man. We should add that he is going to find it extremely difficult to find the sort of work that would otherwise be available to him on leaving the army

(at [15])

before implicitly asking the army to reconsider its decision to discharge him. At one level this statement can be said to be innocuous and even worthy: the judgment makes clear that the offender was appointed RSM at an early age and that he had done sensitive military tasks. On the other hand, however, the statement can be said to be staggeringly naive and insensitive. The court expressly states that they wish to emphasise how impressed they have been at *all* they have learnt about the offender (my emphasis). Presumably they learnt that he downloaded over 350 indecent photographs of children, including at level 4, and that there had been distribution. Presumably the court was not impressed by that. Even setting aside the unfortunate wording used by the court, the language of the judgment downplays the seriousness of the offence. The court notes that there has been distribution but states immediately afterwards 'not for personal gain but as a necessary part of this applicant's sexual practice' (at [3]). The use of the phrase 'necessary as part of this applicant's sexual practice' seems to imply that the offender had no control over what he had done and that he was suffering from an illness rather than participating in a deviant sexual practice. The offender was caught as a result of other offenders being arrested for, *inter alia*, conspiracy to kidnap and rape children (at [3]). Whilst there is no evidence to suggest that the offender was involved in this, it does make clear that this was not a case of a solitary individual downloading material from the internet but was instead a person who was active in discussing his sexual practices and desires with others on the internet. Is this really worthy of mitigation?

It is submitted that *Gardener* is a regrettable case and a paradigm of Ashworth's comment about social accounting. Whilst he undoubtedly performed his career to the best of his ability should this take away from the fact that the offender committed a serious offence and one that has caused secondary harm to the victims portrayed in the photographs? Not only has this been taken into account as mitigation it appears to have cancelled the (substantial) aggravating features of the offence, resulting in a suspended sentence of imprisonment (at [14]) when distribution should ordinarily be punishable by immediate imprisonment and, depending on the level of material distributed, potentially by a significant period of time (SGC, 2007: 113 and see the discussion below).

Character is also controversial in other jurisdictions, with courts being unclear as to whether it acts as a mitigating factor or not. In *R v Johannson* 2009 SKQB 12 the fact that the defendant had no criminal record was specifically considered to be a mitigating factor (at [17]) and a discount was given almost without comment. In *R v Kwok* (2007, unreported) the Ontario Superior Court of Justice made specific reference to the issue of character. The facts of this case were complicated but a summary is that the offender was found to have a computer containing over 2,000 images and 60 movie clips, all amounting to child pornography. The court stated that it 'would appear that apart from his problems with child pornography Mr Kwok has been a person of good character, which is a mitigating factor' (at [18]). Some of the detail is given which includes a statement that his offending in respect of child pornography had lasted 14 years (at [21]). Given this it must be questioned whether it can truly be said that the offender was of good character. He had not 'been out of trouble' for 14 years – he had offended, he simply was not caught. Whilst, of course, this can be true of many crimes, the fact that this can be proven in this case must make it relevant. It is notable that later in the judgment the court, when discussing what his friends would have thought of him, noted 'they did not know his true character then' (at [53]). Thus the court on the one hand is saying that the offender is of good character and on the other is saying that he is of poor character. It would have been more appropriate to decide that either the offender was not of good character or, given the length of offending, stated that it did not count for much.

The position is also somewhat equivocal in Australia. In the Australian Capital Territory the courts have held that good character should be taken into account as a mitigating factor and have specifically rejected the suggestion that the discount should not apply to child pornography cases (*Forbes v The Queen* [2008] WASCA 233 at [11]). Yet other jurisdictions within Australia adopt the opposite stance. Under Commonwealth law the courts have held that good character should count for very little (*DPP (Cth) v D'Alessandro* [2010] VSCA 60) and the same is true of New South Wales. Indeed, in *R v Gent* [2005] NSWCCA 370 the court took a strong line, saying, 'it appears to be a common feature of [these] offences . . . that the offender is otherwise of good character, is in good employment and of sound reputation' (at [68]). Other states would seem to take the approach of considering the relevance of character to mitigation on the facts of each case (for the State of Victoria see *R v SLJ (No. 2)* [2010] VSCA 32 but cf *DPP v TDJ; DPP v MS* [2009] VSCA 317).

In the United States an offender's character is something that must be taken account of at federal level (see 18 USC §3353(1)) but the extent to which it is relevant remains for the judge to decide. Certainly there are cases that show that a court is prepared to receive evidence as to the offender's good character (see, for example, *US v Serrata* 425 F.3d 886 (2005) and *US v Howe* 543 F.3d 128 (2008)) but it has been held that character by itself is not ordinarily a reason to justify departure from sentencing guidelines (*US v O'Brien* F.3d 301 (1994) and *US v Winters* 174 F.3d 478 (1999)). The author has not identified a case where a federal court has significantly altered a sentence due to good character and thus the position in the U.S. would seem to be similar to the position in England and Wales in that it is taken account of but should not ordinarily be particularly relevant as a mitigating factor.

Viewing images

It was noted at the beginning of this section that the SGC included a number of additional mitigating factors and one of these is where a person views but does not store images (SGC, 2007: 114). The origins of this mitigation would appear to be the SAP's approach to the decision in *R v Smith; R v Jayson* [2003] 1 Cr App R 13 (discussed in Chapter 6). Following their recommendation as to how possession should be treated (as discussed above) they noted that in *Jayson* the Court of Appeal had held that calling an image to the screen amounted to the offence of making. The SAP, after describing the behaviour of viewing material, stated 'the Panel suggests that the starting point for sentence should be lower in such a case than in one where the offender has actively saved the material' (SAP, 2002: 7). This was endorsed by the Court of Appeal in *Oliver* where the Court of Appeal said, 'merely locating an image on the internet will generally be less serious than downloading it' ([2003] 1 Cr App R 28 at p. 467) and eventually the statement was included in the definitive sentencing guideline.

At first sight it would seem appropriate to link the issue of accessing indecent photographs of children to that of possession. In Chapter 6 there was a discussion of the ruling in *Smith; Jayson* and it can be accepted that it was a natural progression of the ruling in *Bowden* but it is perhaps a more important case since, in *Bowden*, had the argument not succeeded the offender would, at the very least, have been guilty of the crime of possession whereas the same is not true of viewing. If the image is not downloaded then a person cannot be said to be in possession of the image, especially where it is housed in the cache without their knowledge or ability to access it. The SAP and SGC have adopted the approach that viewing should be considered less serious than possession. It is perhaps easy to see why they have adopted this approach. Someone in possession of an image has actual custody of it and it could, for example, be accidentally discovered meaning that someone would be exposed to its contents. As has been discussed already, a physical collection of images (including those stored on a computer) can also be sorted and catalogued, which could be an indication of the degree to which an offender is involved with pictures.

However it must be questioned whether technological changes mean that this position is no longer appropriate. For example, is 'cloud storage' a matter of possession or viewing? It will be remembered from Chapter 6 that it can be argued that a person who stores material on virtual storage devices may not necessarily possess it because they cannot exercise full control over it. It is also known that many sites, including commercial sites (and it would seem that these are becoming increasingly prevalent) organise their material quite efficiently. Since broadband coverage has meant that high-speed internet access has become ubiquitous it means that offenders may have less need to actually download material. In the days of 'dial-up' downloading the material was a necessity as accessing it could take a considerable time, so repeated access was difficult. However with instant-access internet this is no longer true and a person can repeatedly access an image by locating it on the same website or file-sharing site. Is this any less damaging than possession? Certainly in terms of the secondary victimisation caused to the victim it is unlikely that there is much difference between the accessing and possession of an image. Setting aside the cataloguing issue (which may not be as relevant with commercial or file-sharing sites where the categorisation usually occurs automatically by the site and those who upload them) the only principal difference is that there is a reduced risk that an innocent third party could encounter the material when it is merely viewed, but it must be questioned whether this by itself justifies a reduction in sentence since there may be other physical requirements that minimise third-party discovery in possession cases (e.g. password protection, encryption, sole access to a computer, etc.).

Separate to the issue of photographs being housed on the internet there is the issue of webcasts, which are arguably more problematic. If an offender views footage, including live footage, which is being broadcast within a small group of offenders this could only be considered viewing or accessing. However, far from being the least intrusive conduct, it could be argued that this is an aggravated form of behaviour since the offender's involvement in the abuse of children may be significant. For example, if there are only six people who know about the existence of this webcast then even if one is only viewing it rather than making suggestions as to what abuse is featured, he must still be considered to be highly involved with the material, and the sentence should reflect this.

Possession

Whilst not featuring in the formal list of mitigating points for indecent photographs, the SGC stated that sentences for the possession of photographs should be lower where, *inter alia*, 'the photographs are retained solely for the use of the offender' (SGC, 2007: 110). This would seem a rather unusual statement to make. It was seen from Chapter 6 that there is a separate offence of possessing photographs with the intention of showing or distributing images and so there must be a presumption that the offence of possession (or, making when it has been used solely for downloading, a point discussed earlier) must always be catering for situations where the photographs are for the sole use of an offender. Where there is evidence to suggest that the offender possessed them in order to show or distribute them then the correct approach would be to charge the offence under s. 1(1)(c), PoCA 1978.

With a maximum sentence of five years' imprisonment there is of course a need to differentiate between the different types of conduct inherent in possessing indecent photographs of children but this should not involve the sentencing guidelines council, in effect, blurring the boundaries between the different offences. It is perfectly permissible for the Council to consider the appropriate sentence for cases arising under s. 1(1)(c) but it should not do so by stating that simple possession is a mitigating factor. Parliament has stated that the simple possession of child pornography is a criminal offence and, as noted in Chapter 6, this is a simple offence; an offender knowingly possesses an image. Stating that this is a mitigating factor would appear to circumvent the intention of Parliament in creating this offence as one distinct from situations where the photographs are held for the benefit of another or to show or distribute them.

Thresholds

So far what has been discussed are the aggravating and mitigating circumstances that vary a sentence but what are the guidelines that the SGC have produced? In this section it is not intended to consider the SAP and *Oliver* guidelines in depth as they have now been superseded although reference will be made to them as and when appropriate.

The SGC produced a table that explains the guidelines (Table 10.2). The guidelines are interesting in a number of respects. The key issues that need to be discussed are the issue of quantity (which quite clearly is important in this context) and the custody threshold.

Quantity

Perhaps the key issue in the guideline is the notion of quantity. It has been noted already that quantity can act as both an aggravating or mitigating circumstance but the guidelines above also make clear that the issue of quantity is relevant to the various thresholds. For example, the possession of a 'small' number of level 4 or 5 images has a starting point of 26 weeks' custody but the possession of a 'large' quantity has a starting point of 12 months' imprisonment. Similar terminology was used by the SAP (e.g. see SAP, 2009: 9) but nowhere in the document was the meaning of the term 'large' or 'small' ever explained. The same approach was adopted in *Oliver* where the Court of Appeal made reference to large and small quantities but did not provide any guidance as to what these terms mean. Yet at the same time, when discussing the fact that quantity could aggravate the sentence, the court stated 'it is impossible to specify precision as to numbers. Sentencers must make their own assessment of whether the numbers are small or large' ([2003] 1 Cr App R 28 at p. 469). With respect to the Court of Appeal and the SAP and SGC, if it is impossible to specify what is large or small quantities then it would seem illogical to use this as the basis of discriminating between different categories of sentences. If the purpose of a guideline is to assist in the development of consistent sentencing practice then some guidance should surely have been given as to what amounts to a small or large quantity.

It is not necessarily easy to ascertain what amounts to a large or small quantity although in some instances it is perhaps obvious. For example, in *R v Tatam* [2005] 1 Cr App R (S) 57 the offender had over 495,000 images in his collection including nearly 3,500 images at levels 4 and 5 and in *R v Davenport* [2009] 2 Cr App R (S) 38 the offender was found to have over 19,000 images in his possession, including nearly 5,000 at levels 4 and 5. In both instances there was no question that this was anything other than an extremely large collection. At the opposite end of the scale it was said in *R v Joy* [2007] EWCA Crim 3281 that two images at level 4 and 15 at level 5 was a small quantity, something that would seem obvious. However between the two extremities it does not appear that the courts have been particularly consistent in their approach. Akdeniz suggests 'it appears

Table 10.2 Sentencing guidelines

Type/nature of activity	Starting point	Sentencing range
Offender commissioned or encouraged the production of level 4 or 5 images	Six years' custody	Four to nine years' custody
Offender involved in the production of level 4 or 5 images		
Level 4 or 5 images shown or distributed	Three years' custody	Two to five years' custody
Offender involved in the production of, or has traded in, material at levels 1 to 3	Two years' custody	One to four years' custody
Possession of a large quantity of level 4 or 5 material for personal use only	Twelve months' custody	Twenty-six weeks to two years' custody
Large number of level 3 images shown or distributed		
Possession of a large quantity of level 3 material for personal use	Twenty-six weeks' custody	Four weeks to eighteen months' custody
Possession of a small number of images at level 4 or 5		
Large number of level 2 images shown or distributed		
Small number of level 3 images shown or distributed		
Offender in possession of a large amount of material at level 2 or a small amount at level 3	Twelve weeks' custody	Four weeks to twenty-six weeks' custody
Offender has shown or distributed material at level 1 or 2 on a limited scale		
Offender has exchanged images at level 1 or 2 with other collectors, but with no element of financial gain		
Possession of a large amount of level 1 material and/or no more than a small amount of level 2, and the material is for personal use and has not been distributed or shown to others	Community order	Appropriate non-custodial sentence

Source: SGC, 2007: 113–114.

that a "large quantitiy" will be regarded as thousands rather than hundreds of images at levels 4 or 5' (Akdeniz, 2008: 81) although it is not clear that he meant to say 'at levels 4 and 5' since the cases that he cites do not necessarily lead to this conclusion.

In *R v Hardy* [2005] EWCA Crim 1636 the Court of Appeal said that the court in *Oliver* had been 'careful' not to define what 'large' and 'small' meant and that the court had not intended to set out defined rules in other cases where they have considered quantity (at [7]). However this does beg the question how the guidelines are to be implemented in practice if no indication is to ever be given. Despite the comment in *Hardy* the Court of Appeal has made a series of rulings that could assist in identifying the meaning of quantity. In *R v Gibson* [2009] EWCA Crim 2081 the offender had, *inter alia*, 39 images at level 4 which the court described as not a great number (at [10]) and certainly the sentence imposed would appear to confirm that it was treated as a small number of level 4 or 5 images.

In *R v Reast* [2006] 1 Cr App R (S) 70 the Court of Appeal stated, 'it is difficult . . . to regard no less than fifty images . . . as necessarily amounting to a "small number" ' (p. 357) although this may, admittedly, have been influenced by the fact that at least some of the material took the form of video clips (something discussed earlier in this chapter). In *R v Thompson* [2004] EWCA Crim 503 the Court of Appeal held that 88 indecent images was not a large quantity of material (at [8]). Certainly this would appear to suggest that at relatively modest levels of images there appears to be doubt as to what amounts to a 'large' collection. It would seem more certain where the size of the collection reaches the hundreds (see, for example, *R v McAdie* [2004] EWCA Crim 3521, where 225 images at level 4 were considered large; *R v Colbear* [2009] EWCA Crim 1383, where 33 images at level 5 and 264 at level 4 were described as large, and *R v Barrow* [2008] EWCA Crim 2808, where 758 level 4 images were considered to be a large quantity) but this does not, of course, assist us in understanding collection size.

Even if we set aside the fact that it has been seen that there appears no settled view about what 'large' and 'small' means for sentencing purposes, there remain more fundamental difficulties with the use of quantity as a threshold. The first is that the concept must change with time. As technology develops and storage devices becoming increasingly large and internet speeds become ever quicker, it becomes significantly easier to amass a large quantity of material. In the early days of the internet it would take a considerable length of time to download individual images or movies whereas with fibre-optic cable or super-fast broadband, a movie or folder with hundreds of images contained within it can be downloaded in moments. Presumably this means that the thresholds change with technology. So whereas hundreds of images may have been considered to have constituted a large collection some years ago (on general sizes see Taylor and Quayle, 2003: 159 f.) it is no longer unusual to seize hundreds of thousands of images. Are we really saying that the behaviour of the offender now is any worse than the offender before the Internet Age? Is it not equally possible that an offender in the present age has an opportunity to gather more material than past offenders ever imagined? Taylor and Quayle also note that placing an emphasis on quantity is arguably missing the point:

... an emphasis is placed on the number of child pornography pictures recovered, as if this in some sense represents a measure of risk, or a reduction in the vulnerability of children. The reality is that large collections are more a reflection on an individual's ability to use the internet.

(Taylor and Quayle, 2003: 205)

Whilst it is conceded that quantity is perhaps an issue that should be taken into account for sentencing its importance must be questioned. It is perfectly acceptable to consider a very small collection to be a mitigating factor (e.g. an offender that has only a handful of images) and very large collections can be treated as an aggravating factor but they should not be used for deciding the bands of a sentence. As Taylor and Quayle note, it is simply indicating that an offender may actually have the time and technology to gather a large number of images.

How then should sentencing deal with collections? It has been noted already that the main emphasis on sentencing should be the offender's involvement with photographs and quantity does not easily fit within this. As technology changes the quantity of material is likely to continue to increase and it would seem inappropriate to continuously alter our perception of what a 'small' quantity of material is just because of these shifts in technology. A better approach to considering involvement may be to look at how long a person has been involved with photographs. Keeping and accessing photographs for three years may be more pertinent than the fact that an offender has a collection of 100,000 images, many of which he will never be able to access.

An alternative may be to consider an analysis of the collection. In *R v Hardy* [2005] EWCA Crim 1636 the Court of Appeal stated 'what is a large quantity . . . may depend on what exactly the practice of the particular defendant was' (at [7]) and perhaps considering the practice of the defendant may be a better approach. It was noted earlier in this chapter that there were some questions raised about the idea of categorising images and what it tells us about offender behaviour. An interesting issue that has not necessarily been discussed in depth is whether a better approach may be to consider whether a proportionate analysis of a collection may better inform a sentence. The only case to have considered the proportions of a collection was *R v Hazeldine* [2003] EWCA Crim 3612 where the Court of Appeal analysed the collection as 51 per cent at level 1; 13 per cent at level 2; 24 per cent at level 3 and 11 per cent at level 4 (at [3]). In that particular case not much may have turned on this analysis other than to show that the majority of the offender's behaviour would seem to be at level 1. However this is not always true and this can be seen, for example, in *R v Wrall* [2008] EWCA Crim 3162. The offender's collection was described by the court in totals but Table 10.3 presents it as both a number and a proportionate analysis.

Whilst 69 images at level 4 may not be particularly significant, it is perhaps more significant that nearly one-third of his collection consisted of level 4 and 5 images. This may demonstrate the type of images that an offender is actively seeking and storing. A more illustrative case is perhaps *R v Biddulph* [2009]

Table 10.3 Wrall's collection

Level	No.	%[a]
1	111	48
2	14	6
3	33	14
4	69	30
5	2	1

Note
a Percentages are expressed as rounded numbers.

Table 10.4 Biddulph's collection

Level	No	%[a]
1	767	61
2	24	2
3	2	0
4	16	1
5	448	36

Note
a Percentages are expressed as rounded numbers.

EWCA Crim 1776, where the collection is as shown in Table 10.4. There is no doubt that 448 level 5 images would be considered a large collection but the proportionate analysis perhaps shows something about his behaviour. Thirty-six per cent of his collection was found to be of level 5 images and yet very little of the collection was within either levels 2 to 4, something that may inform our understanding of how an offender is establishing his collection. In *Bidulph* the Court of Appeal reduced a sentence of 30 months' imprisonment to one of two years, in part because the guideline states that the sentencing range for the possession of a large quantity of level 4 images has a maximum of two years. However should this remain true where it can be seen that an offender appears to be deliberately seeking out and retaining level 5 images? Two years' imprisonment is less than half the maximum sentence set by Parliament and yet this is the worse type of material that the law classifies. Whilst it was noted earlier that there are questions as to whether this means anything for dangerousness, a marked preference for level 5 images may be something that a sentencing court should take account of.

Another notable example where this may be of relevance is *R v Thompson* [2004] EWCA Crim 503. This was mentioned above because the Court of Appeal held that 88 images were not a 'large' collection. Whilst it was noted that this was in conflict with other decisions of the Court of Appeal it could be argued that, in isolation, it may be an understandable conclusion by the court. However when the facts are examined more closely it would seem that this is perhaps an example of when we should take heed of the comment of the Court of Appeal in *Hardy* as noted above. The offender had, in his drawer, hard copies of images that he had printed from the internet. By implication therefore the offender has been viewing images on the internet and printing those images he wished to keep. The total collection was 120 pictures and 88 of these (73 per cent) were level 4, with the next highest proportion being level 3 images (at [2]). Whilst therefore 88 images may not be large, is it relevant for a sentencing purpose that an offender appears to be taking care to collect only level 4 images, i.e. those that depict the penetrative assault of children. If one of the mischiefs of the offence of possession is to punish those who seek sexual gratification from their keeping of indecent photographs of children then perhaps the sentence should increase where it can be seen that they appear to deliberately seek out the more graphic forms of indecent photographs of children.

Of course a difficulty with proportionate analysis is it may lead to situations where the analysis could be considered inappropriate in all the circumstances. An example of this could be *R v Lee* [2010] EWCA Crim 1783 where the offender had in excess of 1 million images in his collection (see the analysis in Table 10.5). In addition to this there were 879 videos across all five levels, which have not been included in the analysis above. How should this offender be sentenced? A proportionate analysis would show that 98 per cent of his collection is at levels 1 and 2 but this disguises the fact that he had over 10,000 images at levels 4 and 5. Should this offender be sentenced on the basis that a small proportion of his collection is held at levels 4 and 5? If proportionate analysis were to be adopted then it would seem that the answer is 'yes' although perhaps the overall size of the collection could be taken into account. The alternative would be to say that some collections are so extraordinary that they should be sentenced on the basis that their collection does not fit the guidance. The Court of Appeal in *Lee* rejected this last argument when they stated:

> The number of level 4 and 5 photographs and films, while large, was not, in the judgment of the court, so exceptionally large as to call for a significant departure from the guideline.

(at [13])

This is, it is submitted, somewhat surprising since a collection of 10,000 level 4 and 5 images is exceptional and this perhaps should have been reflected by the court. Certainly a collection of 1 million images is still somewhat unusual and the court should perhaps take this into account.

An exceptionally large collection perhaps also raises questions about the discount awarded for pleading guilty discussed earlier in this chapter. If a person has an exceptionally large collection could this be a reason to reduce the discount

Table 10.5 Lee's collection

	No	%*
Level 1	983,327	96
Level 2	19,971	2
Level 3	12,576	1
Level 4	9,900	0.9
Level 5	693	0.07

* percentages are expressed as rounded numbers.

for guilty plea since an offender can do little other than to plead guilty when faced with charges relating to such a significant collection? The Court of Appeal appears uncertain as to this. In *Lee*, above, the court gave a discount of 50 per cent for plea (reducing the notional sentence from three years to 18 months' imprisonment: see at [14]) which is a much higher discount than the recommended one-third. It is difficult to see why the court took this approach and certainly there is nothing within the transcript that would suggest other significant forms of mitigation. In the same month the case of *R v Fox* [2010] EWCA Crim 1702 was heard. Here the offender had a collection of over 100,000 images across all levels and the court said, 'in view of the overwhelming nature of the case against the appellant, a one-third discount for a plea might be regarded as generous' (at [14]). It is submitted that *Fox* is the preferable position and that it was inappropriate for the court in *Lee* to discount the sentence so heavily as the offender had, in effect, no choice but to plead guilty.

Custody threshold

The second issue that perhaps has to be examined is the custody threshold. The SAP, in their advice, stated 'the choice between a custodial and non-custodial sentence is a particularly difficult one for a sentence dealing with an offence of this nature' (SAP, 2002: 8). This is a very pertinent point and it has not diminished in the following years. The consequences of the threshold were discussed at the beginning of this chapter in terms of rehabilitation and sex offender treatment programmes. It was recognised that the issue has not been fully resolved and serious questions must be asked about the purpose of a short custodial sentence that prevents an offender from receiving treatment to remedy his deviant behaviour.

Allied to the issue of the custody threshold is the important issue of its relationship to treatment. The balance between incarcerating a person and allowing him to remain in the community is perhaps complicated by questions on whether an offender imprisoned will be given the opportunity to address their behaviour and undertake treatment that could assist them in rehabilitation.

Whilst it was seen in Chapter 2 that the evidence for any link between the posses-sion of child pornography and contact offending was uncertain, the evidence was clearer that offenders exhibit inappropriate, and perhaps harmful, sexual behaviour. A response to this could be to encourage an offender to address his behaviour which should, in turn, prevent the offender from relapsing into further offending. This rationale is behind the use of sex offender treatment programmes (SOTP).

Sex offender treatment programmes have been in use for nearly two decades (Middleton *et al.*, 2009: 6) and whilst they remain somewhat controversial, they do appear to have a level of success (Middleton *et al.*, 2009: 6 citing NOMS, 2008). Traditionally an offender who was convicted of a child pornography offence and who was eligible for an SOTP would be sent on the default programme, i.e. the same one that was used for contact offenders. It was decided that this would be inappropriate and a specific SOTP was developed. Whilst the iSOTP is a relatively new vehicle, early analysis would appear to suggest that it does bring with it a measure of success (Middleton *et al.*, 2009). The programme appears to assist offenders in understanding their behaviour and recognise and minimise factors that are likely to lead to re-offending (Middleton *et al.*, 2009: 15) although the authors concede that the exact success will not be able to be gauged accurately until a longitudinal offending survey takes place (Middleton *et al.*, 2009: 17), although it will be some time before such an approach can be adopted with those who first went through the programme.

Whilst it would seem that SOTPs do have a measure of success therefore, a difficulty with them is the eligibility of offenders. SOTPs exist both within a custodial setting and whilst in the community. However the choice of sentence will have a direct impact on the eligibility of offenders to participate in the progress. The iSOTP programme has developed a twin-track approach; either an individual programme of 20 to 30 sessions, each of approximately 90 minutes' duration, or a group programme involving 35 sessions, each lasting 90 minutes (Middleton *et al.*, 2009: 9). The duration of the programme will therefore last several months. This can pose a significant difficulty for an offender who is incar-cerated. Where a person is sentenced to gaol for a determinate period he will be released after serving 50 per cent of his sentence, the balance being served on licence (s. 244, CJA 2003). The consequence of this is that an offender must be sentenced to a term of imprisonment of sufficient length to complete the course. This could be a reasonably long term since the initial months in gaol will be taken up by administration and possibly even appeals. An offender who is given a short custodial sentence is therefore not given an opportunity to undertake a SOTP and address their behaviour. Where it is believed that sexual deviance can pose a risk of reoffending (Cortoni, 2009: 43) then this may mean that offenders are being set up to re-offend. If, however, they were given a community punishment then it is likely that they could complete a community SOTP as part of the conditions of that sentence (although a recent report by HM Inspectors of Police and Probation noted that community SOTPs were subject to delays of several months; HMIC, 2010: 33 f.).

The fact that SOTP is not available for short-term prisoners poses a dilemma for judges faced with sentencing an offender. On what basis should they impose a sentence? It has been noted that the public generally consider incarceration to be the only sentence that is purely punitive. Whilst there have been a number of initiatives over the years by governments to recognise community sentences as 'true' punishment, politicians and the press will continue to present them as a 'light' alternative. Accordingly a judge who opts to impose a community sentence on, for example, an offender who has downloaded child pornography will run the wrath of society and the press even though it may offer the better opportunity to prevent re-offending. The guideline on sentencing child pornography offences (discussed below), its reference to the custodial threshold (SGC, 2007: 114), and its recommendation that short custodial sentences should be imposed (ibid.) perhaps demonstrates that the SGC recognise the perception that incarceration is the only 'true' punishment.

Recently the issue of short custodial sentences has become a political issue. During the 2010 general election the Liberal Democrats suggested that there should perhaps be a minimum term before someone could be sentenced to prison, and below that term non-custodial punishments should be used (Liberal Democrat Website). The Secretary of State for Justice and Lord Chancellor (Kenneth Clarke QC) has also stated that there should be a review of short custodial sentences (Clarke, 2010). Unusually the review was received without a maelstrom of adverse comment and it is quite possible that there will be a shift away from very short custodial sentences. That said, it is not clear that any changes would apply to all offences. Preventing sexual offenders from being sent to prison, even for short terms of imprisonment, is unlikely to be welcomed by many in the press or by certain politicians. It will be interesting to see what, if anything, happens as the current position does not appear sustainable in that short custodial sentences do not allow an offender the opportunity to address their behaviour.

Chapter 11

The international dimension

It is trite to state that the internet has allowed the issue of child pornography to become truly global. The internet, and related resources, mean it is possible for users from across the world to talk to each other and to exchange information. As early as 1992 an international operation (led by the United States) was held to identify individuals participating in an international 'ring' (Krone, 2005: 4). The issue perhaps became more noticeable after Operation Starburst in 1995. This was a truly international operation that involved law enforcement agencies in five countries working together and apprehending 37 suspects from across the globe. By 1998 the reality of international collectives was apparent from Operation Cathedral (known as Operation Cheshire Cat in the United States). Cathedral involved law enforcement agencies infiltrating a secretive network known as the 'w0nderland club' (Krone, 2005: 3). This operation involved law enforcement agencies in 11 countries arresting 107 individuals and identifying vast quantities of child pornography. The scale of international networking was evident from Operation Avalanche (which was known as Operation Ore in the United Kingdom) which involved the tracing of those who had subscribed to Landslide Productions, one of the largest commercial hosters of child pornography. In the UK alone Operation Ore led to over 7,000 people being identified (HMIC, 2008).

In a 2001 editorial *The Lancet* said:

> [Child pornography] is surely precisely this sort of borderless problem that requires firm action from one of the international agencies.
>
> (357 *Lancet* 569).

As will be seen, by 2001 the issue of child pornography had already begun to feature on the international agenda, but the fact that *The Lancet* felt it necessary to make such a call perhaps demonstrates that this fact was not readily understood.

This chapter seeks to identify how international bodies seek to regulate child pornography. Chapter 2 presented various definitions of child pornography that were set out in international instruments and this will not be rehearsed here.

However international responses continue to be important and they will be examined in three ways:

- Global initiatives.
- European initiatives.
- Jurisdiction.

The latter, jurisdiction, is arguably a domestic approach but, as will be seen, the securing of jurisdiction by individual countries and the increasing decision to adopt an extraterritorial approach to such matters has been largely at the bequest of international agreements. Accordingly the issue of jurisdiction will be discussed in this chapter.

Global initiatives

The first issue to examine is how the issue of child pornography features on the global policy agenda and how international law is being used to regulate child pornography.

The issue of child sexual exploitation and, in particular, child pornography was somewhat hidden until the second half of the twentieth century and did not feature on the international agenda in any real significance until the 1990s, something noted by the UN Special Rapporteur (whose office is discussed below), who stated, 'the 1990s ushered in a new international concern for children. This attention is long overdue' (Muntarbhorn, 1995: 4). In 1989 the UN Convention on the Rights of the Child was unveiled for signature and it quickly achieved almost universal ratification (Buck, 2008). Article 34 of the Convention, as will be identified in the next section, seeks to 'protect [the] child from all forms of sexual exploitation and sexual abuse' but the Article does not define what is meant by sexual exploitation or abuse nor does it state how signatory states should identify that duty. That said, it provides a statement in international law that the sexual exploitation or abuse of children was not appropriate.

The issue of child pornography was quickly considered to be an issue that required special treatment. In the 1980s a series of researchers began to operate on a policy level and they decided in 1990 to create a global NGO to be known as ECPAT (originally meaning 'Ending Child Prostitution in Asian Territories' but now meaning 'Ending Child Prostitution And Trafficking'). Very quickly ECPAT had established itself as the leading NGO in this area and from the very beginning it considered the issue of child pornography to be an important issue that required specific responses. By 1996 ECPAT was working in partnership with the United Nations and they were an intrinsic part of the First World Congress (discussed below). Since then other NGOs have become established but ECPAT continues to have a truly global presence and one that has a significant impact on the policy level (see, for example, Manners, 2009: 233 when discussing ECPATs role in developing EU policy on this area).

United Nations

The United Nations has had a role in tackling the proliferation of child pornography for many years. The mandate for protecting children from sexual exploitation appears to have derived from its previous recognition of the harm caused by childhood exploitation through, for example, labour and other activities prejudicial to health (van Bueren, 1994: 52). By the 1980s however attention had shifted to sexual exploitation and there was recognition that some areas of the globe were sexually exploiting children as an industry (van Bueren, 1994: 53).

The United Nations is involved in a variety of ways through, for example, its High Commissioner for Human Rights, UNICEF (known as the United Nations Children Fund although it is now a formal agency rather than a fund for distributing aid) and UNESCO (United Nations Educational, Scientific and Cultural Organisation). In 1999 UNESCO organised an experts meeting on child pornography which considered a number of aspects of law enforcement, including harmonising laws and co-operation between law enforcement agencies. UNESCO also established an internet education and safety programme (Akdeniz, 2008: 221) which sought to raise awareness of sexual exploitation facilitated by the internet.

UNICEF has arguably taken the lead in recent years as they have a mandate in respect of protecting children from violence, exploitation and abuse. Along with funding research, UNICEF operates on both the policy and action levels. In terms of policy, they have used their position to place considerable pressure on national governments to alter their laws to deal with child pornography. Perhaps a good example of the work of the United Nations is in relation to Japan where, in 2008, UNICEF complained that the law in Japan was not adequate for combating child pornography. The United Nations does not operate simply on the policy level, it also undertakes project work. A good example of this is the work of UNESCO in 2006 when it operated an awareness-raising project in South Africa that sought to demonstrate the reality of child pornography and sought to establish an action plan for its elimination (UNESCO, 2006: 2).

World congresses

In 1996 the First World Congress Against Commercial Sexual Exploitation was held in Stockholm, Sweden. The Congress was empanelled and co-hosted by the United Nations, ECPAT and the Swedish government. The Congress brought together most of the key UN agencies (including INTERPOL) together with national and international NGOs, national governments together with law enforcement agencies, child protection agencies, academia and the industry in an attempt to discuss issues relating to the (commercial) sexual exploitation of children. Subsequently two more World Congresses have been held, in 2001 (Yokohama, Japan) and 2008 (Rio de Janeiro, Brazil).

The World Congresses have three principal themes, one of which is child pornography. Each World Congress has been guided by a background report on each of the three themes (the child pornography ones being: ECPAT, 1996; Carr, 2001 and Quayle *et al.*, 2008)). The background reports are usually written in conjunction with subject experts (in the first report the experts were primarily from law enforcement but by the third report the experts were drawn from academia, NGOs, child protection and law enforcement). A common theme across all three background reports is the need to harmonise laws. In the first report it had been noted that there was no single definition of child pornography (ECPAT, 1996) and a similar point was raised in 2001 although it must be conceded that the Optional Protocol had only just been developed by then. By the Third World Congress it may be thought that this would have been resolved but the thematic report continued to note that there were uncertainties in definitions (Quayle *et al.*, 2008).

In 2002 the Special Rapporteur questioned whether there had been any progress between the First and Second World Congress (Petit, 2002: 13) and the latest report of the Special Rapporteur, whilst not stating so expressly, would seem to arrive at the same conclusion, with the Rapporteur noting that there remain some countries with no legislation covering child pornography and there being significant differences in national responses to the phenomenon (Maalla, 2009: 12). It could therefore be questioned whether the World Congresses achieve anything but to an extent this would be a negative reading of the position. The World Congresses undoubtedly ensure that child pornography is kept on the policy agenda and a review of the thematic reports and outcome documents of each World Congress does suggest that there is increasing recognition of the problem of child pornography and the need to act. Also, the latest report of the Special Rapporteur does note that there is clear evidence of increased international co-operation (Maalla, 2009: 21), something that was called for during the First and Second World Congress.

Legislative instruments

Perhaps the most notable example of the United Nations work in this area is shown in its legislative instruments. The first to note is the 1989 Convention on the Rights of the Child, which quickly achieved almost universal acceptance (Buck, 2008: 168). Some provisions of the UNCRC have been discussed already, most notably in Chapter 2 when it was noted that Article 1 of the Convention presumes that a child is a person under the age of 18. The principal provision of the UNCRC of relevance is Article 34, which provides (in part) '[s]tate parties undertake to protect the child from all forms of sexual exploitation and sexual abuse'. The decision not to distinguish between sexual abuse and exploitation has been criticised by some (van Bueren, 1994) although this is presumably because the definition of these terms remains open to debate and it was intended not to leave any gap. Article 34 is intended to be a preventative measure but it would appear that it is limited to the circumstances listed in Article 34 (van Bueren, 1994: 53). These circumstances set out in Article 34 are:

   (a) The inducement or coercion of a child to engage in any unlawful sexual activity.

   (b) The exploitative use of children in prostitution or other unlawful sexual practices.

   (c) The exploitative use of children in pornographic performances and materials.

Whilst child pornography is therefore expressly mentioned, the CRC is imprecise about its extent or definition. For example, it requires there to be the *exploitative use* but no definition is given as to what exploitation means, including as some would argue (van Bueren, 1994) it requires there to be a commercial context. The first Special Rapporteur noted that vague language can cause difficulties in assessing the adequacy of (national) legal frameworks (Muntarbhorn, 1991) which can make the task of protecting children more difficult. Others prefer to be more optimistic on the effect of Article 34, noting that it has acted as the platform upon which other developments on tackling sexual exploitation have been built (Doek, 2009: 775).

Article 34 was arguably never intended to be a definitive statement on the protection to be offered to children from sexual exploitation and in 1995 the UN Commission on Human Rights established a working group to examine the possibility of an optional protocol to the CRC to provide specific safeguards to children from sexual exploitation (CHR Resolution 1994/90). The First World Congress (discussed above) placed considerable emphasis on the need for international law to reconsider its approach to the issue of, *inter alia*, child pornography (see the *Declaration and Agenda for Action: First World Congress against Commercial Sexual Exploitation of Children*, p. 3) and this was echoed by the then Special Rapporteur who questioned whether Article 34 appropriately covered all types of child pornography, particularly those involving new technologies (Calcetas-Santos, 1997: 12). Whilst the Special Rapporteur encouraged the wording of Article 34 to be developed, the view was instead taken that this provided further evidence that a new instrument was required and in 2000 the Optional Protocol on the Rights of the Child on the sale of children, child prostitution and child pornography was opened for signature.

The Optional Protocol has not quite had the same level of take-up as the UNCRC itself but by 2008 (the last year for which information is provided) some 122 countries had signed the Protocol, with it being ratified by 119 countries (UN, 2008: 1). It is notable that the United States, which had signed but not ratified the UNCRC, ratified the Optional Protocol but the United Kingdom was slightly less forthcoming; whilst it signed the Protocol in 2000 it did not ratify it until 2009.

As was noted in Chapter 2 a significant difference between the Optional Protocol and the UNCRC is the detail of its definitions. The Optional Protocol provides a clear definition of what constitutes child pornography (Article 2) and also, unlike the UNCRC, provides specific requirements on signatory states to criminalise specific actions in respect of child pornography (Article 3(c)). As these have been discussed elsewhere they will not be reiterated here. The Optional Protocol goes further however and mandates states to undertake a variety of action in order to safeguard children from sexual exploitation. This includes securing jurisdiction (Article 4: discussed below), facilitating extradition (Article 5) and co-operation in investigations (Articles 6 and 10). States are also required to ensure that goods and material used in the sexual exploitation of children are forfeited (Article 7), which in the context of child pornography may reduce secondary victimisation. The protection of the victim is then taken further in Article 8 and Article 10 mandates, *inter alia*, the provision of educational initiatives to try and minimise the likelihood of offences taking place. This will include, for example, co-operation with industry and NGOs to facilitate safer internet schemes. Article 10 also calls on Member States to address the 'root causes' of sexual exploitation, including poverty, which is an important provision. It is incumbent on states to not only ensure that their own laws are effective but also that they assist those in some countries who continue to see the exploitation of their own children as a route out of poverty.

Special Rapporteur

One representative of the UN deserves to be considered separately. In 1990 the UN Commission on Human Rights (UNCHR) appointed a Special Rapporteur on the sale of children, child pornography and child prostitution (Resolution 1990/68 on the Rights of the Child). Since 1990 the mandate has been continuously renewed, and the current Special Rapporteur (Najat M'jid Maalla) is the fourth to hold the office. Since 1991 an annual report has been made by the Special Rapporteur.

The mandate of the Special Rapporteur is set by the Human Rights Council and is extended at three-year intervals. The latest resolution (Resolution 7/13) was made at its fortieth meeting in March 2008. The current mandate includes:

- To consider matters relating to the sale of children, child prostitution and child pornography.
- To continue, through continuous and constructive dialogue with Governments, intergovernmental organisations and civil society . . . the analysis of the root causes of the sale of children, child prostitution and child pornography; addressing all the contributing factors, especially the demand factor.
- To identify and make concrete recommendations on preventing and combating new patterns of sale of children, child prostitution and child pornography.
- To continue . . . to promote comprehensive strategies and measures on the prevention of sale of children, child prostitution and child pornography.

(Resolution 7/13 §2)

In support of this mandate the Council encourages all governments to co-operate with the Special Rapporteur (Resolution 7/13 §3) and requests the Secretary

General and the Commissioner for Human Rights to 'provide all the human, technical and financial assistance' to the Special Rapporteur (Resolution 7/13 §4).

The mandate is suitably wide and allows the holder of the mandate sufficient flexibility to decide how to discharge the mandate. Whilst the annual reports will detail the specific countries and tasks undertaken in the past year, some will also discuss key thematic findings from research and visits undertaken by her. The annual report is made to the Human Rights Council which in turn reports to the General Assembly. Also the reports are made public and so they by themselves act as a policy-influencing document although the views are technically personal and without a resolution of either the Council or Assembly will not become UN policy.

The Special Rapporteur undoubtedly undertakes valuable work and the annual reports have been important in identifying weaknesses in domestic and international responses, together with highlighting potential good practice and areas to develop. In 2004 the annual report of the then Special Rapporteur, Juan Miguel Petit, concentrated on the thematic issue of child pornography (Petit, 2004). This was one of the first pieces of international policy research and involved a questionnaire being replied to by 51 separate countries (Petit, 2004: 2).

The Special Rapporteur considered a definition of child pornography (Petit, 2004: 7–8) and, as discussed in Chapter 2, differentiated between child erotica (broadly classed as soft-core pornography) and child pornography itself. The Special Rapporteur also sought to include virtual child pornography, arguing it should be prohibited for seeking to normalise the sexual exploitation of children (Petit, 2004: 8 but see Chapter 5 for a discussion of this argument). Having considered international instruments the Special Rapporteur noted the limitations of the Optional Protocol (Petit, 2004: 9) but also noted that it did provide a basic framework on which to operate. Of some concern was the fact that the Special Rapporteur noted that some countries did not have, or had very basic, laws relating to child pornography (Petit, 2004: 22). Whilst it may be thought that being named in a report such as this could help incentivise countries to produce laws, the Special Rapporteur did not name those countries that had no, or inadequate, laws. By failing to name those countries it could be argued that there is likely to be less pressure placed on the country to adopt an appropriate framework of laws. The fourth mandate holder has altered this approach and, for example, in the 2009 annual report the Special Rapporteur noted that she had sent letters to six governments relating to allegations (Maalla, 2009: 5) although she only received two responses. What is notable, however, is that the correspondence was exhibited as an addendum to the report and this suggests that the Special Rapporteur may be beginning to use the sanction of public disclosure, albeit as a measure of last resort.

The Special Rapporteur is an important policy-level initiative that provides a focus for much of the national and international initiatives. Each annual report notes how many keynote addresses and conferences the holder of the office delivers and it is clear that her presence is in demand. Similarly the Special

Rapporteur visits individual countries each year, in part to assess their laws and procedures, but also to identify good practice that can then be disseminated. However some have questioned whether the Special Rapporteur can discharge her mandate. For example Buck, 2008 notes:

> The work of the Special Rapporteur has been valuable . . . However . . . it is regrettable that the [post] remains under-resourced. In such a context, progress by the Special Rapporteur is likely to be somewhat mixed, its work being over-reliant on the research and other resources made available via the individual efforts of each mandate holder.
>
> (p. 170)

The complaint of under-resourcing is one that will be familiar to most working in the policy arena. However there is undoubted truth in what Buck concludes; despite the fact that the Human Rights Council called upon the Secretary General and High Commissioner for Human Rights to resource her work, it would seem that the Special Rapporteur has limited funds. The mandate holder does not have a team of researchers or staff and primarily works alone. This must, by necessity, mean that the amount of research that can be undertaken is limited.

The Group of Eight (G8)

Recent global initiatives include those of the G8 in this area. The G8 owes its origins to an economic summit in 1975 attended by the five richest countries (France, Germany, Japan, United Kingdom and the United States). By the end of the decade the group had expanded to become the G-7 with the addition of Italy and Canada. During the 1990s the Soviet Union (then Russia after the dissolution of the USSR) were invited to attend the meetings which had begun to stray beyond mere economics and would involve geopolitical issues. In 1998 the group formally changed from the G-7 to the G8.

Whilst the G8 remains a primarily economic vehicle, its move into geopolitical issues has also included it developing a role in preventing the commercial sexual exploitation of children. In 2001 at the Milan summit they sought to develop a strategy to combat child pornography and in October of that year a group known as the Lyon/Roma group was created to tackle international crime. A sub-group of the Lyon/Roma group was specifically tasked to examine the issue of sexual exploitation and in the Paris summit of 2003 a strategy was created (G8, 2003 §15–17).

In 2009 a group of experts were brought together in Chapel Hill, North Carolina, to consider the issue of child pornography regulation and their work led directly to the ministerial declaration of 30 May 2009 in Rome. The declaration ('The Risk to Children posed by Child Pornography Offenders') reaffirmed their commitment to tackling child pornography. The declaration notes that the nature of internet child pornography requires international co-operation (G8, 2009: 5). This is explained:

Effective international co-operation would be achieved through a wider membership in multilateral task forces, sharing specialised software and closely co-ordinating on line [SIC] undercover investigations and other international law enforcement operations.

(G8, 2009: 6)

Whilst an important statement it is notable that the declaration does not state how this can be achieved. The G8 is, to an extent, a discussion forum and whilst there may be informal and quasi-formal agreements to co-operate these do not have the same status as a Convention or Treaty (although, of course, many treaties (including both the UNCRC and Optional Protocol) are not binding and simply rely on reports as a monitoring mechanism: Buck, 2008: 172–175).

A criticism that can be levelled at the G8 is whether it has double standards. The Rome declaration stated that '. . . in some countries, effective legislation has not yet been adopted'. Whilst there was no clarification of what 'effective legislation' means serious concerns have been raised as to the state of law in two G8 countries. UNICEF has noted that both Japan and Russia do not currently criminalise the possession of child pornography. It will be remembered from Chapter 2 that although criminalising possession remains controversial to some it is now broadly accepted as a necessary part of the regulation of child pornography. This is reinforced by the UN Special Rapporteur who has consistently argued that the criminalisation of possession is a necessary, and not merely a desirable, step in the protection of children (Petit, 2004: 23; Maalla, 2009: 23). Accordingly it would be difficult to see how Japan and Russia's failure to criminalise the possession of child pornography could be considered to be effective.

Aside from the criminalisation of child pornography there has also been concern as to whether G8 countries are appropriately controlling the hosting of child pornography (see for example Travis, 2008). The hosting of child pornography is quite clearly an inherent part of the process of distribution and access and it is of concern that some countries of the G8 continue to host this material whilst at the same time purporting to sign up to a strategy to tackle child pornography. It may be politically difficult for the G8 to put pressure on other countries to combat child pornography or to tighten their laws when members of the G8 themselves are lacking in this very approach.

Interpol

An agency that is of particular interest in this area is Interpol, which is an international law enforcement agency. Interpol is surprisingly old with its origins dating back to 1923 when European governments decided that inter-country crime meant that greater co-operation was required (McCulloch, 2005: 145). It was not until 1989 however that Interpol began to became active in combating child sexual exploitation and not until 1993 that a comprehensive strategy was devised that allowed the agency to, *inter alia*, seek to control child pornography (McCulloch, 2005: 145).

Interpol now has a significant role in combating child pornography. Its first role is in respect of co-ordinating action between countries that belong to Interpol. Arguably its more notable work in this area was in respect of the operation that followed the US Postal Inspection Service's action against Landslide Productions. This was a major website operated by Thomas and Janice Reedy which was responsible for hosting child pornography material. The US Postal Inspection Service acted against the US citizens but it quickly became apparent that subscribers from all over the world had subscribed to this site. As the US Postal Inspection Service had no jurisdiction over citizens of other countries, Interpol volunteered to analyse the subscription listings to identify individuals from other countries and pass the relevant information to national police agencies (McCulloch, 1995: 146). The UK version of this operation – Operation Ore – will be discussed in Chapter 12.

The global nature of the internet means that co-operation is increasingly important not least because there is a real risk that a national operation could interfere with another nation's operation. If, for example, country X decides to act against a virtual group found in their country it is quite possible that this will 'tip off' the members of the group in other countries. If country Y was investigating the group because they believed that they were abusing a child (and broadcasting that abuse over the internet) then the action taken by country X could cause real difficulties for country Y, potentially preventing the successful identification and recovery of the child victim. Interpol's co-ordination policy is designed to try and stop this and national law enforcement agencies are asked to inform Interpol when such operations are to take place (McCulloch, 2005: 148).

An increasingly important aspect of Interpol's work is in respect of the development of a database for victim identification. Whilst many countries had developed their own repository of child pornography images the G8 and other global policy leaders, had suggested that global co-operation was required. The initial database was known as ICAID (Interpol Child Abuse Images Database) and this was largely the result of the COPINE repository (the COPINE project was based at University College Cork, Ireland and they had developed a repository of images as part of their legitimate and important academic work: see Holland, 1995). The development of ICAID was welcome but there were difficulties in ensuring that material was sent to Interpol (McCulloch, 2005: 147) and although one of the primary justifications for its development was to facilitate victim identification, very few children had ever been identified (Holland, 2005: 76).

ICAID was eventually replaced and the new database is known as ICSE DB (Interpol Child Sexual Exploitation image Database) which is a major step forward. A difficulty with ICAID was that only Interpol could access it. Therefore if an investigator wished to identify whether an image they had found was already known (which could be useful in tracing a victim, see Chapter 12) they had to submit it to Interpol who would then process it and send the result back. This was cumbersome and perhaps accounted for some of the reluctance to submit material. ICSE DB on the other hand has secure off-site access meaning that law enforcement agencies can gain real-time access to the database allowing for much quicker responses.

Its other roles in the field of child pornography include the provision of training for national law enforcement officers and being a member of the Virtual Global Taskforce (VGT). The VGT was established in 2003 and consists of law enforcement agencies in Australia, Canada, Italy, the United Kingdom and the United States together with Interpol. The VGT operate child safety initiatives and also conduct operations against child pornography. Their most famous initiative is perhaps Operation PIN (Krone, 2005). This is a reactive policing site that purports to be a site offering child pornography but which, in fact, is operated by the VGT (the propriety of such sites is discussed in Chapter 12). If a person accesses this site their details are recorded and passed to the appropriate law enforcement member of Interpol.

The VGT also has an increasingly important role in offender identification. As with victim identification this is based on the premise that photographs are pictures of a crime scene and can be used as evidence to identify those who are abusing a child. Perhaps the most famous example of this is the arrest of Christopher Neil who had recorded himself abusing children and then placed these images on the internet. Neil had disguised himself by using manipulation software to obscure his face but the VGT managed to reverse engineer the manipulation and then, with the co-operation of Interpol, traced him which ultimately led to his arrest.

European initiatives

Whilst child pornography features heavily on the global policy agenda it also features at the geopolitical regional levels. Arguably the most active region to consider international approaches to child pornography is that of Europe. Outside of Europe it is not always understood that there are two international bodies operating in Europe; the Council of Europe (which consists of 47 countries and which is the elder body) and the European Union (which consists of 27 countries). Whilst becoming a member of the Council of Europe is a prerequisite of joining the EU the two bodies remain distinct although they do co-operate with each other on certain projects. As with the previous section, the purpose of this section is to provide an overview of some of the key initiatives. In the space allowed it is not possible to provide a comprehensive analysis but an interesting summary of the issues can be found in Akdeniz, 2008: 165–208.

Council of Europe

As noted already the Council of Europe is the elder body. Whilst its best known instrument is the European Convention on Human Rights a number of other instruments exist in this area. Periodically throughout this book it has been noted that the ECHR has a direct impact on the law relating to child pornography but the purpose of this section of the chapter is instead to detail the initiatives that are to be found in its other instruments.

As with other institutions it was not until comparatively late that the Council of Europe began to consider issues relating to the commercial sexual exploitation of children with its initial statement coming in 1991 (Akdeniz, 2008: 193). The initial action came by way of a recommendation on sexual exploitation, pornography, prostitution and trafficking of children which was, in essence, a policy statement by the Council to consider harmonising their laws to combat this behaviour (Akdeniz, 2008: 193). The recommendation was completely non-binding and required no formal action to comply: it was simply a statement of intent.

Since the 1990s however increasing attention has been paid to formal legislative instruments and for our purposes two are relevant; the Convention on Cybercrime (CETS No. 185) and the Convention on the Protection of Children against Sexual Exploitation and Sexual Abuse (CETS No. 201). The Convention on Cybercrime is the earlier of the two conventions. It is unnecessary to go into the background to this Convention but Akdeniz, 2008 provides a useful summary of the policy decisions that led to the Convention. Whilst the Cybercrime Convention was not aimed specifically at the sexual exploitation of children, Article 9 sought to tackle child pornography. Article 9.2 provided a definition of child pornography which included visual depictions of a minor engaged in sexual activity, a person appearing to be a minor engaged in sexual activity or realistic images representing a child engaged in sexual activity (in other words virtual child pornography). The requirement that it focuses on sexual activity would, at first sight, seem to suggest that nudity or the display of the sexual genitalia of a child would not be covered but the explanatory notes accompanying the Convention states that the lascivious exhibition of genitals was intended to be covered. The UN Special Rapporteur, writing in 1994, suggested that the definition put forward in the Cybercrime Convention was one of the most comprehensive (Petit, 2004: 10). A minor was defined under Article 9.3 as someone under the age of 18 although signatory states were allowed to reduce this age to 16 if they wished.

Article 9.1 listed a series of actions in respect of child pornography that should be criminalised. These included the production, offering, distribution and procurement of child pornography together with its possession. However Article 9.4 allowed a signatory state to 'opt out' of criminalising the procurement or simple possession of child pornography. As a Cybercrime Convention all the offences relate to child pornography created, accessed, distributed or stored on a computer system and does not include off-line pornography. However the Cybercrime Convention was one of the earliest international instruments that sought to create specific criminal offences in connection with child pornography. The Convention was also notable in that although it was technically a regional instrument for the Council of Europe, a number of countries outside of the Council of Europe also signed the treaty, the most prominent additional signatory being the United States.

Whilst the Cybercrime Convention was a notable step forward, the Council was concerned that it was restricted to child pornography facilitated by computers but also that it did not cover wider issues of sexual exploitation. The work of the

Council ultimately led to the passing of the Convention on sexual exploitation. Again the background to the drafting of this Convention will not be set out. The Convention on sexual exploitation is a much wider instrument and goes far beyond just child pornography, with it covering various forms of child sexual abuse and exploitation. A considerable amount of the Convention is spent considering non-criminal justice interventions. So, for example, Chapter II of the Convention deals with preventative measures, including examining the issues of recruiting and working with children and educational provision. Chapter III of the Convention requires signatory states to consider how they will co-ordinate responses at a local, national and international level.

Chapter IV of the Convention deals with the protection of victims but it also includes provision under Article 13 for hotlines. Whilst many of the provisions of Chapter IV are more relevant to other forms of sexual exploitation and abuse (although it should be remembered that many victims of child pornography will also be victims of sexual abuse since the material will depict their sexual abuse) some will be relevant and these will be discussed in Chapter 12. Chapter V relates to the establishment and provision of intervention programmes that seek to prevent the sexual abuse or exploitation taking place. Chapter VI of the Convention turns to the substantive criminal law. Article 20 of the Convention discusses the criminalisation of child pornography. As with the Convention on Cybercrime the production, dissemination and possession of child pornography is criminalised (although under this Convention there is no need for the material to involve the use of a computer) but Article 20.1(f) provides the additional requirement that states will criminalise 'knowingly obtaining access, through information and communication technologies, to child pornography'. This provision will tackle those who browse the internet for child pornography but who do not download it or who access peer-to-peer networks or newsgroups without downloading material. The justification for this was discussed in Chapter 2 and reference should be made to that.

Article 20.2 defines child pornography as visually depicting a child engaged in real or simulated sexually explicit conduct, including the depiction of a child's sexual organs for a sexual purpose. However Article 20.3 allows a Member State the right not to criminalise the production or possession of virtual child pornography or the possession of material that has been created by a child aged over the age of consent and who possesses it themselves. This latter point is analogous to one of the exceptions created by the Canadian Supreme Court in *R v Sharpe* 2001 SCC 2 and this was discussed in detail during Chapters 8 and 9.

Article 25 deals with the important issue of jurisdiction. This is something that will be addressed in more detail in the final section of this chapter but it is worth noting here that Article 20.2 requests that extraterritorial jurisdiction is based on the victim of the offence and Article 20.4 states that the principle of dual criminality (discussed below) should not apply. Article 20.7 provides for the prosecution of non-nationals who are resident in a signatory state's territory but whom they will not extradite. Again this will be discussed below but in the context of more general sexual exploitation it can be an important provision to ensure that people with financial means do not avoid justice by staying in extradition-free states.

Article 27 discusses the penalty that should be imposed for breaching the offences and states that they should be punished by 'effective, proportionate and dissuasive sanctions' (Article 27.1). Most international instruments will not set a minimum penalty that should be imposed but Article 27.1 is clearly requiring states to consider these matters as serious. Article 28 considers a series of factors that will be considered to aggravate the offences and some of these (e.g. acts that are prejudicial to the welfare of the child, acts against a family member, previous convictions or the involvement of organised crime) will be relevant to crimes of child pornography.

Chapter VII concerns the investigation and prosecution of offences, setting minimum standards for how offences relating to the sexual exploitation of a child should be prosecuted. Important provisions within this part are Article 33 that requires States to consider carefully the imposition of a statute of limitation and Article 34 which requires that the persons who are to investigate these crimes are suitably trained. Chapter VIII requires states to record data relating to offenders and Chapter IX provides a series of measures to facilitate international co-operation.

The Convention is not yet in force as it will come into force only when five states of the Council of Europe have ratified it (Article 45.3) and so far only three (Albania, Denmark and Greece) have done so. That said, 38 Member States have signed the Convention (the United Kingdom doing so on 5 May 2008) and it is likely to enter into force relatively soon and it is submitted that it is likely to be an important source of international rules within the Council.

European Union

The Treaty of Maastricht established three pillars of the European Union, with the third pillar being known as the Justice and Home Affairs pillar (although subsequently renamed Police and Judicial Co-operation in Criminal Matters) which provided for co-operation in, *inter alia*, the field of criminal justice. The Treaty of Lisbon abolished the pillar structure but judicial co-operation remains a central part of the EU with it being incorporated into Articles 67–89 of the Treaty on the Functioning of the EU. It will also ultimately lead to the European Court of Justice and European Commission gaining competence over the implementation of legislation made under these provisions.

It has been noted that children were not mentioned in EU legislation until 1996 (Manners, 2009: 229) although this is perhaps not surprising since, until that time, the EC (as it was then named) was considered to be purely an economic institution. However from the mid-1990s the EU became increasingly interested in the issue of children's rights, including sexual exploitation (Akdeniz, 2008: 167). An early indication of this was Joint Action 97/154/JHA on action to combat trafficking in human beings and sexual exploitation of children. By the new millennia attention remained focused on this issue and Council Decision 2000/375/JHA on combating child pornography was passed. This instrument included requirements on Member States to encourage internet users to report suspicions of child pornography distribution to law enforcement agencies (Article 1.1) and to create specialist units to tackle child pornography (Article 1.2). The Decision also required Member States to co-operate on the investigation and prosecution of child pornography (Article 2) and work with industry to develop ways of eliminating child pornography (Article 3).

As a policy statement the Council Decision was important although its execution was perhaps more questionable and no comprehensive analysis exists to understand how the Decision continued. Whilst Decision 2000/375/JHA was important as the first time community legislation was directed specifically towards child pornography it was not without failings. The Decision did not define what was meant by child pornography nor did it provide any detail as to how Member States were to fulfil its objectives. Realistically the Decision was more the approach of a series of policy objectives than a definitive series of actionable pronouncements.

This changed with the adoption of Council Framework Decision 2004/68/JHA on combating the sexual exploitation of children and child pornography. Unlike the 2000 Decision, the 2004 Framework Decision was more precise as to its purposes and was written in language that purported to require Member States to comply. The Decision provided for a definition of child pornography which is based on the Optional Protocol to the CRC and covers sexually explicit conduct, lascivious exhibition of the genital or pubic area of a child, depictions of a person appearing to be a child and virtual child pornography (Article 1(b)).

In terms of offences, the Framework Decision required the production, distribution, supply and possession of child pornography to be criminalised (Article 3). As with the Council of Europe conventions there is provision to 'opt out' of criminalising the possession of material that appears to be a child but is, in fact, of an adult and virtual child pornography (Article 3.2). Unlike most international instruments, the Framework Decision also sets a minimum accepted maximum penalty that should be imposed for these offences, with child pornography being between one and three years imprisonment (Article 5.1) except for the production of child pornography which should have a maximum of between five and 10 years' imprisonment (Article 5.2). As with the other international instruments the Framework Decision requires Member States to adopt an extraterritorial stance to the offences contained within it (Article 8). There is also provision relating to the treatment of victims (Article 9).

Despite the fact that Member States should have complied with the Decision by 20 January 2006 (Article 12.1) there is considerable evidence that many States have not done so. Perhaps the most illustrative example was highlighted in Chapter 2 where it was noted that many Member States have not altered the age of a 'child' to 18 as required by the Decision. In 2007 a somewhat optimistic analysis was undertaken by the European Commission (in order to discharge its duties under Article 12 of the 2003 Decision) which concluded that there had been broad compliance but ultimately noting that there were significant omissions by some Member States and some even failed to provide information about compliance (EC, 2007). This has been subsequently confirmed in later documents and the EU is now proposing to replace the Framework Decision with a new Directive (see EU Commission Proposal for a Directive on combating Sexual Abuse, Sexual Exploitation and Child Pornography, repealing Framework Decision 2004/68/JHA COM (2010) 94 2010/0064(COD)). Under the Treaty of Lisbon this should mean that for most countries this will mean that the Commission and European Court of Justice can ensure compliance, although some countries (most notably the United Kingdom) have an 'opt-out' from these provisions.

The proposed Directive tightens the definition of 'child pornography'. Whilst it is broadly similar to the original Framework Decision, it drops the reference to 'lascivious' exhibitions and instead includes 'any depiction of the sexual organs of a child for primarily sexual purposes' (Article 2(b)(ii)). The original Decision included depictions of the pubic area of a child and this has now been dropped, presumably meaning that a decision such as that which took place in *US v Knox* 32 F.3d.733 (1994) (discussed in Chapter 4) could not happen since the proposed Directive is clear that it applies only to the depiction of the genitalia and not the area. One issue that does arise, of course, is that genitalia is not defined and so a question must be raised as to whether the female breast comes within this definition as it was noted in Chapter 2 that the ordinary definition of the word 'genitalia' means it does not. The definition adopted in the proposed Directive will also cover adults pretending to be children and also simulated sexual activity. The issue of virtual child pornography is tackled with the proposed Directive including, 'realistic images of a child engaged in sexually explicit conduct or realistic images of the sexual organs of a child, regardless of the actual existence of such child, for primarily sexual purposes' (Article 2(b)(iv)). Quite what 'realistic images' means will undoubtedly need to be construed judicially but it would appear that at least some forms of virtual child pornography will be included.

Article 5 of the proposed Directive then mandates that individual states criminalise a number of activities in respect of child pornography, namely:

- Acquisition or possession of child pornography (Article 5(2)).
- Knowingly obtaining access by means of information and communication technology (Article 5(3)).
- Distribution, dissemination or transmission (Article 5(4)).
- Offering, supplying or making available child pornography (Article 5(5)).
- Production (Article 5(6)).

Each activity also contains a minimum standard for what the maximum sentence should be. Whilst this seems a contradiction in terms, it is perhaps best explained by reference to Article 5(6) which states 'production of child pornography shall be punishable by a maximum term of imprisonment of at least five years'. This is mandating that countries introduce a custodial sentence for the production of child pornography and that the sentence cannot be any less than a maximum of five years imprisonment although the maximum sentence could be greater. The penalties suggested in the Directive are quite modest and the original replacement Directive was suggesting both minimum and maximum sentences but this now appears to have been dropped.

The proposed Directive includes a number of other features that are of interest. Article 9 includes a series of factors that should be considered as aggravating factors when a person comes to sentencing. These include the age of the child, their vulnerability and the level of harm inflicted. Article 10 mandates a disqualification from working with children where a person is convicted of a relevant offence and Articles 14–20 present a series of rules that relate to the investigation of crimes, securing jurisdiction and mandating programmes to support and assist victims. Article 21 requires member states to block access to websites that are known to include child pornography. This has proven extremely controversial and it will be interesting to see whether this provision is retained in the final Directive.

Initiatives

Whilst the EU has passed a number of pieces of legislation, their greater impact has perhaps been through the funding of various initiatives. A major initiative is the DAPHNE programme to combat violence against children, young persons and women, specifically including sexual exploitation. The first tranche of the programme (Decision 293/2000/EC) lasted from 2000 to 2003 and was quickly followed by two further tranches (Decision 803/2004/EC and Decision 779/2007/EC) which extended the programme from 2004–2008 and 2008–2013. The DAPHNE project has been used in various ways including the development of academic research and educational initiatives. It has also been used, for example, to develop treatment programmes for those with a sexual interest in children (developed by the COPINE unit).

A major initiative in this area was the Safer Internet programme. This programme ran for five years with a budget of €38.3 million and funded approximately 89 programmes (Akdeniz, 2008: 173). The principal objectives of the plan were:

- To promote the safer use of the internet and communication technologies, particularly for children and young people.
- To educate users, particularly children, parents, carers, teachers and educators in this regard.
- To fight against illegal content and harmful conduct online.

In 2002 the Safer Internet Plus programme was developed as the successor to the Safer Internet programme. This was originally designed as a three-year programme (Akdeniz, 2008: 173) but was extended in 2005 to cover the period up to 2008

(Akdeniz, 2008: 174) and has currently been extended once more to include the period up to 2013 (see Decision 1351/2008/EC). Whilst the emphasis of the latest version of the programme has been extended to include grooming and bullying, a particular emphasis of the programme continues to be targeting child pornography. The budget for the period up to 2013 is €55 million and Article 2 of the Decision states that the following action lines shall be addressed by the programme:

- Ensuring public awareness.
- Fighting against illegal content and harmful content on line.
- Promoting a safer online environment.
- Establishing a knowledge base.

These are extensions of the previous actions. Two initiatives have been created under this initiative – the Inhope and Insafe organisations (discussed below) – and the knowledge base has led to significant academic research being undertaken. One of the most important aspects of the knowledge base was a major project examining how children used the internet and related communication technologies (Livingstone and Haddon, 2009).

The two principal initiatives to have arisen out of the Safer Internet Plus programme however are the establishment, and continued funding of, Inhope and Insafe. Inhope is the association of hotline operators. For our purposes, a hotline can be summarised as a point of contact for members of the public to report websites that host child pornography which will then be actioned by the industry or law enforcement. The annex to Decision 1351/2008/EC states that a particular action of the programme is 'providing the public with, and promoting the existence of, contact points and hotlines for reporting online illegal content and harmful conduct' (para. 2.1). Inhope was founded in 1999 under the original Safer Internet programme but continues to receive funding from the Safer Internet Plus programme. As the international association, it assists in the creation of new hotlines and sets minimum standards that hotlines must adhere to in order to receive formal recognition. Inhope also allows for the sharing of information relating to the hosting of information (allowing a website to be blocked or removed in more than one country) and also provides educational initiatives.

Insafe is the second major body to receive funding from the Safer Internet Plus programme. Insafe, like Inhope is a network. This time the network is a series of awareness centres that are tasked to educate the community on the safe use of the internet and communication technologies by children and young persons. The education is not however restricted to young people and will include parents and teachers. The annex to Decision 1351/2008/EC provides direct support for their work when it states that an action point is to 'provide contact points where parents and children can receive answers to questions about how to stay safe online . . .' (para. 1.2). There are awareness centres in all Member States except Estonia and the programme also includes centres in the non-EU countries of Iceland and Norway (although they are part of the EEA).

Europol

Further evidence of the EU's intention to tackle issues relating to child pornography in ways other than by legislation is the work of Europol, the European law enforcement agency. Established under the authority of the Treaty of Maastricht and coming into existence in 1998, this agency acts as a central point of contact between the law enforcement agencies of each country: assisting through, for example, intelligence sharing, crime analysis and facilitating co-operation of national agencies. From its inception Europol was considered to have a role in preventing the sexual exploitation of children and as early as 2000 it had established pan-European investigations relating to child pornography (*Annual Report*, 2000), something that it continues to do (see subsequent annual reports). The fact that Europol was tasked in this way from its very existence provides further support for the suggestion that by the end of the 1990s the EU was operating an active policy agenda on issues relating to child pornography.

Jurisdiction

The final section of this chapter examines the issue of jurisdiction. As noted at the beginning of the chapter, in the context of child pornography this is not a concept of international law *per se*, but is instead an exercise of the sovereign jurisdiction of a country to prosecute for acts undertaken outside of its territory. The ordinary rule of jurisdiction is territorial, i.e. the State will only prosecute offences that occur within its sovereign territory. It has been explained that this is ordinarily not simply that the courts lack jurisdiction (as they may, in fact, have jurisdiction) but rather it is that the *actus reus* of a crime requires it to be committed within the territory of a country (Hirst, 2003: 11; Card *et al.*, 2008: 37).

It should be noted at the outset that certain forms of conduct undertaken outside of the territory of England and Wales are ordinarily actionable. These primarily relate to conduct on British-registered or owned ships, aircraft and members of the Merchant Navy or armed forces (Card *et al.*, 2008: 37). This form of jurisdiction will not be discussed in this section of the chapter as it will rarely be an issue in terms of child pornography although, of course, it would be of obvious relevance where a person takes an indecent photograph of a child on a UK-registered cruise ship. Instead this section discusses what is commonly known as extraterritorial jurisdiction, i.e. the jurisdiction that the UK has claimed in respect of dealing with child sexual exploitation, including child pornography, that takes place in a foreign country.

There are a number of different approaches to extraterritorial jurisdiction. The four most common are based on the protective principle, the active personality principle, the passive personality principle and universal jurisdiction. The latter are situations which are, in essence, crimes under international law and can be tried regardless of where they were committed (Hirst, 2003: 54). Obvious examples of crimes in this classification are slavery, piracy and war crimes. The sexual exploitation of children is not considered a crime under international law (and note the international instruments discussed in the preceding sections obligated Member States to criminalise conduct rather than creating crimes under international criminal law) and thus universal jurisdiction is not raised. The same can be said of the protective principle which can be summarised as 'acts done wholly abroad may be criminalised if they involve attacks on or threats against a state's security or vital national interests' (Hirst, 2003: 48). Child sexual exploitation does not amount to a threat to the State or national interests and this too can be discounted. This leaves the two personality principles; the active and the passive. The active is arguably the most common (Fredette, 2009: 18) and is based on the nationality of the offender whereas the passive personality operates on the basis of the victim's nationality (Hirst, 2003: 51).

Under the active personality a state may extend its jurisdictional ambit to criminalise the acts of its own citizens that take place abroad. It has been suggested that the justification for the active personality extension of territorial jurisdiction is that citizens of a country are able to seek benefit and protection as a result of their citizenship and accordingly they owe a comparable duty not to act against the interest of their state (Blakesley and Stigall, 2004: 123). The US federal courts phrased it in similar, but more governmental, language when the Naval–Marine Court of Criminal Appeal stated that a sovereign country has the right to 'regulate its own citizens, regardless of their location' (*US v Kolly* (48 MJ 795 (1998) at p. 797).

Increasingly the active personality will also apply to those resident in a country too and this is certainly something that appears to apply in England and Wales (Hirst, 2003: 204 and see s. 72(2), SOA 2003). This extension has certainly been considered appropriate in respect of the sexual exploitation of children where it has been thought that restricting jurisdiction to nationals has led to some persons escaping justice (Svensson, 2006: 655). The move finds support in international instruments with the Optional Protocol to the CRC requiring extraterritorial laws to apply to those 'ordinarily resident in its territory' (Article 4.2(a)). The move is also echoed in the Council of Europe Convention on sexual exploitation (Article 25.1(e)).

It may be considered somewhat controversial to extend extraterritorial laws to mere residents since arguably they do not owe the same duties as a citizen although it has been suggested that residents owe obligations only when living under the protection of the Crown (Hirst, 2003: 220 in *Joyce v DPP* [1946] AC 347 the House of Lords held that the fact that William Joyce (a.k.a. 'Lord Haw Haw') had applied for, and been granted, a British passport meant that he was under protection whilst abroad although many would argue that his subsequent actions would appear to demonstrate the repudiation of any such protection). Certainly there is little difficulty in stating that D, a citizen of country X, should adhere to the laws of country Y when he resides or visits there. It is perhaps more problematic to state that D should also adhere to the laws of country Y when he visits country Z. Where he has a passport issued in country Y then perhaps the 'protection' argument can apply and a person who seeks protection by country Y should expect to adhere to the standards set down by that country, but where he retains a passport under country X it is less easy to see why he should be liable for prosecution in country Y for his actions in country Z. Again it is perhaps understandable from the perspective of seeking to tackle those who travel solely for the purpose of sexually exploiting a child, but its application to people within a country raises questions about whether it is one country trying to impose its laws and customs on another.

Along with the active personality principle it will be recalled that there also exists the passive personality principle; here jurisdiction is based on the nationality of the victim. This has historically been considered one of those most controversial and opposed bases for extraterritorial jurisdiction (Hirst, 2003: 51). In the field of child sexual exploitation, including child pornography, it has become increasingly seen as a useful method of securing jurisdiction and this is evident from international instruments. It was noted earlier that both the Optional Protocol to the CRC and the Council of Europe Convention on sexual exploitation call for states to adopt the passive personality principle (Articles 4.2(b) and 20.2 respectively). This is perhaps more relevant to other forms of commercial sexual exploitation but it could still have an application to child pornography. An example could be where D, a citizen of country X, is in a relationship with V's mother, a citizen of country Y. Whilst in country X, D takes indecent photographs of V and these are discovered when D is in country Y. Adopting the passive personality principle would allow D to be charged with the creation of child pornography rather than mere possession which is probably all that could be charged unless jurisdiction was extended.

Ordinarily extraterritorial jurisdiction is subordinate to the territory on which the crime took place (Blakesley and Stigall, 2004: 123) but with some offences, including offences relating to the sexual exploitation of a child, this can be problematic as certain countries are known not to take the issue of child sexual exploitation seriously. The principle of subordination will ordinarily also lead to difficulties over the issue of double jeopardy, something that is particularly strong in common-law countries. Put simply the rule against double jeopardy states that a person should not be criminalised twice for the same action. In this context it means that where D, a resident of country X, commits a crime in country Y he should not be subject to prosecution in both country X and Y. The UN Special Rapporteur has suggested that the principle of double jeopardy should not apply (Maalla, 2009: 23) but it is notable that none of the current international instruments have gone this far. The UNCRC Optional Protocol is completely silent on this point and the Council of Europe Convention on the sexual exploitation of children simply states that in a conflict between jurisdictions, the countries seeking a prosecution should 'consult with a view to determining the most appropriate jurisdiction for prosecution' (Article 25.8). This is perhaps not surprising since the principle of double jeopardy is so entrenched in many legal systems. Even systems that have partially abrogated the rule (e.g. England and Wales) have done so only in respect of previous acquittals (see Part 10, Criminal Justice Act 2003) and not in respect of punishments. It is unlikely many countries would allow an offender to be punished twice for the same action.

A key principle in the issue of extraterritorial jurisdiction is that of dual criminality. Many jurisdictions ordinarily require that a citizen not only commits an offence under their own law but that it should also be a criminal offence in the territory where the crime took place (for the historical position in England and Wales see Hirst, 2003: 49–50). In the context of child sexual exploitation this can be problematic in that some countries may not criminalise certain activities (Svensson, 2006: 655). As a response to this some jurisdictions have begun to remove the dual criminality rule (in England and Wales see s. 72, Criminal Justice and Immigration Act 2008 which removed the requirement under s. 72, Sexual Offences Act 2003). Some international instruments have also sought to remove the principle, most notably the Council of Europe Convention on the sexual exploitation of a child which specifically calls for its removal (Article 25.4 although Article 25.5 allows states to derogate from that provision). This is echoed in the draft EU framework directive (Article 13.3 but note that Framework Decision 2004/68/JHA does not include this call) but it is perhaps notable that the Optional Protocol to the CRC does not do this.

It has been suggested that abrogating the principle of double criminality is controversial (see, for example, Card *et al.*, 2008: 40) in part because it could mean that a citizen is criminalised in his country of nationality for undertaking activity that is perfectly lawful in another country. So, for example, in Iceland the age of consent is fourteen. If D, a UK citizen, went to live in Iceland and had sexual intercourse with a 15 year-old girl no criminal offence is being committed in Iceland. However under the provisions of s. 72, Sexual Offences Act 2003 a crime is being committed under English law. Should the law of the United Kingdom apply in these circumstances? Would it alter our perception of the answer if the example above had not involved Iceland but had, for example, involved a country that is often thought of as having a sex tourism problem (e.g. Sri Lanka which, until recently, had the age of consent set at twelve)? It is this dilemma which is at the heart of the difficulty of adopting extraterritorial laws to sex offences. Whilst many would have no difficulty in extending the laws to tackle those who exploit a child, identifying what amounts to exploitation is more difficult. There is no uniform age of consent across the world or indeed within regions. It was seen from Chapter 4 that differences can exist even in countries (where, for example, it was seen the age of consent differs between states within the United States and within Australia), and it should be noted from the earlier discussion of international legal instruments that none of these instruments have attempted to define a uniform age of consent.

The argument in favour of abolishing the principle of dual criminality is that a state can, in certain contexts, decide that their citizens or nationals should adhere to prescribed behavioural standards wherever they are. However given that citizenship is something not easily defined and where it is possible to hold citizenship without ever having visited the country of nationality (e.g. a baby born to UK parents in Cambodia will still be a UK citizen irrespective of whether he has ever lived or visited the United Kingdom) this can mean that people are being held to standards contrary to the laws of where they live. Child pornography is a classic example of this since it was noted in Chapters 2–4 that although most international instruments defined a child as 18, many countries continue to adopt a lesser age. If D, a UK citizen, takes an indecent photograph of a child in one of those countries then he commits a criminal offence even though it was perfectly lawful to do this in that country. If D is a 'sex tourist' (i.e. he specifically travelled to country X in order to take indecent photographs of children under the age of 18) then a prosecution may well be appropriate but where D has lived in that country all his life it may not. Of course this perhaps demonstrates the blurring of criminal law and criminal procedure. Where D lives in another country, D (as a UK national) may be technically guilty of an offence under English Law but it is highly unlikely that he would ever be prosecuted for it. That said, the fact remains that he remains at risk of prosecution and can rely only on prosecutorial discretion to prevent a formal criminal justice intervention. Squaring this circle is extremely difficult and it is why the principle remains controversial but the fact remains that if the principle of dual criminality remained then it could cause significant difficulty in the prosecution of child sexual exploitation, including child pornography.

Enacting extraterritorial legislation is relatively easy to do but this, by itself, does not answer all the problems. It has been noted that a significant difficulty with extraterritorial laws is their implementation: 'without effective co-operation and enforcement, the most comprehensive [extraterritorial] legislation is useless to protect the world's children' (Svensson, 2006: 659). This is a most pertinent point. Legislative action is impotent without it being used by law enforcement agencies. Where the conduct has taken place in a different country from that which the law enforcement agency is based then difficulties arise about the gathering of evidence and, for example, witness testimony. That said, it has also been suggested that extraterritorial legislation is more than just a mechanism and that it can serve as a demonstration of principle (Card et al., 2008: 43) and that it could serve to deter people from going abroad to undertake illegal and exploitative behaviour. This is an extremely important point although it is difficult to quantify.

As regards child pornography it is perhaps easier to gather the evidence than for other crimes relating to the sexual exploitation of a child. The principal evidence will be the photographs and, in terms of England and Wales, the relevant legislation would be the Protection of Children Act 1978 (in conjunction with s. 72, Sexual Offences Act 2003). It will be remembered from Chapter 3 that it is not necessary to know the age of the child for the purposes of PoCA 1978 and accordingly it would not be necessary to identify the child in order to consider whether the photograph is of a child. This is perhaps demonstrated by the case of *R v Towner* (2001, unreported but discussed in Card et al., 2008: 42) where the defendant was convicted in the Crown Court for, *inter alia*, taking indecent photographs of a child in Cambodia. The pictures were discovered by his wife when checking her husband's computer, and serves as an example of how child pornography offences could be identified and prosecuted with minimal co-operation from outside of the United Kingdom. Where co-operation is required it will be remembered from the earlier parts of this chapter that this is an integral role of both Interpol and Europol.

Chapter 12

Policing child pornography

This chapter will consider how law enforcement has reacted to the challenges of policing child pornography. Unfortunately due to size limitations it has been necessary to concentrate on traditional law enforcement schemes and it has not been possible, for example, to consider the issue of self-regulation. Arguably this is one of the most important recent developments of the policing of child pornography although realistically self-regulation is something that is restricted to a small number of countries, most notably the United Kingdom (through the Internet Watch Foundation). For a discussion on the issues raised by self-regulation see Walden (2010).

Chapter 11 noted that international bodies, including Europol and Interpol, are increasingly involved in combating child pornography and it was also noted in Chapter 6 that both the security and intelligence services also now have a role in this environment. However it is ultimately still the police who have a direct role in combating child pornography. This section of the chapter will analyse their role and, in particular, will look at three areas: (1) organisation, (2) operation, (3) victims.

Organisation

The first issue to consider is that of the organisation of law enforcement agencies to combat child pornography. It has been remarked that the organisation of the police in the United Kingdom is fragmented and full of fraught political battles (Jewkes and Andrews, 2005: 46). This is certainly true of the policing of child pornography.

Forty-three police forces

Those unfamiliar with the organisation of the police force in England and Wales may be surprised to know that there are 43 separate police forces. Each force covers a geographical area that is, broadly speaking, equivalent to a local authority area with there being two police forces in London. The first, the City of London Police, the smallest police force in the country, covers the territory of the City of

London (roughly one square mile) together with the territories of the Inner and Middle Temple. The second, and far larger, organisation is the Metropolitan Police, the largest police force in the country and which, for some matters, has a national remit.

Whilst it has been said that only three police forces had dedicated paedophile units (West Midlands Police, Greater Manchester Police and the Metropolitan Police (Jewkes and Andrews, 2005: 47)) Devon and Cornwall Police have also had a paedophile unit for a number of years although it is not as large as others. Some units may specialise. For example, Greater Manchester Police were one of the few police forces that actively sought to trace victims from images of child pornography. The paedophile units are ordinarily staffed by police officers who have specialist expertise in this area and ordinarily both proactive and reactive operations will take place within them.

Those forces that do not have a paedophile unit will all usually have dedicated officers that investigate child sexual exploitation, including child pornography. However these officers could be housed in a number of different teams including child protection units, public protection units, hi-tech crime teams and, in a number of forces, POLIT units (Paedophile Online Investigation Teams) (Jewkes and Andrews, 2005: 47). The approach of these teams will very much depend on the officers within it. Some will be experts on the management of sex offenders rather than the investigation of particular types of crime. POLIT units tend to include specialist officers that are capable of undertaking proactive investigations and will also include an intelligence capability. All units are unlikely to have the same level of capability and it has been noted that they may not include the broad range of work that the larger units or the specialist paedophile units have (Jewkes and Andrews, 2005: 47).

Where specialist staff are used then a question that arises periodically is whether officers should have a restricted tenure within the department (Jewkes and Andrews, 2005: 57). Some forces suggest that certain specialist units should have their key personnel rotated. There can be a number of reasons for this including concerns as to the psychological effect of long-term exposure to child pornography, the need to refresh teams and to allow officers exposure to work that is conducive to promotion. It has been noted that some officers are resistant to rotation or tenure, in part because there is a belief that it can waste the expertise of some officers (Jewkes and Andrews, 2005: 57). This can be particularly true where officers have undertaken educational programmes to increase their knowledge of the area. When the Metropolitan Police sought to introduce tenure into their Paedophile Unit there was political and media concern (Hurst, 2003) and the policy was, to an extent, modified.

CEOP

The fragmented nature of policing has, on a number of occasions, led to calls over the amalgamation of forces and raised questions over whether there should be national capabilities in respect of some forms of policing. The policing of child pornography is such an area. Initially national policing was extremely informal with the Metropolitan Police, as the largest and most advanced paedophile unit, providing assistance to local forces (HMIC, 2008: 31). The assistance had to be informal, not least because until comparatively recently a police officer had no automatic right of arrest outside of his force area. Eventually there was recognition that this area required a national focus and initially this was piggy-backed on to existing national structures, most notably the National Hi-Tech Crime Unit (NHTCU) with some intelligence being handled by the National Criminal Intelligence Service (NCIS). The latter was responsible, in part, for receiving the names from the US Postal Inspection Service following the taking down of Landslide Productions, in the action that would become known as Operation Ore in the United Kingdom (discussed below).

A difficulty with this approach however was that child pornography (and other crimes relating to the sexual exploitation of children) was only a minor part of a wider remit held by both the NHTCU and NCIS. The NHTCU, for example, was responsible for a number of other crimes including large-scale financial crimes, hacking, viruses and terrorism. In its early days only one-quarter of its work was related to child pornography (Jewkes and Andrews, 2005: 48). Yet despite this the particular nature of child pornography investigations, particularly following Operation Ore, meant that the NHTCU structures quickly became 'creaking at the seams' (Jewkes and Andrews, 2005: 49).

The experience of NHTCU led many to consider the question of whether a dedicated resource for child sexual exploitation was required. Following extensive discussions and visits to the relevant American national centre (National Center for Missing and Exploited Children) it was decided to establish a UK centre and this came into being in 2006 with the establishment of the Child Exploitation and Online Protection Centre (CEOP). This national centre was established by the Home Office as an affiliate of the Serious and Organised Crime Agency (SOCA) although it had its own Chief Executive and its own Board. The exact relationship between CEOP and SOCA has never been fully clarified and in January 2010 it was announced by the Home Office that they intend to separate the organisation and constitute CEOP as a non-departmental public body (Home Office, 2010), although the coalition government has apparently reversed this decision.

As an affiliate of SOCA, CEOP is not technically a police organisation although it is part of the wider police family and clearly a criminal justice agency. CEOP, from its very inception, however was never designed to be a purely law enforcement organisation and police officers sit alongside social workers and educationalists (Home Office, 2010: 8). Its police officers are on secondment and, whilst they do not exercise any power of arrest, they do assist local police in the investigation of sexual exploitation, particularly that facilitated on the internet, including child pornography.

CEOP has established itself into three 'faculties': Intelligence, Specialist Operational Support and Harm Reduction. CEOP describes its intelligence hub as the 'key to the success of the CEOP Centre' (CEOP website). Within this faculty are both intelligence gathering and intelligence analysis. Intelligence sharing, both within the United Kingdom and with other countries or organisations, also takes place within this faculty. The Intelligence faculty will also examine trends and consider how the intelligence product can be used by other faculties, including Education. The Specialist Operational Support faculty is the part of CEOP that has the most to do with live operations and working with police. It also includes a small financial investigation team. This is commercially supported by the credit card company Visa Europe and aims to trace and seize money and assets that has been earned through the exploitation of a child, together with analysing the new trends that are used to pay for exploitative services (Bains, 2008: 25).

The third faculty is the Harm Reduction faculty, which encompasses a number of innovative features for a law enforcement agency. Along with traditional crime prevention schemes this faculty is also responsible for CEOP's educational initiatives. These initiatives include training for law enforcement and others within the child protection regime and, in combination with the University of Central Lancashire, CEOP has developed a system whereby its training can lead to an educational qualification (Bains, 2008: 25). The Harm Reduction faculty also includes those staff that represent CEOP on the various bodies that have as their aim the prevention of child sexual exploitation (CEOP website).

CEOP is a relatively new organisation and there have been few public evaluations of its work. An important document in this context is the report of an inspection of CEOP by HM Inspectorate of Constabulary (HMIC) that was conducted in 2008. The review was initiated by SOCA (HMIC, 2008: 21) and HMIC undertook the review because under s. 16, Serious and Organised Crime and Police Act 2005, it has the legal duty to inspect SOCA. As CEOP is an affiliate of SOCA this meant HMIC were empowered to conduct the review.

HMIC noted that there was overwhelming support for the concept of CEOP and it was possible to show that it had already made a significant impact on policing in this area (HMIC, 2008: 6). However whilst broadly supportive of its work, HMIC was concerned about a number of aspects of CEOPs governance and structures (HMIC, 2008: 37). It noted that the CEOP budget was provided by central government for a three-year period but that it received additional monies from the EU, other government departments and from certain charities (HMIC, 2008: 56). As an affiliate CEOP receives additional support from SOCA although HMIC found estimating a figure for this support to be problematical (HMIC, 2008: 57). Whilst CEOP currently receives support, both financial and manpower, from charities and the industry HMIC notes that these cannot be guaranteed and that therefore CEOP 'has no certainty on the finances for any long-term strategic development and planning' (HMIC, 2008: 11).

Its governance was the cause of most concern (it being concluded that 'if not addressed [it] will prevent the CEOP Centre from achieving its objectives' (HMIC, 2008: 36)). The HMIC noted that the governance arrangements were convoluted (HMIC, 2008: 9) and that 'no single body/board is providing full active governance' (HMIC, 2008: 10). A particular complaint was that although the then CEO,

Jim Gamble, was considered to be 'inspirational' (HMIC, 2008: 63) there appeared no systematic approach to holding him to account (HMIC, 2008: 10).

Issues were also raised about CEOPs relationship with other bodies. It was noted that some thought that CEOP were trying to do too much: 'CEOP cannot save the world' (HMIC, 2008: 64) and that the relationship with industry was the subject of tensions (HMIC, 2008: 75). These tensions continue to the present day. During 2009 and 2010 the then CEO of CEOP, Jim Gamble, complained that, in his opinion, some industry members were not dealing with the issue of reporting sexual exploitation seriously. The complaint arose after one social networking site – Bebo – agreed to provide a 'report button' on their site that allowed users to contact CEOP directly to report abusive content or behaviour. The link was to CEOP and Jim Gamble complained that not every social networking site would provide this link. Industry responded that they took abuse seriously but they were not all convinced that a direct link to CEOP was either necessary or desirable. The dispute undoubtedly showed tensions exist between CEOP and industry and it should be questioned whether the CEO of CEOP should be publicly berating industry using emotive language during broadcasts with the media. That said, CEOP would probably retort that its aim was to protect children. However given that industry co-operation is crucial to the fight against child pornography it can be questioned whether such public tensions are helpful. That is not to say that the industry should have a veto – far from it – but is public disagreement conducive to the establishment of effective relationships?

CEOPs relationship with the police is even more complex. Officers that had contact with CEOP were generally positive about the experience (HMIC, 2008: 70) but strategically there was some concern about the exact relationship between CEOP and individual forces, with an absence of any memorandum of under-standing or service-level agreement prepared (HMIC, 2008: 71). It is perhaps not surprising that there is tension here since, as was noted previously, the history of policing is littered with territorial and political battles (Jewkes and Andrews, 2005: 46) and HMIC note themselves that one of the criticisms is that some forces believe that CEOP are encroaching on to their territory (HMIC, 2008: 71). The absence of formal partnership agreements perhaps allows for this distrust to arise but CEOP is arguably not experiencing anything different to other national law enforcement agencies which, by their very nature, will impinge on some functions traditionally exercised by local forces.

Many of the problems that HMIC identified for CEOP were not, to be fair, of its own making. The funding of CEOP for example is a matter primarily for government. Similarly its governance is largely an issue for others although there was concern about whether those sitting on its board were truly independent of CEOP and the extent to which CEOP itself recruited and appointed members of its board. In 2010 it was announced that the government intended to establish CEOP as a non-departmental public body (NDPB). CEOP was an affiliate of SOCA because it allowed the organisation to be created without the need for primary legislation and because it allowed it to develop its own structure and strategy. As an affiliate of SOCA it could use its parent agency for legal powers to conduct covert surveillance, etc. The difficulty with the arrangement however is that it was never fully explained how SOCA would superintend CEOP and this created some of the governance issues that were discussed above.

Transforming CEOP into an NDPB could have assisted in ensuring that the problems identified above would not be faced in the future. As an NDPB its sponsoring government department would need to be clear about its budget and also its abilities to seek additional monies from elsewhere. That said, caution must be exercised in depending on money from charities or the internet industry as neither sources can be guaranteed. Charities may need money for other purposes and HMIC also notes that charity rules may even raise legal difficulties for their continued support (HMIC, 2008: 11).

As an NDPB its governance arrangements would be set out in statute. This would include a requirement for an independent board and their appointment would be subject to the ordinary rules of public-sector governance. An important part of the NDPB status would be to clarify the rules on CEOP's relationship with other sectors, particularly the police, and also who it would be audited or inspected by.

CEOP is undoubtedly a step forward. A national resource to deal with the issue of, *inter alia*, child pornography has to be welcomed. A national resource can minimise some of the 'local' problems identified above. That said, it must be recognised that CEOP was created in a hurry and its early years have seen shifts as to its remit and also meant that the law enforcement response to child sexual exploitation had to be rethought. This has, as HMIC noted, created tensions between the various players. The proposed move to NDPB status could have resolved some of these tensions but the new coalition government formed in 2010 are reviewing this decision. Whilst the decision is theoretically the subject of consultation it would seem that the government has decided not to give CEOP NDPB status but instead to continue the status quo by integrating it into the new National Crime Agency. Jim Gamble, who set up CEOP and became its first chief executive, resigned over the decision and many children's charities disagreed with the decision. However, it would seem the government does not intend to back down and CEOP is likely to form part of the new agency. It is to be hoped that the new arrangements answer the criticisms of HMIC.

Forensic capability

It was noted that the policing of child pornography is somewhat fragmented, it being divided between the national centre (CEOP) and 43 separate police forces, all of different sizes. This can mean that there is a discrepancy in resources and this is particularly apparent in the forensic capability of police forces. Forensics, as will be seen, can be a fundamental aspect of any investigation into child pornography but it is also an expensive resource. This is an issue that is only likely to get worse. Sanderson, an independent forensic expert, contrasts two arrests of the same offender. The first arrest took place in 1995 and:

> At that time, a total of approximately eighty videos, fifteen magazines, ten indecent covers and four computer discs were seized.
>
> (Sanderson, 2006: 190)

The second arrest took place in 2003. This time:

> There were eight computers, thirty-nine separate hard drives, over 400 CD/DVDs, more than 200 floppies, in excess of 100 Zip disks, and approximately 100 videos. The computer hard drives alone contained 800 Gb of digital evidence.
>
> (Sanderson, 2006: 190)

That was an arrest in 2003. Since that time media storage has grown in size and sophistication. We are now accustomed to solid-state storage devices (a.k.a. memory or data sticks) that are several gigabytes in size and as small as a thumb-nail. Hard drive development has continued to accelerate and now it is possible to purchase a one terabyte (about 1,000 Gb) hard drive for less than £50. This means that the amount of data that can be seized by the police is almost incomprehensible. The reality that this brings is even more profound:

> It could take one officer the whole of his working career to thoroughly investigate the contents of a 10 Gb hard drive.
>
> (National Hi-Tech Crime Unit spokesman, quoted in Jewkes and Andrews, 2005: 52)

Multiply this by the amount of storage that is now being discovered and it is quickly apparent that there are real difficulties in the way that the police are structured and can operate.

Smaller forces will, by their very nature, not be able to resource as large a forensic capability as some other forces. Many forces use outside forensic service providers as it may be difficult to justify an adequate internal forensic capability (which would entail employing a number of technicians to cover sickness, leave, etc.). Maintaining an internal forensic capability can also be problematic since many forensic experts could earn more money in the private sector than the public sector (Jewkes and Andrews, 2005: 56) and this will mean that, once trained, the police service may lose them to an outside agency requiring them to recruit and retrain their replacement. It may be thought that using police officers trained as forensic analysts could solve this problem but this is unlikely to be true since although it may solve the issue of retention, the costs of employing a police officer far exceed the cost of employing civilian staff due to pension and leave arrangements. The specialised nature of this work also means that an officer is unlikely to gain a broad range of experience which could fatally harm his promotion prospects (Sommer, 2005: 25). Accordingly an officer who has any desire for advancement during his career is unlikely to choose to enter the field of computer forensics.

An additional problem with forensic capability is that traditionally there was no common understanding of what was required to become a forensic expert (O'Brien, 2005: 159). Historically it was simply that someone 'knew about computers' but where they were not within the police family or did not have regular contact with the police then questions began to be raised about the integrity of evidence. Certainly during Operation Ore there began to be concern about the validity of some expert evidence provided (O'Brien, 2005: 159). One expert in particular, Jim Bates, caused concern when he was convicted at Leicester Crown Court for offences relating to false witness statements given in a trial (where he misrepresented his qualifications) and perjury. It was reported in the press that this caused the CPS to review a number of cases (Doward, 2008) although there is no evidence to suggest that any successful appeal has been brought or any case halted as a result of his convictions, and it was noted that he was considered to have been one of the leading experts in the field.

As will be noted below there is considerable debate between expert witnesses about the success or otherwise of Operation Ore and some disquiet about who precisely can call themselves an expert. In *Bates v Chief Constable of the Avon and Somerset Police* [2009] EWHC 942 (Admin) the Divisional Court held that a judge in the Crown Court could not rule who can, or cannot, act as a defence witness. Whilst a judge can state that a person may not provide admissible expert evidence, this decision must be based purely on the question as to whether the person has sufficient expertise (at [22]). That said, the Divisional Court also noted that if a person was to give evidence their credibility would be important when the jury decide how much weight to give to the testimony.

Forensic capability undoubtedly remains one of the significant challenges of a law enforcement response to child pornography. Clearly from the standpoint of safeguarding the integrity of the evidence and law enforcement operations it would be better if the forensic capability was within the police family (although there will always be a need for reserve capacity where, for example, unexpected investigations arise and this raises the question discussed above about who 'qualifies' as an expert). Establishing this capacity will however be expensive. Some of the smaller forces will struggle to establish sufficient internal capacity. This is undoubtedly one of the difficulties with the current police organisational structure, where each of the 43 separate police forces in England and Wales might as well be a fiefdom. Regional co-operation between local forces could ensure greater resilience but it has to be said that there is not an illustrious history of police co-operation on any matter: individual chief constables are ordinarily loathe to surrender any of their autonomy, especially in matters relating to their budget.

Operational

It has been remarked that since the 1970s 'there has been a technological race between child pornographers and the police forces who wish to combat them'

(Jenkins, 2001: 143). The advent of the internet and related communication technologies has transformed the operational work of police officers in this way. The preceding section has identified how the structure of law enforcement in England and Wales has reacted to this change, including the development of specialist police units and the establishment of CEOP. In this section the operational challenges that exist in the policing of child pornography will be considered.

It has been suggested (Krone, 2005: 2) that there are in essence four types of police operation in respect of child pornography on the internet:

- Against an individual.
- Against covert groups.
- Against those who subscribe to websites.
- Those who are caught as a result of a police 'sting' operation.

The first group is that of individuals and Krone notes that it is quite possible that offenders will operate without being part of a collective. Such persons are, in effect, likely to be those who download information rather than trade material (downloading behaviour was discussed in Chapter 2 and see also Taylor and Quayle, 2003: 182). Individuals are likely to come to police attention through a complaint (by, for example, a victim or through someone in the family) or because a person gains access to the individual's computer (e.g. when a computer is being repaired) (Krone, 2005: 2).

An individual may also, of course, feature within the third category of Krone's typology, that of a person who subscribes to a website. Indeed, some would probably argue that those who subscribe to websites are the paradigm of the actions of an individual but Krone argues the groups are separate. The primary basis would seem to be the suggestion that group one individuals may (although they do not need to) be technically proficient whereas Krone argues the third category are somewhat naive: 'it may be that subscribers are less experienced offenders . . . many offenders [are] willing to sign up with their personal credit card details to obtain access to websites containing child pornography' (Krone, 2005: 3). There is arguably some truth to this and it will be seen below that many offenders will use sophisticated anti-surveillance strategies whereas subscribers are frequently happy to provide personal data. Offenders within this third class are detected ordinarily when the website is infiltrated by the police and the list of subscribers is detected. The most prominent example of this in recent years is Operation Ore which will be discussed below.

The second category identified by Krone is that of covert groups. It is implicit within his analysis that this is meant to tackle those who belong to a collective and he refers, in particular, to the security adopted by its members (Krone, 2002: 2). Whilst this will be discussed below it must be questioned whether this analysis leaves another group uncovered. 'Individuals' and 'Covert groups' may be described as being at opposite ends of a spectrum and between them there will be smaller more informal networks through, for example, newsgroups, peer-to-peer networks or chat rooms. They may not have the same collective identity as a covert group but neither are they necessarily individuals. This could mean that perhaps an additional category in the typology needs to be considered.

The fourth, and final, category is those persons who are detected as a result of a sting operation (Krone, 2005: 2). The anonymity of the internet does allow for a number of so-called sting operations to be used (Krone, 2005: 5–6) although they raise significant ethical and legal issues. The use of sting operations and the ethical considerations that arise will be discussed in more detail below.

Krone's typology is a useful starting point although there have undoubtedly been technological shifts since it was created. For example, Krone argues that 'web sites are the most visible access to child pornography and they provide the widest coverage' (Krone, 2002: 3). Whilst they remain the most visible it is less certain that they provide the widest coverage anymore than with it being suggested that more distribution now takes place over peer-to-peer networks (Bain, 2008: 33). That said, Krone's work remains relevant and demonstrates the broad range of behaviour that the police will encounter.

It will not be possible in this chapter to discuss all the challenges faced in policing child pornography but instead this section will consider focuses. The first focus is to examine Operation Ore which is probably the most notable police operation on combating child pornography in the United Kingdom in recent years. As will become apparent it is arguably the paradigm of Krone's third form of police operations, web subscribers. Other focuses that will be examined are image analysis, counter-surveillance strategies that the police must try to circumvent and then finally sting operations and infiltration. It is submitted that these last two focuses are both examples of Krone's fourth type of police operation.

Operation Ore

Operation Ore is the largest police operation against child pornography to have ever taken place in the UK, and probably one of the largest police operations to have taken place in any aspect of criminality. Operation Ore transformed the public awareness of this crime. Arguably before the operation the issue of child pornography was rarely discussed in the mainstream media but the extensive coverage that Ore received, together with the fact that famous people were caught up in the operation (most notably Pete Townsend, the lead guitarist of The Who), meant that child pornography suddenly became something that the public was aware of.

Operation Ore was the UK part of a global operation that arose after the US Postal Inspection Service arrested Thomas and Janice Reedy who operated Landslide Productions, a website based in the United States. The website did not generally offer pornography itself but rather primarily acted as a portal to other sites: users would pay a subscription to Landslide Productions and then could gain access to numerous websites that were linked to Landslide. Whilst Landslide Productions initially started out hosting adult pornography it soon grew to include sites that specifically catered for child pornography (O'Brien, 2005: 156).

When the US Postal Inspection Service detained the Reedys they were able to access the list of subscribers. The US Postal Inspection Service had jurisdiction only over US citizens but it became apparent that citizens from a number of countries had accessed the site and thus the data was sent securely to Interpol who then dissected the list to identify each country involved. Interpol then sent the UK names to the NCIS (National Criminal Intelligence Service). The NCIS received a list of 7,272 names (HMIC, 2008) and they began to analyse them. Initially, due to the structure of the police in the United Kingdom, the names were broken down into geographical areas and then further analysis was undertaken. Priority was given to those suspects that were in positions of authority (including police officers) and those with access to children (either professionally or personally) (Jewkes and Andrews, 2005: 49).

Operation Ore meant the police had to face something that they never had before: a list of suspects that numbered thousands. In no other form of policing would the police be suddenly handed a list of over 7,000 people that were suspected of committing a criminal offence. More than that, the offence was one that was committed using technology, meaning that there was a need for officers to have an adequate knowledge of information and communication technologies. Where police forces sought to avoid this requirement, through providing technical 'crib cards', it caused difficulties as technically aware offenders simply evaded questions (Jewkes and Andrews, 2005: 55). Each computer that was discovered needed to be analysed and quickly the forensic capability of police forces ground to a halt. This caused the operation to have a slow start with it being reported that in the first year some 1,300 search warrants had been executed with 1,200 arrests being made (Jewkes and Andrews, 2005: 49). Whilst 1,300 persons accounts for only 18 per cent of the names on the list it should be noted that for the police to execute 1,300 warrants in respect of a single investigation is unprecedented.

At the beginning of Operation Ore the fact that it related to Landslide Productions was not widely known but inevitably it became widely known and eventually it was known to even the public through media attention. When the police executed some search warrants this meant that some people either had disposed of their computer or had a replacement computer. Questions were raised as to whether this meant that suspects escaped liability even where there was evidence from their credit card transactions that they had purchased material from Landslide Productions. The Crown Prosecution Service decided that possession of material was not necessary and they initiated prosecutions for the common-law offence of inciting the distribution of child pornography (see *R (on behalf of O'Shea) v Coventry Magistrates' Court* [2004] EWHC 905 (Admin) discussed in Chapter 6). As noted earlier in the book this was a somewhat controversial decision as it certainly broadened the previous understanding of the circumstances under which incitement could take place.

    As Operation Ore unfolded it began to be the focus of criticism. By its comple-
tion 2,450 individuals had 'been held to account' with a 93 per cent rate of guilty
pleas (HMIC, 2008: 27). This is, on the one hand, a large number of offenders
from a single operation but accounts for only 34 per cent of the names on the list.
The figure of 93 per cent is also interesting because it is presumably based on
those that are charged rather than arrested: some reports note that of the initial
3,500 individuals arrested, less than half were charged (O'Brien, 2005: 156).
No detailed public analysis of Operation Ore has yet taken place. Such analysis
would allow the public to know how the operation proceeded although it should
be noted that internal reviews have taken place and it is widely acknowledged
within the criminal justice system that Operation Ore would run differently if it
arose again.
    The proportion of those convicted has, on the one hand, been criticised, it being
observed by some as an inadequate response (Jewkes and Andrews, 2005: 49) and
yet on the other hand has also been labelled as evidence of a flawed operation.
Arthur suggests that the US authorities collected 35,000 names of US citizens
from Landslide but that this led to only 144 arrests and 100 prosecutions (Arthur,
2007: 7). He questions how, with a list one-fifth as large, a conviction rate nearly
thirty times greater was achieved although the latter is obviously an exaggeration
if HMIC figures are correct and only 2,450 have been convicted. That said, the
disparity does seem extraordinary and probably cannot be explained simply by
differences in law enforcement organisation (Landslide was primarily executed
by federal agencies in America whereas both state and federal law was arguably
breached) and legal definitions.
    Certainly in recent years Operation Ore has been subject to a number of attacks
by commentators. The attacks have been heightened by the fact that a number of
suicides took place as a result of people being under investigation in Operation
Ore (Campbell, 2007 suggests there has been 39 suicides) which brings an additional emotive factor, especially since in at least one of these cases the suicide was
of a person who was innocent of the charges. (Commodore David White,
Commander of the Royal Navy in Gibraltar committed suicide after being
suspended whilst investigated as part of Operation Ore.) That said, the police
argue that there are many reasons why someone might take their own life and that
whilst they can implement strategies to minimise the risk, the possibility of suicide
cannot be a reason to abandon an operation such as Ore. The criticisms tend to
focus not on those where indecent photographs of children were discovered
(whilst in the early days of Operation Ore there were some who argued that
images had been downloaded after a computer had become infected with a Trojan
virus, there is no evidence to suggest that this defence succeeded in any great
numbers) but rather on those situations where no images were found and recourse
was made to incitement. It is not known precisely how many offenders were
charged in this way but it was used extensively. Some criticisms were based on
the list and suggestions that the list of names passed to the NCIS was not original
but rather a copy prepared by non-law enforcement officers (O'Brien, 2005: 157)

although given the extensive checks made by the police in this country it is not clear that any transcription errors ever occurred.

There are two principal attacks levelled at Operation Ore. The first is based on credit card fraud and the second is based on the operation of Landslide itself. From the early days of Operation Ore there has been concern as to whether credit card fraud would mean that an innocent person could be caught up in this activity (Arthur, 2007). It is suggested that credit card fraud was endemic and that criminal gangs would create sites that purported to offer (legal) pornography and charge a subscription for entry. Once a person had entered their credit card details the gangs would then trade the card details for profit (Campbell, 2007). There is some doubt as to the validity of this attack. Bates, a forensic expert who has alleged the police take the issue of fraud into account (Campbell, 2007), has been somewhat discredited after being convicted for offences of perjury and making a false witness statement (Doward, 2008). That said, it must be noted that the convictions do not necessarily negate his experience as a forensic expert (see *Bates v Chief Constable of Avon and Somerset Police* [2009] EWHC 942 (Admin)) and so it is quite possible his attack remains credible.

Other forensic experts question the attack, noting that fraud has been alleged over recent years and yet no tangible evidence has been adduced to support the argument (Laville, 2009). CEOP also states that, to the best of their knowledge, no conviction for incitement to distribute child pornography was ever based solely on a single credit card and that other supporting evidence was used (Laville, 2009). In the absence of any case where an offender is shown to have been wrongly convicted through fraud this would seem to be an example of an attack that is easily stated but less readily proved.

The second attack is on the operation of the site itself. Operation Ore was always premised on the basis that those who subscribed to (parts of) Landslide Productions were deliberately seeking to obtain child pornography. However some question this and suggest that the portal did not, as was alleged, contain only child pornography but also included (lawful) adult pornography (O'Brien, 2005: 158). This attack has not yet been fully tested in court but if true it would be more difficult to refute than the attack based on credit card fraud. However there is no requirement that the portal be used exclusively for access to child pornography although the offence of incitement required proof that the offender sought access to those types of images. At present it is mere assertion that the portal could have been used to access lawful pornography but if it were proved that a subscription to a particular site allowed access to lawful pornography without displaying child pornography then this could render a conviction for incitement unsafe.

Operation Ore continues to provoke emotive reactions. On one side of the debate are the police, who state that, whilst they would run the operation differently if it was undertaken again, it did lead to the detection of a high number of offenders and the safeguarding of real children from abuse. On the other hand others, particularly some within the media, allege that it was a flawed operation that has led to innocent people being convicted. Without a public audit of the operation it is unlikely that suspicion will ever be removed but it should be noted that there have been few acquittals or successful appeals, which could act as an indicator in itself. In 2009 it was reported that Anthony O'Shea, the first person to be convicted of incitement, was seeking leave to appeal his conviction on the basis that the evidence used in Operation Ore was flawed (Laville, 2009: 1). Media stories reported how this would lead to the acquittal of 'hundreds' and yet the Court of Appeal comprehensively rejected the aguments (*O'Shea v R* [2010] EWCA Crim 2879) stating the case raised no new points. No doubt the final act of Operation Ore has yet to play out but it did provide a useful learning tool for the police and others in terms of how future operations should be conducted.

Image analysis

It has been noted already that storage capacity is rising exponentially with devices capable of storing terabytes of information becoming commonplace. The cost implication of forensic examination was highlighted above but it does also raise an operational issue: to what extent does all the media seized have to be examined? If indecent images are discovered then does all the material have to be analysed?

There are two principal reasons for examining the material seized. The first is to assess the material held by the offender and the second is in respect of victim identification. The latter will be discussed in more detail below but it is clear that there is a desire to examine the material for this purpose:

Any still images of video files found on the suspect's computer hard drives or portable devices should be analysed to determine whether they contain previously unidentified victims who need to be safeguarded from further abuse.

(Bains, 2008: 12)

However the initial reason for examining material is based not on victimhood but as a criminal justice response. The initial check will be to see whether the material is illegal and to classify it. In terms of sentencing it was seen in Chapter 10 that the Sentencing Guidelines Council (following earlier work by the Sentencing Advisory Panel and the Court of Appeal (Criminal Division)) adopted a five-point scale on which material is to be graded. The appropriateness of this will not be discussed in this chapter but because sentencing depends on its grading this means that material must be classified, something evident from the decision in *R v Thompson* [2004] EWCA Crim 669 where the Court of Appeal indicated its preference that the quantity of material in each level should be set out by counsel.

A question that is frequently then asked is how much of the material must be classified. There is no legal requirement to classify all the material but the courts will only sentence on the basis on which an offender is convicted or pleads guilty to (following the decision in *R v Canavan* [1998] 1 All ER 42). The rule in

Canavan is now subject to the statutory principle in ss. 17–21, Domestic Violence, Crime and Victims Act 2004 which allows for sample counts to be heard by a judge alone although there is no evidence that this provision is being used widely in respect of indecent photographs of children, in part because a count alleging multiple possession is perhaps easier to prove.

Some law enforcement officers believe that it is necessary to classify all of the material but there is no legal requirement to do this. Realistically once a collection is over a particular threshold it is unlikely that a sentence will increase and thus tactically it may not be necessary to classify each image. However a reason for looking at the whole collection is that it may show the offender is not just a collector but is also a contact offender. It may, for example, contain images of an offender's own child. If a collection is only partially analysed then it is possible that this may be missed which could have a direct impact on the welfare of the child.

How then is a collection analysed? The traditional approach is for a civilian analyst or police officer to examine the content of each storage device. As storage capacities increase this becomes increasingly difficult, especially with large-scale organisations where several suspects are being dealt with at once. A criticism of Operation Ore was the time taken between arrest and any decision to prosecute, this being caused in part by the amount of time it takes to analyse a storage device.

Technology has begun to offer a (partial) solution to this. Some programs, for example C4P (Categorising for Pictures) operate automatically to scan storage devices and to identify duplicate photographs (Bains, 2008: 35). It is quite possible that a collection will involve a number of duplicates and accordingly this may speed up the process by ensuring that offenders need only examine original images. However even this can be vast and so classification protocols are being developed and automated systems are also beginning to appear. Computer analysis is able to differentiate what is likely to be a photograph through, for example, the number of individual colours to be found in a picture (a photograph is likely to have thousands whereas drawings and computer graphics are likely to have a smaller file depth), its size and the dimensions of an image (Sanderson, 2006: 192). Using such systems allows vast quantities of images to be gradually reduced. Additional filters could be used so that, for example, the computer could estimate the proportion of an image that was likely to involve human flesh (Sanderson, 2006: 194). The use of this software can lead to a significant reduction in suspicious images. Similar strategies would be to examine common filename extensions (i.e. those that indicate a series of images) which may lead to further identification. The pool of resulting images is then examined as thumbnails as it was discovered that an experienced person could discard non-suspicious images relatively quickly (Sanderson, 2006: 193).

Ultimately however the resulting images must be examined individually and then classified. The protocols and automated systems merely reduces the amount of images that have to be classified. This remains time consuming and therefore the question as to how much material must be analysed remains unanswered. Initially at least it can be argued that sufficient analysis must be made to be demonstrative of the offending behaviour but, as noted above, an incomplete analysis may mean that contact offending is missed. Some forces are however having to contemplate this in order to ensure that there is not an unreasonable delay between initial investigation and prosecution.

Counter-surveillance

In 2001 it was stated:

> Reading the boards, we must be struck by the relative lack of serious concern about law enforcement activity – as distinct from the constant nagging paranoia that X or Y is a police provocateur, activity that seems to represent almost a pastime.
>
> (Jenkins, 2001: 151)

The issue of so-called 'sting' operations will be discussed below but by the latter half of the decade it would seem that the position of ambivalence towards police operations had changed, with offenders increasingly adopting more sophisticated strategies to avoid detection by law enforcement agencies, as evidenced by this statement from an offender:

> Yes, one always thinks about it. Every time you put on the computer. You notice how it blinks like hell and one starts to wonder who the hell it is, sometimes one wonders if it is the cops. Of course one thinks of it, every time one is out there.
>
> (Eneman, 2009: 8)

There is evidence that offenders are becoming more sophisticated in their strategies to avoid detection and this poses challenges for the police themselves. There are a number of different strategies but one of the most important would appear to be technological choices. At the beginning of the decade it would seem that web-based or newsgroup-based circulation of images was the primary method of distribution. This has now changed however and recent analysis suggests that peer-to-peer distribution is now the predominant means of image distribution (Bains, 2008: 34). The shift away from the web is viewed by offenders as necessary because the web is considered to be (largely) insecure (Eneman, 2009: 9). That said, offenders also considered peer-to-peer systems to be vulnerable if they were not aware of who both parties were (Eneman, 2009: 9).

There was, in the latter half of the decade, some concern as to the issue of encryption. Whilst it has been stated that its use has not become widespread (Bains, 2008: 37) it would appear to be used by the security conscious. Certainly Eneman notes that some offenders consider the use of encryption to be important when using peer-to-peer systems (Eneman, 2009: 9). Current encryption techniques are quite complex and thus many offenders will not use them because of the time it can take to encrypt and de-encrypt the material but as programs become easier to use and computer processing speeds make the complex algorithms quicker to process it is likely that encryption could become more problematic. In England and Wales the government responded to the issue of encryption by enacting legislation that can require the police to demand access either to the unencrypted data or the key that allows access (s. 49, Regulation of Investigatory Powers Act 2000: for a discussion see Walden, 2007: 282–295). In *R v S* [2009] 1 All ER 716 the Court of Appeal rejected the suggestion that this provision breached Article 6 of the ECHR by ruling that s. 49 did not infringe the privilege from self-incrimination, in part because the encryption 'key' could not of itself be incriminating as it was simply a matter of fact: the suspect either has a 'key' or does not, and he either complies with the order or does not.

Strategies to evade detection are based primarily on the security of the system. Eneman notes that a secure system will allow a small number of people to build the site and members of the site would be provided with a manual detailing what security to use (Eneman, 2009: 10). This finding supports previous understandings of secure systems. Some of the more 'successful' collectives involve the use of sophisticated security arrangements. One of the most prominent examples of this was found in the 'w0nderland club' which was an online international 'ring' that traded child pornography. The club operated a system whereby membership was gradually conferred on individuals and several layers of security would be required before full access given (Taylor and Quayle, 2003: 141). A similar approach was adopted by the 'Shadowz Brotherhood' which was another prominent international ring. Membership was based on a 'star' rating and this indicated what level of access to the community a member had (O'Donnell and Milner, 2007: 162). If used properly, such security makes it extremely difficult for a group to be compromised. However the security of a group is only as good as its membership and it is notable that 'w0nderland' fractured because there were some members who refused to obey the rules (Taylor and Quayle, 2003: 143).

In terms of individual security and ability to evade detection the growth of wireless technology has created a new opportunity for offenders. An insecure wireless connection allows anyone to gain access to it and if illegal material is downloaded then it will be traced to the owner of the wireless connection and not the user (Bains, 2008: 37). This is one reason why criminal justice agencies are increasingly seeking to raise public awareness of this issue and persuade them to encrypt their connections. An analogous issue is the growth of 'Pay and Go' wireless services (Bains, 2008: 38). These do not require a user to register for their use and some (in particular airports) access is given by a voucher that can be bought in a machine or in a shop for cash. In these instances there will be no forensic trace that could be used to track offenders. The growth in these services (which are becoming increasingly common in cafes, pubs, etc.) does potentially allow for a new way of evading contact and may prove a more popular alternative than a cyber café where there is a danger that objectionable material will be witnessed by others.

Sting operations

It has been noted already that one of the four types of operation identified by Krone is that of the sting operation. It is not the place of this book to make a detailed analysis of the laws relating to these type of operations (for fuller details see Mitchell *et al.*, 2005 and Gillespie, 2008b and for a fuller discussion on the law in a wider context see Squires, 2006).

Krone describes a 'sting' as the position whereby the police actively solicit offenders on the internet (Krone, 2005: 4) although it is commonly accepted that it is more than this: it is usually considered to be the position whereby the police use pretence to imply that they are prepared to supply child pornography. There are a number of different methods of doing this and whilst one ordinarily thinks of it as a police officer actively posing as an offender (Jenkins, 2001: 145 presents an example of this) it is submitted that a sting could be either active or passive.

The difference between an active and passive sting is perhaps questionable as both involve the police taking action but the distinction is, it is submitted, through how the operation begins. With a passive sting an operation is established and the police become involved when it is 'triggered'. Perhaps the most obvious example of this is Operation PIN which is operated by the Virtual Global Taskforce (VGT). The VGT operate a series of sites that purport to advertise child pornography (Krone, 2004: 4; Walden, 2007: 229). The sites do not include any real images but include a series of portals whereby users click to indicate that they are interested in viewing images that would constitute child pornography. If the user reaches the point whereby images would ordinarily be displayed then a message is produced which states that the attempt has been recorded and that local police (i.e. the VGT member state) will be informed (Krone, 2005: 5). Operation PIN is not the only website that operates in this way and others will act as a bulletin board or hosting site, inviting users to contribute material (Walden, 2007: 229 reports one instance where this led to the arrest of an offender).

An active, or dynamic, sting differs in that the police are active from the very beginning of the operation. In the context of child solicitation (a.k.a. 'grooming') this type of operation is not uncommon (Gillespie, 2008b) but it can be used equally in respect of child pornography. Jenkins provides an early example of this type of operation:

> Instead of claiming to be a thirteen-year-old girl, another FBI agent might claim to have a video of his niece taking a shower and offer that in exchange to a like-minded pervert.
>
> (Jenkins, 2001: 145)

Sting operations, even when they involve operations against those who seek to exploit a child, are extremely controversial with some arguing that they amount to a 'thought crime' or are an example of the police creating, rather than detecting, crime (see Gillespie, 2008b: 199). From a legal perspective law enforcement agencies will argue strongly that they only capture those that are seeking to commit a criminal offence. Operation PIN, for example, is not triggered until a user accesses several parts of the site: it is not enough that an offender simply comes across the site; he must take a number of steps in the knowledge that he is trying to access child pornography. Even where (as in England and Wales) a country does not have a substantive defence of entrapment the law will ordinarily set the boundaries in which the police can operate, with the usual distinction being that the police cannot seek to lure someone into committing a crime they would not ordinarily commit.

An interesting question that arises in the context of sting operations relating to child pornography relates to the contents of the site. Operation PIN, it will be remembered, has no material on it and simply consists of promises that such material will be available. Is a site without images likely to catch the sophisticated offender or the one who is naive as to the availability and access of child pornography? Krone notes that a question that remains unanswered is whether police are able to use real child pornography as part of a sting site (Krone, 2005: 5). Some authors believe that only a site that involves real images will be effective but that this raises difficulties:

> To attract traffic, the honey trap would have to include hundreds or thousands of genuine images, which once made available would continue to circulate ad infinitum. It would be deeply embarrassing for a law enforcement bureaucrat to admit to a [Parliamentary] investigation that his or her agency had regrettably become one of the world's largest distributors of child pornography, no matter how good a cause.
>
> (Jenkins, 2001: 160)

This quote contains a number of important points. The first is recognition that a site without images is likely to be of only limited assistance with many offenders being sceptical of the fact that they are not shown any material. Sites often receive traffic through recommendations from others and this is likely to be missing with no images being present. However whilst the use of images may lead to more people being identified, Jenkins notes two difficulties with such an approach. The first is that the images, once placed on the internet, circulate indefinitely. It has already been noted that once an image has been placed on the internet it is, in essence, on the internet permanently due to mirroring, etc. (Taylor and Quayle, 2003). The effect that this has on a victim has also been discussed (Palmer, 2004 and see the discussion in Chapter 2). The second difficulty identified by Jenkins relates to the political consequences. Even if the police would wish to use such tactics, is it likely that they would be permitted to do so? It is unlikely that the

Home Secretary or other Home Office minister would welcome the finding that a law enforcement agency is actively involved in the unrestricted distribution of child pornography given the reaction this is likely to provoke in members of the public and sections of the media.

A sting site may not necessarily be created by the police, and the possibility of continuing a pre-existing site has also been raised by Jenkins although he argues this would be equally problematic:

> Only somewhat less embarrassing would be the statement that . . . [a law enforcement agency] knew that a given site was distributing such material, but that the agency had tolerated its existence for six months or a year.
>
> (Jenkins, 2001: 160).

Whilst it may be tempting to keep a site active in an attempt to trace those who seek to access this site the same ethical problems as creating a sting site must arise. The law enforcement agency will still be complicit in the distribution of child pornography and, depending on the nature of the material, perhaps be complicit in the production of child pornography (e.g. if it is a site which invites users to upload pictures themselves). An interesting alternative to this is discussed by Walden who notes that after one site was taken down by police, they then pretended to be an administrator seeking a new person to take over the site (Walden, 2007: 229). When a person contacted them and showed an interest in taking over the site he was arrested. Obviously this tactic will only capture a small number of persons but it is likely to mark the limits of what the public are likely to consider acceptable in terms of the operation of websites.

Infiltration

The sting is perhaps the classic example of a proactive operation and, as discussed above, can bring about results. However it has been argued '. . . the vast bulk of arrests still involve low-level or plainly careless perpetrators, and this is likely to remain the case for the foreseeable future' (Jenkins, 2001: 143). Whilst not specifically said in the context of proactive operations the point is one of direct relevance. Although there have been several high-profile arrests relating to quite sophisticated groups (Krone, 2005: 4) the vast majority of arrests relate to individual offenders who are found in possession of the material. How are such networks brought down? Jenkins argues that the 'w0nderland club' was brought down through traditional police work by persuading some of the members to become informants until its members could be identified and arrested (Jenkins, 2001: 152). However others have suggested that it was unlikely that every member was identified and suggest that some members escaped detection and they created another organisation (Taylor and Quayle, 2003: 146).

Tackling a group may require infiltration especially where it is based on either multi-layer access or through a peer-to-peer system. The difficulty with a peer-to-peer system is that there is no central node that can be the subject of surveillance (Walden, 2007: 233). Whilst a bulletin board or FTP site can be covertly monitored and the IP addresses of those who access this site can be logged and reported, the same is not true of a peer-to-peer network. Where, however, the bulletin board or FTP site provides multiple layers of security the same position is likely to be raised as law enforcement will not necessarily know the existence of the sites to be monitored. Anti-surveillance techniques, such as anonymising IP addresses (discussed in part above), may also mean that online surveillance will not be effective. In both situations it is therefore more likely that infiltration will be required, either by a covert law enforcement officer or by turning an existing member into an informant.

Infiltration however raises similar ethical issues to that discussed above in respect of sting sites. If an existing member is to become an informant is this the police acquiescing to the activities of that person? It would immediately raise suspicions if, for example, they suddenly stopped discussing their fantasies or stopped trading images. However if the police allow them to trade is this not condoning their activity? Infiltration perhaps raises further issues. An infiltration requires a new person to be introduced and interviews with offenders demonstrates that an important consideration as to whether a person was allowed into a collective is trust, with new members demonstrating that they are trustworthy (Taylor and Quayle, 2003: 145). How is this trust built up? Perhaps the most obvious method is by providing material. It is known that for some collectives entry is through the production of material (this was true of the w0nderland club: see, for example, Krone, 2005: 3). Where does this leave the police?

It has been noted that the question of whether the police can use indecent images in this way has not yet been answered although it has been raised (Krone, 2005: 5). The difficulty is of course that they are not simply images. If, as many believe, abusive images of children amount to the revictimisation of a victim then are the police not complicit in this revictimsation? It is unlikely that the revictimisation will be lessened by the fact that the police are involved and indeed the converse may be true as the victim may believe that his or her victimisation is somehow condoned by the State. Of course if this tactic is not used then it may mean that targeting collectives – which may not be restricted solely to the distribution of images (for example in the 'w0nderland' case there was evidence that some of the group were contact offending and distributing the material to members) – becomes extremely difficult where they employ security. Ultimately the answer is probably similar to those involving sting sites: how would the public react if they knew the police had become a distributor rather than detector of child pornography?

Costs

One implication of proactive policing is their cost. Whilst the creation of a site such as that used in Operation PIN may not require much financial resourcing, its operation might. Staff will need to be trained in the operation of the site and the costs of infiltration will be more significant. It has been noted that in many instances an aim of a proactive operation would be to try and trace an individual through, for example, an email identity or IP address. The UN Special Rapporteur has noted that the ability to use these tracing methods is an important step in the fight against child pornography and she praises the efforts of countries, such as the United Kingdom, which has speeded up the process by changing the law to allow ISPs to disclose this information, without a court order (Maalla, 2009: 15). However these requests are not without cost:

> In the UK, for example, an initial subscriber check to identify the suspect or victim behind a username or Internet Protocol address can cost £40–£65. This has significant cost implications for law enforcement agencies, regardless of their investigative capacity: such checks cost CEOP £100,000 per year . . .
>
> (Bains, 2008: 14)

The costs referred to apply only to one organisation (CEOP) and if this is multiplied across all the various forces that undertake such analysis it can be seen that it will quickly reach seven-figure sums. The police only have limited resources and high-tech investigations compete for the same resources, and even when resources are identified they must be shared across other high-tech priorities (Jewkes and Andrews, 2005: 49). After the 11 September/7 July bombings, a considerable amount of resources were devoted to terrorism. Even with a large operation such as Operation Ore the Home Office turned down requests for additional funding (Jewkes and Andrews, 2005: 50).

As much of the work is hidden (and as noted already many proactive operations may only identify a limited number of offenders) it is questionable how many forces are prepared to devote sufficient resources to undertake proactive operations. This is perhaps exacerbated by the fact that despite some media interest it remains a relatively low-profile crime. As will be seen below, few victims are identified, and without it being in the public's consciousness it rarely features on the performance targets inherent within policing priorities (Jewkes and Andrews, 2005: 50).

Victims

The role of victims should be considered briefly in this chapter. An earlier section of this chapter discussed image analysis and it was noted that the police argue that this is necessary not just for the prosecution of an offender but also to identify any potential victims. In recent years the issue of victimhood has become increasingly recognised in the criminal justice system and in policing in general. This is arguably particularly true in the area of child pornography where it has been suggested that the issue of victims has traditionally been ignored:

A substantive criticism of the criminal justice system's response to child pornography is that it has over-focused on offender issues, at the expense of victim issues. At worst, the child victim becomes an object around which adults (offenders, police and social services) devote resources to sustain their own construction of events, and their own vested interests, rather than those of the child.

(Taylor and Quayle, 2003: 206)

Implicit within this criticism is the recognition that law enforcement agencies primarily see their role as the apprehension of offenders (Taylor and Quayle 2003: 204) and not necessarily the detection of victims (save where it leads to the identification of perpetrators). If, as many would suggest, child pornography is the depiction of a crime it would seem logical to examine the images in the hope of identifying either a victim or offender. A difficulty with photographs and images from the internet is, of course, that they are not necessarily easy to date at first glance. It has been noted that this has caused police resources to be dedicated to the investigation of a picture that is 30 or 40 years old (Taylor and Quayle, 2003: 206). Does this matter? With finite resources it could be argued that it would be more appropriate to prioritise the identification of children that are currently at risk of abuse and where intervention may prevent the further abuse of children.

In Chapter 11 it was noted that Interpol has produced a database of child abuse images and some countries also have their own databases (including the United States where it is based at the National Centre for Missing and Exploited Children, and the United Kingdom where it is based at CEOP). The use of image analysis software linked to these databases allows the police to assess whether an image of a child contained within a collection is to be found in other images within the database. The analysis can be very sophisticated and it is possible, for example, to use algorithms to identify whether any of the images contained in the database is the same victim at a different age (Interpol web site). An advantage of this is that it allows the police to focus their investigation. For example, the police identify a picture of child X aged five. The database suggests that pictures of child X is already to be found in the database but aged eight to 10. The police now know that there is no point in focusing their resources on finding a child aged five, they are looking for a child aged at least 10. That is not to say that the image of her aged five should not be analysed, as it may provide clues to her identity (especially where, for example, a school uniform is shown), but it does at least mean that the police will not waste resources trying to locate a child who is five years younger than she actually is.

A difficulty with victim identification is highlighted by the UN Special Rapporteur, where she remarks that image analysis is 'a highly specialised and rigorous process that requires a great deal of time, enormous expertise and leading-edge computer technology. It is an expensive instrument that the developing countries cannot afford' (Maalla, 2009: 15). Interpol would probably argue that this is one reason for them to host the database since the analysis can be undertaken by their officers although this perhaps only masks the problem since Interpol's budget could itself be placed under strain if there were a large number of referrals.

Whilst computer-assisted identification is of considerable use it is not the 'magic bullet' solution; as with most police work some aspects of the analysis will ultimately have to be dealt with by a human investigator. Victim identification is extremely detailed work that involves examining the slightest of clues. Holland (2005: 82–83) presents a well known example that shows the level of detail that can be required to identify a child. The matter began with a GMP officer who detected a number of images that he believed were of British origin. Through consulting an architectural historian they were told the type of house that the images had been recorded in (which dated to the early 1900s). The abuse took place on a girl portrayed in a school uniform and by circulating the uniform they were able to narrow down a group of schools that used that uniform. Most of the evidence came from a scene where the child was abused in a bedroom. In the background there were computer boxes and by contacting the manufacturer of the computers a timeline could be established (when those units were sold) and a longlist of names of those who had bought the computers. Further analysis of the images showed they had been taken by a specific type of camera. By cross-referencing the list of customers who bought the camera with those who bought the computer, two people were found. An analysis of their personal data (child benefit payment, age, etc.) showed a likely offender and he was later convicted of offences relating to this, and two children were identified and removed from an abusive situation.

This example demonstrates the level of detail that is sometimes required to identify a child. Holland notes that GMP had no way of knowing where the child was and, whilst the officer was given clearance to conduct his investigation, it was limited to a period of six weeks (Holland, 2005: 83). GMP, as noted above, is one of the forces that had a dedicated paedophile unit. If it was a smaller force it must be questioned whether an officer would have been allowed to undertake this investigation. This is now (partly) resolved by the fact that CEOP takes the lead on identification although it is questionable whether sufficient resources have been allocated to this task.

It is easy to see from the example above how complicated image analysis is. Also, as the methods of victim identification have become known there would seem to be some evidence that offenders are being more careful and abusing children in rooms that are devoid of traceable objects (Jewkes and Andrews, 2005: 58). Also, the subjective nature of image analysis means that human error is always a possibility (Holland, 2005: 81). In the example presented above, the senior investigating officer noted that they jumped to conclusions with certain evidence and believed, for a time, that they were looking for one particular building whereas, it turned out, there were in fact two separate locations where the abuse took place (Holland, 2005: 81).

Victim identification is obviously important but it should be noted that the success rate remains relatively small. In 2004 it was estimated that only 267 children had ever been identified from images on the internet (Holland, 2005: 87) and whilst it has been suggested that this figure had risen to over 870 by 2009 (Maalla, 2009: 15) the UN Special Rapporteur has still stated that victim identification remains 'difficult' (Maalla, 2009: 15).

Image analysis and victim identification would obviously seem an important consideration but they are not without ethical dilemmas. Two are of particular note here. The first concerns the establishment of databases of victim photographs. It has been noted already that these are proving to be a valuable resource and making a considerable contribution to the identification of both perpetrators and victims. The UN Special Rapporteur however notes:

> ... the consequences of storing and exchange [SIC] of images for the victims must not be ignored. Victims do not necessarily draw a distinction between the persons looking at their images or the reasons they are looking at them.
>
> (Maalla, 2009: 17)

This is an interesting point. If, as would appear likely, victims suffer from secondary victimisation through the photographs depicting their abuse and exploitation remaining in circulation, is this necessarily reduced by the fact that it is the police who retain the image? The image continues to exist and, from the victim's perspective, it continues to be in circulation. Some victims may not understand the need for the image to be retained and why it is not destroyed. Whilst the UN Special Rapporteur is not suggesting that image databases should not be used – and indeed arguably the opposite is true – the comments are perhaps a warning that law enforcement agencies must think carefully how they use image banks. Victims who are identified and who are able to understand the process should perhaps be told why the image is being retained and how it is being used. Clarity should be given as to who is entitled to access the image and in what circumstances. A strong ethical policy on storage and access may not remove the victim's fears but it can perhaps reassure them that their image is being used sensitively.

The second ethical dilemma arises from who should be identified from the databases. Whilst there would seem few that would challenge the idea of seeking to identify children the position is arguably less certain of those who are now adults:

> It is less easy to justify commitment of resources to seek to identify children who are now adults who were involved in older pictures. There are two reasons for this: unless detection is very straightforward, the deployment of the specialist resources necessary should presumably focus on the ongoing abuse, rather than past abuse, because this is where need is greatest. However, another and more important issue relates to the effects of identification of a

child on that individual as an adult, and their family. Victims' rights to retain control over their own experience are important here.

(Taylor and Quayle, 2003: 206)

This is an interesting statement. It is difficult to argue with the first point made. Resources are finite and it has been noted that the identification process is extremely resource-intensive and attention should probably be focused on attempting to protect children from abuse that is currently happening. The second statement however raises more interesting ethical questions. Law enforcement agencies have traditionally operated on the basis that where a serious crime has been detected it should be investigated. Whether it ultimately leads to a formal criminal justice intervention is something different and in England and Wales would require an examination of whether it is in the public interest to prosecute. The police would argue that contacting any victim that is identified may be ultimately preventing future abuse since the person who offends in the photograph may continue to have access to children and may be abusing them.

However Taylor and Quayle question whether the police have the right to seek out victims:

When an individual seeks help, by disclosing events in the past, then it is reasonable to follow through on such disclosure. But it cannot be right to force disclosure on someone who has come to terms with his or her own past, and who fears the loss of control over that experience which will inevitably come about in a police investigation.

(Taylor and Quayle, 2003: 207)

It is quite possible that a victim may not know that she had been photographed until the police contact the victim or the victim may not have known that the image has been circulating. A victim may, as Taylor and Quayle suggest, have come to terms with the abuse that they have suffered and they could well have hidden it from their family, including a partner. If the police were to contact the victim then this may mean that the trauma they suffered could resurface. It may also lead to the situation where family members become involved. Child sexual abuse is an emotive topic and not everyone reacts in a calm and supportive way. It is quite possible the actions would be divisive to the family, causing additional emotional challenges to the victim.

This is not an easy issue to resolve. Whilst Taylor and Quayle might be correct to state that the police contacting a victim could be traumatic and unwelcome where a victim has come to terms with their abuse, there could be many other reasons as to why a victim has not disclosed the abuse. It is quite possible that the victim is concerned that the authorities would believe she was complicit in her abuse (because, for example, the photograph shows the child smiling or actively participating). Whilst, of course, it is extremely unlikely that the authorities would react in this way, a victim may not know this. It is not uncommon for perpetrators to state that the victim was at fault or state that a victim will not be believed. It is possible that a victim may welcome contact from the police as it may allow them to address their isssues, but a victim may prefer the past to be left alone. A law enforcement agency cannot know whether the victim would welcome or reject an approach until they have made contact, by which time it is of course arguably too late for the victim that wishes to be left alone. Whilst victim identification remains time-consuming and expensive this is perhaps an ethical dilemma that will arise infrequently but it is something that needs to be considered at a policy level.

Chapter 13

Conclusion

What conclusions can be drawn about child pornography? Instead of trying to summarise the book as some conclusions do, this chapter will instead focus on a small number of key themes to consider what the analysis in this book has shown. It is not intended to conclude as to what each chapter has detailed but rather consider more general issues. The purpose of this chapter is to consider whether there are any lessons that can be learnt by the law.

Terminology revisited

The first conclusion entails revisiting an important theme from the introductory chapter. It will be remembered from Chapter 1 that some academics, law enforcement agencies and child protection bodies have called for the term 'child pornography' to be avoided and new terms to replace it. The logic behind such calls is simple. The term could be interpreted as misrepresenting or even trivialising the true nature of the material. Advocates of change all appear to agree that the term 'child pornography' is problematic but it will be remembered from Chapter 1 that there is no consensus amongst advocates as to what term should replace it, in part because the existing alternative labels could be seen as self-limiting the type and nature of the material.

Not everyone agrees with the need for change and it has been seen that in the international arena the term 'child pornography' remains used in both legislative and policy contexts. It will be remembered from Chapter 11 that the UN Special Rapporteur has the term 'child pornography' as part of her title and her mandate. Individual countries also continue to use the term, with it being suggested that the United States is one of those countries that are committed to its use (Davidson *et al.*, 2010: 121). Even where the term is not used in a legislative capacity (for example, England and Wales, where it will be remembered from Chapters 3 and 6 that the legislative term is 'indecent photograph of a child') it continues to be used in the policy arena (see, for example, Protecting the Public (Cm 5668)).

Should we worry about what the material is called? In Chapter 1 it was decided that this book would use the term 'child pornography' and the justification for this was that it continues to be used in both the legislative and policy arenas at both the international and domestic levels. However was that a way of simply avoiding an 'awkward' question? Certainly in other writings I have acknowledged the difficulty of the term 'child pornography' (Gillespie, 2005, 2008) and yet each time I have used the term for the justification put forward in Chapter 1 of this book.

As an academic it is not necessary for me to use the official language of policy or law, save where I am reproducing verbatim quotes of the various instruments. Presumably therefore I could have chosen to do that in this book and to avoid using the term 'child pornography'. Perhaps the conclusion to this book is a good time to consider whether it was right to continue to use the term 'child pornography' within the book and indeed its title.

It has been seen that whilst the term 'child pornography' may be problematic so are the other alternative labels put forward. It will be remembered that each alternative tended to carry its own difficulties, especially when it perhaps misrepresented what it covered. The classic example of this is perhaps 'child abuse images' when this term does not map out what many countries' legislation considers to be child pornography. 'Images' suggests any type of pictorial representation and yet many countries remain photograph-based, and 'child abuse' does not properly describe the range of material that many countries' legislation will encompass. Whilst 'child exploitation' can, at least, broaden the range of material, it also carries with it problems, not least the fact that 'exploitation' is a slightly vague term and its differential to abuse is perhaps unclear (Buck, 2010: 262 f.).

If, for a moment, we set aside domestic legislation and consider international action then continuing to use 'child pornography' does, it is submitted, carry with it certain advantages. Whilst some have argued that child pornography is a tainted term it is at least recognised: as has been seen throughout this book it is used extensively in international instruments and policy documents. It is unlikely that 'child abuse images' or 'child exploitation material' carries with it the same understanding as the term 'child pornography'. The ability to have a recognisable term is important in the international arena where the simplicity of language and the ease of translation can be crucial. It has been noted in this book that there are cultural differences between what amounts to child pornography and the same certainly applies to what amounts to abuse or exploitation.

Within an academic bubble the term 'child pornography' remains problematic as it does have the appearance of a link to (lawful) adult pornography and can suggest that it is part of the wider sex industry which, some (but certainly not all) will argue is largely legitimate. There can be no doubt that child pornography is inherently different from adult pornography. Whilst there is doubt as to whether all adult material necessarily shows the consensual behaviour of adults there is at least a substantial body of material that would seem to have been produced legitimately. The same is not true of child pornography (for the moment concentrating on children below the age of consent: the issue of the age of a 'child' is considered below). Even where a child has not been coerced into producing the material, the power imbalance that exists between the child, the person filming it and the distributor is such that any apparent consent given is simply not valid. In any event a significant (and apparently growing: Taylor and Quayle, 2003; Bains, 2008; IWF, 2010) amount of material depicts obviously non-consensual sexual assaults on young children. In this regard child and adult pornography are intrinsically different and there should not be any pretence as to a link between them.

However child pornography does not exist within the academic bubble; it exists in the real world. It is submitted that to effectively combat child pornography requires an international solution. Child pornography in the modern era is a transient crime that is facilitated primarily through cyberspace. Whilst national laws are important, because it allows nationals complicit in the acquisition, production or dissemination of child pornography to be the subject of criminal sanction, it is only when there is a truly global network of laws that it will become difficult for material to be stored or indeed produced. It has been seen that it is difficult to identify a common definition for child pornography let alone agree a single term. Considerable progress needs to be made at the international level before even a minimum definition is agreed (Gillespie, 2010b) or before there is coherency as to the definition of the base crimes required to combat child pornography. Should time be spent on producing an agreed alternative term? If there was evidence to suggest that there was a real risk that people truly believed that child pornography was akin to adult pornography and that the children depicted were consenting to their behaviour then the answer would probably be 'yes'. However it is submitted that there is currently no evidence to suggest this and that it is more likely that people are now aware of the reality of child pornography. Given this it must be questioned whether moving to an alternative label is appropriate. It would require a considerable amount of time to be given as it will be agreed at an international policy level, followed by an awareness programme so that the general public and those working in the area were aware of what the label was. Realistically relabelling child pornography must be of a lower priority than trying to tackle its creation and proliferation. Much still has to be done on this (see below) and therefore it is submitted that the time would be better spent on that rather than a discussion of its label.

Defining child pornography

The first focus of this book examined the definition of child pornography and it has been seen that this is something that continues to defy a coherent definition. It has been seen that individual countries define child pornography in different ways and sometimes (for example, the United States and Australia) the definitions will differ within the country. The position is no better at the international level where instruments all differ in their definition, even when they have been produced by the same organisation (for example, within the Council of Europe the definition adopted in the Convention on Cybercrime differs from that adopted in the Convention on the Protection of Children against Sexual Exploitation and Sexual Abuse).

Defining child pornography poses a number of interesting questions, especially when one considers international law. The failure of the international community to take a lead on these issues will be discussed below but in this section it will be questioned whether it is possible to identify a definition of child pornography that could be used within legal instruments. In an article published in 2010 I questioned whether a difficulty with international instruments is that they try to do too much (Gillespie, 2010b). By this I meant that the existing international legal instruments adopt the approach of defining 'child pornography' in an idealised way: that the definition covers what we would hope a law would cover. Yet the reality is that some countries will not be at this level and whilst it may be easy to sign an instrument that defines certain material as 'child pornography' and criminalises such actions, implementing it becomes somewhat problematic.

Of course identifying a minimum standard would not prevent countries going beyond this minimum and indeed that would remain the key aim to provide the most appropriate laws that safeguarded vulnerable members of society. The countries examined in this book are good examples of this: each country has adopted strong laws and they have proactively amended them to tackle emerging threats. However key questions do remain in respect of these laws and the definitions they use.

Child

The first part of any definition of child pornography is the question of who amounts to a 'child'. Many jurisdictions differentiate between the age at which a person is considered a child for the purposes of child pornography and the age for the purposes of consent. It was suggested in Chapter 2 that this brings a number of challenges. The age of 18 has been chosen by many states because of the belief that a child of 16 may not understand the consequences of the behaviour they are engaging in. During Chapter 2 it was argued that this can be true of other forms of sexual behaviour but it is submitted that this line of argument can be carried only so far. Whilst other forms of sexual contact may have permanent consequences the fact remains that in many of these instances there remains an element of control by the child in terms of their effect (e.g. through medical treatment (for sexually transmitted diseases), contraception, abortion or adoption) whereas the same is not necessarily true of child pornography. Once an image is placed on the internet then it is believed that it is outside of the child's control and the image will never be recovered. There is perhaps also the question as to the power imbalance involved in child pornography where an adult will ordinarily be involved, even if it is off-camera (Taylor and Quayle, 2003). The same is not necessarily true of offline sexual contact and perhaps this does demonstrate a difference that could justify a higher age of a 'child'.

Perhaps it is not the definition of a 'child' that matters but the consequences of this definition in terms of criminalising the actions of those involved in child pornography. What concerns me is that by choosing the age of 18 it potentially criminalises 16 and 17 year-olds who record themselves partaking in ostensibly lawful conduct. At the same time I can accept that a child of 16 may not be in a position to understand the consequences of becoming involved in the commercial distribution of child pornography. It may be difficult to differentiate between these in terms of a definition but it would be possible to differentiate between them in terms of criminalising conduct. It was noted in Chapter 9 that in many countries there is a question over whether children should ever be prosecuted for consensual behaviour but certainly in some countries, such as the United States and England and Wales, this possibility continues to exist. Therefore the law relating to child pornography should mirror the legal position in respect of the regulation of consensual sexual activity between minors. Personally I believe that non-criminal responses should be invoked for such matters. This is not to minimise the consequences of behaviour but rather a question as to whether criminalising adolescents is an appropriate response. However at the very least I do believe that the laws relating to child pornography should recognise the fact that adolescents have a sexual life.

The law should, it is submitted, differentiate between personal consensual behaviour and exploitative, or potentially exploitative, behaviour. Of course many will argue that such a differential is particularly difficult, especially when notions of power are factored into individual relationships. However there will be some adolescents above the age of consent who do, for example, wish to provide a sexualised photograph to their partner in the same way that some adults do. Should the law criminalise this? It is submitted the answer is 'no'. England and Wales recognises this, in part, through the rather absurd defence contained within s. 1B, PoCA 1978 but a more appropriate response is to be found within the ruling of the Supreme Court of Canada in *R v Sharpe* 2001 SCC 2. It is submitted that the inclusion of a similar ruling within other legal systems would render the discussion of the age of a child as less controversial. It is beyond doubt that 16 and 17 year-olds can be exploited but not all adolescents are. *Sharpe* differentiated between the personal taking and possession of an image and its showing or dissemination. It could be argued that such a distinction is difficult to sustain. It will be remembered that research shows us that once an image is placed on the internet it is likely to be mirrored and exist perpetually. However does the fact that this can happen justify blanket criminalisation of all images by adolescents? Would a better solution not be to criminalise those who show or distribute the images to another? It was suggested in Chapter 9 that a person has the right to sexual autonomy and it is submitted that this encompasses sexual images of oneself. As part of that autonomy it should be possible for a person to take a picture of themselves or give such a photograph to another, but if a person were to further distribute this image then it is a violation of that autonomy and the law could respond accordingly. If this approach were to be adopted then perhaps the definition of a 'child' would be easier.

Nature of the material

Perhaps the most difficult part of the definition is that which relates to the nature of the material. It was seen in Chapters 3 and 4 of this book that there are a variety of different approaches that have been used to define the nature of child pornography in the various jurisdictions. It was seen from Chapters 3 and 4 that all the definitions include representations of sexual activity with a child, something that must be an absolute minimum requirement. Subject to the discussion on age above, where sexual activity with a child is illegal under domestic law it should follow that the representation of a (real) child engaged in such activity should also be illegal. Where the definitions diverge is in respect of what else constitutes child pornography.

It was seen from Chapter 3 that England and Wales adopts the test of indecency. It is submitted that for the reasons contained within that chapter that this is the worst of the definitions considered in this book. It will be remembered that 'indecent' is not defined in the Protection of Children Act 1978 and the courts have not identified a precise definition either, it simply being judged against contemporary standards of decency (*R v Graham-Kerr* [1988] 1 WLR 1098; *R v Smethurst* [2002] 1 Cr App R 6) and it being clear that it is a derivative of obscenity (*R v Stanford* [1972] 2 QB 391). The principal difficulty with indecency is that its imprecise definition will conceivably criminalise the innocent taking of a photograph (for example, the parental photograph of a child in the bath) whilst at the same time potentially ignoring the activities of those with a sexual interest in children. It is not necessary to rehearse the arguments set out in Chapter 3 but the current definition of indecency is, it is submitted, no longer fit for purpose if it ever were.

The question is what should replace it. Chapter 4 noted that there are a variety of different approaches taken by the jurisdictions examined. The law in America is based on lasciviousness which it was seen also defies a precise definition. As with indecency it is a derivative of obscenity and the focus would seem to be on the image itself rather than the impact it may have on the viewer (although cf the sixth factor contained in *US v Dost* 636 F. Supp. 828 (1986)). The focus of lasciviousness would appear to be based on the sexualised nature of the photograph and thus an emphasis is placed on the pose of the child depicted (see, for example, *US v Boudreau* 250 F.3d 279 (2001)). Of course it was seen in Chapter 4 that lasciviousness could be broader than indecency in at least one context since it can include images of clothed children in apparently sexually suggestive poses (the most notable decision being *US v Knox* 32 F.3d 733 (1994)).

Canada and some Australian jurisdictions adopt the approach of examining what the purpose of the material is rather than simply looking at the image in isolation. In *R v Sharpe* 2001 SCC 2 McLachlin CJC noted that the Canadian test requires the tribunal of fact to consider whether its dominant characteristic is the depiction of the child's sexual organs for a sexual purpose, meaning to provide sexual stimulation to the viewer. Similar logic is adopted in the Australian Capital Territory and South Australia where the law, *inter alia*, applies to the depiction of the sexual parts of a child for the sexual gratification of an offender. Such approaches mean that the law is able to better differentiate between the types of material and, in particular, its purposes.

It is submitted that any test relating to the nature of material should not concentrate on the isolated examination of material. It was noted in Chapter 2 that a wide variety of material can be used by offenders for the purposes of sexual gratification and this does pose challenges for the law. However it is submitted that there must be a minimum level of severity before an image can amount to child pornography and that where ostensibly innocent images of clothed children are classed as child pornography there is a danger that the law itself starts to sexualise children (see Adler, 2001). That is not to say, of course, that a picture of a clothed child can never amount to child pornography but it should be restricted to situations where there is the depiction of a child engaging, or appearing to engage, in sexual conduct (discussed below). Of course this raises an interesting issue as to whether the presence of annotations can transform such material into harmful content. Where the emphasis of the law is simply on a photograph then perhaps the answer is 'no' but where context is allowed to be taken into consideration then annotations may be relevant. In Chapter 2 it will be remembered that the primary justification for the criminalisation of child pornography is that it can be said to cause harm to a child, either in its primary or secondary sense. Annotations could conceivably contribute to the harm suffered by a child. Where, for example, a photograph is accompanied by text that suggests that the child is engaging in sexual conduct then this may attract the characteristics of secondary victimisation although this is something that would depend on the nature of the photograph, the nature of the annotations and its location. This is an area that would benefit from research as little is known about annotated imagery and its possible impact on those portrayed within it.

It is perhaps unsurprising that the nature of child pornography defies a precise definition since society's expectations of what is, or is not, acceptable will change according to cultural standards. However it is submitted that a degree of certainty must be brought to the law of child pornography and it should be possible to ascertain the type of material that should be criminalised. In Chapter 3 it was suggested that a degree of certainty could be brought to the law in England and Wales by using a hybrid test and it is submitted that this is the most appropriate way to classify child pornography in terms of its nature. In England and Wales this could (theoretically) be achieved by the courts simply deciding that the test of indecency as applied is inappropriate, although in terms of *stare decisis* it would be difficult to do so, and realistically it would require a ruling from the Supreme Court, although that Court (and its predecessor, the House of Lords) is traditionally slow to depart from established precedent. It would be more appropriate for the change to be made in statute.

The term 'indecent' should be rejected in any change. It was seen earlier in this chapter that the term 'child pornography' was disliked because it carried with it negative connotations and it is submitted that 'indecent' as a term is not particularly helpful either since indecency suggests a low threshold, hence the debate in Chapter 2 surrounding the possibility that parents could breach child pornography laws through the taking of what could seem innocent photographs. Any statutory change should use more appropriate language. The language of the Optional Protocol is perhaps closer when it refers to the nature as being sexual. The term 'sexual' at least has parity with the language of the Sexual Offences Act 2003, which is the legislative instrument concerning other offences relating to the sexual exploitation and abuse of children. The definition within the SOA 2003 is derived from the decision of the House of Lords in *R v Court* [1989] AC 28 and it is submitted that a derivative of this would be appropriate for offences relating to child pornography.

It is submitted that child pornography should be defined in a way compatible with the Optional Protocol and it could be stated as:

> The representation of a child engaging, or appearing to engage in, sexual activity or the representation of the child's genitalia, anus or (female) breasts for primarily sexual purposes.

'Sexual purposes' would then be defined in a very similar way to s. 78. The test would, in essence, be:

(a) whatever its circumstances or any person's purpose in relation to it, it is because of its nature sexual; or
(b) because of its nature it may be sexual and because of its circumstances or the purpose of any person in relation to it (or both) it is sexual.

Using the language of the Optional Protocol to include the representation of a child for sexual purposes rather than it being a sexual representation of a child is important as it could mitigate the fears expressed in *R v Graham-Kerr* [1988] 1 WLR 1098 surrounding the need to prove the motivation of the maker or taker of the photograph and not the one who is 'using' it.

If we use the example of a person taking a photograph or downloading an image from the internet first, the new definition would be relatively easy. The premise of the expanded definition is that some images that do not depict sexual activity will be obviously sexual. This could, for example, include a child who is posed in such a way as to expose her genitalia in an obviously sexualised way. In these instances it would not be necessary to consider the motivation of the photographer or downloader, the image is inherently sexual and would constitute child pornography. Other images could be more debatable, e.g. a young child naked in a bath or on the beach. Such an image is not obviously sexual but it is submitted that it is capable of being sexual. Accordingly the definition would require that the motivation of the photographer or downloader is ascertained (through the police interview or through other means, e.g. an analysis of the collection or other evidence which may show purpose). If the motivation was innocent (e.g. a parent taking an innocuous photograph of their child) then the image would not be child pornography but if it were for a sexual purpose then the image would be classed as child pornography and the offender could be culpable. The test is arguably stronger for the downloading of images since if the offender has downloaded other images of child pornography then this could be put before the tribunal of fact as evidence of a sexual purpose.

What of the distributor? Again the test would differentiate between the obviously sexual and those images that are capable of being sexual. In respect of the latter the motivation would not be of the photographer or downloader but of the distributor. This addresses the exploitative aspect of child pornography. For example, a parent takes a picture of their child naked in the bath and, because the child was moving, it shows the child's genitalia. For the reasons discussed above it is an image that is capable of being sexual but is not obviously sexual. The taking of the photograph was innocent and therefore it would not constitute child pornography. The parent then sends it to an aunt. Again, as it is capable of being sexual then the motivation of the offender is relevant and this is for an innocent purpose and so there is no question of the parent being culpable for the distribution of child pornography. The partner of the aunt (X) sees the photograph. He has a sexual interest in children. He sends it to Y, whom he knows from a paedophile web site. Here the motivation is sexual: he is posting it so that Y can receive sexual gratification from the photograph. In these circumstances it can be said that X has distributed child pornography because it is sexual as a result of 'the purpose of any person in relation to it'.

This approach could also have been of assistance in the seizure of images from art exhibitions. Where the image is obviously sexual then it is submitted that the seizure could be justified because of the secondary harm that can be caused to the child. Where, however, the image is capable of being sexual (and the images by Tierney Gearon and Nan Goldin may seem to fall within this definition) then the purposes of the showing would need to be examined. Where it is on display within a public art gallery it is highly unlikely that it could be said to be displayed for a sexual purpose. Where, however, X shows the image at his house to Y and Z, both paedophiles, in order for the purposes of sexual gratification it would become culpable.

The effect of this change would be to remove the focus of the law purely from the image. It is submitted that when the law becomes fixated by the image and not the circumstances which surround it, there is a risk that the law does not achieve its primary aim: the protection of children. Arguably this has happened in England and Wales and it is a matter to be regretted.

Virtual child pornography

The definition above deliberately did not discuss the issue of virtual child pornography, nor did it discuss the types of material. Realistically this is because the comments contained within Chapter 2 on the type of material are largely self-standing. Whilst text is undoubtedly problematic, it is difficult to see how one could encapsulate a law that captures the writings of paedophiles that does not criminalise Nabokov's *Lolita*. Of course the argument could be, as many jurisdictions do, to exempt those that have been published but this raises a number of problems, especially in modern society where e-books are increasingly common and where it is possible to self-publish books for very little money from internet websites.

The more interesting debate relates to the issue of virtual child pornography, something discussed in Chapter 5. There is no doubt that this has become the latest frontier in respect of the arguments for and against the regulation of sexualised material of children. To proponents of free speech the regulation of virtual child pornography is a step too far because it cannot be for the purpose of protecting children from abuse or exploitation since at least some virtual child pornography is the product of fantasy. No child, they argue, is directly harmed by a computer-created depiction of a child engaged in sexual activity. Those that argue for its regulation suggest that it is difficult to differentiate between real and virtual child pornography and that it is as equally offensive as 'real' child pornography. In Chapter 5 a distinction was drawn between what was labelled 'fictitious' child pornography and that which relates to a real person. It is submitted that this distinction is crucial to understanding the limits of any law (for an extremely interesting discussion on this see Ost, 2010).

It was seen in Chapters 3 and 5 that the law in England and Wales does not currently criminalise all pictorial representations of an identifiable child engaging in sexual activity. It is submitted that this is wrong and that the focus of the law should be the protection of children and this includes non-photographic forms of representation, particularly computer-generated or computer-manipulated images. Only where such representations are of photographic quality will they come within the definition of a pseudo-photograph and it is likely that few images will be of this level. What of those images that do not depict an identifiable child, i.e. those which are products purely of the imagination? It was noted in Chapter 5 that there is no single argument that can justify the criminalisation of these images. Whilst many seek to draw a link between such images and the abuse of children there is no research evidence that demonstrates such a link exists. Does that mean that criminalisation cannot be justified? The answer to this must be 'no'. It was noted in Chapter 5 that there are a number of arguments that can contribute to a conclusion that criminalisation can be justified but at the heart of any argument must be morality.

Whilst the use of morals to justify the criminalisation of an activity is controversial, it is clear that at least in a philosophical sense it is possible to justify such criminalisation (see Ost, 2010: 235 f.). Governments have sought to avoid using morality as a justification for criminalising such material relying on other justifications, but the reality of the situation is that, at least in respect of fictitious representations, morality is the only justification that can be sustained. Within the context of the European Convention on Human Rights this approach can be justified relatively easily since Articles 8 and 10 of the Convention allow interference for, *inter alia*, the protection of morals and, as was noted in Chapter 5, the ECtHR has traditionally given signatory states a wide margin of appreciation in terms of domestic standards of propriety. Criminalising the production and distribution of virtual child pornography would probably therefore be upheld. Of course there is the question as to what threshold is chosen for the nature of such material. Those international instruments that do seek the criminalisation of virtual child pornography (including the Optional Protocol and the Council of Europe Convention on the Protection of Children against Sexual Exploitation and Sexual Abuse) do not differentiate between virtual and 'real' child pornography suggesting the same test be adopted. This would appear to be the position in some countries (for example certain jurisdictions within Australia) but it is perhaps notable that both England and Wales and the United States adopt a different approach and criminalise only those that are classed as obscene. It is submitted that this latter approach is correct. It has been noted that reducing the standard of obscenity for child pornography can be justified because of the harm it causes to children. Where there is no direct harm, however, then it becomes difficult to justify departing from the threshold of obscenity, a standard that courts have considered marks the appropriate balance between the rights of an individual and the standards society can expect of its citizens.

Of course the question then becomes whether it is possible to justify criminalising the mere possession of fictitious virtual child pornography. This is perhaps a more difficult question. In England and Wales and the United States the traditional approach has been that the criminalising of mere possession cannot be justified. That said, at least in England and Wales this has been the subject of two recent qualifications. The first was offences relating to extreme pornography contained in the Criminal Justice and Immigration Act 2008 and the second being the prohibited images legislation contained within the Coroners and Justice Act 2009. However the government in neither case put forward a particularly strong justification for criminalising the possession of such material (for interesting critiques of the legislative justification (or lack of it) in respect of these laws see Murray, 2009 and Ost, 2010). Whilst it is accepted that many pictures that fall within these definitions will be unpleasant, so is a lot of material that is classified as obscene. Indeed, some obscene material could be considered harmful and yet its possession is not illegal. For example, a video of a woman being raped is undoubtedly obscene. If it were distributed it would easily fall within the OPA 1959 and yet its simple possession is not illegal. It is submitted that the secondary harm that could be caused to the victim is comparable to that experienced by a child victim of child pornography and so there is a strong case for criminalising possession and yet this has not been suggested.

Can the simple possession of virtual child pornography be justified? It is likely that a challenge to the provisions in England and Wales would invariably fail. The Human Rights Act 1998 requires courts to act in a way compatible with the ECHR but, as noted in Chapter 5, it is highly likely that criminalising possession of such material would be compatible with Articles 8 and 10 of the ECHR because a legitimate aim under those provisions is the protection of morals. Given the importance the ECtHR has placed on morality it is unlikely that criminalising possession would be considered disproportionate. However many theorists will question the validity of criminalising simple possession, especially in relation to fictitious child pornography where no evidence of a link of harm can be shown. To many, criminalising the possession of fictitious material purely on the basis of morality will be seen as a paternalistic step by the State.

Offences

It was argued above that the law has, to an extent, lost focus on what the purpose of child pornography is and it is submitted that this is borne out, at least in England and Wales, in respect of the offences too. It was seen in Chapter 6 that the decision in *R v Bowden* [2000] QB 88 has had a dramatic impact on the law relating to indecent photographs of children. Its importance cannot be overstated and this decision has, in essence, had a more significant impact on the law than many of the legislative amendments that have been made to the Protection of Children Act 1978. Bowden was probably a creature of necessity at that time. The law was not fit for purpose by the time of *Bowden*. The internet had begun to have an impact on child pornography and collections were expanding at a considerable rate (see the discussion in Taylor and Quayle, 2003). Simple possession, at that time, was punishable only by six months' imprisonment, and it is perhaps not surprising that the police and Crown Prosecution Service sought to achieve higher sentences by arguing that the downloading of images actually amounts to the making of an indecent photograph rather than mere possession.

A literal interpretation of PoCA 1978 does support the ruling in *Bowden*. A file now exists that previously did not exist. However to an extent that was true in other circumstances. If X purchased a photograph from Y then a photograph came into his possession that he previously did not have. What differs is the point of creation: with downloading it is created by X whereas when it is purchased in hard-copy then it is created by Y. However, is the reality any different? In both situations X now has an image that he never had before and, at least in common parlance, one would probably say that X possesses that image.

Bowden in essence started a series of cases where the court ceased to look at what the offender is doing and instead began to look at the technical processes of a computer. *R v Jayson* [2003] 1 Cr App R 13 is perhaps the paradigm of this approach where the court adopted similar technical reasoning to decide that the viewing of an image amounts to its creation, even where no image is stored in the cache. That is not to decry the objective of *Jayson* as it is submitted that criminalising the viewing of child pornography can be justified, but it is an exercise in the interpretation and manipulation of language rather than an examination of what it is that the offender was doing. That this reasoning can cause difficulties is evident from the decision in *R v Porter* [2006] 1 WLR 2633 where the Court of Appeal held, quite properly, that a person cannot be guilty of possessing an image that is stored in an area of the computer he cannot access. It will be remembered from Chapter 6 that this concerned images that have been deleted. Where an offender is charged with making an image then the fact that it has been deleted and is stored on the computer is irrelevant yet where the offender is charged with possessing it then it amounts to a defence. Given that the behaviour of the offender is the same on each occasion it must be questioned to what extent the law is coherent. Problems were also identified in respect of the use of peer-to-peer technologies and whether this amounts to distribution or possession with intent to distribute. Again, it is submitted that the offender's actions seem less important in these decisions than the workings of the computer and servers.

It is submitted that a rationalisation of the law is required. PoCA 1978 was written for a time before the Internet Age, and whilst the courts have, perhaps valiantly, sought to interpret the legislation to take account of technological advances this has, almost certainly inadvertently, created a position where the law ceases to be coherent. England and Wales are not alone in this and it was seen in Chapter 8 that other jurisdictions have similar problems, particularly where there is an overlap between the downloading and possession of material and questions being raised as to what the meaning of, for example, possession is.

The law should be simplified wherever possible whilst leaving flexibility to adapt to future technological changes. Certainly there is no evidence that technological advancements are slowing down and even five years ago few would have thought that 'cloud technology' would be as prevalent as it is now. The growth of cloud technology is likely to pose a number of challenges to legal systems, not least in respect of jurisdiction. In deciding what conduct should be criminalised an analysis should be made of offender behaviour with legislation responding to this. In Chapters 2, 6 and 8 an analysis was made of offender behaviour and current offences and it is submitted that no single country has a perfect system; each has their own problems and difficulties. However it is possible to consider the offences already in existence to formulate new proposals.

The first, and most obvious, action to criminalise is the creation of child pornography. All countries obviously include this and it was seen from Chapter 8 that in most countries the construction of this term tends to lead to an overlap between this offence and simple possession when one discusses downloading. Whilst England and Wales uses a very technical definition – taking or making – most countries adopt a slightly more purposeful approach and talk about the 'production' of child pornography. It is submitted that this would be a more appropriate term to use. Production should mean the creation of material but should this mean the creation only of original material? There is an attraction to such argument since this would differentiate between the producer and the downloader but it could cause difficulties. For example, what of the person who is creating duplicate copies of a DVD to be mailed out to someone? If X takes the photographs and Y does the actual posting then Z, who duplicates the material, would not fit into the definition of either the creator or the distributor. However by allowing duplication to be included within the offence it undoubtedly creates the potential for overlap between the offences: a person who downloads material has, in essence, duplicated the material. Perhaps this is inevitable. One solution would be to use inchoate liability to cover those who duplicate existing material for others to distribute (i.e. the duplicator would be an accessory to the distributor) or alternatively guidance could be issued to prosecutors so as to ensure that the offence is not used for the downloading of material for personal possession but is instead used against those who are, in its narrower sense, complicit in the production of child pornography.

The next offence to consider is that of the dissemination of child pornography. Whether this is dealt with by one offence ('distributing child pornography' with 'distributing' then defined) or a series of offences, there are a number of behaviours that will need to be captured by such an offence. These were summarised in Chapter 2 but will include the sending of material, the selling of material and the showing of material. Each of these are linked by the notion of an offender disseminating material to another person. It was seen in Chapter 10 that it is common for a commercial element to be treated as a significant aggravating factor. It is for this reason that many offences will differentiate between the selling of material and distribution without profit. However it has been questioned whether this is necessarily an appropriate response given that the exact proportion of commercial child pornography remains the subject of some debate (Bains, 2008; Petit, 2004). The distribution of child pornography causes direct harm to a child as it increases the number of people who see the material and take sexual gratification from it. This has a direct impact on the secondary victimisation a child suffers and thus its criminalisation can be justified. In many instances distribution is very simple to criminalise, either through a general offence (such as that contained within the Canadian or Irish legislation) or through a series of offences linked to dissemination (as in the US federal law and, to a lesser extent, the position in England and Wales). However it was seen that new technology perhaps raises challenges to offences relating to the dissemination of child pornography.

Peer-to-peer technology has raised a number of issues in respect of distribution. In England and Wales and America the courts have been called upon to rule how peer-to-peer technology fits within distribution (see Chapters 6 and 8). In part this is because most of the legislative instruments pre-date this technology and so criminalisation is based on the premise of possession with intent to sell or distribute. However this does not necessarily cover the situation with peer-to-peer technologies: possession with intent suggests that a person has a specific purpose to disseminate whereas a peer-to-peer user may be prepared to allow people to copy material but it may not necessarily be a specific purpose. It was noted in Chapter 2 that the distribution of child pornography is a serious matter. It has a direct impact on the child as it increases the secondary victimisation and, through mirroring and copying, keeps the image 'alive' and in circulation.

It is submitted that it is perfectly acceptable to criminalise not only those who are prepared to distribute images but also those who allow their images to be accessed by others. A person should not be in possession of child pornography and, given the direct harm that is caused by its dissemination, it is permissible to require that a person who does illicitly have such material does not allow others to access it. In Chapter 10 it was seen that an absence of distribution has been treated in some cases as a mitigating factor. That is wrong. Victims of child pornography should be protected and this means punishing distribution and requiring people to ensure that images are not distributed. In Chapter 8 it was noted that both Canada and certain Australian jurisdictions have the offence of 'making available' child pornography and it is suggested that this is an appropriate form for an offence to take. A person who allows others to access child pornography that they possess should be culpable because of the direct harm caused.

'Making available' can also include an inchoate element in that it should not be necessary to prove that distribution *has* happened but it will include situations where the police can prove that it is *possible* to gain access to the images stored. Requiring proof of actual distribution could require detailed forensic analysis yet the reality is that by allowing access an offender has ignored the harm that could be caused. What should the mental element of the crime be? Given the harm that can be caused it is submitted that proof of specific intent is not necessary: it is not unreasonable for the law to expect that a person should not distribute or make available child pornography. That is not to say that a strict liability offence should be permitted but perhaps the more appropriate mental requirement is that approved by the South Australian Court of Criminal Appeal in *R v Molloy* [2008] SASC 352 where it was stated that the prosecution must prove an intention to make material available, knowledge that material is available or is reckless as to whether material is made available (at [43]). Whilst recklessness may be a lower standard than is found in other child pornography offences, it is submitted that the harm nexus present in distribution means that it can be justified in the offence of making material available.

The next offence to consider is that where an offender takes possession of child pornography. This will encompass the downloading of child pornography, the purchase of material and its importing. One solution would be to simply criminalise the possession of child pornography (as Canada does). Other countries adopt the approach of differentiating between the different methods by which a person can come into possession of the material, particularly when it involves either purchasing or importing child pornography (see the discussion in Chapter 8). An argument in favour of making this distinction is that the importation or purchase of material does show a commercial element to the transaction and, as noted in Chapter 10, commerce has traditionally been considered a serious aggravating feature.

A difficulty with the offence of simple possession is that it does create problems where a person has deleted the images and they are no longer recoverable without special forensic software. It was seen in Chapters 6 and 8 that in most jurisdictions this would defeat an allegation of possession because it could not be said that the offender has custody or control of the images. Whilst it can be argued that an offender is in possession of them before the time of deleting (or, using the logic of the Canadian case of *R v Chalk* 2007 ONCA 815, it can be argued that the deleting of the images itself can be seen as an exercise of the control requirement inherent in possession) in some jurisdictions this could cause difficulties because there are time limitations on some offences. On the one hand it could be argued that this situation is not a problem since if the offender is not in possession of the images any more he cannot view them and thus the harm caused to the child is, at least in respect of that individual offender, neutralised. The counter-argument of course is that it is evidence that an offender may have been involved with child pornography before deletion. Where this is true then it could be questioned why an offender should evade liability simply because he deleted the image, not least because there may be a number of different reasons why the image was deleted.

A possible solution to the problem of deleted images would be to criminalise the acquisition of child pornography. This could cover the downloading, purchase or receipt of child pornography. Whilst it would not automatically solve the issue of deleted images – as it would still be necessary to prove who received them – it would at least ensure that a person who has deliberately sought child pornography could be culpable. Sentencing guidance could differentiate between commercial and non-commercial acquisition. Criminalising the acquisition of child pornography would also mean that it was not necessary to engage in the linguistic gymnastics currently required in England and Wales in respect of the incitement to distribute child pornography. It will be remembered in Chapter 6 that since *R (on behalf of O'Shea) v City of Coventry Magistrates' Court* [2004] EWHC 905 (Admin) the courts have found it necessary to use the law of incitement (now causing or encouraging) in order to prosecute those who have purchased child pornography where they have then disposed of the material. If the acquisition of child pornography were to be criminalised then it would not be necessary to differentiate between the different methods. Thus downloading would be caught by this provision as would receiving an item from peer-to-peer or receiving an item through the post.

It would of course be necessary to include a mental requirement if the acquisition of child pornography were to be criminalised. As with possession, there is the potential that those who acquired child pornography unsolicited could be culpable. What should the mental requirement be? Certainly intention or knowledge should be included: those who intentionally acquire or acquire material knowing that it is child pornography should be culpable. What of those who are merely reckless as to whether the material is child pornography? In England and Wales recklessness requires foresight: a person is consciously taking the unjustified risk that, in this context, material they acquire is child pornography (see *R v Cunningham* [1957] 2 QB 396). In Chapter 2 it was noted that the acquisition of child pornography does directly harm a child through secondary victimisation. It is submitted that it could be justified to use recklessness in this context. A person who is trawling lawful adult pornography sites would ordinarily not be considered reckless but where, for example, they download an image that has a name tag that implies child pornography (e.g. 'young cuties, 'lolita', 'young and fresh', etc.) then it is submitted that it can be justified to require them to take particular care and assess, for example, whether they believe the site is respectable, whether there is certification of the age of those presented, etc.

Of course criminalising acquisition is not without difficulties. The prosecution would be required to prove which particular person acquired the material. This is similar to the existing requirement where the prosecutors seek to use the offence of 'making' (or equivalent in other jurisdictions) where the defendant must be shown to be the person who has made the material. For the offence of possession, however, one need not prove who actually downloaded or received the material, they need only prove that it is in their custody and control.

A further difficulty with the offence of simple possession is that there is doubt as to what extent it can be said that it applies to 'cloud storage'. The difficulty with cloud storage is that there is an argument that a person does not have custody of the space that the material is stored on. They do not own the space and the point of a cloud is that the files need not remain in the same place: they will be shifted between servers depending on space and the person who 'owns' the material will never know where precisely they are located (simply accessing them through a file transfer protocol). The files are therefore at the whim of the person who is hosting the files as part of the cloud and if that person decided to delete them then the person whose files they are would have no way of preventing this from happening. If possession requires both custody and control then it is possible that the cloud may cause difficulties. Of course possession could be redefined to cope with virtual housing spaces. Perhaps the most appropriate definition is that included within the Canadian Criminal Code where it defines possession as:

A person has anything in possession when he has it in his personal possession or knowingly:

(i) has it in the actual possession or custody of another person; or
(ii) has it in any place, whether or not that place belongs to or is occupied by him, for the use or benefit of himself or of another person

Code, s. 4(3)(a))

This is an interesting and comprehensive definition of possession and it would cover the situation discussed above in respect of clouds. As regards a cloud it could not be said that a person has the material in his personal possession nor is it necessarily in the actual possession of another person (as they have the files but they cannot gain access as cloud storage would ordinarily be encrypted so that only the file owner has access) but it would meet the definition of paragraph (b). The files are in any place for his benefit. Paragraph (b) expressly contemplates that the file owner does not own the place where they are stored and accordingly this would apply to cloud storage, freenet and other forms of transient storage.

Where possession may not assist is where a person looks at streaming material on the internet (which is not recorded in the cache) or views child pornography in a location where any files that are created are not within his possession (e.g. a cyber-cafe). In the Canadian case of *R v Carswell* 2009 ONCJ 297 the Ontario Court of Justice held that a person viewing child pornography 'has possession of it on their screen, and they are able to view it, download it, or store it at that point in time' (at [398]) which is an attractive submission if possession is taken to encompass control rather than physical custody. The Canadian court is stating that the child pornography exists on the screen and therefore the person who has called that image to the screen is in possession of it. Similar reasoning was adopted by the English Court of Appeal in *R v Jayson* [2003] 1 Cr App R 13 where it held that calling an image to the screen meant that the image was made. The logic of these decisions is that there is nothing within the legislation that requires child pornography to be tangible property: an image on a screen is as much child pornography as a physical photograph. To that extent it can be argued that calling up an image may amount to possession (cf the decisions of the US courts in *US v Stulock* 308 F.3d 922 (2002) and, in particular, *US v Navresad* 66 MJ 262 (2008)) although it does require the courts to adopt this reasoning.

Some countries have decided that in order to put the matter beyond doubt an offence should be created of viewing or accessing child pornography (see, for example, the provisions in the United States at 18 USC §2252A(a)(5) or those in the Canadian Criminal Code at s. 163.1(4.2)). The advantage of this approach is that there is no doubt that the deliberate viewing of material is culpable but the disadvantage is that it could, of course, lead to duplication between this offence and possession (see the discussion on this in Chapter 8 in respect of the provisions of the United States, Canada and Australia). To an extent this can be minimised by prosecutorial guidance but the possibility of duplication must certainly be recognised. Can such crimes be justified? It is submitted that the answer is 'yes'. It will be remembered from Chapter 2 that it was argued the viewing of child pornography does contribute to the harm against a child and that, in essence, it was comparable to the possession of child pornography. Certainly with modern technology the distinction between physical possession and viewing online must break down. Internet speeds now mean that it is possible to get almost instant access to websites. Viewing a photograph stored on a website is now undoubtedly as easy as physically storing it on one's computer. The same is especially true of the streaming of movie files where it is possible to view files that are not easily downloadable. States should ensure that the law covers such behaviours.

The international dimension

International law

It has been mentioned in this chapter already, but a conclusion of this book is that international action will be required to effectively tackle child pornography. This is undoubtedly an area where further work is necessary and this book has simply scratched the surface of this issue but the comment from the Lancet in 2001 that child pornography is 'surely the sort of borderless problem that requires firm action from one of the international agencies' (357 *The Lancet* 569) remains equally true today. However a conclusion that could also be drawn is the fact that this quote remains as accurate because, as with other aspects of the sexual exploitation of children (see, for example, Watson, 2009) there has been a failure of international law to safeguard children from abuse and exploitation.

The failure of international law is because there has been a failure to exercise leadership. It is not clear which body is seeking to exercise leadership in this area and yet there is a need for a body to stake a claim to taking the lead on the eradication of child pornography. At the regional level Europe has at least attempted to take a stand against the issue of child pornography and both the EU and the Council of Europe have been active in this respect. However the Council of Europe could be characterised as a toothless tiger in this respect. Whilst it is impressive that there is now in existence the Convention on the Protection of Children against Sexual Exploitation and Sexual Abuse one must look to the implementation of such a treaty. Whilst at the time of writing (summer 2010) 32 out of 40 Member States have signed the Convention, only seven have ratified it (CofE website). Most of the major countries have failed to ratify it (those ratifying it are Albania, Denmark, Greece, the Netherlands, San Marino, Serbia and Spain). Whilst the effect of ratification will differ depending on each country's laws, it is a necessary step that shows a country is committed to upholding the principles in the Treaty. That said, there is no guarantee that a country that ratifies the treaty will comply with it. There is no enforcement mechanism under the Treaty. The European Court of Human Rights, the Court of the Council of Europe, has no jurisdiction over the Convention and thus a person who believes that their rights under the Convention are infringed has few options to secure their rights.

The position in EU law should be more certain. It is a central tenet that a country, when it joins the EU, accepts that some elements of EU law become an intrinsic part of domestic law (Article 249 of the Treaty on the Functioning of the EU). Some parts of EU law automatically become part of domestic law but in respect of others the country can decide how to implement the law. A good example of this in England and Wales is the Data Protection Act 1998 which was passed primarily to comply with an EC Directive (Directive 95/46/EC). Since 1997 the EU has mandated action in respect of the exploitation of children and Council Framework Decision 2004/68/JHA was a major step forward which set out, in detail, a minimum standard for laws relating to, *inter alia*, child pornography. Yet although all countries within the EU undertook to comply with the Framework, few complied fully. A new Directive should be passed within the next year but even though the Treaty of Lisbon has improved the enforcement mechanism of EU law it is yet to be seen whether the Commission and, ultimately, the European Court of Justice will have the stomach to enforce this Directive. It is also worth noting that not every EU Member State has an obligation to comply with the Directive. The EU's ability to legislate in the criminal justice arena is very controversial and some countries secured 'opt-outs' from this legislation, including most notably England and Wales.

Whilst regional bodies may encourage action to be taken, their influence is of course limited and perhaps one would expect global bodies to take a lead on this. Yet realistically there is little leadership being exercised here. It will be recalled that the UN produced the Optional Protocol to the Convention on the Rights of the Child, on the Sale of Children, Child Prostitution and Child Pornography. This has been signed by 122 countries and has been ratified by 119. Accordingly it would be thought that this means that 119 countries have committed themselves to adhering to the principles within the Protocol but there is no effective system of ensuring compliance. As with other international instruments (Aust, 2005: 248) there is no court that has jurisdiction over the Optional Protocol or, indeed, the Convention on the Rights of the Child. A committee (the Committee on the Rights of the Child) is established under the CRC to receive reports in respect of both the CRC and the Optional Protocol (Article 13(1) of the Optional Protocol requires signatory states to submit an initial report followed by a report every five years) and they can then comment on these reports. This is comparable to the Human Rights Committee that is responsible for monitoring the International Covenant on Civil and Political Rights (Aust, 2005: 249) and indeed other treaty-based global bodies (Schmidt, 2010: 404).

Is reporting an effective manner of enforcing the Protocol? Buck notes that signatory states are almost routinely late (Buck, 2010: 98) which could be taken as a sign that countries do not take the matter seriously although Schmidt argues in some instances this is because countries have ratified numerous human rights treaties, each requiring their own report, leading to a backlog (Schmidt, 2010: 408). No sanction exists if a country does not submit a report (Buck, 2010: 94) although Schmidt believes that the threat of public criticism of a failure to submit a report has meant that most reports are ultimately submitted (Schmidt, 2010: 408).

A backlog of reports exist in the Committee on the Rights of the Child (Buck, 2010: 98) and it has been questioned whether this means the eventual conclusions of the Committee relate to the current position within a country or whether they are obsolete by the time of their publication (Rehman, 2010: 598). The scrutiny of the reports is supposed to be facilitated by the inclusion of NGOs, who are permitted to attend and present information (Rehman, 2010: 594), but there is concern that too much information could swamp the committee (Schmidt, 2010: 408) with some questioning whether the NGOs are even listened to by the committee (Rehman, 2010: 599).

It is clear that the reports can criticise the activities of some states (see Buck, 2010: 157 for examples) but it ultimately has no means of ensuring compliance. All the committee can do is to publicise its findings, including bringing any failures to the attention of (ultimately) the General Assembly but it has been noted that without a judicial sanction it is relatively easy for a state to ignore such criticism and fail to adhere to their obligations (Aust, 2005: 246).

If the UN cannot take a lead what of the G8? It was noted in Chapter 11 that the G8 has increasingly become a global political body with significant influence. Whilst its origins were in finance – and this probably remains its most important function – it has recognised that its membership carries with it responsibilities and influence on other issues. It was noted in Chapter 11 that the G8 has begun to turn its attention to the issue of the sexual exploitation of children and has specifically considered the issue of child pornography. The G8 may seem therefore an ideal body to take leadership in this area. Its influence means that it could use its economic power to encourage action by individual states. However it is difficult to see how this leadership could be exercised. The G8 is an informal grouping and it does not possess any permanent institutional framework. It exists through the co-operation of the Member States but has no staff or infrastructure. Even if this could be set aside for a moment it must be questioned whether the G8 has the moral authority to take a lead in this area. Whilst it has, through various proclamations, made credible statements about the need to tackle child pornography, two of its members are frequently criticised for failing to adopt adequate provision in their own country. Japan continues to refuse to criminalise the possession of child pornography, with the latest refusal coming in 2010. Its definition of child pornography is also considered to be incompatible with the Optional Protocol. Russia, the most recent member of the G8, is considered to be responsible for the majority of commercial child pornography being produced (Sheehan and Sullivan, 2010: 144). How can an organisation such as the G8 put pressure on other countries to counter child pornography when even its own Member States fail to do so?

The failure to exercise leadership is not, of course, an issue that is restricted to child pornography or indeed the sexual exploitation of children, but it is realistically something that will be required in order to effectively combat child pornography. The enforcement of international law is controversial and it can be difficult to achieve in international human rights law where identifying a remedy can be problematic. International law has traditionally been a body of laws that applies to disputes between countries and thus a remedy would favour, or permit action by, one party over the other (Mégret, 2010: 146). However this cannot apply in international human rights law where the violation is likely to be by one state against its own citizens. Some treaties establish a court with competence (the most obvious examples being the European Court of Human Rights or the Inter-American Court of Human Rights) but the global courts such as the International Court of Justice and International Criminal Court have no jurisdiction over the treaties discussed in this book.

The absence of a competent court means that those who believe they are failing to be protected by the State have limited options open to them. One possibility is to approach a competent court in a tangential way. For example, a complaint could be brought to the European Court of Human Rights not on the basis that a signatory state has failed to adhere to its obligations under the Optional Protocol or the Council of Europe Convention on the sexual exploitation of children but rather in an attempt to badge it as a breach of human rights (through the right to personal integrity). However there is little evidence to suggest that the courts are willing to widen their jurisdiction to encompass such arguments and the failure of international treaties to produce a common definition would complicate such an application.

If a court cannot be petitioned then it is likely that a citizen will need to rely on the reporting procedures discussed earlier. However an additional complication with relying on this method is that there is no right of individual petition under the Council of Europe Convention, CRC or Optional Protocol. Thus X, a citizen of country Y, has no right to petition the relevant investigatory committee (e.g. the Committee on the Rights of the Child). They are reliant on the failure being picked up in the reporting process, something that is relatively unlikely. A welcome step therefore is the establishment by the Human Rights Council of an Open-ended Working Group on an additional optional protocol to the Convention on the Rights of the Child to provide a communications procedure (Resolution HRC/RES/11.1, June 2009). This additional protocol would allow an individual of a country who signed the protocol to communicate a complaint directly to the Committee on the Rights of the Child (see the proposal for a draft optional protocol produced by the chair-rapporteur of the working group: A/HRC/WG.7/2/2). The HRC has extended the mandate of the working group (A/HRC/RES/13/3, April 2010) and it is to be hoped that the work comes to fruition. That said, this will only assist so far. Whilst it will allow a matter to be brought before the Committee they are not a court and they will not have any power to enforce a remedy for breach, although they would be able to publish their considered response to the communication, including a conclusion as to whether the individual has suffered a breach of protection. It would be hoped that public reporting would place political pressure on a country to comply with their obligations under the treaty.

International action

Slightly distinct from the issue of international law is the issue of international action. It was noted in Chapter 11 that there is increasing co-operation between governments and law enforcement agencies and this is something to be welcomed. It was noted in Chapter 11 that the Virtual Global Taskforce has been welcomed by the UN Special Rapporteur and for good reason. The VGT provides an excellent opportunity for law enforcement agencies to work closely together to prevent the sexual exploitation of children.

The internet, and related communication technologies, has ensured that child pornography now has no borders. Images can be easily stored on the internet and accessed anywhere in the world (the IWF annual reports discuss where most material is hosted). This provides challenges for domestic law enforcement agencies. Whilst they may be able to target those who access such material they cannot, by themselves, target those who are actively hosting or disseminating the material. This difficulty is increasing as technology develops. The growth of cloud technology presents particular challenges for the law as the information within the cloud can be moved frequently and the location of the cloud is unlikely to be identifiable from the access point. A user will access cloud space from a particular URL but the content will be stored in various locations. This means that law enforcement agencies in many countries will need to be involved. The storage of the data on various servers, etc. is also likely to be encrypted with the physical host almost certainly not having access to the encrypted material. Thus even where the store is located it is unlikely to be of assistance without being able to identify the cloud owner.

An important aspect of international co-operation must also be assisting those countries that do not have the same expertise, facilities and resources as the developed countries. It was noted in Chapter 12 that a modern child pornography operation can require significant resources to be devoted to it. This includes law enforcement officers familiar with technology, the use of specialist forensic software and, not infrequently, the use of covert intelligence. In many countries it is simply unrealistic to expect that local law enforcement agencies will have these resources. Part of an international co-operation strategy is therefore providing these countries with, for example, a forensic capability and training for local law enforcement agencies. To be fair to the international community this does appear to be happening and alongside individual countries, both Interpol and Europol devote considerable time towards this. International co-operation on victim identification is also important and the ever-evolving Interpol database is a key strength in this area.

The victim

Perhaps the final focus arises as much from its omission as its inclusion. Reference has been made to 'the victim' several times in this book, usually when referring to the harm that can be caused by child pornography. It is clear that I do not believe that, as some allege, child pornography is a victimless crime. However the precise status of the victim is difficult to ascertain in child pornography. Very little is known about the impacts of child pornography on a victim (for an interesting discussion on the position in Germany see von Weiler *et al.*, 2010). Perhaps this is because law enforcement operations tend to concentrate on those who possess and distribute child pornography and not its creation. That is not a criticism of law enforcement, it is a very secretive form of behaviour, and identifying the creators is extremely difficult. However this does mean that the victim is perhaps one step removed from the operations.

In their seminal work on child pornography Taylor and Quayle criticise the criminal justice system for being 'over-focused on offender issues, at the expense of victim issues' (Taylor and Quayle, 2003: 206). It is difficult to argue against this point, particularly in common-law countries such as England and Wales, where traditionally the victim has no formal role in criminal justice investigations. The role of the police, in many jurisdictions, is to detect crime and bring perpetrators to justice. If a victim is identified then the police will liaise with other agencies to seek to protect the child but where the interests of the victim and prosecution collide it will often be the case that the interests of the victim become of secondary importance. This is not restricted to child pornography, it is a criticism that has been levelled in respect of the sexual exploitation of children for some time. Chapter 12 raised difficult questions about how a law enforcement operation should proceed where the victim portrayed in an image is no longer a child but an adult. Should the adult be informed that the images are circulating? Should the victim be required to co-operate? These issues are outside the scope of this book but it is clear that further research is needed on these issues as they raise interesting and important issues about the ethics of criminal investigations and the role a victim has in proceedings.

Where a victim can be identified as a child then it is obviously imperative that the police intervene. Traditionally few resources have been dedicated to victim identification and certainly this continues to be the case in many jurisdictions, including England and Wales. Whilst CEOP do have a victim identification unit it is under-resourced and it is simply one unit. It is perhaps understandable why victim identification has had a low priority given what has been said above about the priorities of the police but if the police do not fund such work who does? Social services budgets are based on locality (as are police but local authorities are even more fragmented than the police). How likely is it that a rural district council will fund work to trace a child who may not even be a British citizen or resident let alone resident in their locality? This is one of the reasons why a national unit is important but it must be properly resourced. The police treat photograph-based images of children very carefully and for good reason. However this does mean that the opportunities for NGOs to assist in the identification of a victim are restricted? This is an issue that needs to be reconsidered. Identifying child victims should be a priority even though it is a complex operation. Funding must be provided and this is something that central government, police forces, NGOs and local authorities need to consider carefully.

Of course if child victims are identified then new problems arise. It has been noted elsewhere that the treatment of child victims of abuse and exploitation by the criminal justice system is generally unsatisfactory. There is no reason to suppose that this is any different in respect of child pornography and indeed arguably it may be worse as people may not understand the way technology works and the manner in which a child is re-victimised. International instruments require signatory states to provide assistance to victims and protective measures in respect of any litigation that arises. It is crucial that this occurs and yet doubt exists about the will to do so, especially in common-law countries where there is scepticism as to whether treatment and counselling contradict the central principle of fairness towards the defence.

Conclusion

So what is the conclusion that can be drawn? Child pornography has existed for hundreds of years but, realistically, it is only in the last 30 years that the law has begun to consider the issue. Advances in technology have led to seismic changes in this field. Child pornographers were relatively few, in part because of the difficulties in finding material, and the costs and risk involved in producing it. Technology meant that this changed dramatically. Through the internet and related resources it was suddenly possible to find hundreds of thousands of images and be able to talk to like-minded individuals in real time. Digital technology meant that the risks and cost involved in the production of child pornography decreased markedly. Anyone with a digital camera and internet connection could take photographs or video footage and upload it for viewing by others in a matter of seconds. Now the process is even quicker and easier since mobile telephones have photographic qualities to rival most cameras and include computer processing power that was unimaginable even a decade before.

It could seem that we are fighting a losing battle. Despite the fact that law and policy have sought to tackle child pornography for 30 years there remains a vast amount available and reports of arrests, prosecutions and convictions appear almost daily in newspapers. However it is easy to be downcast but steps forward are being taken. Filtering and blocking are controversial steps and do raise significant issues in terms of personal freedoms, but if done carefully and proportionately these processes can assist in the removal of one stage of the child pornography cycle. Law enforcement agencies are becoming more adept at the detection of child pornography and infiltrating those who seek to proliferate it. International bodies are beginning to realise the responsibilities that they have.

In training courses or public lectures I have often likened the fight against child pornography to a game of chess. Every time law enforcers, legislators or policy makers make a move their shadows try to counter it. We should not forget that many child pornographers are intelligent professionals who include law enforcement, lawyers and computer specialists amongst their ranks. They can anticipate what moves are being made and push technology to try and counter the moves. It is perhaps easier for the 'shadows' to act because they do not have the delays inherent in changing law or policy. However it is possible to anticipate threats and to train agents to understand patterns of behaviour and begin to gain the advantage. Child pornography is not something that is going to disappear in the near future and it is incumbent on international bodies, governments and those in authority to ensure that we do not fall behind those that are complicit in the sexual abuse and exploitation of children. That is a considerable challenge but one that must be met.

Bibliography

ACPO/CPS (2004) *Memorandum of Understanding between Crown Prosecution Service and the Association of Chief Police Officers concerning Section 46 Sexual Offences Act 2003* (http://www.cps.gov.uk/publications/docs/mousexoffences.pdf, last accessed August 2010).

Adler, A. (2001a) The perverse law of child pornography 101 *Columbia Law Review* 209–273.

Adler, A. (2001b) Inverting the First Amendment 149 *University of Pennsylvania Law Review* 921–1002.

Adler, A. (2007) All porn all the time 31 *New York University Review of Law and Social Change* 695–710.

Akdeniz, Y. (2001) Governing pornography and child pornography on the internet: the UK approach 32 *University of West Los Angeles Law Review* 247–275.

Akdeniz, Y. (2007) Possession and dispossession: a critical assessment of defences in possession of indecent photographs of children cases *Criminal Law Review* 274–288.

Akdeniz, Y. (2008) *Internet Child Pornography and the Law: National and International Responses* (Aldershot: Ashgate Publishing).

Altheide, D.L. (2009) Moral panic: from sociological concept to public discourse 5 *Crime Media Culture* 79–99.

Archbold (2010) *Criminal Pleading, Evidence and Practice*. London: Sweet & Maxwell.

Arthur, C. (2007) Is Operation Ore the UK's worst-ever policing scandal? *Guardian*, Thursday 26 April.

Ashworth, A. (2000) *Sentencing and Criminal Justice* (3rd edn) (London: Butterworth).

Ashworth, A. (2005) *Sentencing and Criminal Justice* (4th edn) (Cambridge: Cambridge University Press).

Aust, A. (2005) *Handbook of International Law* (Cambridge: Cambridge University Press).

Ayre, P. and Barrett, D. (2000) Young people and prostitution: an end to the beginning? 14 *Children and Society* 48–59.

Bain, V. (2008) *Online Child Sexual Abuse: The Law Enforcement Response* (ECPAT, Bangkok, Thailand).

Balin, R., Handman, L. and Reid, E. (2009) Libel tourism and the duke's manservant: an American perspective. *European Human Rights Law Review* 303–331.

Bamford, A. (2004) *Cyber-bullying*, AHISA Pastoral Care National Conference.

Basbaum, J.P. (2010) Inequitable sentencing for possession of child pornography: a failure to distinguish voyeurs from pederasts 61 *Hastings Law Journal* 1281–1305.

Beech, A.R., Elliot, I.A., Birgden, A. and Findlater, D. (2008) The internet and child sexual offending: a criminological review 13 *Aggression and Violent Behaviour* 216–228.

Benedet, J. (2008) Annotation to R v Garbett *Carswell Ont* 1147.

Bjarkman, K. (2004) To have and to hold: the video collector's relationship with an ethereal medium 5 *Television and New Media* 217–246.

Blakesley, C.L. and Stigall, D. (2004) Wings for talons: the case for the extraterritorial jurisdiction over sexual exploitation of children through cyberspace 50 *Wayne Law Review* 109–159.

Blanchard, R. (2009) Reply to letters regarding pedophilia, hebephilia and the DSM-V 38 *Archives of Sexual Behaviour* 331–334.

Blanchard, R., Lykins, A.D., Wherrett, D., Kuban, M.E., Cantor, J.M., Blak, T., Dickey, R. and Klassen, P.K. (2009) Pedopilia, hebephilia and the DSM-V 38 *Archives of Sexual Behaviour* 335–350.

Bloxham, A. (2010) Facebook profile 'could damage job prospects' *Telegraph*, 29 January, News.

Bocij, P. (2004) Camgirls, blogs and wish lists: how young people are courting danger on the internet 3 *Safer Communities* 16–22.

Bourke, M.L. and Hernandez, A.E. (2009) The 'Butner study' *redux:* a report of the incidence of hands-on child victimization by child pornography offenders 24 *Journal of Family Violence* 183–191.

Brady, M.J. (2007) Prosecution responses to internet victimization 76 *Mississippi Law Journal* 623–637.

Buck, T. (2010) *International Child Law* (2nd edn) (Abingdon: Routledge).

Buck, T. (2008) 'International Criminalisation and Child Welfare Protection': the Optional Protocol to the Convention on the Rights of the Child 22 *Children and Society* 167–178.

Calcetas-Santos, O. (1997) *Report of the Special Rapporteur on the sale of children, child prostitution and child pornography.* UN Economic and Social Council. E/CN.4/1997/95.

Cameron, K.A., Salazar, L.F., Bernhardt, J.M., Burgess-Whitman, N., Wingood, G.M. and DiClemente, R.J. (2005) Adolescents' experience with sex on the web: results from online focus groups 28 *Journal of Adolescence* 535–540.

Campbell, D. (2007) Operation Ore flawed by fraud *Guardian*, Thursday 19 April.

Card, R., Gillespie, A.A. and Hirst, M. (2008) *Sexual Offences* (Bristol: Jordan Publishing).

Carr, A. (2004) *Internet Traders of Child Pornography and other Censorship Offenders in New Zealand* (Wellington: Department of Internal Affairs).

Carr, J. (2001) *Theme Paper on Child Pornography: A Conference Paper presented at the 2nd World Congress on the Commercial Sexual Exploitation of Children* (www.ecpat. net/eng/ecpat_inter/projects/monitoring/wc2/Yokohama_Theme_Child_Pornography. pdf, last accessed April 2010).

Carr, J. (2002) *Sentencing of Offences involving Child Pornography: A Letter to the Sentencing Advisory Panel* (http://www.chis.org.uk/uploads/56.pdf, last accessed August 2010).

Cattaneo, C., Ritz-Timme, S., Gabriel, P., Gibelli, D., Giudici, E., Poppa, P., Nohrden, D., Assmann, S., Schmitt, R. and Grandi, M. (2009) The difficult issue of age assessment on pedo-pornographic material 183 *Forensic Science International* e21–e24.

Cavanagh, A. (2007) Taxonomies of anxiety: risks, panics, paedophilia and the internet. *Electric Journal of Sociology* 1–16.

Choo, A. (2006) *Evidence* (Oxford: Oxford University Press).

Clarke, K. (2010) The government's vision for criminal justice reform, speech to the Centre for Crime and Justice Studies, London, 30 June.

Cohen, S. (2002) *Folk Devils and Moral Panics* (3rd edn) (Abingdon: Routledge).

Coleman, S. (2008) You only live twice: how the First Amendment impacts child pornography in Second Life 29 *Loyola of Los Angeles Entertainment Law Review* 193–232.

Collier, Richard (2001) Dangerousness, popular knowledge and the criminal law: a case study of the paedophile as sociocultural phenomenon, in P. Alldridge and C. Brant (eds) *Personal Autonomy, the Private Sphere and the Criminal Law* (Oxford: Hart Publishing).

Cortoni, F. (2009) Factors associated with sexual recidivism in Beech, A.R., Craig, L.A. and Browne, K.D. (eds) *Assessment and Treatment of Sex Offenders* (Chichester: Wiley).

Critcher, C. (2002) Media, government and moral panic: the politics of paedophilia in Britain, 2000–2001 4 *Journalism Studies* 521–535.

Curry, A. (2005) Child Pornography legislation in Canada: its history and current developments 29 *Canadian Journal of Information and Library Sciences* 141–170.

Davidson, J., Quayle, E. and Morgenbesser, L. (2010) Editorial 16 *Journal of Sexual Aggression* 121–124.

DeClue, G. (2009) Should hebephilia be a mental disorder? 38 *Archives of Sexual Behaviour* 317–318.

Doek, J.E. (2009) The CRC 20 years: an overview of some of the major achievements and remaining challenges 33 *Child Abuse and Neglect* 771–782.

Doward, J. (2008) How police put their faith in the 'expert' witness who was a fraud *Observer*, Sunday 23 March.

Dworkin, R. (1966) Lord Devlin and the enforcement of morals 75 *Yale Law Journal* 986–1006.

Eardley, A. (2006) Libel tourism in England: now the welcome is even warmer 17 *Entertainment Law Review* 35–38.

Easton, S.M. (1994) *The Problem of Pornography: Regulation and the Right to Free Speech* (London: Routledge).

Easton, S. and Piper, C. (2005) *Sentencing and Punishment: The Quest for Justice* (Oxford: Oxford University Press).

EC (2007) *Report from the Commission based on Article 12 of the Council Framework Decision of 22 December 2003 on combating the Sexual Exploitation of Children and Child Pornography.* COM(2007) 716.

EC (2009) *Proposal for a Council Framework Decision on combating the Sexual Exploitation of Children and Child Pornography, repealing Framework Decision 2004/68/JHA.* COM (2009) 135, 2009/0049 (CNS).

ECPAT (2006) *Child Pornography: An International Perspective* Available on line at: http://csecworldcongress.org/PDF/en/Stockholm/Background_reading/Theme_papers/ Theme%20paper%20Pornography%201996_EN.pdf (last accessed 5 January 2010).

Edge, S. and Bayliss, G. (2004) Photographing children: the works of Tierney Gearon and Sally Mann 5 *Visual Culture in Britain* 75–89.

Edwards, S.S.M. (1998) The contemporary application of the Obscene Publications Act 1959 *Criminal Law Review* 843–853.

Edwards, S.S.M. (2000) Prosecuting 'child pornography': possession and taking of indecent photographs of children 22 *Journal of Social Welfare and Family Law* 1–21.

Egan, R.D. and Hawkes, G. (2008) Girls, sexuality and the strange carnalities of advertisements: deconstructing the discourse of corporate paedophilia 23 *Australian Feminist Studies* 307–322.

Eichenwald, K. (2005) Through his webcam, a boy joins a sordid online world *New York Times*, 20 December.

Elliott, I.A. and Beech, A.R. (2009) Understanding online child pornography use: applying sexual offense theory to internet offenders 14 *Aggression and Violent Behaviour* 180–193.

Emmett, S. (2001) The camgirls: how are teenagers persuading complete strangers to send them gifts and money? *Guardian*, 28 August.

Endrass, J., Urbaniok, F., Hammermeister, L.C., Benz, C., Elbert, T., Laubacher, A. and Rossegger, A. (2009) The consumption of internet child pornography and violent and sex offending 9 *BMC Psychiatry* 43: 1–7.

Eneman, M. (2005) The new face of child pornography, in Klang, M. and Murray, R. *Human Rights in the Digital Age* (London: Cavendish).

Eneman, M. (2009) Counter-surveillance strategies adopted by child pornographers 5 *International Journal of Technology and Human Interaction* 1–17.

Evans, D.T. (1993) *Sexual Citizenship: The Material Construction of Sexualities* (Abingdon: Routledge).

Fortin, J. (2009) *Children's Rights and the Developing Law* (3rd edn) (Cambridge: Cambridge University Press).

Fowler, R. (1995) Julia Sommerville defends 'innocent family photos' *Independent*, Sunday 5 November.

Fredette, K. (2009) International legislative efforts to combat child sex tourism: evaluating the Council of Europe Convention on Commercial Child Sexual Exploitation 32 *Boston College International and Comparative Law Review* 1–43.

G8 (2003) *Meeting of G8 Ministers of Justice and Home Affairs: Presidents' Summary* (http://www.g7.utoronto.ca/justice/justice030505.htm, last accessed 28 December 2009).

G8 (2009) *The Risk to Children posed by Child Pornography Offenders: A Ministerial Declaration by G8 Justice and Home Affairs Ministers* (Rome, 30 May).

Garland, D. (2008) On the concept of moral panic 4 *Crime Media Culture* 9–30.

Gillespie, A.A. (2003) Sentences for offences involving child pornography *Criminal Law Review* 81–92.

Gillespie, A.A. (2004) 'Grooming': definitions and the law 154 *New Law Journal* 586–587.

Gillespie, A.A. (2005a) Indecent images of children: the ever-changing law 14 *Child Abuse Review* 430–443.

Gillespie, A.A. (2005b) Child pornography: balancing substantive and evidential law to safeguard children effectively from abuse 9 *International Journal of Evidence and Proof* 29–49.

Gillespie, A.A. (2006a) Cyber-bullying and harassment of teenagers: the legal response 28 *Journal of Social Welfare and Family Law* 123–136.

Gillespie, A.A. (2006b) Indecent images, grooming and the law *Criminal Law Review* 412–421.

Gillespie, A.A. (2007) Diverting children involved in prostitution 2 *Web Journal of Current Legal Issues*.

Gillespie, A.A. (2008a) Adolescents accessing indecent images of children 14 *Journal of Sexual Aggression* 111–122.

Gillespie, A.A. (2008b) Cyber-stings: policing sex offences on the internet 81 *Police Journal* 196–208.

Gillespie, A.A. (2010a) Legal definitions of child pornography 16 *Journal of Sexual Aggression* 19–32.

Gillespie, A.A. (2010b) Defining child pornography: challenges for the law 22 *Child and Family Law Quarterly* 200–222.

Gillespie, A.A. (2010c) Sexual exploitation, in Buck, T. (ed.) *International Child Law* (2nd edn) (London: Routledge).

Hanson, R.K. (2009) How should we advance our knowledge of risk assessment for internet sexual offenders? G-8 colloquium seminar. Chapel Hill, NC.

Harrison, C. (2006) Cyberspace and child abuse images: a feminist perspecive 21 *Affilia* 365–379.

Hebenton, B., Shaw, D. and Pease, K. (2009) Offences involving indecent photographs and pseudo-photographs of children: an analysis of sentencing guidelines 15 *Psychology, Crime and Law* 425–440.

Herman-Giddens, M.E. and Slora, E.J. (1997) Secondary sexual characteristics and menses in young girls seen in office practice 99 *Pediatrics* 505–512.

Hirst, M. (2003) *Jurisdiction and the Ambit of the Criminal Law* (Oxford: Oxford University Press).

HMIC (2008) *A Review of the Child Exploitation and Online Protection Centre* (London: HMIC).

HMIC (2010) *Restriction and Rehabilitation: Getting the Right Mix* (London: HMI Probation and HMI Constabulary).

Holland, G. (1995) Identifying victims of child abuse images: an analysis of successful identifications in Quayle, E. and Taylor, M. (eds) *Viewing Child Pornography on the Internet* (Lyme Regis: Russell House Publishing).

Holland, G. (2005) identifying victims of child abuse images: an analysis of successful identifications, in Quayle, E. and Taylor, M. (eds) *Viewing Child Pornography on the Internet* (Lyme Regis: Russell House Publishing).

Home Office (2010) *Child Exploitation and Online Protection Centre: The Way Forward.* Cm 7785.

Howitt, D. (1995) *Paedophiles and Sexual Offences against Children* (Chichester: Wiley).

Hughes, M. (2009) Blogger who wrote about killing Girls Aloud cleared *Independent*, 30 June 30, news.

Humbach, J.A. (2009) *'Sexting' and the First Amendment* (http://digitalcommons.pace.edu/lawfaculty/596).

Hurst, P. (2003) Police tackling child sex offenders may be given new jobs to cut stress. *Independent*, 25 August, p. 2.

Ito, K. (2005) A history of Manga in the context of Japanese culture and society 38 *Journal of Popular Culture* 456–475.

IWF (2007) *Annual Report* (Cambridge: Internet Watch Foundation).

IWF (2010) *Annual Report* (Cambridge: Internet Watch Foundation).

Jenkins, P. (2001) *Beyond Tolerance: Child Pornography on the Internet* (New York: New York University Press).

Jenkins, P. (2009) Failure to launch: why do some social issues fail to detonate moral panics? 49 *British Journal of Criminology* 35–47.

Jewkes, Y. (2010) Much ado about nothing? Representations and realities of online soliciting of children 16 *Journal of Sexual Aggression* 5–18.

Jewkes, Y. and Andrews, C. (2005) Policing the filth: the problems of investigating online child pornography in England & Wales 15 *Policing and Society* 42–62.

Jones, G, (2003) 'Ladies' comics': Japan's not-so-underground market in pornography for women 22 *US–Japan Women's Journal* English supplement 3–30.

Kaplowitz, P.B., Slora, E.J., Wasserman, R.C., Pedlow, S. and Herman-Giddens, M.E. (2001) Earlier onset of puberty in girls 108 *Pediatrics* 347–353.

King, M.L. (2007) Concepts of childhood: what we know and where we might go 60 *Renaissance Quarterly* 371–407.

King, P.J. (2008) No plaything: ethical issues concerning child pornography 11 *Ethic Theory and Moral Panic* 327–345.

Kinsella, S. (1996) Change in the social status, form and content of adult Manga 8 *Japan Forum* 103–112.

Kinsella, S. (2000) *Adult Manga: Culture and Power in Contemporary Japanese Society* (London: Curzon Press).

Kleinhans, C. (2004) Virtual child porn: the law and the semiotics of the image 3 *Journal of Visual Culture* 17–34.

Kollock, P. and Smith, M.A. (1999) *Communities in Cyberspace* (London: Routledge).

Krone, T. (2004) A typology of online child pornography offending 279 *Trends and Issues in Crime and Criminal Justice* 1–6.

Krone, T. (2005) International police operations against online child pornography 296 *Trends and Issues in Crime and Criminal Justice* 1–6.

Lane, F.S. (2001) *Obscene Profits: The Entrepreneurs of Pornography in the Cyber Age* (New York: Routledge).

Lanning, K. (2005) Compliant child victims: confronting an uncomfortable reality, in Quayle, E. and Taylor, M. *Viewing Child Pornography on the Internet* (Lyme Regis: Russell House Publishing).

Laville, S. (2009) Legal challenge to web child abuse inquiry *Guardian*, Thursday 2 July.

Leary, M.G. (2007) Self-produced child pornography: the appropriate societal response to juvenile self-sexual exploitation 15 *Virginia Journal of Social Policy and the Law* 1–50.

Levy, A. (2005) Schoolgirls put topless pictures on the internet *Daily Mail*, 21 April, News.

Levy, N. (2002) Virtual child pornography: the eroticization of inequality 4 *Ethics and Information Technology* 319–323.

Li, Q. (2007) New bottle but old wine: a research into cyberbullying in schools 23 *Computers in Human Behaviour* 1777–1791.

Liberty (2009) *Liberty's Second Reading Briefing on the Coroners and Justice Bill in the House of Commons* (London: Liberty).

Livingstone, S. and Haddon, L. (2009) *EU Kids Online: Final Report* (London: London Schoool of Economics).

Longo, R. E. (2004) Young people with sexual behaviour problems and the internet in Calder, M.C. *Child sexual abuse and the Internet: Tackling the new frontier* (Lyme Regis: Russell House Publishing).

Luehr, P.H. (2005) Real evidence, virtual crimes: the role of computer forensic experts 20 *Criminal Justice* 14–25.

Maalla, N.M. (2009) *Report submitted by the Special Rapporteur on the sale of children, child prostitution and child pornography*. UN Human Rights Council. (A.HRC.12.23).

Manchester, C. (1995) Criminal Justice and Public Order Act 1994: obscenity, pornography and videos. *Criminal Law Review* 123–131.

Manchester, C. (1996) Computer pornography and the Court of Appeal's decision in Fellows *Criminal Law Review* 5–8.

Manners, I. (2009) The EU's international promotion of the rights of the child in Orbie, J. and Tortell, L. (eds) *The European Union and the Social Dimension of Globalization: How the EU influences the World* (London: Routledge).

McCarthy, M.A. and Moodie, R.A. (1981) Parliament and pornography: the 1978 Child Protection Act 34 *Parliamentary Affairs* 47–62.

McCulloch, H. (2005) Interpol and crimes against children in Quayle, E. and Taylor, M. (eds) *Viewing Child Pornography on the Internet* (Lyme Regis: Russell House Publishing).

Mégret, F. (2010) Nature of obligations, in Moeckli, D., Shah, S. and Sivakumaran, S. *International Human Rights Law* (Oxford: Oxford University Press).

Melville-Brown, A. (2009) Publish and be damned – by the court 85 *European Lawyer* 16–17, 47.

Middleton, D., Mandeville-Norden, R. and Hayes, E. (2009) Does treatment work with internet sex offenders? Emerging findings from the Internet Sex Offender Treatment Programme 15 *Journal of Sexual Aggression* 5–19.

Mieszkowski, K. (2001) *Candy from Strangers*, (http://www.salon.com/tech/feature/2001/08/13/cam_girls/index.html).

Mitchell, K.J., Wolak, J. and Finkelhor, D. (2005) Police posing as juveniles on line to catch sex offenders: is it working? 17 *Sexual Abuse: A Journal of Research and Treatment* 241–67.

Moser, C. (2009) When is an unusual sexual interest a mental disorder? 38 *Archives of Sexual Behaviour* 323–325.

Moultrie, D. (2006) Adolescents convicted of possession of abuse images of children: a new type of adolescent sex offender? 12 *Journal of Sexual Aggression* 165–174.

Muntarbhorn, V. (1991) *Report of the Special Rapporteur on the Sale of Children, Child Prostitution and Child Pornography.* UN Economic and Social Council (E/CN.4/1991/51).

Muntarbhorn, V. (1995) *Report of the UN Special Rapporteur on the sale of children, child pornography and child prostitution.* UN Economic and Social Council. E/CN.4/1995/94.

Murray, A.D. (2009) The reclassification of extreme pornographic images 72 *Modern Law Review* 73–90.

NCH (2005) *Putting U in the Picture* (London: NCH Publications).

O'Brien, M. (2005) Clear and present danger? Law and the regulation of the internet 14 *Information and Communications Technology Law* 151–164.

O'Connell, R, Price, J. and Barrow, C. (2004) *Cyber-stalking: Abusive Cyber Sex and Online Grooming* (Preston: UCLAN).

O'Donnell, I. and Milner, C. (2007) *Child Pornography: Crime, Computers and Society* (Cullompton: Willan Publishing).

Ormerod, D. (2001) Indecent photographs of children: making an indecent photograph of a child whether breach of European Convention on Human Rights, Articles 8 and 10 *Criminal Law Review* 657–659.

Ormerod, D.C. (2004a) Incitement *Criminal Law Review* 948–951.

Ormerod, D.C. (2004b) Indecent photograph: possession of indecent pseudo-photograph of children *Criminal Law Review* 1039–1041.

Ormerod, D.C. (2006) Indecent photograph of a child: possession of indecent photograph of child *Criminal Law Review* 748–751.

Ormerod, D.C. (2009) *Smith and Hogan's Criminal Law* (12th edn) (Oxford: Oxford University Press).

Ormerod, D.C. and Fortson, R. (2009) Serious Crime Act 2007: the Part 2 offences *Criminal Law Review* 389–414.

Ost, S. (2004) Getting to grips with sexual grooming? The new offence under the Sexual Offences Act 2003 26 *Journal of Social Welfare and Family Law* 147–159.

Ost, S. (2009) *Child Pornography and Sexual Grooming: Legal and Societal Responses* (Cambridge: Cambridge University Press).

Ost, S. (2010) Criminalising fabricated images of child pornography: a matter of harm or morality? 30 *Legal Studies* 230–256.

Palmer, T. (2004) *Just One Click: Sexual Abuse of Children and Young People through the Internet and Mobile Technology* (London: Barnardo's).

Palmer, T. (2005) *Behind the Screen: Children who are the Subjects of Abusive Images* in Quayle, E. and Taylor, M. (eds) *Viewing Child Pornography on the Internet* (Lyme Regis: Russell House Publishing).

Parker, M.R. (2009) *Kids these Days: Teenage Sexting and how the Law should deal with it* (http://works.bepress.com/michael_parker/1).

Paul, B. and Linz, D.G. (2008) The effects of exposure to virtual child pornography on viewer cognitions and attitudes toward deviant sexual behaviour 35 *Communications Research* 3–38.

Persky, S. and Dixon, J. (2001) *Kiddie Porn: Sexual Representation, Free Speech and the Robin Sharpe Case* (Vancouver: New Star Books).

Petit, J.M. (2002) *Report of the Special Rapporteur on the Sale of Children, Child Prostitution and Child Pornography* UN Economic and Social Council (E/CN.4/2002/88).

Petit, J.M. (2004) *Rights of the Child: Report submitted by the Special Rapporteur on the Sale of Children, Child Prostitution and Child Pornography*. UN Economic and Social Council (E/CN.4/2005/78).

Peysakhovich, S. (2004) Virtual child pornography: why American and British laws are at odds with each other 14 *Albany Law Journal of Science and Technology* 799–823.

Phoenix, J. (2002) In the name of protection: youth prostitution policy reforms in England and Wales 22 *Critical Social Policy* 353–375.

Quayle, E. (2007) Assessment issues with young people who engage in sexually abusive behaviours through the new technologies, in Calder, M.C. *New Developments with Young People who Sexually Abuse* (Lyme Regis: Russell House Publishing).

Quayle, E. and Taylor, M. (eds) (1995) *Viewing Child Pornography on the Internet* (Lyme Regis: Russell House Publishing).

Quayle, E. and Taylor, M. (2006) Young people who sexually abuse, in Erroga, M. and Masson, H. (eds) *Children and Young People who Sexually Abuse Others: Current Developments and Practice Responses* (2nd edn) (London: Routledge).

Quayle, E., Erooga, M., Wright, L., Taylor, M. and Harbinson, D. (2006) *Only Pictures? Therapeutic Work with Internet Sex Offenders* (Lyme Regis: Russell House Publishing).

Quayle, E., Lööf, L. and Palmer, T. (2008) *Child Pornography and Sexual Exploitation of Children Online* (Bangkok: ECPAT International)

Rehman, J. (2010) *International Human Rights Law* (London: Routledge).

Renold, E. and Creighton, S.J. (2003) *Images of Abuse: A Review of the Evidence on Child Pornography* (London: NSPCC).

Rheingold, H. (1993) *The Virtual Community: Homesteading on the Electronic Frontier* (Reading, MA: Addison-Wesley).

Roberts, J.V. and Doob, A.N. (1990) News media influences on public views of sentencing 14 *Law and Human Behaviour* 451–468.

Robertson, G. (1979) *Obscenity: an Account of Censorship Laws and their Enforcement in England and Wales* (London: Weidenfeld & Nicolson).

Rook, P. and Ward, R. (2008) *Rook and Ward on Sexual Offences* (London: Sweet & Maxwell).

Rowan, D. (2002) Menace on the Net *Observer*, 7 July.

Rowbottom, J. (2006) Obscenity laws and the internet: targeting the supply and demand *Criminal Law Review* 97–109.

Sanderson, P. (2006) Mass image classification 3 *Digital Investigation* 190–195.

SAP (2002) *Offences involving Child Pornography* (London: SAP).

Schmidt, M. (2010) United Nations, in Moeckli, D., Shah, S. and Sivakumaran, S. *International Human Rights Law* (Oxford: Oxford University Press).

Seto, M.C. (2004) Pedophilia and sexual offences involving children 15 *Annual Review of Sex Research* 321–361.

Seto, M.C. (2008) *Pedophilia: Psychopathology and Therapy*, in Laws, D.R. and O'Donohue, W.T. (eds) *Sexual Deviance: Theory, Assessment and Treatment* (2nd edn) (London: Guilford Press).

Seto, M.C. and Eke, A.W. (2005) The criminal histories and later offending of child pornography offenders 17 *Sexual Abuse: A Journal of Research and Treatment* 201–210.

Seto, M.C., Cantor, J.M. and Blanchard, R. (2006) Child pornography offences are a valid diagnostic indicator of pedophilia 115 *Journal of Abnormal Psychology* 610–615.

Seto, M.C., Reeves, L. and Jung, S. (2010) *Explanations given by child pornography offenders for their crimes* 169–180.

SGC (2007a) *Definitive Sentencing Guideline* (London: SGC)

SGC (2007b) *Reduction in Sentence for a Guilty Plea* (London: SGC).

Sheehan, V. and Sullivan, J. (2010) A qualitative analysis of child sex offenders involved in the manufacture of indecent images of children 16 *Journal of Sexual Aggression* 143–167.

Sheldon, K. and Howitt, D. (2007) *Sex Offenders and the Internet* (Chichester: Wiley).

Smith, J.C. (1988) Commentary on R v Land *Criminal Law Review* 120–121.

Smith, M. (2004) Fantasies of childhood: visual culture and the law 3 *Journal of Visual Culture* 5–16.

Smith, S.F. (2008) Jail for juvenile child pornographers? A reply to Professor Leary 15 *Virginia Journal of Social Policy and the Law* 505–544.

Sommer, P. (2005) Emerging problems in digital evidence 58 *Criminal Justice Matters* 24–25.

Squires, D. (2006) The problem with entrapment 26 *Oxford Journal of Legal Studies* 351–76.

Svensson, N.L. (2006) Extraterritorial accountability: an assessment of the effectiveness of child sex tourism laws 28 *Loyola of Los Angeles International and Comparative Law Review* 641–664

Tate, T. (1990) *Child Pornography: An Investigation* (London: Methuen).

Taylor, M. and Quayle, E. (2003) *Child Pornography: An Internet Crime* (Hove: Brunner-Routledge).

Taylor, M., Holland, G. and Quayle, E. (2001) Typology of paedophile picture collections 74 *Police Journal* 97–107.

Travis, A. (2000) *Bound and Gagged: A Secret History of Obscenity in Britain* (London: Profile Books).

Travis, A. (2008) Fewer than 3,000 websites produce bulk of child porn *Guardian*, 17 April, News.

Tromovitch, P. (2009) Manufacturing mental disorder by pathologizing erotic age orientation 38 *Archives of Sexual Behaviour* 328.

Udagawa, Y. (2007) Compensated Dating in Japan: An Exploration of Anomie and Social Change. Postgraduate dissertation (University of Central Missouri).

UNESCO (2006) *Commercial Sexual Exploitation: Child Protection Information Sheet.* (http://www.unicef.org/protection/files/Sexual_Exploitation.pdf, last accessed 6 January 2010).

Van Bueren, G. (1994) Child sexual abuse and exploitation: a suggested human rights approach 2 *International Journal of Children's Rights* 45–59.

Vandebosch, H. and van Cleemput, K. (2008) Defining cyberbullying: a qualitative research into the perceptions of youngsters 11 *Cyberpsychology and Behaviour* 499–503.

Von Weiler, J., Haardt-Becker, A. and Schulte, S. (2010) Care and treatment of child victims of child pornographic exploitation in Germany 16 *Journal of Sexual Aggression* 211–222.

Waites, M. (2005) *The Age of Consent: Young People, Sexuality and Citizenship* (London: Palgrave).

Walden, I. (2007) *Computer Crimes and Digital Investigations* (Oxford: Oxford University Press).

Walden, I. (2008) Porn, pipes and the State: censoring internet content 44 *Barrister* 16–17.

Wasik, M. (2008) Sentencing guidelines in England and Wales: state of the art? *Criminal Law Review* 253–263.

Watson, A.M.S. (2009) Too many children left behind: the inadequacy of international human rights law vis-à-vis the child 12 *Sociological Studies of Children and Youth* 249–271.

Wells, M., Finkelhor, D., Wolak, J. and Mitchell, K.J. (2007) Defining child pornography: law enforcement dilemmas in investigations of internet child pornography possession 8 *Police Practice and Research* 269–282.

White, M. (2003) Too close to see: men, women and webcams *New Media and Society* 7.

Williams, K.S. (2004) Child pornography law: does it protect children? 26 *Journal of Social Welfare and Family Law* 245–261.

Winder, B. and Gough, B. (2010) 'I never touched anybody – that's my defence': a qualitative analysis of internet sex offender accounts 16 *Journal of Sexual Aggression* 125–142.

Wolak, J., Finkelhor, D. and Mitchell, K.J. (2005) *Child Pornography Possessors arrested in Internet-related Crimes* (Washington: NCMEC).

Wortley, S. and Smallbone, S. (2006) *Child pornography on the Internet. Problem-orientated Guides for Police*, Guide No. 41 (Washington DC: US Department of Justice).

Ybarra, M.L. and Mitchell, K.J. (2005) Exposure to internet pornography among children and adolescents: a national survey 8 *Cyberpsychology and Behaviour* 473–486.

Zander, T.K. (2009) Adult sexual attraction to early-stage adolescents: phallometry doesn't equal pathology 38 *Archives of Sexual Behaviour* 329–330.

Zanghellini, A. (2009) Underage sex and romance in Japanese homoerotic Manga and Anime 18 *Social and Legal Studies* 159–177.

Zekos, G.I. (2007) State cyberspace jurisdiction and personal cyberspace jurisdiction 15 *International Journal of Law and Information Technology* 1–37.

Index

Printed in Great Britain
by Amazon